Babylon
or
New Jerusalem?

Perceptions of
the City in Literature

32 DQR STUDIES IN
LITERATURE

Series Editors

C.C. Barfoot - A.J. Hoenselaars
W.M. Verhoeven

Babylon
or
New Jerusalem?

Perceptions of
the City in Literature

Edited by
Valeria Tinkler-Villani

Amsterdam - New York, NY 2005

Cover design: Aart Jan Bergshoeff

The paper on which this book is printed meets the requirements of
'ISO 9706: 1994, Information and documentation - Paper for documents -
Requirements for permanence'.

ISBN: 90-420-1873-9
©Editions Rodopi B.V., Amsterdam - New York, NY 2005
Printed in The Netherlands

CONTENTS

LIST OF ILLUSTRATIONS

PREFACE

I could tell you how many steps make up the streets rising like stairways, and the degrees of the arcades' curves, and what kind of zinc scales cover the roofs; but I already know this would be the same as telling you nothing. The city does not consist of this, but of relationships between the measurements of its space and the events of its past ....

... each man bears in his mind a city made only of differences, a city without figures and without form, and the individual cities fill it up.[1]

This book and the voices it carries enter what has been one of the fastest growing forums of discussion in recent years. Unreal city, modernist metropolis, urban landscape, five-gated city, word-city and city as text – these and many more terms have multiplied in the attempt to contain and describe the inherent multifariousness of the perceptions provoked by the challenge of the city. This exonerates me from entering into yet another introduction to the basic themes contained within this topos. In fact, it is tempting to simply juxtapose more than two passages from Italo Calvino's *Invisible Cities*, effectively studded on a page, and thereby provide a suggestive and dynamic introduction to the forms and shapes of the literatures of the city. However, something must be said about the space the present book hopes to occupy within this arena. Rather than drawing critically from one or a few specified theoretical frameworks, these essays draw a map of the city in literature, but then as a kind of grid (like the map of the London underground) rather than as a dictionary (an A to Z).

Although the book does not aim to provide a comprehensive treatment of the subject, it does attempt to be representative. The title foregrounds one basic antithesis or binary opposition informing the topos of the city, and it reflects other sets of concepts that are articulated in binaries. It is the liberating dynamism of the city as well as the imprisoning marginality of

---

[1] Italo Calvino, *Invisible Cities* (1972), trans. William Weaver, San Diego, 1974, 10, 34.

one's existence within it that engenders creativity, as Deborah Parsons shows. This same liberating vitality and spaciousness is dissected by boundaries into classified areas of activity or zones – with the difficulty that this involves in crossing them, and the threat of claustrophobia within any one of them. Such crossings are traced in many of the articles, as is that other antithesis: the multiplicity of languages and signs resulting in the impenetrability of the city and of urban life. Again, the flux through the network of streets acquires meaning because of the confinement within the labyrinth formed by the streets or within the underworld they counterbalance. Disguise as revelation is a further opposition Eugène Sue exploits in *Les Mystères de Paris*, as Sara James describes.

A number of the contributors refer to real cities, and here the forms of explorations are many. The historical centrality of a capital city within the mechanics of a system – in this case, London as the centre of a web, literally, of correspondences (with the correspondents being aware of this) – is revealed by James How. The socio-political emphasis and the use made of the reality of the Victorian city is not just discussed but actually charted by Robert Druce, whose demonstrates how statistics attempt to order the disturbing spectacle of an over-complex urban development. The transformation, in terms of progress, of real cities such as London and Paris, improved by legislation on cemeteries (see Alan Shelston's article) by lighting (in Karlien van der Beukel's piece), or by projects of urban renewal (in the Paris of Maxime du Camp, as discussed by Philip Rand) – all these are basic aspects of a study on the city. From Renaissance plays to contemporary novels, uses of real cities in literature yield comparative and contrastive analyses. Rocco Coronato's scrutiny of the formalized "scena di città" in Renaissance Ferrara and its transposition onto Jonson's Venice fills an important gap in the chronological survey as well as in the formal landscape of images of the city in literature; its major contribution is the focus on visual impact. At the other end of the temporal and formal spectrum, Wim Tigges's analysis of the violent life in Belfast traces the intricate and ironic workings of the language, the verbal impact, in which it is articulated. The voices of the inhabitants of violent and violated cities are recorded also in the two final contributions in the collection, where Françoise Besson scrutinizes gaps in imaginings of broken cities, and John Stotesbury dissects the layers of South African urban existence and its deliberate destruction.

In contrast to such reflections on real cities are the diverse images of the city in worlds specifically forged by the writers: William Blake's expressive exploration of multiple usurpations, considered by C.C. Barfoot, and the monuments James Thomson places in his city, huge stone structures dwarfed by the apparently even larger and more substantial shape of Dürer's Melancholia, that I discuss. Neither imagined cities nor real cities belong to a ghetto of interpretative systems separate from each other; what a volume such as the current one hopes to do is articulate such opposition into a complex binary for the reader to reflect on.

Other contributors give some of these general considerations a more specific focus: Daniel Karlin adds the indispensable voice of Elizabeth Barrett Browning and of her *Aurora Leigh* – the voice of poets, and of what London can mean for their poetry and identity. Kasia Boddy's analysis of urban structures and strictures in the vision of the city as a boxing ring indicates the urban transformation of a specific cultural and leisure activity and thereby complements and extends Doc Rossi's analysis of jazz as guiding metaphor for urban life. Similarly, the transformation of the real into the unreal city, or into the word-city or the city as text – however one's allegiance to systems of perceptions might lead one to phrase it – can be viewed as yet another rich strand of the city in literature: hence, the importance of the comparative element. For although the original aim was to have two articles, and consequently two perspectives, on each facet represented here, in the case of the Modernist city this was extended in order to reflect the crucial node this period forms in the lifespan of the literary city. The essays by Annelise Ballegaard and Fredrik Tygstrup amplify the focus on the roles of the modernist metropolis by adding a strong comparative element as well as the indispensable focus on the role of memory.

The articles are arranged chronologically with the exception of the very first (von der Thüsen's formal analysis, which also offers us a useful survey of texts from Wordsworth to the Modernists). Since it has an analogous formal approach, I had thought of continuing with my own piece and then with Ian Almond's essay on Augustine and Wordsworth, which carries on a discussion of the poet of *The Prelude*, but also sets up a useful method of thesis and antithesis. But finally I decided to simply follow as closely as possible a plain chronological thread, with the reader being invited to identify patterns of significance for his or her own self.

However, there are three points in particular the present essays reinforce, which I would like to foreground and present for the reader's consideration. First, that the binary oppositions which create the dynamism of writing on the city are indeed more correctly described as binary structures, for they are necessary and fruitful, multiplying sets of double perspectives by means of which the writers or narrators engage with the multiplicity of urban experience. The second point follows closely from the previous but takes it one step further into the very first antithesis proposed by the title: Jerusalem *is* Babylon – the spiritual is the temporal, whether in Blake's strife in London or in the public and private troubles in Belfast. At the close of his essay, Doc Rossi comments, about the novel he analyses, that "the key to spiritual evolution comes from the involution of the spirit that can only take place in Babylon" (203); the same is true for more textual cities. Even the murder of cities, as John Stotesbury shows, can mean the awakening of its inhabitants – and of the texts' readers. The third and final point is that, quite apart from providing writers with contents (a setting, a set of more or less conventional images, characters and languages), or a collection of themes and motifs, or tools such as symbols and myths, the challenge of the city has indeed determined the very form and course of literature. This becomes strikingly clear in the Modernist moment – in the case of the novel, for example, in the shift from "narrated cities" to "urban narratives", discussed by Frederik Tygstrup. But every century or even generation has responded to the historical changes in the city by reshaping its literature. Indeed, from that first early modern beginning – Dante Alighieri's civic divine comedy, inscribed in the vulgar language of urban exchange – literature has been the textual architecture of the mind corresponding to the cities on the ground, creating analogous memorializations and erasures. One cannot but begin to scrutinize urban geography and its developments to envisage what forms the literature of the future will take.

Valeria Tinkler-Villani

ACKNOWLEDGEMENTS

Thanks are due to all the contributors to this volume, including the students who took part in the "City in Literature" course, and the organizations that have helped with funding: the Leiden Faculty of Letters, the KNAW (the Royal Dutch Academy of Sciences) the Netherlands Graduate School for Literary Studies and Editions Rodopi BV, Amsterdam.

THE CITY AS METAPHOR, METONYM AND SYMBOL

JOACHIM VON DER THÜSEN

Literary images of the city cannot really be seen in isolation from other forms of image-making of the city. American city sociologists have pointed to the fact that it is not only travellers who need images for the ordering of their experiences, but city dwellers also have to orient themselves by images.[1] In addition, inhabitants bond themselves to cities/neighbourhoods by specific forms of image-making. Architects and planners, too, develop images of the city when complementing or changing parts of an urban landscape. In this last case, the term "image-making" seems to retain its original sense: that of drawing and mapping. However, if one looks more closely at the underlying principles that produce the mental images which steer all perceptions of the city, one discovers that the image-making process follows procedures which are basically linguistic operations. Image-making of the city is concerned with the assignment of meaning to an otherwise meaningless medley of heterogeneous phenomena. The three main linguistic operations that govern images of the city are the symbolic, the metaphoric and the metonymic.

On the symbolic level, the city is seen as an image of something larger than the city itself. Here, the city often becomes "an image for the articulation of an encompassing ideal".[2] Image-making on this level has a very long tradition; it reaches back to the very beginning of city dwelling. When in antiquity, for instance, the city was mapped as a crossroad within a walled confine, this was meant to be representative of the cosmos itself. Another projection was the city of Jerusalem as heaven on earth, foreshadowing the divine *civitas* and pointing

---

[1] See especially the seminal study by Kevin Lynch, *The Image of the City*, Cambridge: Mass, 1959.

[2] Thomas A. Reiner and Michael A. Hindery, "City Planning: Images of the Ideal and the Existing City", in *Cities of the Mind: Images and Themes of the City in the Social Sciences*, eds L. Rodwin and R.M. Hollister, New York and London, 1984, 133-47, esp. 133. I have based my classification of city images on the introductory remarks in this article: Reiner and Hindery talk about three "planes" of image-making. Overlooking, however, the basic linguistic procedures involved, the authors do not employ the terms "metaphoric", "metonymic" and "symbolic".

to "the human potential for holiness".[3] In the construction of medieval cities the same topos was used. Thus the medieval layout of Utrecht, the largest city in the Low Countries before 1500, shows a cross formed by the cathedral, marking the centre, and four churches at the end of the bars. On less sacred ground, the fact that utopias have often been given an architectural and urban form points to the same pattern: the city represents human existence in its most ideal form.

We could say, then, that on this symbolic level the city reveals through its form a more general truth. This does not always have to be an ideal; the city can represent a neutral entity as well. Thus a particular city may be seen as the expression of a culture or of a phase of civilization, as in the nineteenth century when London became the representative image of industrial capitalism. In our own time, a city like New York provides us with one of the most radical and most telling images of modern life itself.

Literature is full of such images of the city with a representational and symbolic function, especially when we think of the urban novel or the great city-poem of the last two hundred years. Literature has both celebrated the city as the supreme expression of wealth, of energy, of the amalgam of living styles and, conversely, as representative of modern society's ills, its anonymity, egotism, oppression and anxiety.

On the metaphorical level of image-making, the city is expressed in terms of relatively concrete constructs and processes that often have no overt connection to urban life. Thus the city is seen as body, monster, jungle, ocean or volcano. Such metaphorical equations usually have an ideological quality. The traveller who perceives eighteenth-century London as "the great Wen" passes an unmistakably negative judgement, while the visitor or flâneur who sees this same city as "the great bazaar" usually assigns an attractive quality to it. Some metaphors, however, can be used in a fairly neutral sense: aquatic metaphors – such as river, stream, sea, ocean – commonly have this quality.

City metaphors have a holistic tendency. Speakers who use them search for the one encompassing image that will contain the potentially unstructured and will give meaning to the otherwise incomprehensible energies that threaten the onlooker. Literature, however, frequently demonstrates how difficult it is to stick to one such holistic image. As the testing ground of ideologies, literature often shows how inadequate a first guiding metaphor proves to be: in its stead, a whole cataract of metaphors appears. Such subsequent images complement each other or, as more often happens, cancel each other out.

Nature, the safe haven of metaphorical meaning, often proves insufficient for the comprehension of city life – of that form of existence which is so stunningly new and utterly non-natural. Literature frequently demonstrates that the holistic thrust of the city metaphor precludes precisely that which it is supposed to describe: the new experience. Thus, when all the big metaphors are shed,

---

[3] Reiner and Hindery, 134. See also Lewis Mumford, *The City in History*, Penguin, 1961, rpt. 1979, 282-87.

literature often comes into its own as the tentative and experimental scription of that which, as yet, neither has a name nor a familiar cognitive pattern.

On the metonymic level of image-making, a totally different procedure emerges. Here, the image of a city is made up of the customs, structures and buildings which are specific to that particular city. For example, the image of Paris is co-determined by the Eiffel Tower, the image of Athens by the Acropolis, that of Cologne by its cathedral. Customs and traditions that are associated with certain cities can also contribute to their images: thus Siena's image is in part defined by the Palio, while the image of New Orleans is determined by its jazz tradition and its carnival, the Mardi Gras.

As my examples on this level of image-making show, the tourist cliché and the advertisement slogan are never far away. But not all is banal and trite on this plane. One must not forget that city residents also orient themselves along metonymic lines. To be sure, inhabitants of a big city gain little by identifying the whole of their town with one or two monuments or customs, but they are always guided by markers within their own city. Orientation takes place through characteristic buildings, peculiar architectural ensembles, the form of open spaces, the rumour attached to neighbourhoods, and so forth. Residents also identify with their city by taking over the rhythm of its customs and festivities. American sociologists have conducted extensive studies on this internal mapping of cities.[4]

It is clear that on this level of image-making there is hardly any holistic tendency. Rather, the city appears as an aggregate of diverse images, as a collection of partial visions which are marked by a certain degree of heterogeneity. The city is not represented by a distinct phenomenon outside itself, as in the metaphoric mode, but by various parts of itself. It might therefore be more correct to call this the synecdochic mode, but, as the word "metonym" is frequently used in its broader sense which includes synecdoche, I prefer to retain the term "metonymic".

Let me illustrate these three modes of image-making with some examples from literary descriptions of London between 1800 and 1930. In the nineteenth century, London was the city that posed the greatest challenge to its observers. Nobody had seen anything like it. The growth of London was unparalleled; its traffic was overwhelming, and the intensity of its economic life was beyond comparison. London was the capital of the technologically most advanced nation, indeed the very centre of the largest empire of modern times.

It comes as no surprise, then, that the Romantics (with their basically Rousseauistic view) looked with horror upon this new form of life. But there were exceptions. Wordsworth, for one, was able to write a tranquil sonnet on an

---

[4] See the references in Kevin Lynch, "Reconsidering *The Image of the City*", in *Cities of the Mind*, 151-61.

early morning departure from London, "Composed upon Westminster bridge, September 3, 1802":

> Earth has not anything to show more fair:
> Dull would he be of soul who could pass by
> A sight so touching in its majesty:
> This City now doth, like a garment, wear
> The beauty of the morning; silent, bare,
> Ships, towers, domes, theatres, and temples lie
> Open unto the fields, and to the sky;
> All bright and glittering in the smokeless air.
> Never did sun more beautifully steep
> In his first splendour, valley, rock, or hill;
> Ne'er saw I, never felt, a calm so deep!
> The river glideth at his own sweet will:
> Dear God! the very houses seem asleep;
> And all that mighty heart is lying still![5]

We see a panorama of serene quiet, a vista of a city at some distance. To be on this bridge means distancing oneself from the potential din and turmoil of the city. Another distance is added: a temporal detachment from the city's daytime activities. The visual sense dominates the experience; the eye as the sensory organ of distance creates order. Indeed, order and silence are the dominant impressions. There is but slight motion, that suggested by the effect of light ("glittering") and the gliding of the river.

What is perhaps most surprising in a poem of the Romantic age is the fact that the city is not opposed to nature. Instead, the city is embedded in the great cosmic order, "lying open unto the fields and to the sky". The place of culture ("towers, domes, theatres, and temples") is integrated into the realm of nature, the whole of nature being suggested by "earth", "fields", "sky", "sun" and "river". In this context of reconciliation of culture and nature, the bridge has an added significance; it is, after all, a tangible symbol of connection.

Looking at the metaphors in the poem, one discovers that lines 4 and 5 are governed by the theatre image:

> This city now doth, like a garment wear
> The beauty of the morning ....

This resonates with the beginning of the poem. The first line, "Earth has not anything to show more fair", already points to a theatre/stage situation. What is suggested here is, of course, a traditional image, well-known from Renaissance and Baroque art: "the world as a stage."

Not surprisingly, this traditional metaphor disappears as the poetic

---

[5] William Wordsworth, *Selected Poems*, London, 1963, 254-55.

description progresses and enters the domain of nature. The end of the sonnet shows the city as the heart of a large body. The Romantic metaphor – "nature as organism" – takes over. The city becomes the central organ of nature itself, which in turn is conceived as a living body. This also means that the bridge as a supportive symbol has become superfluous. The end of the sonnet does not deal with the reconciliation between two antagonistic forces; instead, it thematizes an ultimate unity.

Such tranquil and consoling images of the city cannot be found in the famous London passages of Wordsworth's long autobiographical poem *The Prelude*:

> Rise up, thou monstrous ant-hill on the plain
> Of a too busy world! Before me flow, 150
> Thou endless stream of men and moving things!
> Thy every-day appearance, as it strikes –
> With wonder heightened, or sublimed by awe –
> On strangers, of all ages; the quick dance
> Of colours, lights, and forms; the deafening din;
> The comers and the goers face to face,
> Face after face; the string of dazzling wares,
> Shop after shop, with symbols, blazoned names,
> And all the tradesman's honours overhead:
> Here, fronts of houses, like a title-page 160
> With letters huge inscribed from top to toe;
> Stationed above the door, like guardian saints,
> There, allegoric shapes, female or male,
> Or physiognomies of real men,
> Land-warriors, kings, or admirals of the sea,
> Boyle, Shakespeare, Newton, or the attractive head
> Of some quack-doctor, famous in his day.
>
> Meanwhile the roar continues, till at length,
> Escaped as from an enemy, we turn
> Abruptly into some sequestered nook, 170
> Still as a sheltered place when winds blow loud!
> At leisure, thence, through tracts of thin resort,
> And sights and sounds that come at intervals,
> We take our way. A raree-show is here,
> With children gathered round; another street
> Presents a company of dancing dogs,
> Or dromedary, with an antic pair
> Of monkeys on his back; a minstrel band
> Of Savoyards; or, single and alone,
> An English ballad-singer …. 180
> ….
> Thence back into the throng, until we reach,
> Following the tide that slackens by degrees, 190
> Some half-frequented scene, where wider streets
> Bring straggling breezes of suburban air.

> Here files of ballads dangle from dead walls;
> Advertisements, of giant-size, from high
> Press forward, in all colours, on the sight;
> ....
>   Now homeward through the thickening hubbub, where
> See, among less distinguishable shapes,
> The begging scavenger, with hat in hand;
> The Italian, as he thrids his way with care,
> Steadying, far-seen, a frame of images
> Upon his head; with basket at his breast
> The Jew; the stately and slow-moving Turk,
> With freight of slippers piled beneath his arm!
>
>   Enough; – the mighty concourse I surveyed,   220
> With no unthinking mind, well pleased to note
> Among the crowd all specimens of man,
> Through all the colours which the sun bestows,
> And every character of form and face: ....[6]

Here, the speaker is in the middle of things. For a moment, he looks at the city as a scene, but he cannot keep this distance. Structure, overview, order – they are all lost. He has to give up the facile nature metaphor that comes to him first ("monstrous ant-hill"). The dominant image of the following lines is the metaphor of flowing water ("endless stream of men and moving things").

Eventually, the speaker himself starts moving. He perceives "shop after shop", while he becomes the medium forming the links in the endless chain of things ("the string"). The speaker has become part of the dynamics of the city. This corresponds to the fact that sounds take over ("deafening din", "roar"), taking from him the last vestiges of distance granted by the visual sense. The individual has become powerless, giving way to the turmoil against which there is no protection.

Having fled into an alley and having regained some of his composure, the speaker eventually experiences the great city as a bazaar. The city appears as a fair, with travelling artists and exotic animals. This image is extended when the visitor comes upon advertising walls and encounters representatives of other nations and cultures: Italian, Jew, and Turk. But even the relatively comforting image of the bazaar cannot be retained for long. The restless dance of images is taken up again in the passages that are to follow.

As may be clear by now, in such a text no stable significance of the city can be found. Where confrontation with the city is actively sought, no one metaphor will suffice. Images pile up, and it may be that it is only in the endless stream of metaphors itself that the new experience of the London traveller can be adequately expressed. There is a sense that life in the city is recognizable as life,

---

[6] William Wordsworth, *The Prelude: A Parallel Text*, ed. J.C. Maxwell, Penguin, 1986, 259-63, lines 149-80, 189-95, 211-23 (the version quoted is the 1850 version).

too, yet that the ways in which it moves can only offer glimpses of potential meaning. The whole of it remains unreadable.

There are many authors in the nineteenth century who tried to capture some of the novelty and the shock of the London experience, as Wordsworth had done before them. The well-known study by Raymond Williams, *The Country and the City*, lists many of the metaphorical techniques employed by writers such as Cobbett, Dickens, Gissing, and Hardy.[7] I will not, therefore, go into further details here but would like to point to the fact that the rural authors – with their usually negative outlook on the big city – were the most likely to cling to one reductive metaphor. Not willing to open themselves up to the complexities of modern urban life, these writers tried to contain their perceptions within a single overarching image.

Alongside these metaphorical reactions to London in nineteenth-century literature, we also find examples of the symbolic mode. The city as symbol was less prominent in literature around 1800, but gained momentum in the later Victorian era. By then, the newness of the London experience had lost some of its sharp edges. After 1850 the urban landscape of London changed: squares and thoroughfares were widened, monumental buildings were erected. With these changes, the comments of many observers changed as well.[8] London now tended to be seen as the symbol of the force and grandeur of the British Empire itself. Yet, since the squalor had by no means completely disappeared, some observers stressed additional symbolic relationships. In the juxtaposition of London's West End and East End, for instance, they saw an image of the dichotomy between rich England and its exploited colonies.

Even before 1850, there had been occasional references to a wider symbolic horizon: no other city represented modern industrial capitalism the way London did. The German visitors Heinrich Heine, Georg Weerth and Friedrich Engels were among the socially conscious authors who pointed to this connection. In their view, one only had to study the lonely mass of Londoners in order to get a vivid and gruesome picture of capitalism in the working. Engels wrote:

> The very turmoil of the streets has something repulsive, something against which human nature rebels. The hundreds of thousands of all classes and all ranks crowding past each other, are they not all human beings with the same qualities and powers, and with the same interest in being happy? And have they not, in the end to seek happiness in the same way, by the same means? And still they crowd by one another as though they had nothing in common, nothing to do with one another, and their only agreement is the tacit one, that each keep to his own side of the pavement, so as not to delay the opposing streams of the crowd, while it occurs to no man to honour another with so much as a glance. The brutal

---

[7] Raymond Williams, *The Country and the City*, Oxford and New York, 1973. See esp. ch. 19, "Cities of Darkness and of Light".

[8] See *The Idea of the City in Nineteenth-Century Britain*, ed. B.I. Coleman, London, 1973, 120-23.

indifference, the unfeeling isolation of each in his private interest becomes the more repellent and offensive, the more these individuals are crowded together, within a limited space. And, however much one may be aware that this isolation of the individual, this narrow self-seeking is the fundamental principle of our society everywhere, it is nowhere so shamelessly barefaced, so self-conscious as just here in the crowding of the great city. The dissolution of mankind into monads, of which each one has a separate principle, the world of atoms, is here carried out to its utmost extremes.[9]

Literature increasingly made use of this symbolic mode when the perspective was broadened even further. Only when authors proclaimed that the experience of the big city stood for the experience of modern life in all of its facets was the representational force of city life fully exploited. The first to use this equation, however, was not a Londoner but the Parisian poet Baudelaire. For him the city offered the most compressed and most exciting experience of modern existence.[10]

   Later in the century, this view was taken up by Henry James who said that London offered "the most complete compendium of the world".[11] Henry James had tried to illustrate the modern condition in his city novels, yet the first London novel that succeeded in portraying the city experience as the epitome of contemporary life was Virginia Woolf's *Mrs Dalloway*. Whereas Henry James had not been able to shed the traditional negative judgements – there is something old-fashioned about the horror that his notebook entries betray – Mrs

---

[9] Friedrich Engels, *The Condition of the Working Class in England in 1844*, with a pref. written in 1892, trans. F. K. Wischnewetzky, London, 1968, 24. See the Appendix for the original text.

[10] First explored by Walter Benjamin in his studies on Baudelaire (1937-1939). The completed parts were published as *Charles Baudelaire: Ein Lyriker im Zeitalter des Hochkapitalismus*, Frankfurt am Main, 1974.

[11] James said the following about his London experience: "It is difficult to speak adequately or justly of London. It is not a pleasant place; it is not agreeable, or cheerful, or easy, or exempt from reproach. It is only magnificent. You can draw up a tremendous list of reasons why it should be insupportable. The fogs, the smoke, the dirt, the darkness, the wet, the distances, the ugliness, the brutal size of the place, the horrible numerosity of society, the manner in which this senseless bigness is fatal to amenity, to convenience, to conversation, to good manners – all this and much more you may expatiate upon. You may call it dreary, heavy, stupid, dull, inhuman, vulgar at heart and tiresome in form. I have felt these things at times so strongly that I have said – 'Ah London, you too then are impossible?' But these are occasional moods; and for one who takes it as I take it, London is on the whole the most possible form of life. I take it as an artist and as a bachelor; as one who has the passion of observation and whose business is the study of human life. It is the biggest aggregation of human life – the most complete compendium of the world. The human race is better represented there than anywhere else, and if you learn to know your London you learn a great many things" (*The Complete Notebooks*, eds Leon Edel and Lyall H. Powers, New York, 1987, 355).

Dalloway's city experience is one of fascination and delight. For Clarissa Dalloway, the city is a place of benign anonymity and of ravishing abundance. She enjoys the unlimited movement and the feeling of freedom that results from this. Freedom also means that everybody is the creator of his own city:

> For having lived in Westminster – how many years now? over twenty, – one feels even in the midst of the traffic, or waking at night, Clarissa was positive, a particular hush, or solemnity; an indescribable pause; a suspense (but that might be her heart, affected, they said, by influenza) before Big Ben strikes. There! Out it boomed. First a warning, musical; then the hour, irrevocable. The leaden circles dissolved in the air. Such fools we are, she thought, crossing Victoria Street. For Heaven only knows why one loves it so, how one sees it so, making it up, building it round one, tumbling it, creating it every moment afresh; but the veriest frumps, the most dejected of miseries sitting on doorsteps (drink their downfall) do the same; can't be dealt with, she felt positive, by Acts of Parliament for that very reason: they love life. In people's eyes, in the swing, tramp, and trudge; in the bellow and the uproar; the carriages, motor cars, omnibuses, vans, sandwich men shuffling and swinging; brass bands; barrel organs; in the triumph and the jingle and the strange high singing of some aeroplane overhead was what she loved; life; London; this moment of June.
>
> For it was the middle of June. The War was over .... And everywhere, though it was still so early, there was a beating, a stirring of galloping ponies, tapping of cricket bats; Lords, Ascot, Ranelagh and all the rest of it; wrapped in the soft mesh of the grey-blue morning air, which, as the day wore on, would unwind them, and set down on their lawns and pitches the bouncing ponies, whose forefeet just struck the ground and up they sprung, the whirling young men, and laughing girls in their transparent muslins who, even now, after dancing all night, were taking their absurd woolly dogs for a run; and even now, at this hour, discreet old dowagers were shooting out in their motor cars on errands of mystery; and the shopkeepers were fidgeting in their windows with their paste and diamonds, their lovely old sea-green brooches in eighteenth-century settings to tempt Americans ... and who should be coming along with his back against the Government buildings, most appropriately, carrying a despatch box stamped with the Royal Arms, who but Hugh Whitbread; her old friend Hugh – the admirable Hugh!
>
> "Good-morning to you, Clarissa!" said Hugh, rather extravagantly, for they had known each other as children. "Where are you off to?"
>
> "I love walking in London", said Mrs. Dalloway. "Really, it's better than walking in the country."[12]

The fact that the city consists of signs which are difficult to grasp is no reason for despair anymore. The very openness of meanings is a challenge and an offer of adventure for Clarissa Dalloway. She is an upper-class figure and, as such, she shares some of the features of the nineteenth-century flâneur. This means that she reacts in an aesthetic way to the vibrant and heterogeneous world that

---

[12]Virginia Woolf, *Mrs Dalloway*, New York, 1925, 6-7.

surrounds her.[13]

It is doubtful, however, whether she is quite as free and detached from her environment as the nineteenth-century flâneur had been. The fact that she does not leave "her district", Westminster, makes for rather restricted movements, even resulting in circular patterns of motion.[14] Mrs Dalloway's activities are connected to surroundings that have historical depth and that she can relate to. As a consequence, she is never fully exposed to the shock of the new.

In this context, the tower of Big Ben has a special function. It is the stable orientational sign for the movements for all of the characters in the novel. Thereby the third mode of image-making comes into play: *the metonymic*. Clarissa Dalloway and the other characters relate to Big Ben, not only because Big Ben is their major topographical marker, but also because it creates order in the temporal sense: the sound of Big Ben divides the continuous flow of life in the city.[15] Big Ben establishes what could be called a common rhythm. In addition, Big Ben has a symbolic quality: some of the characters view the tower as the sign of British power and of a shared history.

Ultimately, however, there are no fixed meanings on the metonymic level. Even though Big Ben has a shared basic significance, each character projects his own personal meaning onto the building. This is a phenomenon we come across in other twentieth-century urban novels as well: every individual reads and interprets his city in his own manner.

In the modern urban novel, then, the symbolic and the metonymic modes of image-making come together. On the symbolic level, life in the city becomes an image of the modern condition itself, mirroring its curiosity, its craving for adventure and its mobility. On the metonymic level, the novel foregrounds the specific markers of a city – precisely because its inhabitants are depicted as isolated individuals who are in need of an orientational network and cannot thrive on the freedom of movement alone.

In closing, we might ask whether all of this means that in the twentieth-century city novel the metaphoric mode has disappeared altogether. At first glance, this seems to be the case. Since metaphor curbs what is incomprehensible and controls what is heterogeneous in city life, the metaphoric mode must necessarily become the least adequate form of image-making in the modern urban novel. Consequently, straightforward metaphors of the city are few and far between in modern city texts. Yet, viewed from a different angle, the matter is somewhat more complicated. For one could rightfully ask whether there is not something intrinsically metaphoric about the modern city novel. After all, it depicts urban experience as a continuous "flow" of phenomena, as a never-

---

[13] On this point, see especially Hana Wirth-Nesher, *City Codes: Reading the Modern Urban Novel*, Cambridge, 1996, 188-89.

[14] As has been shown by Avrom Fleishman, *Virginia Woolf: A Critical Reading*, Baltimore, 1975, 71-73.

[15] See Wirth-Nesher, 184.

ending "stream" of perceptions. On its presentational level the modern city novel follows "aquatic patterns": its narrative arrangement of perceptions and episode has "meandering" and even "oceanic" qualities. Some novels indeed thematize these structural characteristics. Thus, the literary presentation of the very openness and boundlessness of modern city experience resonates with a metaphoric field that has always been one of the least ideological of all metaphoric domains. Yet it is precisely here that a borderline is reached: in such "aquatic" images the metaphorical tendency to arrest all fleeting impressions and to contain the incomprehensible is reduced to a minimum.

APPENDIX

Schon das Straßengewühl hat etwas Widerliches, etwas, wogegen sich die menschliche Natur empört. Diese Hundert-tausende von allen Klassen und aus allen Ständen, die sich da aneinander vorbeidrängen, sind sie nicht Alle Menschen, mit denselben Eigenschaften und Fähigkeiten und mit demselben Interesse, glücklich zu werden? und haben sie nicht Alle ihr Glück am Ende doch durch ein und dieselben Mittel und Wege zu erstreben? Und doch rennen sie aneinander vorüber, als ob sie gar nichts gemein, gar nichts miteinander zu tun hätten, und doch ist die einzige Übereinkunft zwischen ihnen die stillschweigende, daß jeder sich auf der Seite des Trottoirs hält, die ihm rechts liegt, damit die beiden aneinander vorüberschießenden Strömungen des Gedränges sich nicht gegenseitig aufhalten; und doch fällt es keinem ein, die andern auch nur eines Blickes zu würdigen. Die brutale Gleichgültigkeit, die gefühllose Isolierung jedes Einzelnen auf seine Privatinteressen tritt um so widerwärtiger und verletzender hervor, je mehr diese Einzelnen auf den kleinen Raum zusammengedrängt sind; und wenn wir auch wissen, daß diese Isolierung des Einzelnen, diese borniertе Selbstsucht überall das Grundprinzip unserer heutigen Gesellschaft ist, so tritt sie doch nirgends so schamlos unverhüllt, so selbstbewußt auf als gerade hier in dem Gewühl der großen Stadt. Die Auflösung der Menschheit in Monaden, deren jede ein apartes Lebensprinzip und einen aparten Zweck hat, die Welt der Atome ist hier auf ihre höchste Spitze getrieben.[16]

---

[16] Friedrich Engels, *Die Lage der arbeitenden Klasse in England. Nach eigner Anschauung und authentischen Quellen*, 1845, in Karl Marx and Friedrich Engels, *Werke*, 10 vols, Berlin, 1972, II, 257.

WORDSWORTHIAN COMPARISONS WITH AUGUSTINE'S *CIVITAS DEI*: THESIS AND ANTITHESIS

IAN ALMOND

If we begin with the observation that a metaphor is not a device but a perspective, and/or that metaphors *a priori* do not exist until that uncanny moment when we decide the author is trying to "say something else", and/or that any text has the potential to become a metaphor the moment an enigmatic intention or an occult, secondary meaning is suspected, then the rest of our discussion must endure a peculiar kind of oscillation. It is an uncertainty instigated by two very basic questions. First, when poets or thinkers write about real cities, when should we consider them to be metaphors? Secondly, when writers use cities as metaphors, how often can we look for the "real city" – a Bruges or a Babylon – as the source of their imagery?

Augustine taught at Milan – then Mediolanum – under St Ambrose from 382 to 387. One wonders what he would have thought of today's Milan, with its six million inhabitants and twenty-six suburbs. One can almost imagine the fourth-century bishop, huffing and puffing with his mitre from one *strada* to another, frowning with moral disapprobation at the ice-cream parlours, the roar of the vespas, the kissing couples in the Piazza Mercanti. Although Augustine, unlike Wordsworth, would never have the chance to visit a modern industrial city, his aversion towards the earthly metropolis permeates every page of *City of God*: "The larger the city, the more is its forum filled with civil law suits and criminal trials."[1] For Augustine, there is no earthly city comparable to the urban paradise which, one day, will manifest itself as *Civitas Dei*, the City of God.

To call *City of God* an extended metaphor would be an understatement, to say the least. In twenty-two books and eleven hundred pages, Augustine painstakingly plots the course and appointed ends of two cities, one of which "consists of those who live by human standards, the other of those who live according to God's will". The dwellers of the earthly city, unlike those of the City of God, are lovers of the temporal and the transient, not the permanent and

---

[1] *City of God*, trans. Henry Bettensen, ed. David Knowles, Penguin, 1980, Book XIX:5, 859. All further quotations are taken from this translation.

enduring. They seek not the will of God but the "infinite variety of pleasure with crazy extravagance". Thus the earthly city itself is the "slave of base passions" and as a result is divided against itself by "litigation, by wars, by battles". In contrast to the harmony of the divine city, whose inhabitants seek a common end, worship a common God, "united by a common sense of right and by a community of interest", Augustine paints the earthly city as the site of a constant warring of wills, a Hobbesian nightmare where "unbridled" lusts forever vie with one another for the satisfaction of their own individual appetites.[2]

"City" is a rather loose term for Augustine. Throughout the book, it could be construed as meaning "community", "society", "race", on occasions "Church" and even "world-view". The two cities constitute two groups of people in the world, one that wishes to live in accordance with God's (unchanging) laws, and the other that lives following its own human (ever-changing) standards and customs. For a number of reasons, however, the metaphor retains its literality. Firstly, Augustine's book was provoked by the sacking of Rome in 410, an event which "to all thinking men in the Latin world ... was a psychological shock without parallel".[3] However, it was not so much the image of chaotic forces overwhelming an ordered metropolis that prompted Augustine's book, but rather the allegations that Christianity and the Christian God were to blame for Rome's downfall: "This fired me with zeal for the house of God and I began to write City of God to confute their blasphemies and falsehood."[4] Secondly, the names Rome and Babylon are never far from mind when reading about the "earthly city" in Augustine. Following an Old Testament tradition which sees the city as an increased opportunity for collective sin and communal blasphemy (Nineveh, Sodom, etc.), Babylon – and later Rome, which is a "second Babylon" – is seen as the example *par excellence* of the earthly city, if only because its name means "confusion". At the very beginning of the *City of God*, Augustine tells us about the "city of this world, a city which aims at dominion ... but is itself dominated by that very lust of domination". The earthly city, exemplifying the illusion of human independence from God, deifies itself by exercising the "right" to enslave others. It is an angle which gives Augustine's prose an oddly contemporary ring – murder, torture, oppression and injustice are all qualities of the earthly city, all consequences of the confusion of warring wills. Augustine points out that the first founder of a city was a murderer (in Genesis 4:17, Cain murders his brother Abel and then goes on to establish a city), the product of a "fratricide".[5] Augustine, fond as ever of his etymologies, is quick to note the assonance to the word Cain as meaning "possession" (from Kayin, Kãnãh, meaning "to get").[6] The city of this world, conceived in a murder and cursed with a desire to possess,

[2] *Ibid.*, XV:1, 595; I:30, 42; XV:4, 599; XIX:24, 890.

[3] Knowles's note in *City of God*, xv.

[4] From *Retractions*, 2, 43, 2, as quoted in Knowles's "Introduction", *ibid.*, xvi.

[5] *City of God*, XVIII:2, 764; XVI:18, 677; I:1, 5; XV:5, 600.

[6] *Ibid.*, XV:17, Knowles's note, 626.

forever seeks the temporal at the expense of the eternal, the sensual at the expense of the spiritual, and the transient in exchange for the immutable.

To put the case in slightly more postmodern terms: Augustine's history of the two Cities represents the progression of two different language games, two different understandings of the word "society". In the Heavenly City, harmony is achieved through the unity of direction, the unanimous accordance of a common centre – in this case, "the one supreme God" who "forbids sacrifice to any being except Himself alone". In the Heavenly City, there are no superfluous components or errant elements – Augustine's vision is one of perfect holism: "A man's house ought to be ... a small component part of the city ... and every component part points to the completeness of the whole."[7] Domestic peace contributes to communal peace; the peace of the home forms part of the peace of the city. Even marital discord, ultimately, affects municipal stability. In the Heavenly City, the direction of play is always monolinear, always monocentric: there are no isolated incidents, no idiosyncrasies wholly unrelated to their environments, no pockets of rebellious particularity within the all-encompassing scheme of the General.

If Augustine uses the metaphor of the city, then Wordsworth uses cities as metaphors. There are "good" cities and "bad" cities in Wordsworth, and the "good" cities invariably invoke the same characteristics as Augustine's Jerusalem: silence, light, stillness, tranquillity, immutability. Such cities are rarely glimpsed at midday, amidst the cries of street vendors and the whinnying of horses. "Incident at Bruges", the two sonnets concerning "Bruges" and "Westminster Bridge", and "St Paul's" all take place in the early morning or late evening. The pictures of folly we are presented with in Book Seven of *The Prelude*, the "foolishness ... and madness in parade", the "blank confusion" of the "overflowing streets", the street festivals with their "anarchy and din/Barbarian and infernal" make no appearance in the aforementioned poems, all of which display a noticeable absence of human movement, a thoroughly static sense of the sublime.[8] Perhaps the oddest thing about the cities in these poems is their silence, a quality which Wordsworth insists upon so often that one begins to grow suspicious:

> In Bruges town is many a street
> Whence busy life hath fled;
> When, without hurry, noiseless feet
> The grass grown pavement tread.

("Incident at Bruges", 1-4)

---

[7] *Ibid.*, XIX:23, 890; XIX:16, 878.

[8] William Wordsworth, *The Prelude: A Parallel Text*, ed. J.C. Maxwell, Penguin, 1986; Book VII, 284, 286 290, 292; lines 588, 695, 613, 659-60 in the 1805 version. All further references to Book VII in the text will be by line numbers to this edition and version. References to other works by Wordsworth are to *The Oxford Authors: William Wordsworth*, ed. Stephen Gill, Oxford, 1984.

O gentle Power of Darkness! these mild hues;
Obscure not yet these silent avenues...

("Bruges I", 11-12)

Hence Forms that slide with Swan-like ease along;
Hence motions, even amid the vulgar throng,
To an harmonious decency confined:

("Bruges II", 6-8)

And all that mighty heart is lying still!

("Westminster Bridge", 14)

However haunting the imagery, however enticing the cadences, one might be forgiven for thinking that, in Wordsworth's cities, people simply get in the way. Is a subtle misanthropy at work here? What is it about noise and movement that seems to be so incongruous with Wordsworth's idea of a desirable city?

To understand this a little better, we have to return to Augustine and his fundamentally etymological preference for Jerusalem (literally "vision of peace") over Babylon (literally Babel, "confusion"). The association of silence not just with divinity but with the proper reception of divinity is an age-old one – "Be still and know that I am Lord", writes Augustine at the end of *City of God*, quoting the forty-sixth psalm.[9] Wordsworth echoes the sentiment in "Star-gazers", whose joy rejects "all show of pride" because it is "not of this noisy world, but silent and divine".[10] If silence is divine, proper, *profound*, then noise is inauthentic, trivial, superficial. Silence is the opposite of what biblically has always been considered to be "chatter" or "foolish talk"; it constitutes the desire to occupy oneself with – and be occupied by – the significant in life, namely God. That which is not God or related to God – thoughts which do not lead you back to the centre, as it were – are vain, transient, death-seeking. Silence implies that one empties oneself of all worldly (trivial) thoughts, in order to be filled with divine (significant) ones. Once we understand the Sabbath as a day when one puts aside all worldly work and occupations to think about God, we can begin to see why Augustine calls the City of God a "sabbath without end",[11] a perpetual sabbath. In Augustine's New Jerusalem, there will be no idle chatter, no sensual diversions, nothing to distract the city-dwellers from their voluntary, joyful, endless contemplation of the Holy.

True to Augustinian doctrine, Free Will reigns supreme in both cities, the only difference being that, whereas in the Heavenly City the populace correctly exercise their own freedom to turn their thoughts towards God (Augustine's creator forces no-one to think about Him against their will), the inhabitants of the

---

[9] *City of God*, XXII:30, 1090.

[10] "Star-gazers", lines 27-28, 323.

[11] *City of God*, XXII:30, 1090.

earthly city abuse this freedom by turning their attention to what is temporal and fleshly, away from what is permanent and enduring. Whereas the Heavenly City is concerned with the love of God, the contemplation of something *external* to itself, the citizens of Babylon are inevitably besotted with their own ever-changing desires – an attitude Augustine conveniently sums up as "self-love reaching the point of contempt for God".[12]

Thesis: Westminster and Bruges – cities of harmony
Wordsworth, too, makes a similar distinction between worthy thoughts and trivial ones, although in a less openly theological way. "Bad" cities flood the senses with an array of vain and foolish things; for the narrators of poems such as *The Prelude* and "Tintern Abbey", these "bad" cities are places where one literally cannot stop and think, so immersed is the speaker in "the same perpetual flow/Of trivial objects, melted and reduced/To one identity" (702-703). The multiple and dazzling diversity of the particular blinds the poet's eye to that holy sense of the General, the moment when one "sees the parts/As parts, but with a feeling of the whole" (711-12). The "bad" city confuses the senses, distracts the faculties, blinds one to the eternal through the insistent presence of the transient, and ultimately loses the individual in the parts so that he loses any sense of "the whole". Wordsworth's "bad" cities deny depth: they convince their inhabitants that the world of the senses is the only world there is.

A poem such as "Star-gazers" exemplifies this attitude. In the middle of "Leicester's busy Square", a crowd of onlookers gather around a telescope set up on a frame, waiting to glimpse the moon for a farthing. Wordsworth's narrator interprets the scene with all the zeal of a medieval allegorist: the city-dwellers, "men of the multitude", bored with the banality of the present and the immediate, yearn for a glimpse of the immutable, the transcendental. Here the city – to employ that ancient metaphor of the carnal – is the cage of the soul. One by one, members of the crowd pay their farthing, peer at the moon and then "slackly go away, as if dissatisfied" (32). For a moment, Wordsworth's telescope offers an escape from "this noisy world" with its "show of pride", a moment's release from the urban chaos of plurality into the "silent and divine" encapsulation of a singular and unchanging reality. If Augustine's earthly city, with its confusion and babble, prevents the soul from seeing God, then Wordsworth's London prevents their inhabitants from thinking that "deep and earnest thought" (25) which all profundity entails.

This slowly brings us to an important paradox in both Augustine and Wordsworth's understanding of "good" and "bad" cities. Wordsworth's "good" cities do not exist in any earthly, empirical way – we do not smell their rivers, hear their streets, feel their stonework. We are permitted a vision, that is all – a vision untainted with actuality, blissfully bereft of any human activity, carefully removed from the sensual, the real, the actual.

---

[12] *Ibid.*, XIV:28, 593.

A sight so touching in its majesty:
This City now doth like a garment wear
The beauty of the morning: silent, bare,
Ships, towers, domes, theatres and temples lie
Open unto the fields, and to the sky.
All bright and glittering in the smokeless air.[13]

The same impulse which prefers the child to its father seeks out the city in the early hours of daylight, before it becomes polluted with the dismal banality of midday – its textures, cries and smells. Such cities exemplify "ideas" in the most etymological sense of the word – from *idein*, meaning to see. Unchanging images of silent rivers, morning skylines and deserted boulevards are as far as Wordsworth's "good" cities ever come to being realized. Constituting nothing more than images, than *signs*, these cities remain forever anchored in the world of the possible – unpeopled, unrealized, intact.

With regard to the allure of the unrealized, Augustine's Heavenly City has a similar status: "This image was also called the Holy City, in virtue of its pointing to that other City, not as being the express likeness of the reality which is yet to be." The City of God is an ongoing, as yet unfinished project, the cumulative progress of an inscrutably divine will. Despite lengthy descriptions in the closing pages of *City of God* of what the Heavenly City will be like, the New Jerusalem still remains an incomplete signifier, a nebulous, unfinished splendour, tantalizingly half-glimpsed within a flurry of inadequate symbols. Of course, the difference between the Wordsworthian "good" city and the Augustinian one is a question of eschatology: the "reality which is yet to be" of Augustine's celestial community will inevitably render itself tangible, sooner or later, in accordance with a divinely arranged schedule. Wordsworth's "good" cities, however, remain frozen in the silence of their dawns or dusks, rather like the "little town" on Keats's Grecian urn, enigmatically robbed of its populace. Whether or not a paradox occurs here all depends on the extent to which "unrealized" is synonymous with "uncertain". Both writers' "good" cities embody certainty, at least in one sense of the word. The Heavenly City epitomizes certainty because it is governed by one whose will "continues unshaken and steadfast" and is not the subject of man's capricious, unpredictable desires. It "stands in the security of its everlasting seat" and is the same picture of "changeless tranquillity" that God is. The eternal and unchanging nature of God's goodness reassures the certainty of the Heavenly City. It is a city where nothing is hidden (God will "bring all things to light"), where everyone's actions have a common motivation, a common interest, a common goal. The world, for Augustine, is a fundamentally uncertain place, where we are "tossed about at the mercy of chance and accident", where the truth is always hidden, where torture is elected as the only way of procuring

---

[13] "Westminster Bridge", lines 3-8.

certainty in an uncertain world.[14] Thus Augustine's Heavenly City, a haven from the *mundum* of accident and chance, does not only exemplify political certainty (freedom from tyranny, social instability and injustice) but also epistemological certainty – people will mean what they say, and say what they mean. As Kevin Hart has pointed out in *The Trespass of The Sign*, in the New Jerusalem symbols and metaphors will no longer be necessary, as the sign was a consequence of the fall. Misunderstandings belong to the world and worldly comprehension – in the New Jerusalem, everyone will understand one another perfectly.

In the cities of "Composed Upon Westminster Bridge" and "Bruges", chaos, uncertainty and confusion are equally absent. London's skyline lies "open unto the fields, and to the sky", free of any menacing obscurity or sinister smog – no hidden alleyways, twisting side streets, dark lanes, nothing which might conceal the unpredictable, the unexpected. It is the perfect scenario for an urban determinism – all the constants are cited, all the variables are known. The only source of motion in the poem is the river, which "glideth at his own sweet will". The city's inhabitants – the only chaotic factor in what is otherwise a calm and ordered metropolis – have yet to flood the streets with their shouts and cries, their wares and traffic.

If harmony, order, stasis and silence are (divine) aristocratic attributes, then motion, noise and chaos are distinctly proletarian. In Wordsworth's Bruges, at least, the inhabitants know how to behave themselves:

> Hence motions, even amid the vulgar throng,   7
> To an harmonious decency confined:
> As if the streets were consecrated ground,
> The City one vast Temple   10

Wordsworth, in effect, transcendentalizes his "good" cities, harmonizes them, desecularizes their earthly ends, and anchors them somewhere outside the sphere of the immediate and the unpredictable, so that even the more vulgar, unruly elements amongst them are "from jarring passions freed". This is a phrase which returns us once more to the Augustinian holism we encountered earlier, where the actions of every citizen ultimately contribute towards – or detract from – the common Good of the City. For this very reason, Wordsworth's cities are Newtonian in every sense of the word – operating along the lines of classical physics, where every movement is accounted for, where every effect has a cause, where the sum of all the parts *always* constitutes the whole. These cities, "all bright and glittering in the smokeless air", possess no "fuzzy" pockets of quantum uncertainty, no "undecidable" variables, none of the "anarchy" and "overflowing streets" we see in the London of *The Prelude*. Wordsworth stabilizes his cities by de-humanizing or depopulating them, rendering their structures certain through the removal of their uncertain inhabitants.

---

[14] *City of God*, XV:2, 597; I:16, 26; I:I, 5; XV:25, 642; XXIII:18, 1160; XIX:4, 825.

Antithesis: the London of *The Prelude* – a different Jerusalem?

> Their books are also different .... Those of a philosophical nature
> invariably include both the thesis and the antithesis, the rigorous pro and
> con of a doctrine. A book which does not contain its counterbook is
> considered incomplete.
>
> Borges, "Tlön, Uqbar, Orbis Tertius"[15]

In the first part of this paper, we took some pains to show how Wordsworth's
"good" cities – via texts such as "Bruges", "Westminster Bridge" and "St
Paul's" – exhibited all the characteristics of Augustine's City of God: silence,
light, immutability, tranquillity, unity. What I would like to do in this section is
suggest the opposite hypothesis: that there exists an Other Wordsworth, one
whose Jerusalem manifests itself not in the deserted boulevards of silent cities,
but in the noise and clamour of the "Babylon" presented to us in Book Seven of
The Prelude.

The infernal possibility that one might *confuse* Jerusalem and Babylon is by
no means a recent one – as early as 1764, Voltaire was already having doubts
about the etymology of the word "Babel" in his *Dictionnaire philosophique*:

> I do not know why it is said in Genesis that Babel signifies confusion, for *Ba*
> signifies father in the Oriental tongues, and *Bel* signifies God; Babel signifies the
> City of God, the holy city. The Ancients gave this name to all their capitals. But it
> is incontestable that Babel means confusion, either because the architects were
> confounded after having raised their work up to eighty one thousand Jewish feet,
> or because the tongues were then confounded ....[16]

Voltaire, subtly mocking as ever, suggests that confusion, far from being a lapse
into incoherence away from the clarity of the divine, might actually be the
natural state of divinity. Babylon as the City of God, confusion as *civitas dei* –
what kind of God would ever wish to have Babylon as His city? (One thinks
immediately of the dynamic, unfathomable deity of Eckhart's Godhead and
Boehme's Unground,[17] the primordial Nothingness of apophatic theology). A
God who rejoices in multiplicity and plurality, as opposed to harmony and

---

[15] *Labyrinths*, Penguin, 1987, 37.

[16] Quoted in *A Derrida Reader: Between the Blinds*, ed. Peggy Kamuf, trans. Joseph F.
Graham, London, 1991, 245.

[17] Cf. Eckhart: "In this power, God glows and burns without ceasing ..."; Boehme: "For all
is comprised in the will, and is an essence which, in the eternal Unground, eternally takes
its rise in itself, enters into itself, grasps itself in itself ... and this shines forth out of the
essence in itself and from itself." Eckhart as quoted in Reiner Schuermann's *Meister
Eckhart*, Bloomington, 1978, 6; Boehme as quoted in Walter Kaufmann's *From
Shakespeare to Existentialism*, New York, 1960, 35.

unity? (The God who says to Hosea: "I have multiplied visions for their benefit ...."[18] By questioning the original meaning of "Babel", Voltaire does much more than simply challenge a biblical etymology: he offers a different version of the deity, a concept of divinity whose principle is grounded in motion, not *stasis*, whose very *arché* resides in anarchy.

Voltaire's suggestion that "Babel" might have originally meant "holy city" does prompt the question: what kind of Wordsworth would have the London of *The Prelude*, with its "anarchy and din ... infernal", as his Jerusalem? What kind of Wordsworth would prefer the "blank confusion" of the metropolis (695), with "the whole swarm of its inhabitants" (698), to the "silent avenues" of Bruges, "attired with golden light"? Which Wordsworthian moment would shun the singular "beauty of the morning" on Westminster Bridge, in favour of the "overflowing streets" (613) of midday? One would have to fabricate a Wordsworth more interested in *expressing* "the essential passions of the heart" rather than curbing them, a Wordsworth drawn nearer to extravagance than moderation, closer to excess than sufficiency.[19] In Book Five we read:

> These mighty workmen of our late age   370
> Who with a broad highway have *overbridged*
> The froward chaos of futurity,
> *Tamed* to their bidding; they who have the art
> To *manage* books, and things, and make them work
> Gently on infant minds, as does the sun
> Upon a flower; the Tutors of our Youth
> The *Guides*, the Wardens of our faculties,
> And stewards of our labour, watchful men
> And *skilful* in the usury of time,
> Sages, who in their prescience would *controul*   380
> All accidents, and to the very road
> Which they have fashioned would *confine* us down,
> Like engines, when will they be taught
> That in the unreasoning progress of the world
> A wiser Spirit is at work for us,
> A better eye than theirs, most prodigal
> Of blessings, and most studious of our good,
> Even in what seem our most unfruitful hours?
>
> (my italics)

A distinct aversion towards the language of certainty pervades the piece, an explicit resentment of the notion of limit, system, structure, even to the point of celebrating the "chaos of futurity". In nineteen lines Wordsworth elevates the uncertain over the certain, castigating the Augustinian desire to "controul/All

---

[18] Hosea, 12:10.

[19] "Preface" to *Lyrical Ballads* (1802), *The Oxford Authors: William Wordsworth*, ed. Stephen Gill, Oxford, 1984, 597.

accidents", painting as tyranny the "taming" of chaos, the commodification of daylight ("the usury of time"), the harnessing of a certain energy which – the narrator seems to feel – would be better left unharnessed. In this lengthy and remarkable affirmation of the errant over the pathbound, of the accidental over the necessary, of the spontaneous over the purposeful, Wordsworth's anti-Enlightenment sentiments find their voice within a fearful kind of claustrophobia. Unwilling to march within the parameters of the age's "broad highway", Wordsworth wishes to wander – *without* a guide.

One finds Wordsworth employing a similar vocabulary in the 1802 "Preface", where the words "overflow", "excitement" and "overbalance" occur so often that one ends up overlooking the unconvincing selection of *caveat* ("tempering and restraining") which the poet tries to place after his remarks. Having asserted the aim of poetry to be the production "of excitement in co-existence with an overbalance of pleasure", Wordsworth is quick to check the spontaneous overflow of his conjectures by noting the "danger" that such "excitement may be carried beyond its proper bounds". Such phraseology seems to both affirm and deny a vocabulary of disharmony and dynamism, a vocabulary almost completely absent from the gliding rivers and morning skylines we are presented with in "St Paul's" and "Westminster Bridge". There may have been something about that "overflow" which Wordsworth feared, something about its superfluity, its gratuitous status which unsettled him – a pre-Kierkegaardian incommensurability, perhaps, which did not quite fit into the Hegelian schemes of his "wiser Spirit". The word "overflow" itself is interesting, as it conveys the image of a limit being extravagantly superseded, an excess which in the "Preface" is seen as positive and productive, as long as it is presented "truly and judiciously".[20] Such proliferation constitutes an energy which, I would like to suggest, the Wordsworth who subsequently denounces "extraordinary incident", "extravagant stories" and "outrageous stimulation" will never really feel at ease with – a fact which accounts for the strange ambiguity of the seventh book of *The Prelude*.

Overflowing streets, overflowing feelings; wandering through the London of *The Prelude*, it becomes difficult to separate metaphor from *mimesis*, allegory from observation, the sketch from the symbol. Are we in Babylon or Jerusalem? It would be easy to compile an immediate list of the negative sense-impressions the narrator of Book Seven records: a labyrinthine web of "streets without end" and "unsightly lanes"(195), filled with "the whole swarm of its inhabitants" (698); courts dominated not by Justice but by "brawls of Lawyers" (520); clergy preaching not sincerity but simply pedantic erudition, a "crook of Eloquence" with which to dazzle a "captivated Flock" (565); unashamed prostitution ("the pride of public vice", 419); spontaneous outbreaks of violence ("mobs" and "riots"), freak shows, kitsch art and street theatre eager to win the "uproar of the rabblement" (295). In short, a whole "Grimacing, writhing, screaming" (672) pot

---

[20] *Ibid.*, 609, 603.

of particularities with no common law, centre or direction – and therefore, concludes Wordsworth, "no meaning" (705). For the Wordsworth in love with "harmonious decency",[21] meaning will always be synonymous with direction – the clear and unambiguous text which knows where it is going, which refuses to wander from its path, which is not – in Augustine's words "tossed about at the mercy of chance and accident".[22]

However, if one forgets the "tempering and restraining" Wordsworth for a moment and concentrates on the Wordsworth more interested in a certain "infinite complexity of pain and pleasure",[23] then a gradually different version of *The Prelude*'s London begins to develop out from beneath the deceptive veneer of ungodly chaos. The metropolis of the poem, far from being an artless collage of shallow shapes and gaudy colours, starts to emerge as a dynamic hub of genuine creative power. With such a Wordsworth in mind, one begins to see through the wall of adverse adjective – "miserable", "perverted", "trivial", "barbarian" – to perceive a more encouraging series of phenomena: the "animating breeze", for example, which meets Wordsworth "issuing from the City's Walls" (3), the City as that which breathes *anima* into the poet, the City – no matter how Babylonian – as *cause* of the poem.

In the rich profusion of images which constitutes the London of *The Prelude*, we see how the "strife of singularity" (574) ultimately belies a multifaceted emanation of creativity – a city bristling with shows, circus acts, sermons, comedies, pantomimes, oratory and fairs. In contrast to the graceful motions conveyed in the cities of "Bruges" and "Westminster Bridge" – meandering, gliding and sliding – the force of the city in Book Seven is irruptive, almost to the point of attributing a kind of sentience to the city. Maritime metaphors of current and flow abound; "endless stream of men" (158), "following the tide" (206), "great tide of human life" (631), "the same perpetual flow" (702) and, of course, those "overflowing streets" (595) once more. What I would like to suggest is that Wordsworth's description of the city's traffic adopts, to a large extent, the same terminology as that used in the "Preface", when he describes his poems as attempts to "follow the fluxes and refluxes of the mind".[24] If the spontaneous feelings of a poet can overflow profitably onto a page, why can the spontaneous energy of a city not overflow onto its streets? If all "good poetry" is the consequence of such excessive agitation, and if the end of such poetry is to produce that much-desired excitement which, Wordsworth notes, is "an unusual and irregular state of mind" (609), then the volatile and erratic impression of the city in Book Seven, along with the narrator's negative reaction towards it, cannot be read without a certain irony. It would be the irony of a writer who is both fearful of and inspired by an energy whose "accidents" he cannot "controul", a

---

[21] "Bruges", line 8.

[22] *City of God*, XIX:4, 852.

[23] "Preface", 605.

[24] *Ibid.*, 598.

writer who is keen to separate his composition from the "vulgarity and meanness of ordinary life" and yet maintains that "Low and rustic life" affords the greatest possibility for men to incorporate into themselves the "beautiful and permanent forms of nature",[25] a writer who cannot decide whether the "multifarious" array of bizarre signs which greets him in the London of *The Prelude* constitutes a diversity or a perversity, a writer, ultimately, whose accidents are just too many to control, who is unsure exactly which city he is walking through – a Jerusalem where the citizen may glimpse the One through the many, or a Babylon where one is blinded by the many to the One.

To return – on a final note – to the verb "overflow", a verb which expresses not only the positive diffusion of a source of energy, but also the unforeseen exceeding of a prudent limit. The concept of "overflow", in whatever language it is expressed (*überfliessen, déborder, traboccare*) evokes the admittedly familiar yet curiously contemporary dilemma of the city in Romanticism. Does the untrammelled expression of individuality, within the relative safety of Romantic isolation (lime-tree bowers, ruined abbeys, deserted bays) take on a demonic, destructive aspect within the community ethos of the city or not? How profound is the analogous similarity between the Wordsworthian aestheticizing of "excess" in the "Preface" and the surging plethora of creatures and images which the city of *The Prelude* produces? Before dismissing this as yet another private/public conflict *á la* Rorty – and concluding, therefore, that there are some vocabularies which are simply more "dangerous" than others (the word is both Wordsworth's *and* Rorty's), vocabularies which have to be "privatized" for the sake of the public good – perhaps it might be worthwhile examining the genealogy of the image "overflow", a genealogy whose ultimate origins are largely Neoplatonic. Plotinus writes in the *Ennead*: "Seeking nothing, possessing nothing, lacking nothing, the One is perfect and, in our metaphor, has overflowed and exuberance has produced the new."[26] The influence of this dynamic view of the One, the source of all phenomena, is clearly seen in Augustine's own encounter with the divine: "And Thou didst beat back my infirmity, pouring forth upon me most strongly thy beams of light."[27] Ultimately, however, the aspect of this evolution of the concept of "overflowing" most relevant to our own discussion lies in an avid reader of Augustine's, Meister Eckhart, in a passage taken from his Latin works:

---

[25] *Ibid.*, 602.

[26] From the *Ennead*, V.2.1, as quoted in Gerard Watson's *Greek Philosophy and the Christian Notion of God*, Dublin, 1994, 75.

[27] *Confessions*, 7:10, trans. J. Pilkington, Edinburgh, 1876.

Life means a certain overflow by which a thing, welling up within itself, first completely floods itself, each part of itself interpenetrating every other, before it pours itself out and spills over into something external.[28]

Of course, Eckhart is still talking about God – Eckhart's word for "overflow" is ebullition, *ex-bullitio*, literally a "boiling over" of the power of the divinity into creation – and yet his description of "Life" as a "certain overflow" does initiate the secularization of the concept. For the Wordsworth more attracted by an "over-balance of pleasure" than by a "harmonious decency", the London of *The Prelude* is precisely this "Life" of Eckhart's: life in all its "unmanageable", ebullient, overflowing excess.

---

[28] Quoted in John Caputo, *The Mystical Element in Heidegger's Thought*, New York, 1986, 190.

FERRARA IN *VOLPONE*

ROCCO CORONATO

Cuckolds are painfully alert to the urban scene – at least in the Renaissance: as Corvino explains in Ben Jonson's *Volpone*, the *scena di città*, or urban scene, offers a natural habitat for their activities. Both jealous husband and potential bawd to his wife Celia, Corvino rants against the mountebank-show enacted by Volpone, disguised as the quack Scoto Mantuano, as if there were "No house but mine to make [his] *scene*".[1] For the urban scene can be seen in two ways, as Corvino himself well illustrates when he juxtaposes the perspicuity of the show with his own privileged viewpoint over the square: "No windows on the whole Piazza, here,/To make your properties, but mine? but mine?" (II.iii.5-6).

As Corvino learns on his skin, the Italian Renaissance *scena di città* assigned an exemplary value to such properties. Building on the classical treatises on scenography and the tradition of Roman theatre, the urban scene combines the characters' plots and passions within a place endowed with a perspective that naturally calls for a ruler. This perspective also calls for a sense of "publicity", where making private matters go public equates with making them comprehensible. My working assumption is that such is the pervasiveness of the Italian Renaissance *scena di città* that it works even in the absence of any proven contact. In this study of the urban scene in *Volpone*, I will assume that the ideal city of Ferrara is more real than Jonson's mythical Venice, offering as it does the best "windows on the whole Piazza".[2]

---

[1] Ben Jonson, *Volpone*, II.iii.2. All quotations refer to the New Mermaid edition.

[2] David McPherson investigates the connection between theatricality and Venice in *Shakespeare, Jonson and the Myth of Venice*, proving the extent to which Jonson modelled the Venice of *Volpone* on "the reputations of both Imperial Rome *and* Renaissance Venice" (100). For the mediation of Sir Lewis Lewkenor's translation of Gasparo Contarini, see McPherson, "Lewkenor's Venice and Its Sources". The usage of splendour and spectacularity is scrutinized in Leo Salingar and Roberta Mullini in their contributions to *Shakespeare's Italy: Functions of Italian Locations in Renaissance Drama*, eds M. Marrapodi *et al*, Manchester, 1993.

One is advised to look no further: Ferrara was *the* ideal Renaissance city. Starting from the latter half of the fifteenth century, the Este Court hosted Piero della Francesca, Pisanello, Jacopo Bellini, Rogier van der Weyden and Mantegna, who rephrased European and Italian artistic themes in a plastic synthesis of the Renaissance principles of harmony and decorum.[3] This artistic activity mingled with innovations in urban planning such as the Herculean Addition, a pioneering mediation between the medieval structure of the city, the rising needs of mercantilism and the Utopian nature of the ideal city. On a literary and scenographic level, the experimentation in the functional adaptation of Renaissance city architecture was implemented by the appropriation of the classics. In the latter end of the fifteenth century, Ferrara was the first Court to stage translations of the plays of Plautus, immediately followed by autonomous Italian works.[4]

The imitation and remodelling of the classical sources hinged upon the interpretation of the Vitruvian scenography, culminating in the *scena di città*, the "scenographic topos of the real-symbolic square", as Lodovico Zorzi defines it, that would later be adapted in Florence, Venice and other Italian cities.[5] Two elements appealed most to Italian humanists' theory of scenography: the subdivision of the orchestra and the three types of *scena*. The manuscript of Vitruvius' *De Architectura*, found in 1414, did not in fact include any drawings, a lacuna that elicited copious conjectural reconstruction of the edifices described.[6] Vitruvius reports that the design of the theatre is shaped by four equilateral triangles inscribed into a circle, and that "the stage will be made

---

[3] For a general introduction to the study of the Este Court, see *The Renaissance in Ferrara and Its European Horizons*, eds June Slamons and Walter Moretti, Cardiff and Ravenna, 1984. An illuminating description of Ferrara's "*Stadtgeist*", ultimately questioning the canonical distinction between the tyrant courts and the republics, is Werner L. Gundersheimer, "Toward a Reinterpretation of the Renaissance in Ferrara", *Bibliothèque d'humanisme et renaissance*, 30 (1968), 267-81. A still unsurpassed exploration of art in Ferrara is Roberto Longhi's *Officina ferrarese* (Opere Complete, 5 vols, Florence, 1956, V). André Chastel's *Renaissance méridionale* (Paris, 1965) offers a general introduction to Ferrara and other centres of the Italian Renaissance.

[4] The first period, from Carnival 1486 to Carnival 1503 (both marked by the performance of the *Menaechmi*), saw the enactment of Italian translations of Plautus, enriched by choreographic intermezzi, in the palaces and yards adjoining the Palazzo and the Piazza del Duomo. A second period intervenes in the years 1529-1532, with the creation of the Court theatre where the later plays by Ariosto were staged (Lodovico Zorzi, "Ferrara: il sipario ducale", ch. 1 of *Il Teatro e la città; Saggi sulla scena italiana*, Turin, 1977, 17-21, 26-30.

[5] *Ibid.*, 7. The translations in the text are mine.

[6] For the appropriation of Vitruvius during the Italian Renaissance, see Ferruccio Marotti, "Per un'epistemologia del teatro nel Rinascimento: le teoriche sullo spazio teatrale", and Cesare Molinari, "Il teatro nella tradizione vitruviana da Leon Battista Alberti a Daniele Barbaro", both in *Biblioteca Teatrale*, 1 (1971), 15-29 and 30-46 respectively.

wider than that of the Greeks because all the actors play their parts on the stage, whereas the orchestra is allotted to the seats of the senators" (*De Architectura*, V.vi.1-2). He also associates the three theatrical genres with three differing types of scene. Thus, the comic subjects "have the appearance of private buildings and balconies and projections with windows made to imitate reality, after the fashion of ordinary buildings" ("imitatione communium aedificiorum rationibus" – *De Architectura*, V.vi.9).[7]

Inaugurating the Quattrocento interpretation of Vitruvius, Leon Battista Alberti reports that the befitting place of the orchestra hosts senators and magistrates, separated by the populace ("patres et magistratus certo et dignissimo loco segregati a plebe"). While reiterating the Vitruvian distinction between the three scenes, Alberti omits however to specify the representation of the comic scene. He only adds that the elevated spaces ("exaggerata spatia") in front of the doors were decorated with columns and floors in the fashion of houses ("ex domorum imitatione" – *De Re Aedificatoria*, V.vii.40).[8]

In his activities at the Ferrara court, Pellegrino Prisciano merged the Vitruvian doctrine of Alberti with the material preparation of Ferrara Court festivals. Prisciano prescribes the imitation of houses, with a central door on the stage ("imitatione de case, cum ussi, porte et cum una in mezzo"), and places senators and magistrates in the orchestra. He also matches up the three theatrical genres with their respective scenes, urging that the comic scene be composed of "edifici privati et da citadini cum sue fenestre ed ussi ad similitudine de communi edificii". Yet Prisciano volunteers a peculiar interpretation of the *pulpitum*, which was divided into three parts: the *scena*, where ordinary houses were represented, the proscenium, where the actions were played, and the orchestra – located in front of the proscenium – where senators and magistrates were seated (*Spectacula*, 62-63).[9]

The creation of the *scena di città* also took up the other aspect of Prisciano's seminal activity at Court, the pictorial design of the Schifanoia frescoes.[10] A

---

[7] Daniele Barbaro similarly comments that "i Comici rappresentano cose quottidiane, & attioni di gente bassa, però la scena loro dimostraua forme di priuati edificij" (Vitruvius, *I dieci libri dell'architettura, tradotti e commentati da Daniele Barbaro* [1567], Milan, 1987, 256; translations are from *De Architectura [On Architecture]*, trans. Frank Granger, The Loeb Classical Library, London and Cambridge: Mass, I, 1955.)

[8] In *Storia documentaria del teatro italiano: Lo spettacolo dall'Umanesimo al Manierismo. Teoria e Pratica*, ed. Ferruccio Marotti, Milan, 1974.

[9] Leone de' Sommi provides an alternative explanation for the pervasive connection between comedy and the urban scene with a reference to *Scèhonà*, meaning "'contrada' o 'strada dove siano molte case di vicinanza'" (*Quattro dialoghi in materia di rappresentazioni sceniche*, ed. Ferruccio Marotti, Milan, 1968, Dialogue I, 14).

[10] Aby Warburg, "Italienische Kunst und internationale Astrologie im Palazzo Schifanoia zu Ferrara", *Gesammelte Schriften*, ed. G. Bing, Leipzig and Berlin, 1932, vol. II; and Paolo D'Ancona, *The Schifanoia Months at Ferrara*, trans. Lucia Krasnik, Milan, 1954,

suburban residence within easy reach of the cathedral and the castle, Palazzo
Schifanoia received extensive additions in the 1460s by Borso d'Este.[11] Among
these luxurious additions, the *Salone dei Mesi*, a cycle of frescoes by Francesco
del Cossa, Baldassare d'Este and others, eulogized the life of Borso and his
enlightened rule over Ferrara in a belaboured mixture of mythological and
courteous homage.[12] The cycle includes twelve panels, further divided into three
horizontal bands, each atop the other. The top band sees the triumph of the
mythological gods and goddesses presiding over each month; the middle band
depicts the signs of the Zodiac and the decani; the bottom band stars Borso as the
main character. The overall design celebrates the identification between Borso
and justice, which was so obsessively solemnized in Ferrara. A bronze, seated
columnar monument had been erected to him in the main square. In the March
panel, he is both depicted while administering justice and portrayed with a bust
in a lunette above the word "Justitia".[13]

Within this allegorical cycle, the fresco of April by Francesco del Cossa
(1469-70) shows Borso attentively scrutinizing the urban scene (**fig. 1**). In the
bottom band, the multiple narration has the figure of Borso both in the left
corner, returning from the hunt, and in the bottom right corner while, attended by
his courtiers against the backdrop of a magnificent loggia, he is giving a coin to
his fool.

The most intriguing appropriation of classical scenography is represented in
the top left corner, devoted to the *Palio di San Giorgio* (**fig. 2**). The race, thus
called because the prize was a *palio*, generally of cloth of gold,[14] was a
humiliating feast where citizens of lower status were ridiculed in front of both
the public and the Court.[15] A popular feast in honour of the patron Saint of the
city, it featured a disharmonious range of riders, here placed by Cossa in the
same space: swift Berber horses and their elegantly clad riders head the

---

12. See also Charles M. Rosenberg, "Notes on the Borsian Addition to the Palazzo
Schifanoia", *Musei ferraresi*, 3 (1973), 32-42.

[11] D'Ancona, 7-10; Charles Rosenberg, "The Iconography of the Sala degli Stucchi in the
Palazzo Schifanoia in Ferrara", *The Art Bulletin*, LXI/3 (1979), 377.

[12] Described as "one of the most extensive and enigmatic secular fresco cycles of the mid-
quattrocento" (Rosenberg, "The Iconography", 377) or as "a kind of Renaissance book of
hours writ large" (Gundersheimer, "Toward a Reinterpretation", 278), the Schifanoia
cycle is almost unique in being "the most remarkable instance of a set painted in the
Renaissance on a non-religious subject" (D'Ancona, 10).

[13] This fact would probably explain the omission of the figure of Justice in the frieze of the
adjoining Sala degli Stucchi (Rosenberg, "The Iconography", 381-82). See also Werner
Gundersheimer, "Clarity and Ambiguity in Renaissance Gesture: the Case of Borso
d'Este", *Journal of Medieval and Renaissance Studies*, XXIII/1 (1993), 13, and *Ferrara:
The Style of a Renaissance Despotism*, Princeton, 1973.

[14] Gunderscheimer, "Towards a Reinterpretation", 278.

[15] Zorzi, 10-11.

Figure 1: Francesco del Cossa,"April" (Salone dei Mesi, Palazzo Schifanoia, Ferrara)

Figure 2: Francesco del Cossa, "April", detail: The Palio di San Giorgio (Salone dei Mesi, Palazzo Schifanoia, Ferrara)

competition in front of recalcitrant donkeys all but ready to change course. Then follow coarse runners: discomposed youths, a paunchy, almost naked man, and two lascivious women that show their private parts in the heat of the rush.

Cossa stages the representation of festivity in Ferrara within the Renaissance appropriation of Vitruvian architecture as exemplified by Prisciano. A Roman scene of columns occupies the highest, most external level, combined with an elegant palace from whose windows some gentlewomen exchange amorous glances with young gallants down below.[16] The front level hosts the proscenium, where the *palio* is enacted; in the orchestra sit judges and courtiers, closely contemplating the spectacle. Borso is easily discernible in the right-hand corner of the orchestra, perusing the scene with benevolent, yet vigilant liberality.[17] The chief spectator of festive misrule, Borso will turn into "th'observed of all observers" – the most scrutinized, if elusive actor of the urban scene represented by the theatrical works set in Ferrara.

On-stage Ferrara presents the ruler with a less ideal portrait of the city.[18] In his city comedies, Ludovico Ariosto mingles the pragmatic moralism of the honest city officer with the satire of manners, presenting the power of the Duke as "external and superior" to the theatrical action.[19] Ferrara is observed through an alternation between "two orders of space distribution", the scene, which assumes the real shape of a city street with houses and shops, and "a purely mental space ... entrusted to the imaginative abilities of the spectator".[20]

---

[16] Cf. the "duas contignationes habens domus" reported by Iulius Pollux, where "a distegia lenones quidam prospiciunt, et vetula mulier despicit" (*Onomasticon*, liber IV caput XVIII, in *Storia documentaria del teatro italiano*, 81).

[17] For the interpretation of this panel, see D'Ancona, *The Schifanoia Months*, 35-37; Alberto Neppi, *Francesco del Cossa*, Milan, 1958, 15-18; Eberhard Rhumer, *Francesco del Cossa*, Munich, 1959, 74-75.

[18] According to D'Amico, the interplay between desire and the city rests on "the harmonious blending of structures employed in the *prospettiva* of Italian comedy", which "represents an ideal civic order" against which the playwright projects images of disorder "to create fluid perspectives that dissolve obstructions and reshape the urban world of comedy" ("The Treatment of Space in Italian and English Renaissance Theatre: The example of *Gl'Ingannati* and *Twelfth Night*", *Comparative Drama*, XXIII/3 [1989], 266). Similar associations with the ideal city as "an expression of values" that can "be represented and imagined before being explained" are in Giovanni Tocci, "Perceiving the City: Reflections on Early Modern Age", trans. Patrizia Lombardo, *Critical Quarterly*, XXXVI/4 (1994), 30-38

[19] Siro Ferrone, "Le commedie in prosa dell'Ariosto tra cronaca cittadina e ideologia di corte", *Il Ponte*, XXXII/2-3 (1976), 218.

[20] Riccardo Scrivano, "Towards a 'Philosophy' of Renaissance Theatre", in *Comparative Critical Approaches to Renaissance Comedy*, eds Donald Beecher and Massimo Ciavolella, Ottawa, 1986, 12. Ferrara becomes the "theatrical place of a repetitive, dull and unmodifiable reality" where Machiavellian instincts for predation and self-interest

Ariosto disseminates Borso's privileged viewpoint into an urban scene where publicity is the most heinous taint.[21] In the *Cassaria*, the departure of the old master and father adds to the general absence of any civic authorities (*Cassaria* I.ii, I.iv, I.v): the Borsian view is replaced by the interplay of mutual witnesses. Since the Duke is absent and law becomes an impending presence that will never materialize (IV.ix), all the characters can identify themselves with the reclusive girl who abhors being seen outdoors – "non vuole essere veduta uscire" (V.v).[22] The phobia of publicity returns in the *Suppositi*: Ferrara and its scenes slowly fade in, featuring the city centre where all the characters intently peruse the bystanders, poorly vying with the missing Borsian viewpoint: "Se io avessi auto cento occhi, non mi bastavano a riguardare, or ne la Piazza, or nel Cortile" (II.i). The image of Borso flashes through as the abiding presence, above local law, of the "Principe iustissimo" (IV.viii). Yet the performance of the Duke's law is at least dubious. An abused father is denied satisfaction, for private revenge is forbidden and public denunciation would only divulge his daughter's shame: "publico la mia vergogna" (III.iii). The urban scene is the place where the characters risk exposure, hardly for the benefit of the benevolent ruler's eye.

In the *Lena*, Ariosto offers his Duke the festive disorder of the city. As in the Schifanoia *April*, the ruler is within the picture and contemplates the humiliating spectacle of domestic licentiousness. The play was first staged at the Court of Alfonso I in the 1528 carnival, and then revised with the addition of two scenes for the following carnival.[23] Its plot stages the vain attempts of Flavio to pay Lena, the procuress, for gaining access to Lycinia, the daughter of Fazio, Lena's lover. He is assisted by Corbolo, his Plautine servant, in combating both the paternal license of Ilario and the complacent cuckoldry of Pacifico, Lena's husband. A fake adultery between Flavio and Lena paves the way for both the

---

animate all levels of society. See also Giulio Ferroni, "Per una storia del teatro dell'Ariosto", *Rassegna Letteraria Italiana*, LXXIX/1-2 (1975), 116.

[21] In Ariosto, the terror of publicity builds on the Plautine tradition of domestic scenes that eluded direct enactment, calling for the predominance of expository narrative. Gail Kern Paster noted that the city became "a cold and competitive urban world in which a predatory dynamic and conflicting opposites threaten a whole network of social and familial relationships" ("The City in Plautus and Middleton", *Renaissance Drama* 6 [1973], 32). William Tydeman analyses the rise of London's "positive identity" in its "comedic associations with intrigue and entanglement, amorous escapade and personal humiliation", leaving the "conventional urban background" of Plautus and Terence. "The Image of the City in English Renaissance Drama", *Essays and Studies*, 38 (1985), 29-44.

[22] Ludovico Ariosto, *Commedie: la Cassaria – I Suppositi*, ed. L. Stefani, Milan, 1997; *La Lena*, ed. G. Davico Bonino, Turin, 1976.

[23] G. Davico Bonino argued that the Ducal Court is here finally shown the *other city*, the antithetical version to their refined world (*Lena* xii), while Antonio De Luca remarked the unique freedom and vividness of directions that characterize urban life ("La *Lena* dell'Ariosto", *Rassegna Letteraria Italiana*, LXXXVI/1-2 [1981], 21, 29).

lawful wedding between the two youths and the perpetuation of pandering and cuckoldry.

The *Lena* revives the terror of publicity transpiring from the preceding comedies. Young Flavio keeps his love for Lycinia as "a secret of vital importance that I'd rather lose my property, my honour and my very soul than have it become public knowledge". The only thing that keeps them from satisfying their longing is the "lack of a place to meet" (*Lena* I.i, 64).[24] As a crafty procuress, Lena prevents her neighbours from detecting her manoeuvring in the households, much as her own husband pretends not to get wind of her affair with Fazio. Even at the end of the play, Fazio hushes Menghino, the only character that correctly interprets what has been going on: "Do you want the whole neighbourhood to know about it too?" (V.x, 108). For the play lacks an urban scene where the action may instantaneously become theatrically clear: the public spaces are indirectly described to the Duke who, as Menghino optimistically reports, will "know about it".

Since publicity is forbidden, the *Lena* enhances the role of mediators like panders and servants. Lena thus explains to her husband that impunity derives from publicity: "if I'd taken on all the men you've wanted me to – all the men you've constantly pestered me to accommodate – I'd have been a more public prostitute than the worst tart in the Gambaro." For her subterranean *scena di città* includes doors of an obscene kind: "And when you thought that the front door wouldn't take the traffic, you wanted me to open up the back door for business as well" (V.xi, 109).

The festive theatricality of crime easily recalls the Latin tradition of impunity and salacious wit associated with servants. Corbolo describes himself in explicitly intertextual terms: "What's needed here is the sort of cunning servant I've sometimes seen on the stage, who'd know how to tap the old boy's purse for a sum like that with a few well-thought-out-tricks" (III.i, 77). In fact, Corbolo's portrait of justice generates unfavourable comment on those courtiers and judges that gravely preside over the *palio* in the Schifanoia *April*.

The *Lena* construes justice as an urban scene of mutual deception. Harnessing the argument against publicity, Ilario etches out a disquieting vision of the administration of justice in Ferrara when advised by Corbolo to report to the authorities:

> ... suppose I do go to the duke and tell him the story, what do you think he'll do but refer me to the mayor? And the mayor will just glance up to see if I've got a present for him, and when he sees I haven't, he'll say he has more urgent matters to attend to. And anyway, if I haven't got any evidence or witnesses, he'll think I am a fool. Besides, who do you think commits half these crimes but the very

---

[24] Translations are from Ludovico Ariosto, *Lena*, in *Five Italian Renaissance Plays*, ed. B. Perman, trans. Guy Williams, Penguin, 1978; references are to act and scene numbers from the Italian edition and page number from the Penguin.

people who are paid to catch the criminals? Then the mayor goes shares with one
or other of their officers – they're all in it together (III.ii, 82).

Ariosto's homage to the Court might well be reconciled with lampooning the
local inefficiency of law officers. As the wise Torbido says after having
debunked an attempted theft by the bailiffs, "The duke doesn't have thieves in
his service" (IV.vii, 95). Yet Ariosto, who does not stage these facts in the form
of a public action, represents an urban scene which is different from the *palio*
ideally contemplated by the ruler.

In this underworld *scena di città*, the privileged viewpoint of the ruler is
enforced only when imagined. For the scenes of triumphant justice prevail only
over invented crimes. Corbolo arranges another urban scene of deception,
reporting an intended case of smuggling to two grooms: "You'd never spot it
unless you happened to know it was there, as I do" (V.i, 100). Ilario properly
decodes one of Corbolo's schemes only when another servant unintentionally
blocks the action, confessing that he "was so near to falling into the trap ["m'ha
fatto por gli occhi alla trappola"] – and it was pure chance that the boy let the cat
out of the bag" (V.ii, 100). Even the last bogus story forged by Corbolo portrays
justice as the noxious purveyor of publicity in the urban scene:

> Causing a crowd to collect is against the law of our duke, and the penalty is at the
> discretion of the magistrate. Besides, it could easily lead to manslaughter .... Be
> careful, sir, that you don't end up in serious trouble, with your distress giving
> great pleasure to the hangers-on at court who're always on the look-out for cases
> like this, which give them a chance to go and ask the duke to make them a present
> of the fine-money (V.iii, 103).

The original text refers to those courtiers "che tuttavia tengono aperti gli occhi a
tali casi". Presenting the Court with the other Ferrara, Ariosto envisions a virtual
piazza where domestic plots are offered to the Duke in their making. Yet this
indirect urban scene unveils the negative side of Borso's visual power. Acting on
his lusty master's urge for money, Corbolo hastens to the Piazza to buy quails
and turtledoves, roaming about in the throbbing centre of the city until he is
illicitly helped out by one of the Duke's gamekeepers. His amused words belie
the denial of justice in Ferrara and revile the Duke's officers in front of Alfonso:
"I couldn't help laughing to think how the Duke guards his game with such care,
and protects it with such ferocious proclamations and penalties, and all the time
it's the gamekeepers who do the poaching" (II.iii, 75). Corbolo has sworn
acquiescence on the very icon of justice in Ferrara: "I'll be as silent as Duke
Borso's statue over there" (II.iii, 74).

Literally bringing the figure of Borso into the civic pageant offered to his
successor, Ariosto exposes misrule as a requisite of the fiction of civic order. His
version of the *palio* has Borso silently stand "sopra tutti". Yet the urban scene is
also what makes the Prince visible. The ruler is just another actor set in the
humanist reconstruction of scenography, a distinguished observer reciprocally

eyed by the characters, in a game of mutual complacence and leniency transpiring from the mild reproach that Lena directs against Pacifico: just like the Duke, Pacifico did "know about the whole thing from the beginning", though he "can make it up if he likes; and he can take the whole thing as he pleases" (V.xi, 110; V.xii, 111).

Volpone and Mosca have their own way of taking the whole thing as they please: while Ariosto's characters report the domestic scenes in the context of underworld Ferrara, Jonson stages publicity and its discontents in private households.[25]

Much as in the urban scene of misrule presented to Borso in the Schifanoia *April*, and in Ariosto's divulgation of the private plots, Mosca and Volpone wield Borso's visual control, an eminence enhanced by the default absence of any authority until the dubious appearance of the Scrutineo. Mosca mocks the scenes conjured up by Voltore in his own private theatre of ambition, "What thoughts he has, without, now, as he walks" (I.ii.100). The sequence of visits in the first Act provides a variation of the humiliating *palio*, where the three legacy-hunters "counter-work, the one, onto the other" (I.i.83), each suitor establishing Mosca in the position of the ruler. The first performance occurs at Volpone's house as a private "sport", a grotesque portrait of folly that comments on the humiliating tricks undergone by his fools (I.i.70-73).[26] In the urban scene of acquisitiveness in Venice, the "wise world" peopled by parasites, Mosca can tell apart "those, that have your bare town-art,/To know, who's fit to feed 'em" (III.i.12, 14-15) from

> ... your fine, elegant rascal, that can rise,
> And stoop, almost together, like an arrow;
> Shoot through the air, as nimbly as a star;
> Turn short, as doth a swallow; and be here,
> And there, and here, and yonder, all at once;
> Present to any humour, all occasion;
> And change a visor, swifter, than a thought!

(III.i.23-29)

---

[25] The usage of the domestic scene in *Volpone* recalls the Spanish tradition of the *scena aperta*, where yards were opened into the urban scene to show characters in the secrecy of their households (Leone de' Sommi, *Quattro Dialoghi in materia di rapperesentazioni sceniche*, Dialogue IV, 68).

[26] James D. Redwine connects the usage of "sport" to "a study of man's wolfish compulsion to make others suffer", enacting "almost a morality play on Pride" ("Volpone's 'Sport' and the Structure of Jonson's *Volpone*", *Studies in English Literature*, XXXIV/2 [1994]: 301-302). Howard Marchitell offers a study of the topics of "the will to dominate" and the insistence on reproduction and the master-servant dialectics ("Desire and Domination in *Volpone*", *Studies in English Literature*, XXXI/2 [1991], 287-308).

In this version of the *scena di città*, the fool offers a perspicuous spectacle: "He's the grace of every feast,/And, sometimes, the chiefest guest" (I.ii.77-78). From this show Volpone stands aloof, "since I gain/No common way: I use no trade, no venture" (I.i.32-33). He is an object of admiration for his wealth, which "makes men observe me" (I.i.75). Moral comment is honed in terms of visual control, as Volpone describes his suitors, "their limbs faint,/Their senses dull, their seeing, hearing, going,/All dead before them" (I.iv.147-49).

To such competent Borsian view, the other characters react with dull senses indeed, unable to grapple even with the prodigies reported by Sir Pol. While Ariosto's characters abhor justice as offering a dangerous door for publicity, the fools of *Volpone* ineptly try to stage the public scene of justice. Bonario, the disinherited son, loudly asks Mosca if his sloth is not "Sufficient argument" for punishment (III.ii.10). Mosca takes him to witness his own disinheriting in a domestic space: "I'll bring you,/I dare not say where you shall see, but where/Your ear shall be a witness of the deed;/Hear yourself written bastard" (III.ii.61-64). Within this framework of visual incompetence, Sir Pol provides a ludicrous parody of the secret observation that should uphold an ordered state:

> ... I do love
> To note, and to observe: though I live out,
> Free from the active torrent, yet I'd mark
> The currents, and the passages of things,
> For mine own private use;

(II.i.100-104)

In his Borsian prerogative as the astute observer, Sir Pol closely scrutinizes Volpone-Scoto's gesture, loving "to observe/The state he keeps, in getting up". He misinterprets, however, the local colour and spectacularity of Volpone's show: "I wonder, yet, that he should mount his bank/Here, in this nook, that has been wont t'appear/In face of the Piazza!" (II.ii.32, 25-27).

In fact, Volpone-Scoto has abandoned "the public Piazza, near the shelter of the Portico to the Procuratia" in favour of "an obscure nook of the Piazza", for he loathes those mish-mash *ciarlitani* "that spread their cloaks on the pavement, as if they meant to do feats of activity" (II.ii.35-36, 49-50). Removed "from the clamours of the canaglia", his bank "shall be the scene of pleasure, and delight" (70-72). This is a far cry from the Borsian claim to detect misrule: for the *canaglia* was there to be represented to the Duke, unveiling those "rare, and unknown secrets" (142-3) that could escape his attention.

Volpone's *scena di città* is, in fact, targeted on Celia. As he later reveals to Celia, he has been in the piazza "to see thee at thy window" (III.vii.150). Celia recognizes him as the only one who can see the scene and, as befits a benign, vigilant ruler, grant permission and pardon sins:

> If you have ears that will be pierced; or eyes,
> That can be opened; a heart, may be touched;

> Or any part, that yet sounds man, about you:
> If you have touch of holy saints, or heaven,
> Do me the grace, to let me scape.

(III.vii.240-44)

Volpone celebrates his visual eminence in a peculiar theory of sin he seems to share with Corvino, the enthusiastic cuckold:

> 'Tis no sin, love's fruits to steal;
> But the sweet thefts to reveal:
> To be taken, to be seen,
> These have crimes accounted been.

(III.vii.180-83)

Not only does corrupt law or inefficient censorship naturally thrive in the city: the very fiction of Borso's eye also requires an open space to see and to be seen.

Borso is high above, atop all others – the scenographic tradition of the theatre included a *pulpitum*, or *tribunale*, that characterized the "exaggeratum opus pulpiti" in the orchestra (Alberti, 37 – Prisciano, 56, 62). This argument of the ruler's visibility on an elevated place seems referred to by Jonson in the first scene of the Scrutineo – the tribunal, or indeed the trial – which becomes a veritable school in acquiring a wrong gaze. Justice poorly scrutinizes the public scene of adultery, as Voltore the mediator says, in "this place most void of prejudice" (IV.v.26). Only faked crimes are in fact visible: Voltore unveils "The most prodigious, and most frontless piece/Of solid impudence, and treachery" that ever befell Venice (32-33). Publicity conceals actual criminals, for the Scrutineo is invited to "observe the malice, yea, the rage of creatures/Discovered in their evils" (50-51). The Scrutineo only interprets Voltore's version of the urban scene: Lady Would-Be "had in the open streets/Pursued them" (151-52), and finally a witness "saw 'em/Together, on the water, in a gondola" (149). As Voltore ironically reports, "damned deeds are done with greatest confidence" (IV.vi.53). The first Scrutineo scene exposes the confidence in the administration of justice where the act of seeing and detecting palpable crimes mechanically conjures up a *scena di città*.

After the demise of justice and the defamation of innocents because of the publicity of their non-existent crimes,[27] Volpone and Mosca openly stage their privileged viewpoint in the Venetian urban scene. Volpone gives up his disguise:

---

[27] This is what Stephen J. Greenblatt defines as the "false ending" of *Volpone*, the "false triumph" that preludes to inducing the audience "to reject the theatrical principles of displacement, mask, and metamorphosis" ("The False Ending of *Volpone*", *Journal of English and Germanic Philology*, I/2 [1976], 92, 103).

> Well, I am here; and all this brunt is past:
> I ne'er was in dislike with my disguise,
> Till this fled moment; here, 'twas good, in private,
> But, in your public –
>
> (V.i.1-4)

As Mosca practically observes, their achievement must be frozen as if in a tableau: "We must, here, be fixed;/Here, we must rest; this is our masterpiece:/We cannot think, to go beyond this" (V.ii.12-14). Since the other characters are "so divided 'mongst themselves", they have become even more perspicuous: "Too much light blinds 'em, I think" (20, 23). Mosca and Volpone have created their own *scena di città*. Volpone daringly resorts to publicity: "give out, about the streets ... /That I am dead; do it with constancy,/Sadly" (60-62). His house stages an adroit Scrutineo of the fools: "I'll get up,/Behind the curtain, on a stool, and hearken;/Sometime, peep over; see, how they do look" (83-85). In a topsy-turvy rendition of the Schifanoia *April*, Mosca dispenses justice, separately sanctioning all the three instances of folly. The fools' reactions are imagined in the living space of the city, where Corvino, for instance, is expected "Tomorrow morning, with a rope, and a dagger,/To visit all the streets; he must run mad" (93-94). Their distracted actions bespeak their public humiliation as victims of Volpone and Mosca: "How their swift eyes run over the long deed,/Unto the name, and to the legacies,/What is bequeathed them, there" (V.iii.18-20). In this *scena di città*, Volpone imagines he is enacting his Borsian power of observing the others to the full:

> Mosca, go,
> Straight, take my habit of *clarissimo*;
> And walk the streets; be seen, torment 'em more:
> We must pursue, as well as plot.
>
> (V.iii.104-107)

Being seen *and* taken – such vexation the urban scene offers. Crime walks in the open streets, "at the next corner" (V.vii.23), overly defying the gullible to "publish what you are" (V.viii.21).

The second and final Scrutineo scene reinforces public justice in Venice. Yet it is debatable whether "These things can ne'er be reconciled" (V.xii.1). Another imagined *scena di città* features the public punishment of Corvino, the major theorizer of the open space:

> Thou, Corvino, shalt
> Be straight embarked from thine own house, and rowed
> Round about Venice, through the Grand Canal,
> Wearing a cap, with fair, long ass's ears,

Instead of horns: and, so to mount, a paper
Pinned on thy breast, to the *berlino*

(V.xii.134-39)

In fact, the final dénouement of Volpone, who has fallen into his "own noose" (V.x.13), and of Mosca, "the instrument of all" (19), restores a partial facet of the administration of liberality and justice. Seeing the guilty requires the publicity of both ruler and ruled – the act of seeing Borso looking at his subjects. Yet public punishment restores vigilant discernment only after the fact: "Now, you begin,/When crimes are done, and past, and to be punished,/To think what your crimes are" (V.xii.146-48).

One needs, however, to take a step backwards. *Volpone* overrides Ariosto's exposure of the fiction underlying the Borsian rule. Corvino, the only character to interpret properly the mountebank-show, tries to thwart his wife's visual response. As Volpone says, Celia's "eye first descended on so mean, yet not altogether to be despised, an object" (II.ii.227-28). Here, as Corvino rightly sees, begins an interplay of lecherous gazing between ladies and gallants akin to the scenography envisaged by the Schifanoia *April* right behind Borso's back, describing Celia as a skilful performer:

> ... whilst he,
> With his strained action, and his dole of faces,
> To his drug lectures draws your itching ears,
> A crew of old, unmarried, noted lechers
> Stood leering up, like satyrs: and you smile
> Most graciously! and fan your favours forth,
> To give your hot spectators satisfaction!

(II.v.3-9)

The *scena di città* extends to the windows overlooking the piazza. Celia herself could "mount ... so, [she] may be seen, down to th'foot" (19-20). She is thus transformed into a public whore: "before a multitude[.]/You were an actor, with your handkerchief!" (39-40). Celia's former "restraint" from the public space will now turn into "liberty" as a result of the new regime imposed by Corvino:

> First, I will have this bawdy light dammed up;
> And, till't be done, some two, or three yards off,
> I'll chalk a line; o'er which, if thou but chance
> To set thy desp'rate foot; more hell, more horror,
> More wild, remorseless rage shall seize on thee ....
> And, now I think on't, I will keep thee backwards;
> ....
> Thy lodging shall be backwards; thy walks backwards;
> Thy prospect – all be backwards; and no pleasure
> That thou shalt know, but backwards.

(II.v.50-54, 58-61)

Much like Ariosto's quibble on Lena's backdoor, windows can serve both ways. Claiming that heaven and saints are "blind, or stupid" (III.vii.54), Celia professes to ignore the double usage of the window, which simultaneously offers a view and is offered to the view like the scenographic palace of the Schifanoia *April*. The urban scene of *Volpone* exceeds, in fact, Ariosto's piercing, if ultimately reassuring representation of a city so endemically depraved as to dispense leniency. For Jonson, publicity discloses the *forum conscientiae*, where Celia, like all the individuals in the play, has to retreat further in order to make sense of the spectacle she witnesses. As Corvino had accusingly remarked to Volpone, this is a way "to make your scene", to construct the ruler's privileged perspective where all the characters are reflected in their turn.

A similar mirroring could silently inform the Borsian icon of justice. Prisciano's interpretation of Vitruvius had posited the orchestra as a part of the spectacle, replete with the audience of judges and courtiers one sees in the Schifanoia *April*. This portion of the inset may, in fact, represent a reflected image of the audience, while Borso observes the spectacle riding on the right side of the painting. It is a sort of "vexing irony", as Zorzi observes: "self-contemplation, the discriminating connotation of the theatre of the prince, excludes any necessary intervention by the public. By contemplating his own majesty, the prince is unmasked as self-sufficient" ("Ferrara", 13). In this sense, Jonson extends Borso's self-contemplation to all the characters, since his representation of the city overrides the spectacular myth of Venice or the ideal symbolism of Ferrara. *Volpone* internalizes space: not only does the city enmesh and resolve the single plots of the individuals, it also acts as the ultimate *locus memoriae*, as the attempt to capture life's tricks and turns as a *scena di città* – a feat to be done by moving constantly "backwards" in the Jonsonian scenography of passions and desires.

GEOGRAPHICAL AND TEMPORAL EFFECTS OF THE CITY ON THE CORRESPONDENCE OF THE COUNTESSES OF HERTFORD AND POMFRET, 1738-41

JAMES HOW

The writing of letters in Britain during the eighteenth century has been described by Bruce Redford as "the converse of the pen" and by Linda Zionkowski as a "commerce".[1] But neither of these writers has fully explored the reverse implications of the metaphors they use. For whereas letters may be like conversations or commerce they are certainly not the same as them; and what letters do not have in common with these other forms of human interaction might prove more interesting than what they do have in common with them. The principal difference lies in the medium of transaction. Transactions of conversation and commerce are carried out either face-to-face or by directly appointed agent; whereas the exchange of letters takes place at a distance and within the impersonal network of cross posts, byposts and post roads which constitute the postal system. One of the most important implications of this principal difference is a result of the fact that a postal system always relies upon a centre in order to facilitate sorting and distribution: for such a centre will inevitably mediate or affect what is sent. Richard Rogers reveals the most likely nature of the centre of a postal network when he affirms that "cities ... are the seedbeds of our cultural development ... centres of communication, learning and complex commercial enterprises".[2] From a supposed postmodernist – the architect of the Centre Pompidou and the Court of Human Rights – such a statement might seem a contradiction, given postmodernism's concern with what Linda Hutcheon terms "decentering".[3] And indeed Eric Hobsbawm directly challenges Rogers's maxim when he identifies the twentieth century as the site of:

---

[1] In, respectively, Bruce Redford, *The Converse of the Pen*, Chicago, 1986, and Linda Zionkowski, *The Value of Words: Writing and the Eighteenth-Century Commerce in Letters*, unpublished doctoral thesis, Northwestern University, 1988.

[2] Richard Rogers, "This Is Tomorrow", *Independent on Sunday Review*, 23 November 1997, 15.

[3] Linda Hutcheon, *The Politics of Postmodernism*, London, 1989, 13.

a revolution in transport and communications which virtually annihilated time
and distance ... and for most practical purposes, abolished the cultural
advantages of city over countryside.[4]

But if such a revolution has indeed taken place, how is it possible to explain
what Stephen Bayley terms the continued "gravitational pull of the city", the
phenomemon which accounts for the fact that "half the world's population now
lives in cities and by 2005 it is estimated that fraction will have risen to three-
quarters"?[5] Perhaps with the advent of information technology such a
gravitational pull no longer has anything to do with culture and all to do with
social and economic inequality. More to my purpose, the very ground upon
which this debate is fought – Hobsbawm's siting of his revolution in the
twentieth century – directly implies that in the eighteenth century, at least, the
city was the undisputed centre of culture, transport and communications.

This essay will explore some effects of the centrality of the city upon an
eighteenth-century published correspondence: that of the Countesses of
Pomfret and Hertford. The correspondence was first published in 1805, and –
as in the case of the *Turkish Embassy Letters* (1763) of Lady Mary Wortley
Montagu and the *Letters to his Son and Others* (1774) of Lord Chesterfield –
its publishers evidently hoped for success on the basis of the aristocracy of the
correspondents. Thus, the 1806 edition informs us that the Countesses'
friendship developed at Court in London whilst both were ladies of the
bedchamber to Caroline, the wife of King George II. Certainly, on one level the
correspondence does satisfy the demand for courtly gossip – in one letter alone
there are references to the fact that "the Duke of Marlborough lost 700 pounds
... [and that] Lady Caroline Sackville is to be married".[6] But what neither of the
two editions of this correspondence tells us is that Court life at the time was
highly politically charged, vindictive and unforgiving; and that from the start
the Countesses' friendship became an act of mutual solidarity (a condition
which was later reflected in the letters). On Caroline's death in 1737, the
Countesses retired from London without regret – Hertford to her country
estates at Richkings and Pomfret to travel on the continent. This separation is
the point at which the three-year correspondence begins. In other words, only a
very few of these letters were written from or to London; and probably not one
letter would have been written if the Countesses had not first been separated by
their retirement from London. How then can the city possibly have any

---

[4] Eric Hobsbawm, *Age of Extremes: The Short Twentieth Century 1914-1991*, London,
1994, 12-13.

[5] Stephen Bayley, "Metropolitan Lines", *Independent Saturday Magazine*, 13 December
1997, 10.

[6] Frances Hertford and Henrietta Louisa Pomfret, *Correspondence between Frances,
Countess of Hartford, (Afterwards Duchess of Somerset,) and Henrietta Louisa,
Countess of Pomfret, between the years 1738 and 1741*, ed. William Bingley, London,
1806, I, 75-76.

significant effects upon what was, on the part of one of the correspondents, a travel correspondence? Quite easily, in fact. For since letters rely upon the existence of vast national and international networks, however far letter writers get from the centres of these networks (the cities) they will not be able to escape dependence upon them. Indeed, contemporaneous maps of postal routes resemble primitive anatomical drawings, with the body of the postal network sustained by the bodily organs of the cities, to which all roads lead. Cities are thus as essential to the running of eighteenth-century postal networks as livers, kidneys, or hearts to the animal body.

City forms and city technologies

First, I need specifically to explain what I mean when I refer to the City of London, since any effects of the city upon the Countesses' letters will emanate from this one source, because, according to Daniel A. Baugh, "until the nineteenth century, England was to an unusual degree a single-city kingdom".[7] So, if Baugh is right, it is not surprising that to say – as I have done – that it was absence from London that was the occasion for Hertford and Pomfret's writing is to strike a note of ambiguity. After all, a single-city kingdom is likely to expect multiple functions of that city – which in turn will foster the division of the city into quarters. The Countesses retired from what Max Byrd describes as "the aristocratic Court world that lay along the western curve of the Thames ... physically distinct [from the City and lying] north and west of Charing Cross".[8] And in her letters Pomfret emphasizes only the absence of the effects of *Court*-intrigues once out of London, reminding Hertford that "there is now, dear madam, no reason to dissemble" (I, 56); Hertford, in turn, reminds Pomfret that there is now no longer occasion for the saying of any of the "great many ... unmeaning civil things which both you and I have often heard [at Court]" (I, 51). So, it would seem that as soon as the Countesses were physically absent from the London Court they were freed from any of its effects upon their modes of expression. But the Court constituted only one part of London. The other part, the City with a capital "C", was, according to Max Byrd, to be found:

> East of Temple Bar [where] the crowded, winding alleys and courtyards around St Paul's, Cheapside, the Tower, Wapping, Hockley Hole enclosed the immemorial haunts of London's poor and, more and more in the eighteenth century, the site of its manufacturers as well as its commerce (53).

---

[7] Daniel A. Baugh, "Introduction: The Social Basis of Stability", in *Aristocratic Government and Society in Eighteenth-Century England: The Foundations of Stability*, ed. Daniel A. Baugh, New York, 1975, 2.

[8] Max Byrd, *London Transformed: Images of the City in the Eighteenth Century*, New Haven, 1978, 52-53.

This existence of two distinct districts within one city (a striking example of what the geographer James Vance terms urban morphogenesis) is the cause of the ambiguity I have referred to.[9] Because of this ambiguity, it might not be wise to follow Lewis Namier in labelling the eighteenth-century aristocracy "amphibious [in that] .... It resided part of the year in London and part in its country houses" (quoted in Baugh, 18). For it is very unlikely that any member of the aristocracy ever resided in the City – not when on the other side of London "rapidly developing squares like St. James's, Soho, Golden, Hanover, and Cavendish gave haven" (Byrd, 52). That most class-conscious of all eighteenth-century figures, Samuel Richardson, shows just how rigid the dividing line was between the two Londons in the repeated "joking references to living on 'the wrong side of Temple Bar' (that is, the City, rather than the fashionable West End)" that have been attributed to him by his biographers.[10] It might be more appropriate, then, after Namier, to describe the eighteenth-century aristocracy as semi-amphibious. Yet, despite the fact that the Countesses might not actually ever even have visited the City, the concept of the City was to have insidious effects – which I will describe under the headings of geography and temporality – upon their lives and letters, even as the effects of the Court of London were shed like old skin.

Why might this be? Well, Roy Porter's perceptions go some way to answering this question. He writes that at the time:

> London became the marvel of the world, throbbing with news, spectacles and entertainment. Like New York in the 1920s, it operated as an addictive geography of the imagination, the hero – and often villain – of plays, poetry and Hogarthian prints. Symbolically, the key site for the new public culture was the coffee house.[11]

Again, John Brewer describes this London in his book *The Pleasures of the Imagination* as "rather like late nineteenth-century New York or late twentieth-century Los Angeles: it stood out as the metropolis of the moment".[12] Moreover, Brewer makes it clear that during the eighteenth century "the arts became more commercial and less courtly because they became more urban" (xviii). In other words, the dynamism of London at this time emanated from the City and not from the Court, headed as it was by the deeply unfashionable Hanoverians. Two main points arise from this perception of the City as

---

[9] Byrd notes that "every city encloses extremes of poverty and wealth, but the cleavage between West End and City was especially visible and felt in [Alexander] Pope's time" (*ibid.*, 53).

[10] Elizabeth Bergen Brophy, *Samuel Richardson*, Boston, 1987, 3.

[11] Roy Porter, "Coffee and Culture with Dr Johnson", *Independent Long Weekend*, 24 May 1997, 6.

[12] John Brewer, *The Pleasures of the Imagination: English Culture in the Eighteenth Century*, London, 1997, xxv.

irresistible and universally affecting. First, any effects of the City on the Countesses' letters will indeed be operating within this realm of "an addictive geography of the imagination" – since during the correspondence Hertford avoids London and Pomfret stays on the continent. Perhaps, then, the City will be to the Countesses like one of William Chapman Sharpe's cities "not ... of brick and mortar, but ... 'unreal cities' – cities of mind, cities of word ... 'phantom cities'".[13] Secondly, since the coffee house as a symbolic site for reaction to and participation in the new public culture was largely reserved for men, I propose that it was the letter which assumed this role for women. Hence, the letter will be the site wherein any effects of this new culture on women will most likely be seen.

The coffee house was a defined space – a recognized phenomenon of the social geography of the city. John Brewer even notes that at the time "the coffee house was claimed as a new sort of urban territory, one which was accessible [at least to men] and orderly" (38). But what about letters? Where do *they* exist? Pomfret, suspecting a letter has miscarried, writes "I begin to be ashamed of my persecuting you with my stupid epistles; and I believe that Fate interposes in your favour, and turns aside the flying bits of paper" (II, 210). These "flying bits of paper" clearly exist at some undefined point in between the addresser and the addressee of a letter – somewhere along that distance which the technologies of communication attempt to decrease. In the eighteenth century these technologies were firmly grounded in the City. Any letter that came from or went to the continent had to pass under the eyes of the Foreign Secretary of the Post at the General Letter Office, housed in Lombard Street in the City.[14] The carriage of foreign letters by any other means was strictly forbidden by "the monopolistic nature of the contract" between Parliament and the Post office (Robinson, 44) – especially in a time of war such as the late 1730s and early 1740s.[15] With this knowledge of the restricted route of letters, it is not surprising that aspects of the social geography of the City had an effect upon the imagination of letters during this period.

For Hertford, the knowledge that her private writings – and private writings addressed to her – were wending their way about the streets of east London on their way to the west was a source of anxiety. When a letter was just about to be delivered she could relax and write herself down as playful: "I inquire after the French mail as if I were carrying on a correspondence in order to steal the

---

[13] William Chapman Sharpe, *Unreal Cities: Urban Figuration in Wordsworth, Baudelaire, Whitman, Eliot, and Williams*, Baltimore, 1990, xi.

[14] For details of the Lombard Street Office, see Howard Robinson, *The British Post Office: A History*, Princeton, 1948. For the work of the Foreign Secretary of the Post Office, see Kenneth Ellis, *The Post Office in the Eighteenth Century: A Study in Administrative History*, London, 1958.

[15] In her *Britons: Forging the Nation 1707-1837*, London, 1994, 52, Linda Colley draws attention to the fact that during this period the British were fighting "the wars of Jenkins's Ear and Austrian succession".

dauphin; and actually listen to every double knock at the door, in hopes of the post-man" (I, 93). But when just upon the point of delivering a letter into the postal network she tells Pomfret fearfully: "I have already inserted more in [my last letter] than I should choose any one to see except yourself" (I, 86). Why this anxiety? Linda Colley goes some way to answering this question when she describes the eighteenth-century City as containing:

> Coffee houses, bawds, crowds surging around a gibbet, strolling actresses with overflowing white bosoms, raucous street-criers jostling for space with fiddlers, pick-pockets, fine ladies and fat, glistening clergymen, taut faces of gamblers picked out by greed and candlelight, madmen howling in Bedlam, the damp high walls of Fleet prison ....[16]

Colley explains that this disturbing perception – quite enough to provoke anxiety in a pair of Countesses – was principally propagated by William Hogarth; and I shall return later to that artist's work. In the meantime, it is enough to point out the inhibiting effects of anxiety about the City. Hertford and Pomfret had hoped to develop in their letters an arena of intimacy, analogous to the new "clubs and coffee houses [which] shaped social and cultural life" (Brewer, 36). Thus, Pomfret begins one letter with the following enticing words: "this humbly knocks at your dressing-room door, to welcome you to town" (I, 47). But the calm of this arena is repeatedly shattered by the exigencies of the City technologies used to transmit letters; the air of intimacy is destroyed or invaded. For example, on several occasions Hertford complains to Pomfret of instances of carelessness on the part of the Post Office:

> the courier who had the care of your last letter, dear madam, had used it in so terrible a manner that it was almost impossible to know how to set about opening it; for it had been in the water, and the cover was entirely off at one end. The letter itself was made into a kind of pasteboard ... (III, 197).

At other times Hertford reveals a more serious kind of anxiety, much more likely to affect what she writes: "I could say a great deal to you by word of mouth, which I cannot venture to insert in a letter, lest some one should have the curiosity to open it before it reaches you" (I, 66-67). Nor was this anxiety entirely unfounded. Herbert Joyce notes that one of the chief causes of the "distrust and hostility with which the Post Office appears to have been regarded towards the middle of the [eighteenth] century" was the fact that certain "letters bore evident signs of having been opened at the Post Office [in the City]".[17] Indeed, at one point in the correspondence Hertford almost despairs – at least

---

[16] Linda Colley, "A Very Modern Misfit", *Independent on Sunday Review*, 7 September 1997, 26.

[17] Herbert Joyce, *The History of the Post Office: From its Establishment down to 1836*, London, 1893, 170.

whilst using the General Post – of ever having "an opportunity of sending a letter that does not run the hazard of being opened before it reaches you" (I, 116). Here, the City is perceived as a den of letter thieves – in keeping with the contemporaneous perceptions of Daniel Defoe, who used it as the setting for *Moll Flanders* and *Colonel Jack*, novels which can be seen as the progenitors of crime fiction.

As we have seen, Hertford and Pomfret complained about aspects of the social geography of London; but at the same time they were well aware that in the temporal sphere at least the vitality of the City could potentially be turned to their advantage. In an article about the approach of the new millennium, Hamish McRae notes that "technology, particularly in communications, is racing forward so that distance, for many activities, has virtually ceased to exist".[18] Another journalist, Frances Cairncross, has perhaps precipitately already proclaimed "the death of distance".[19] In the eighteenth century, this distance was only starting to be shortened by City technologies: so, whilst Pomfret is on the Continent, the Countesses repeatedly complain of what they variously describe as being "ever so awkward a distance" (I, 95), "this terrible distance" (I, 170), or "such a distance" (III, 21). The temporal lag between letters produced by this distance has several effects. Hertford decides:

> I cannot determine to wait till I receive another letter from you, before I write. The distance you are at, seems to make a regular return of letter for letter impossible ... (I, 137).

Pomfret, for her part, later abandons the individual letter entirely, because "the extreme badness of the weather and roads makes the post so late" (II, 131). Instead she promises that: "I shall divide my dispatches into seven parts; making them the weekly journal of my motions and observations" (II, 193). Such decisions taken by the Countesses – as a direct result of perceived shortcomings in the efficacy of the Post Office – have profound effects upon a reading of their correspondence. Towards the end of the correspondence, the sensation of dialogue becomes more and more scarce, to be replaced by an inferior rambling species of monologue. And even as Pomfret nears England on her return journey from Italy dialogue is still interrupted – for a reason that she reveals when she complains of "having lived longer without one [of your letters] at Brussels than I did most of the time I was in Italy" (III, 288).

Just such effects as those already observed in the Countesses' letters have been viewed at a theoretical level by Janet Altman. In her analysis of epistolary time structures Altman identifies three temporal registers: the moment of the event narrated within a letter, the moment of the writing of a letter, and the

---

[18] Hamish McRae, "If We Can't Get the Show Right, How Can We Sort out the Century?", *Independent*, 17 September 1997, 23.

[19] Frances Cairncross, "Byte Ride to Everywhere", *Independent on Sunday Section Two*, 14 December 1997, 7.

moment of the reading of a letter. It is not here part of my purpose to delve too deeply into the nature of these complexities, although I would suggest – in the light of what I have already described – that the moment of the transmission of a letter might constitute a fourth temporal register. Rather, I want to re-emphasize the fact that it was the City which set the standard for the technologies of communication in the eighteenth century. Only here were "vigorous efforts ... made to increase the speed of communication" (Robinson, 58). For instance, London had a sophisticated Penny Post of its own as early as 1680, which made deliveries "at frequent intervals, even ten to twelve times a day in the business districts, and four to eight times a day in other parts of the urban area" (Robinson, 71). Nowhere else in Britain had a Penny Post until after 1765. Whilst in London, the Countesses would have used this Post, drastically reducing what Altman refers to as "the disparity between the time of the person who signs the letter and the time of the addressee who receives it".[20] Unfortunately, technology did not yet allow such a service to be expanded beyond a local level. Consequently, whilst Pomfret is on the continent the meaning and possibility of what is contained in the Countesses' letters are altered by the time-lag. Thus, Hertford introduces one anecdote thus: "before this letter reaches Florence, it will be no news to your ladyship ..." (I, 316). Pomfret, for her part, states: "I suppose, before this can reach London, it will be no news that ..." (I, 182). On yet another occasion, Pomfret reveals her growing sense of frustration with the pace of the correspondence when she writes that: "though the post does not go from hence for two days, I cannot forbear sitting down this minute to begin an answer" (I, 180). Here, Pomfret is dreaming ahead to what Frances Cairncross promises – with the advent of the information revolution – will be "a future in which ideas proliferate faster than ever before ... one of breathtaking innovation" (Cairncross, 7). Richard Sennett finds just such a future in his examination of the urban aspects of E.M. Forster's novel *Howards End* – wherein more particularly the link is made between the city and speed of communication, with "London ... a place of 'anger and telegrams'".[21] There is little doubt, then, that much of the impatience the Countesses show in the writing of their international letters – Hertford draws attention to "what an importunate correspondent [I am]" (I, 43) – had been instilled in them by prolonged exposure to the superiors technologies of the City.

[20] Janet Gurkin Altman, "The 'Triple Register': 'Introduction' to Temporal Complexity in the Letter-Novel", *L'Esprit Créateur*, XVII/4 (Winter 1977), 307.
[21] Richard Sennett, *Flesh and Stone: The Body and the City in Western Civilization*, New York, 1994, 323.

"The capital is become an overgrown monster"[22]

The Countesses' abiding perception of the City was not, however, as a source of superior communications; nor was it of an unpleasant but easily avoided place, somewhere to the east of the Court. Their abiding perception – which I will explore in the second half of this essay – is partly revealed by Pomfret when she asks Hertford:

> Why will you treat me so like a tasteless trifler, as to make excuses because your letters are not written in the hurry of business, or the noise of town amusements? Is not one thought of your own more valuable than volumes of the designs, the contrivances ... that fill the scenes of private and of public life in our metropolis of London? (I, 141)

Here, the City is equated with frenzied economic and commercial industry – and hence growth – and with lack of taste. The former perception is given in William Hogarth's engraving entitled *Beer Street* (1751). Although Jan Marsh notes that Hogarth was an habitué of Leicester Fields, located "between the City and the Court",[23] Max Byrd correctly states that he was specifically "expert at portraying the vigorous bustle of London [City] life" (Byrd, 61). Many of the Londoners in *Beer Street* would hardly have been palatable to Hertford and Pomfret; but their beer-fuelled industry is shown to be productive in a variety of ways. Goods are being warehoused, signs painted, orders taken and delivered, newspapers and pamphlets perused; and in the background – behind the nobleman sheltering in his hackney-carriage – scaffolding going up denotes the construction of new buildings or the renovation of old. In reaction to this print Jack Lindsay notes that "it is surprising that the large amount of building in London during these years did not intrude *more* on [Hogarth's] prints".[24] For indeed the mid-eighteenth century was a time of almost unparalleled urban growth, with many, such as James Sambrook, identifying "the growth of London ... [as] the crucial factor in England's transformation ... [in]to a powerful, integrated exchange economy".[25] The phenomenon was much remarked upon at the time – for instance in *Humphrey Clinker*, when Matt Bramble writes to Dr Lewis that "if this infatuation continues for half a

---

[22] Tobias Smollett, *The Expedition of Humphrey Clinker*, ed. Lewis M. Knapp, London, 1966, 87.

[23] Jan Marsh, "A Brush with Kidding Billy", *Independent Long Weekend*, 13 September 1997, 6.

[24] Jack Lindsay, *Hogarth: His Art and His World*, London, 1977, 37. My italics. Lindsay does not draw attention to the builders and stalled building-work that can be seen through the Earl of Squander's study window in the first scene of *Marriage A-la-Mode* (1745). In this series of engravings City-money is shown to finance the building that is going on in the Court.

[25] James Sambrook, *The Eighteenth Century: The Intellectual and Cultural Context of English Literature, 1700-1789*, London, 1986, 78-79.

century, I suppose the whole county of Middlesex will be covered with brick"
(Smollett, 86).

Yet the processes which account for urban growth have only recently begun
to be understood. Geographers such as R. Johnston speak of "a self-propelling
growth process" which can be charted according to the laws of an equation
known as "the *multiplier*".[26] Others, such as the historian E.A. Wrigley, speak
in terms of social and economic changes "at once produced or emphasized by
London's growth and serving in turn to reinforce the growth process, a typical
positive feedback situation, to borrow a term from communication
engineering".[27] The elucidation of such processes helps to explain why no
industry develops in isolation and why urban growth often takes place
exponentially. In contrast, during the eighteenth century such processes were
looked upon with fear and London was seen as "a city gone wild with growth"
(Byrd, 101). The original strategy employed in the face of this fear – which
began to grip long before the 1700s – was brute containment. Thus James
Vance notes that "Elizabeth [I] and her Stuart successors tried bluntly to stop
any expansion [of the City] whatever".[28] But during the seventeenth century
several events conspired to make containment impossible: the chief amongst
these was the rebuilding occasioned by the Great Fire of 1666 and the Glorious
Revolution of 1688, followed by what Colin Nicholson and others have since
termed the Financial Revolution. After the Great Fire, London was
"increasingly organized for productive and expansible economic activities, in
sharp contrast to the rigidly constrained economy of medieval times" (Vance,
233). Therefore, it is not difficult to see why the Court world to the west was
threatened by expansion of the City to the east – for such power as Hertford
and Pomfret had was based on land, not on money or commerce.

Colin Nicholson argues that the Financial Revolution was signalled by the
"emergence of new types of personality, unprecedentedly dangerous and
unstable".[29] These were specifically City "types", with – as identified by Lucy
Sutherland – "the City in what was then a comparatively new sense, that of its
'monied interest'".[30] This newness, this City perception, was again best

---

[26] R. Johnston, *City and Society: An Outline for Urban Geography*, Penguin, 1980, 99-
100.

[27] E.A. Wrigley, "A Simple Model of London's Importance in Changing English Society
and Economy 1650-1750", in *Aristocratic Government and Society in Eighteenth-
Century England: The Foundations of Stability*, ed. Daniel A. Baugh, New York, 1975,
83.

[28] James E. Vance Jr., *This Scene of Man: The Role and Structure of the City in the
Geography of Western Civilization*, New York, 1977, 230.

[29] Colin Nicholson, *Writing and the Rise of Finance: Capital Satires of the Early
Eighteenth Century*, Cambridge, 1994, 20.

[30] Lucy Sutherland, "The City of London in Eighteenth Century Politics", in *Aristocratic
Government and Society in Eighteenth-Century England: The Foundations of Stability*,
ed. Daniel A. Baugh, New York, 1975, 157.

exemplified by William Hogarth. It can be seen in the portrait of Archbishop Thomas Herring (1744). Looking at this portrait, it is not difficult to believe Hogarth's own claim that what first aroused aristocratic opposition to his work was his portraits. Herring himself refused to show the painting; and Lindsay notes that "the Herring circle considered the portrait to show 'features all aggravated and *outrés*', making him look ferocious instead of benevolent" (127). In direct contrast, the portrait of the City merchant Thomas Coram (1740) shows a man overflowing with benevolence and education, surrounded by his books and mathematical instruments. Here, Lindsay notes that Hogarth "sought to preserve the cheerful coarse plebeian vigour of the man ... to say he won his fortune in trade" (113). To my mind, the derivation of Lindsay's word "plebeian" (in its associations with the ancient city of Rome) is of particular interest. For there is indeed something innately of the city about Coram – in the pallor of his skin, the impractical nature of his dress. The high resolution of such perceptions of City types belies H.T. Dickinson's identification of the central importance during this period of a "division between interests which can be labelled Court and Country".[31] For although Dickinson does identify what he refers to as the emergent "separate interest [of] the moneyed men of the City of London" (Dickinson, 106), he comes nowhere near enough to recognizing the extent to which both Court and Country were becoming dependent upon the City. In fact, this was a process which would culminate a century later with Marx's realization in the *Manifesto of the Communist Party* that "the executive of the modern state is but a committee for managing the common affairs of the bourgeoisie".[32]

The problem for the eighteenth-century landed aristocracy was how to contain City perceptions – how to objectify the City. But this was problematized by the geographic nature of London itself. In the first place, "Steen Rasmussen remarks that great cities are of two physical types, either concentrated or scattered, and that London, unlike other European capitals, is a scattered city ... [characterized by] unplanned, privately controlled growth" (Byrd, 24-25). Even today – as a result of London's "physical type" – the British government finds itself continually forced into "protecting our countryside from further suburban sprawl".[33] In the second place, recent geographic theory has drawn attention to what Johnson describes as "the delimitation of the areas joined by social and economic bonds to a particular urban settlement".[34] Geographers have variously termed these areas

---

[31] H.T. Dickinson, *Liberty and Property: Political Ideology in Eighteenth-Century Britain*, London, 1979, 91.

[32] Karl Marx, "Manifesto of the Communist Party", in *The Revolutions of 1848: Political Writings*, ed. David Fernbach, London, 1973, I, 69.

[33] Nicholas Schoon, "Planners put the Squeeze on Cities", *Independent*, 25 November 1997, 11.

[34] James H. Johnson, *Urban Geography: An Introductory Analysis*, Oxford, 1967, 80.

hinterlands, umlands, urban fields, tributary areas, or zones of influence; and in doing so they have only highlighted the increasingly serious problem of defining what is city and what is not city. Despite this jargonistic confusion, two things are certain: first, that "the larger the city, the more complicated are its relations with its surroundings"; and secondly, that "the impact of urbanism on social life extends well away from the immediate vicinity of cities" (Johnson, 89 and 142). In the eighteenth century, the long-term results of urban growth and urban influence would have been unpredictable. The questions the landed aristocracy had to ask themselves were: Where exactly does the influence of the city stop? And how far will cities grow? As far back as the early seventeenth-century James I had clearly been endeavouring to find his own answers to these questions. For in a proclamation of 16 July 1615 he writes: "We doe well perceive in Our Princely wisdome and providence, now, that Our Citie of London is become the greatest, or next the greatest Citie of the Christian world, it is more than time there bee an utter cessation of further new-buildings."[35]

Such questions as those I have drawn attention to become particularly pertinent to the Countesses' correspondence when Hertford embarks upon a trip through the Midlands, intent on enjoying "the finest weather imaginable ... an air of plenty ... [and] every other beautiful appearance of nature" (III, 266). In other words, Hertford hopes to enjoy everything that is not related to cities. But her idyll is shattered when she arrives at Newbury. From thence she writes disconsolately to Pomfret that "there is a manufactory there, which ... adds neither beauty nor pleasure to the town and adjacent fields" (III, 267). Nor was the influence of the City confined to this most literal of spheres. For – as if in anticipation of Linda Zionkowski's interpretation of eighteenth-century letters – Pomfret writes of her correspondence with Hertford that "nothing can be more agreeable than such a commerce, the returns of which never come so soon as desired" (I, 93). Hertford, even more overtly, makes use of the language of high finance when she writes: "as I have no fund within myself to entertain you, I naturally endeavour to furnish myself with the stock of others" (I, 124). This is clear evidence, also seen in a number of other places by a host of eighteenth-century writers, of "the vices of the 'city' ... infecting not only London, but the Court" (Dickinson, 173). Yet, in the light of the Countesses' mutual loathing of "the hurry of business", I cannot agree with Zionkowski in seeing such correspondences as the one I am dealing with as commerce; it is much more likely that the Countesses were indulging each other in a fanciful conceit than that they were themselves really seeing the exchange of their letters in terms of commercial transactions. When analysing their own correspondence, Hertford and Pomfret more often speak of each other's ability to make "a return of amusement" (I, 315). Thus Hertford asks "what return can I make for the most agreeable letters in the world?" (I, 128), while Pomfret wishes in one letter that

---

[35] *Stuart Royal Proclamations*, eds James Larkin and Paul Hughes, Oxford, 1973, I, 345.

she "could give your ladyship any return in this for the entertainment [your last letter] gave me" (I, 182). In this sense, it is more useful to see a correspondence – as does Ellen Strenski – in terms of "the mutual obligation generated by the offering and exchange of gifts".[36] By these means, the Countesses oppose their own aristocratic system of exchange to that of the coarse and undignified – although highly infectious – system of exchange developed after the Financial Revolution in the City of London.

Aristocratic alternatives to the City

To meet what they perceive to be the threat of the ever-expanding City, the Countesses adopt strategies of containment through the medium which their correspondence offers them. I will deal with Pomfret's strategy first. In the course of her travels, Pomfret visited Paris, Lyons, Genoa, Siena, Florence, Rome, Bologna, Venice and Frankfurt. In doing so, she was bound to draw distinctions between the growth of London and the containment of continental cities. Indeed, she enthusiastically describes Florence as "so fine a picture" (I, 223) and reports that "the architecture is esteemed both just and noble" (II, 2). The depth of description of continental cities that Pomfret enters into in some of her letters almost defies reading. She describes cathedrals and public buildings down to the minutest measurement – as for instance the Duomo in Florence with "its length ... a hundred and thirty English ells: the breadth of the tribune, eighty three" (II, 3). It is as if Pomfret is delighting in the elaboration of constraint. Moreover, Pomfret draws particular attention to the pleasing fact that "our English [horse] races are in the country; those of Florence in the city" (I, 326). For Pomfret undoubtedly saw such a practice in terms of the retaining of control of urban space by the aristocracy. The city of Florence even moves Pomfret to verse – as in the following lines:

> This day the circle of the year's complete,
> Since, Florence, I beheld thy pleasing seat ...
> But ere I quite forsake the lov'd retreat,
> There are a thousand things I would repeat.

(II, 140-41)

It is hard to imagine Pomfret expending such a eulogy upon the City of London; and even harder not to balk at the prospect of reading any letter that promises to eulogize – in verse – "a thousand things". The depth of Pomfret's enthusiasm for Italian cities in particular can perhaps be explained by reference to what James Vance describes as:

---

[36] Ellen Strenski, "The Electronic Hybridity of E-Mail: Liminal Subject Formation through Epistolary Gift Exchange", in *The Rhetorical Dimensions of Cyberspace*, http://www, 1996 [site no longer exists].

the fundamental distinction to be drawn ... between a city shaped by land-speculation and land-and-housing market forces in the English world, and a city far more clearly the product of design decisions taken for purposes of "taste" and ostentation on the Continent (Vance, 230).

For, indeed, when Pomfret reaches Rome she is forced to "forbear mentioning porphyry pillars, fountains, &c. for Rome is so full of them, that, if I should take notice of all its treasures of that sort, I should fill my letters with nothing else" (II, 301). Another geographer, Guilio Argan, points out that it was in Italy during the Renaissance that "a theory, or science, of the city was created".[37] This theory concentrated upon schemes for ideal cities contained within permanent city walls, and so permanently controllable by the ruling classes. It is perfectly understandable why Pomfret should, therefore, adopt a strategy of containment that lay in extensive description of such cities within the aristocratic space of letters to another aristocrat.

Hertford stayed in England; and so had to adopt a different strategy of containment of the City. She did so by means of descriptions of the gardens on her country estate at Richkings that are mirrored in detail, length, and tendency to resort to verse only by Pomfret's descriptions of Italian cities. Thus, Hertford describes the changes Lord Hertford has made to her own private garden as follows:

> He has widened the channel of the water that surrounds it, to about thirty feet; and, at two angles, has formed cascades, which, though they do not fall from any considerable height, have still a very good effect, both from their quickening the motion of the current, and making a rushing noise, which is heard in every part of the garden, and, in a hot day, sounds peculiarly cool and refreshing (I, 148-49).

Such a description as this is primarily a record of nice aristocratic response to the country; decidedly anti-urban in its intent. During the elaboration of such descriptions, Hertford often coyly apologizes to Pomfret for attempting "to entertain you with the trifling beauties that please me, whilst you are surrounded by all the magnificence of Italy" (I, 148-50). Yet it is quite evident that Hertford believes with an ideological passion in what she describes, at one point – as if in passing – as the "intrinsic value in home-felt peace" (I, 150) as a means of keeping at bay the encroachments of the expanding city. At the heart of Hertford's epistolary descriptions there is again the concept of aristocratic taste. James Vance notes that:

> throughout the late eighteenth and nineteenth centuries, the ever-expanding "beautification" of the countryside pumped money earned in the cities into the creation of new estates or the support of existing ones ... [and into] the creation

---

[37] Giulio Argan, *The Renaissance City*, trans. Susan Edna Bassnett, London, 1969, 11.

of a vast acreage of new "parks" for the wealthy, wherein a synthetic English landscape was developed (Vance, 300).

Paradoxically it was in order to satisfy just such tastes that the poor were driven out of the country and into the cities, expanding the cities even further and so destroying even more countryside. Such descriptions of gardens as are contained in Hertford's letters, therefore, amount to collaboration in a damaging process of beautification, in that they are involved in the propagation of aristocratic taste.

Hertford and Pomfret's perception of the City as a thing of potentially almost incalculable growth is mirrored today in the British Government's long-standing policy of placing Green Belts of countryside around urban centres, as a means of "stopping towns from growing outwards ever further and joining together".[38] But the Countesses' perceptions were skewed by their rank; and their letters turned into self-defeating strategies of containment which offered models functioning as aristocratic alternatives to the urban. If the Countesses had been merely conversing or indulging in commercial transactions somewhere upon their landed estates, perhaps they could have ignored the City. But the writing – and more particularly the sending – of letters involved them in the vast network of the postal system, with the impossible-to-ignore City at its centre. It did not help that the Countesses had little direct experience of this City and had unrealistic expectations of what cities elsewhere might be. The unrealities of the continental cityscapes described by Pomfret are revealed by Hertford when she writes:

> guess then, dear Madam, how happy your letters make me, which present to my imagination so many beautiful prospects, and magnificent ceremonies, free from the fatigue with which the seeing of them in reality must be attended. Nay, I am persuaded that (if even the inconvenience could be removed) they give me more pleasure in your description than I should find in being a spectator of them myself (III, 104-105).

This skewing of the Countesses' perceptions was largely an effect of the geographic landscape of London – divided as it was between Court and City, so that the Countesses' perceptions are always from the west, looking east. The Court in the west was familiar and known but staid and a suppresser of the technologies of communication which had such beneficial effects upon the letters of the two Countesses. The Court had as a matter of historical policy sought to suppress communication in order that treasonable plots be prevented: the Penny Post itself was the brainchild of William Dockwra, a private individual who sought to profit from the business community of the City.[39] It

---

[38] Nicholas Schoon, "Historic Challenge to the Nation's Green Belt", *Independent*, 16 October 1997, 1.

[39] For more information on Dockwra's innovations see: T. Todd, *William Dockwra and*

was the energy of ideas such as the Penny Post – constantly emanating from the City – which doomed the Countesses' strategies of containment to failure. For such energy fed on the land Hertford described, covering it in urban sprawl, and was stifled by the planned cities Pomfret described in her letters. The very development of the technology which allowed the Countesses to communicate with each other – and so effectively to swap strategies of containment – could not by definition be contained.

---

the Rest of the Undertakers: The Story of the London Penny Post 1680-82, Edinburgh, 1952.

"JERUSALEM" AS CITY AND EMANATION:
PLACES AND PEOPLE IN BLAKE'S POETRY

C.C. BARFOOT

The obvious place for an article such as this to start is with the lyric that everyone knows as "Blake's 'Jerusalem'":

> And did those feet in ancient time
> Walk upon England's mountains green?
> And was the holy Lamb of God
> On England's pleasant pastures seen?
>
> And did the Countenance Divine
> Shine forth upon our clouded hills?
> And was Jerusalem builded here
> Among these dark Satanic Mills?
>
> Bring me my Bow of burning gold:
> Bring me my Arrows of desire:
> Bring me my Spear: O clouds unfold!
> Bring me my Chariot of fire.
>
> I will not cease from Mental Fight,
> Nor shall my Sword sleep in my hand,
> Till we have built Jerusalem
> In England's green & pleasant Land.[1]

In Blake's Preface to *Milton*, this is followed by a quotation from the Bible (Numbers xi 29): "Would to God that all the Lord's people were prophets!" To which we can only say, Amen! – especially after one has paused to consider the ways that "Blake's 'Jerusalem'" as well as Blake's Jerusalem (his concept and dramatization of "Jerusalem") has been hijacked and abused by all sorts of people who have never cared to discover what he might have meant by the name and who would have been outraged if indeed they had ever found out.

---

[1] William Blake, *Milton*, "Preface" (text as in Blake, *Complete Writings*, ed. Geoffrey Keynes, Oxford Standard Authors edn, Oxford, 1966, 480-81).

Consider, for instance, this snippet from *The Observer* the Sunday before the 1997 Conservative Party Conference:

> Last Thursday, in the back room of the Gloucester Museum, the Woman's Institute was having its weekly meeting .... You expected the people present to end the proceedings by singing "Jerusalem", the anthem of both the WI and the Conservative party.[2]

Sadly, one doubts whether most members of the Women's Institute can have more than a sentimental understanding of "Blake's 'Jerusalem'", and they would no more want to build his version of Jerusalem "In England's green & pleasant land" than would the majority of "Last Night" Promenaders, or members of the Tory Party, or English football supporters who now claim the anthem for their own. What kind of "Mental Fight" can we conceive any of these groups being engaged in that Blake could possibly have approved of? Blake's view of the real state of his Jerusalem at the beginning of this new century would not have been very different from his perception of the place and the person at the end of the eighteenth century and the beginning of the nineteenth:

> I behold Babylon in the opening Streets of London. I behold
> Jerusalem in ruins wandering about from house to house.[3]

In this brief essay on what is indeed a vast subject, I am chiefly interested in the way that the symbolism of these two cities, Babylon and Jerusalem, used by Blake not only in traditional, biblical and churchy ways, even in nonconformist chapel ways, as well as in original, idiosyncratic ways, has been assumed and taken over by people in general, and, even more ominously, by specific groups and parties, even political parties, who have very little idea of what Blake was on about. One may even dare to assert that nearly all the people who sing "Jerusalem" with gusto and sincerity, even with tears in their eyes and lumps at the backs of their throats, have no inkling of what the concept of Jerusalem involved in Blake's work, what its place was in his vast and continually evolving mythological narratives, or how he exploited it dramatically to articulate his complex and absorbing ideologies and beliefs.

Blake would not have been surprised by this usurpation, since usurpation is indeed one of the major themes of the myth or myths of his poetry, one of the most frequent elements in his narrative. For Blake, the whole origin of the material universe (as distinct from the spiritual universe) arose from the conspiracy or rivalry between Urizen and Luvah to control the other two Zoas.[4]

---

[2] Andy McSmith and Peter Hillmore, "Hague in the Wilderness", in a section entitled "Psst! Seen any Tories lately?", *The Observer*, 5 October 1997, 19.

[3] William Blake, *Jerusalem*, 74: 16-17 (*Complete Writings*, 714).

[4] For an introduction to the nature of Urizen, Luvah, Tharmas and Urthona, the four "beasts" or "lifes", see the beginning of "Night the First" in *Vala, or the Four Zoas*: "Four

As a consequence of the struggle, the spiritual domain of the Eternals was broken up, and Urizen came to dominate the other eternal elements of spiritual existence, or being, with his own laws. Paradoxically, the creation of material existence and physical life was an attempt to prevent further spiritual disintegration. Therefore, from its very inception the world is a fallen state of being.[5]

The passage which contains my initial two-line quotation from *Jerusalem*, the long prophetic epic and final masterpiece that Blake wrote between 1804 and 1807, and did not complete in its engraved form before 1820, reads:

> Teach me, O Holy Spirit, the Testimony of Jesus! let me
> Comprehend wondrous things out of the Divine Law!
> I behold Babylon in the opening Streets of London. I behold
> Jerusalem in ruins wandering about from house to house.
> This I behold: the shudderings of death attend my steps.
> I walk up and down in Six Thousand Years: their Events are present before
> me
>
> To tell how Los in grief & anger, whirling round his Hammer on high,
> Drave the Sons & Daughters of Albion from their ancient mountains.
> They became the Twelve Gods of Asia Opposing the Divine Vision.
>   The Sons of Albion are Twelve, the Sons of Jerusalem Sixteen.
> I tell how Albion's Sons, by Harmonies of Concords & Discords
> Opposed to Melody, and by Lights & Shades opposed to Outline,
> And by Abstraction opposed to the Visions of Imagination,
> By cruel Laws, divided Sixteen into Twelve Divisions:
> How Hyle roof'd Los in Albion's Cliffs by the Affections rent
> Asunder & opposed to Thought, to draw Jerusalem's Sons
> Into the Vortex of his Wheels, therefore Hyle is called Gog,
> Age after age drawing them away towards Babylon,
> Babylon, the Rational Morality, deluding to death the little ones
> In strong temptations of stolen beauty.[6]

This is neither the place nor the occasion to concern ourselves with all the implications and ramifications of proper names in these lines or of the crimes and their consequences which are alluded to, but the essential drift of this passage is easily grasped – some terrible enormity has taken place, indeed a sequence of atrocities, all as a consequence of the break-up of "the universal

---

Mighty Ones are in every Man: a Perfect Unity/Cannot Exist, but from the Universal Brotherhood of Eden,/The Universal Man, to Whom be Glory Evermore. Amen./What are the Natures of those Living Creatures the Heav'nly Father only/Knoweth. No Individual knoweth ..., nor can know in all Eternity" (*Complete Writings*, 264, where the last two lines are in italics to indicate "Blake's late additions and corrections in the MS").

[5] This is the basic narrative and ideological thrust of *Vala, or the Four Zoas*; see also *The [First] Book of Urizen*.

[6] *Jerusalem*, 74: 14-33 (*Complete Writings*, 714-15).

man", Albion. This tragedy is presented to us in the form of a confrontation between Albion and "the Saviour" at the beginning of Chapter 1 of *Jerusalem*, when the latter (not to be taken as being strictly identifiable with the orthodox Christian Saviour) addresses the divided universal man:

> "Awake! awake O sleeper of the land of shadows, wake! expand!
> I am in you and you in me, mutual in love divine:
> Fibres of love from man to man thro' Albion's pleasant land.
> ...
> Thy Emanation that was wont to play before thy face,
> Beaming forth with her daughters into the Divine bosom:
> Where hast thou hidden thy Emanation, lovely Jerusalem,
> From the vision and fruition of the Holy-one? ..."

But the perturbed Man away turns down the valleys dark:

> "...
> Phantom of the over heated brain! shadow of immortality!
> Seeking to keep my soul a victim to thy Love! which binds
> Man, the enemy of man, into deceitful friendships,
> Jerusalem is not! her daughters are indefinite:
> By demonstration man alone can live, and not by faith.
> My mountains are my own, and I will keep them to myself:
> The Malvern and the Cheviot, the Wolds, Plinlimmon & Snowdon
> Are mine: here will I build my Laws of Moral Virtue.
> Humanity shall be no more, but war & princedom & victory!"
>
> So spoke Albion in jealous fears, hiding his Emanation
> Upon the Thames and Medway, rivers of Beulah, dissembling
> His jealousy before the throne divine, darkening, cold!
>
> The banks of the Thames are clouded! the ancient porches of Albion are
> Darken'd! they are drawn thro' unbounded space, scatter'd upon
> The Void in incoherent despair! Cambridge & Oxford & London
> Are driven among the starry Wheels, rent away and dissipated
> In Chasms & Abysses of sorrow, enlarg'd without dimension, terrible.
> Albion's mountains run with blood, the cries of war & of tumult
> Resound into the unbounded night, every Human perfection
> Of mountain & river & city, are small & withered & darken'd.
> Cam is a little stream! Ely is almost swallow'd up!
> Lincoln & Norwich stand trembling on the brink of Udan-Adan![7]
> Wales and Scotland shrink themselves to the west and to the north!
> Mourning for fear of the warriors in the Vale of Entuthon-Benython[8]

---

[7] "The dark lake of Ulro, a sinister lake in a black forest, a place of indefinite form" (*The Poems of William Blake*, ed. W.H. Stevenson, Longmans' Annotated English Poets, 1971, 632, 5.10n). Ulro is the place furthest from Eden, and represents "chaos, the place of formlessness and non-entity" (*ibid.*, 486).

> Jerusalem is scatter'd abroad like a cloud of smoke thro' non-entity.
> Moab & Ammon & Amalek & Canaan & Egypt & Aram
> Receive her little-ones for sacrifices and the delights of cruelty.[9]

One sees in this passage Blake's wonderful poetic and prophetic skill in speaking about people and places at the same time, and people as places and places as people. Albion is England, and you will have to forgive Blake in this respect, Albion is Britain, and less politically incorrect, Albion is the fallen, created world (as I have already indicated, for Blake the Creation and the Fall are the same – the principal point in which he is neither an orthodox Christian nor even a Jew, indeed it marks him as a heretic to both traditions), the whole material world. But Albion is also an Englishman, an inhabitant of the British Isles, all inhabitants of the British Isles or of the populated globe, even one might say, just in case, the whole inhabited universe. All places are potentially people, since all people are potentially, are actually in the course of the narrative (and not just human people but also original spiritual beings, Eternals, Zoas) transformed, given material shape and form, and fixed as generative or vegetative existences, in order to ensure that they do not cease to exist. Material existence is a means of ensuring that falling, fallen, divided, spiritual beings do not die.

If we return to that earlier quote –

> I behold Babylon in the opening streets of London. I behold
> Jerusalem in ruins wandering about from house to house

– you will notice how unostentatiously Blake links the idea of Jerusalem as a place ("Jerusalem in ruins ...") with Jerusalem as a person fallen on hard times ("Jerusalem ... wandering about from house to house"). In the final part of *Vala, or the Four Zoas* (a very long and incomplete prophetic epic which Blake never finished nor ever engraved), in "Night the Ninth", which celebrates the Last Judgement and the restoration "of Albion the Ancient Man" (see the title on first page of the whole work), "Eternal Man", having risen from his spiritual slumber, which had provoked universal chaos, addresses Urizen, the prime usurper and instrument of destruction:

> And the Eternal Man said: "Hear my words, O Prince of Light.
> "Behold Jerusalem, in whose bosom the Lamb of God
> Is seen; tho' slain before her Gates, he self-renew'd remains
> Eternal, & I thro' him awake from death's dark vale.
> The times revolve; the time is coming when all these delights
> Shall be renew'd, & all these Elements that now consume
> Shall reflourish ....
> ....

---

[8] "The forest in which Udan-Adan is found" (*ibid.*, 632, 5.12n).

[9] *Jerusalem*, 4: 6-8, 14-17, 22-34 and 5: 1-15 (*Complete Writings*, 622-23).

> Thus shall the male & female live the life of Eternity,
> Because the Lamb of God Creates himself a bride & wife,
> That we his Children evermore may live in Jerusalem,
> Which now descendeth out of heaven, a City, yet a Woman,
> Mother of myriads redeem'd & born in her spiritual palaces,
> By a New Spiritual birth Regenerated from Death."[10]

Blake is most explicit here, as if he wants to ensure that the reader grasps the point, "a City, yet a Woman", "we his Children evermore may live in Jerusalem" who is also to be the "Mother of myriads redeem'd & born in her spiritual palaces". While earlier Jerusalem is described as one with "a bosom" ("in whose bosom the Lamb of God/Is seen"), she also possesses "Gates", before which the Lamb of God was "slain". When one makes the burden of Blake's diction and syntax explicit, it seems odder that while reading the poem as a poem, these overlapping identities of place and person and of person and place are all naturally subsumed in the rhetorical flow.

But Jerusalem, of course, is not only "a City, yet a Woman", she is also an "Emanation", a term we have already passed over lightly. To be an emanation you must be a woman, but not necessarily a city. The passage where we first met the term was in that initial confrontation between Albion and the Saviour at the beginning of Blake's epic, the full title of which is *Jerusalem the Emanation of the Giant Albion*. There the Saviour says:

> "Thy Emanation that was wont to play before thy face,
> Beaming forth with her daughters into the Divine bosom;"

And asks:

> "Where hast thou hidden thy Emanation, lovely Jerusalem,
> From the vision and fruition of the Holy-one?"

Albion first dismisses him as:

> "Phantom of the over heated brain! shadow of immortality!
> Seeking to keep my soul a victim to thy Love! which binds
> Man the enemy of man, into deceitful friendships ...."

And assures him that "Jerusalem is not! her daughters are indefinite". The narrator tells us:

> So spoke Albion in jealous fears, hiding his Emanation
> Upon the Thames and Medway, rivers of Beulah, dissembling
> His jealousy before the throne divine, darkening, cold!

---

[10] *Vala, or the Four Zoas*, "Night the Ninth", ll. 202-208, 217-22 (*Complete Writings*, 362-63).

Therefore Jerusalem is not only a city and a woman, she also appears to be a wife and a mother; whereas Albion, in seeking to become macho man, has become less than himself, and is soon to be haunted by his "spectre", usually depicted by Blake as a Dracula bat-like figure, representing the usurping power of reason (see **fig. 3**). In Eternity the whole human is bisexual, for in Eternity there is no sex, no need for sex – Blake has good biblical justification for this belief. When humanity becomes vegetative through generation, the human begins to break down into male and female; and man and his emanation begin to behave as ordinary men and women. Like husbands and wives, they quarrel and fight – they are disloyal to each other, they reject each other, they disown each other. The male becomes aggressive and increasingly destructive. The female, the emanation, becomes flirtatious and apparently sexually predatory, promiscuous, dominating, using her sexual wiles to assume power over universal man, and consequently the fallen generated world, yet at the same time, hypocritically, preaching the need for chastity and purity.

Jerusalem, as we have seen, is a ruined outcast, tramping the streets; Babylon, the scarlet woman, threatens to rule the world (in rivalry and association with all the other emanations on the loose, principally Vala, the emanation of Luvah, the Zoa who represents the passions), but always hidden under the disguise of the conventional morality advocated by the church. In this sense "sex" becomes a superficially enticing tool for the misappropriation of power, operating within a seller's market of "thou shalt not", which not only makes pleasure sinful, but also ensures it is in such short supply that sex and sin are all the more attractive and pleasurable. Since the granting or achievement of such a diversion, either in actuality or in fantasy, is the source of tremendous guilt, sex is all the more powerful as a weapon in the hands of the people who are able to exploit the opportunities they have to provide such thrills and display their gifts as pleasure-givers. It is all an illusion, indeed a delusion, since in reality fallen man (and woman) is threatened either with enforced chastity or with becoming a hermaphrodite or both.

This is to simplify, of course; and I apologize for sounding so theological – the fault of most articles and books on Blake, but understandable and often unavoidable, since his work is a kind of alternative theology frequently aimed at the conventional theology of the churches. But consider this hysterical piece of hate oratory from the fallen Albion's misconceived and misconceiving sons:

"Cast, Cast ye Jerusalem forth! The Shadow of delusions!
The Harlot daughter! Mother of pity and dishonourable forgiveness!
Our Father Albion's sin and shame! But father now no more,
Nor sons, nor hateful peace & love, nor soft complacencies,
With transgressors meeting in brotherhood around the table,
Or in the porch or garden. No more the sinful delights

Figure 3: Two representations of a "spectre" in Blake's *Jerusalem*
(plates 6 and 33)

Of age and youth, and boy and girl, and animal and herb,
And river and mountain, and city & village, and house & family,
Beneath the Oak & Palm, beneath the Vine and Fig-tree,
In self-denial! – But War and deadly contention Between
Father and Son, and light and love! All bold asperities
Of Haters met in deadly strife, rending the house & garden,
The unforgiving porches, the tables of enmity, and beds
And chambers of trembling & suspicion, hatreds of age & youth,
And boy & girl, & animal & herb, & river & mountain,
And city & village, and house & family, That the Perfect
May live in glory, redeem'd by the Sacrifice of the Lamb[11]
And of his children before sinful Jerusalem, To build
Babylon the City of Vala, the Goddess Virgin-Mother.
She is our Mother! Nature! Jerusalem is our Harlot-Sister
Return'd with Children of pollution to defile our House
With Sin and Shame. Cast, Cast her into the Potter's field!
Her little-ones She must slay upon our Altars, and her aged
Parents must be carried into captivity: to redeem her Soul,
To be for a Shame & a Curse, & to be our Slaves for ever."

So cry Hand & Hyle, the eldest of the fathers of Albion's
Little-ones ....[12]

Thus cry, one might interpolate, the voices of all those who appeal to or represent conventional authority, in particular the authoritarian voices of a patriarchal society, outraged by the threat of an independent woman. Rather than accommodate themselves in a materially created world, a fallen world, to the inevitable split between man and woman, and to the inescapable shifts of point of view between the sexes, the sons, who regard themselves as victims, and in no way implicated in the causes of the conflict, demand the branding and expulsion of the offending female, Jerusalem, and her replacement by the apparently conciliatory and accommodating Babylon. "Sin" and "shame" are the perpetually convenient cries for all those, throughout time, who have wished and continue to wish to absolve themselves from all consideration of their own involvement and responsibility for friction and division in society. Therefore Jerusalem is the scapegoat.

Man divorced from his emanation becomes a stone, a rock, bound to a bare unimaginative material existence:

But Albion fell down, a Rocky fragment from Eternity hurl'd
By his own Spectre, who is the Reasoning Power in every Man,

---

[11] The mistaken attitudes of the sons of Albion reflect the conventional Christian view of Christ's death as the consequence of God's demand for a sacrifice for human sinfulness. Blake does not accept Christ's death as a necessary ransom; for him redemption is achieved by freely offered and accepted forgiveness.

[12] *Jerusalem*, 18: 11-37 (*Complete Writings*, 640-41).

Into his own chaos, which is the Memory between Man & Man.[13]

But Albion fled from the Divine Vision; with the Plow of Nations enflaming,
....
But his Spectre rose over the starry Plow. Albion fled beneath the Plow
Till he came to the Rock of Ages, & took his Seat upon the Rock.[14]

Blake's prophetic poems are full of descriptions of rocky places, mountains and caves – the barest, hardest realization of material man, which is the price he has to pay to survive spiritual death. In the meantime, the emanation of Albion, Jerusalem, and the emanations of the other Zoas, having been cast off, either wander forlornly in the wilderness or fall into bad company. Jerusalem is

> ... closed in the Dungeons of Babylon
> Her Form was held by Beulah's Daughters; but all within unseen
> She sat at the Mills, her hair unbound, her feet naked
> Cut with flints, her tears run down, her reason grows like
> The Wheel of Hand incessant turning day & night without rest,
> Insane she raves upon the winds, hoarse, inarticulate.
> All night Vala hears, she triumphs in pride of holiness
> To see Jerusalem deface her lineaments with bitter blows
> Of despair, while the Satanic Holiness triumph'd in Vala
> In a Religion of Chastity & Uncircumcised Selfishness
> Both of the Head & Heart & Loins, clos'd up in Moral Pride.[15]

In this separation of man and emanation – the male and female aspects of humanity – eternal life contracts to mere material existence, without the spiritual life of the imagination. Los, the fallen form of the Zoa Urthona, is the artist who labours in metal, and stone and architecture – just like Blake in painting, engraving, poetry and printing – to contain and to hold these fallen fragments in a form which will preserve them until the moment comes that they are ready for regeneration. This art is seen by Blake as a struggle to enclose and preserve the shattered spirit in such a way that there will still be a chance to unite Albion and Jerusalem in that partnership which is the condition of eternal life. The passage quoted earlier about Albion as he falls as a rocky fragment from Eternity is preceded in Blake's text by the reflection that

> In Great Eternity every particular Form gives forth or Emanates
> Its own peculiar Light, & the Form is the Divine Vision

---

[13] *Ibid.*, 54: 6-8 (*Complete Writings*, 685).

[14] *Ibid.*, 57: 12, 15-16 (*Complete Writings*, 689). Cf. pl. 48 ff. – it is the merciful Saviour who places Albion on the Rock of Ages to await rebirth, but when he is put there, "Eternity groan'd & was troubled at the image of Eternal Death!" (l. 12: *Complete Writings*, 677).

[15] *Ibid.*, 60: 39-49 (*Complete Writings*, 693).

> And the Light is his Garment. This is Jerusalem in every Man,
> A Tent & Tabernacle of Mutual Forgiveness, Male & Female Clothings.[16]

This is not the occasion to dwell in detail on how the story develops, although we will eventually consider the very last phase of the poem. Any attentive reader of the prophetic works will have perceived that Blake's use of places and landscapes and characters – places and landscapes as characters, characters as places and landscapes, real and mythological, actual and imaginative, fearful and consoling – enables him to write long complex poems that are at the same time psychological and cosmological. In his maze-like, multi-layered narratives, we find ourselves in a large world of universal powers and objects; but through this magnification we are also able to observe an inner world that is conscious both of material desires and demands and of spiritual struggles and needs. In his views of the universe and of the human mind, the worlds both within and outside men and women, Blake is far ahead of his time, which partly explains why it is only in the last fifty years or so that he has been properly appreciated. His poems create a pulsating and continuously evolving universe that is psychological and cosmological, and both the psychology and the cosmology reflect social, political and moral realities, present equally in Blake's own day and in our own. How these are related to each other is beautifully demonstrated in the lyric that concludes the Preface to Chapter 2 of *Jerusalem* (see **fig. 4**), which is the gloss everyone giving a hearty rendition of "Blake's 'Jerusalem'" ought to study.

To return to where this essay began. One wonders how much any of what I have hardly been able to touch upon is so much as even suspected by those who are so fond of raising their voices to perform Parry's melodious setting of Blake's most famous and popular lyric – whether they are members of the Women's Institute, sometimes thought of as an organization not only dedicated to "Jam and Jerusalem", but also to "traditional values" of a reactionary tinge; or members of the Conservative Party or even New Labour in search of spiritual profit; or the happy party-goers at the last night of the Proms, waving their flags, in their rapture hardly discriminating between "Rule Britannia", "Land of Hope and Glory" and "Blake's 'Jerusalem'"; or the even more obliviously depressed English football fans. A few years ago there was a minor row in the Church of England when some members protested that "Blake's 'Jerusalem'" was not to be found in the revised Anglican hymnal. One doubts whether either the protesters or the besieged clergy who tried to explain that "Blake's 'Jerusalem'" was not strictly a hymn, really knew why it was not at all appropriate for Blake's poem to be there, and certainly Blake himself would have been horrified at the prospect.

In this essay so far something has been deliberately kept back. Between two passages already quoted there is a line that has not yet appeared. Between the four wonderfully affirmative lines about the eternal nature of emanations –

---

[16] *Ibid.*, 54: 1-4 (*Complete Writings*, 684).

Figure 4: *Jerusalem*, plate 27

> In Great Eternity every particular Form gives forth or Emanates
> Its own peculiar Light, & the Form is the Divine Vision
> And the Light is his Garment. This is Jerusalem in every Man,
> A Tent & Tabernacle of Mutual Forgiveness, Male & Female Clothings –

and the passage about Albion falling –

> Albion fell down, a Rocky fragment from Eternity hurl'd
> By his own Spectre, who is the Reasoning Power in every Man,
> Into his own Chaos, which is the Memory between Man & Man –

there comes another line: "And Jerusalem is called Liberty among the Children of Albion."[17] Indeed earlier in the full page design before the beginning of Chapter 2 (see **fig. 5**) this has been anticipated, for there one reads:

> SUCH VISIONS HAVE APPEARED TO ME
> AS I MY ORDERED RACE HAVE RUN.
> JERUSALEM IS NAMED LIBERTY
> AMONG THE SONS OF ALBION.[18]

If we read and understand "Blake's 'Jerusalem'", his popular anthem or hymn, "And did those feet in ancient times ...", in the light of our consideration of Jerusalem as city and woman, and as Albion's emanation, and comprehend the way in which Blake's potent myth associates the story of Albion and Jerusalem, the four Zoas, and the other Satanic and Divine personages in his tale with the condition of England, Europe and the world in the 1790s and the first decades of the nineteenth century, we are likely to be even more astonished at the enthusiasm of many of those who bawl their lungs out singing

> I will not cease from mental fight,
> Nor shall my sword sleep in my hand,
> Till we have built Jerusalem
> In England's green and pleasant land

Do they really know what they are asking for? It is all very well for Euro-sceptics and Euro-phobes, even for hard-working and public-spirited members of the Women's Institute, to think of Jerusalem as a golden city, free of litter- and lager-louts, football hooligans, and all signs of urban squalor and metropolitan menace, quite compatible with the comfortable cosy rural idyll so dear to the hearts of true English men and women. Loyal members of the Tory party might be able to live with the notion of Liberty, as long as they can define it on their own terms – a freedom from Brussels

---

[17] *Ibid.*, 54: 5 (*Complete Writings*, 684).

[18] *Ibid.*, pl. 26 (*Complete Writings*, 649).

Figure 5: *Jerusalem*, plate 26

bureaucrats and the menace of European politicians and European courts, and the liberty to exploit their own entrepreneurial appetites and other people's vulnerability: in other words, as long as liberty is defined in free-market Thatcherite terms. A Thatcherite Jerusalem, a Little England Jerusalem, a Tory Jerusalem! Excellent! But Blake's Jerusalem? To give them credit most people know that these verses are Blake's. The only problem is they do not appreciate what Blake understood either by "Jerusalem" or by "Liberty".

All of Blake's poetry, not just the prophetic works, is challenging and uncomfortable stuff, for liberals and reactionaries alike, and it is equally difficult for sceptics and for believers, for men and for women. As a commentator one is always faced with the temptation to turn it in the direction of one's own prejudices. That is why one needs to quote so much, in order to let Blake have his own say, even to quote the characters in his fiction he abhorred as well as those he admired and wished us to emulate. This is what Blake understood by the path to Liberty:

> But turning toward Ololon[19] in terrible majesty Milton
> Replied: "Obey thou the Words of the Inspired Man.
> All that can be (can be) annihilated must be annihilated[20]
> That the Children of Jerusalem may be saved from slavery.
> There is a Negation, & there is a Contrary:
> The Negation must be destroy'd to redeem the Contraries.
> The Negation is the Spectre, the Reasoning Power in Man:
> This is a false Body, an Incrustation over my Immortal
> Spirit, a Selfhood which must by put off & annihilated alway.
> To cleanse the Face of my Spirit by Self-examination,
>
> To bathe in the Waters of Life, to wash off the Not Human,
> I come in Self-annihilation & the grandeur of Inspiration,
> To cast off Rational Demonstration by Faith in the Saviour,
> To cast off the rotten rags of Memory by Inspiration,
> To cast off Bacon, Locke & Newton from Albion's covering,

---

[19] Ololon, who only appears in *Milton*, is "the spiritual form of Milton's Sixfold Emanation, she is the truth underlying his errors about women" (S. Foster Damon, *A Blake Dictionary*, London, 1973, 307). "Sixfold" since Milton not only failed to understand his three wives but also his three daughters. Note also Stevenson: "Ololon is a place, and also the dwellers in that place; and they, as is possible in Eternity, later unite into one person" (*Milton*, pl. 21, ll. 15-16n).

[20] There is an obvious difficulty with the repetition of "can be" in this line. Blake's engraved text reads "All that can be can be annihilated must be annihilated". Keynes puts the second "can be" in parenthesis (for no very evident reason); Stevenson, using David V. Erdman's text, omits the second "can be" altogether. The transcription accompanying the facsimile edition of *Milton*, edited by Kay Parkhurst Easson and Roger R. Easson, "published in cooperation with the American Blake Foundation", London, 1979, has "All that can be, can be annihilated, must be annihilated" (129).

To take off his filthy garments & clothe him with Imagination,
To cast aside from Poetry all that is not Inspiration,
That it no longer shall dare to mock with the aspersion of Madness
Cast on the Inspired by the tame high finisher of paltry Blots
Indefinite, or paltry Rhymes, or paltry Harmonies,
Who creeps into State Government like a catterpiller to destroy;
To cast off the idiot Questioner who is always questioning
But never capable of answering, who sits with a sly grin
Silent plotting when to question, like a thief in the cave,
Who publishes doubt & calls it knowledge, whose Science is Despair,
Whose pretence to knowledge is envy, whose whole Science is
To destroy the wisdom of ages to gratify ravenous Envy
That rages round him like a Wolf day & night without rest:
He smiles with condescension, he talks of Benevolence & Virtue,
And those who act with Benevolence & Virtue they murder time on time.
These are the destroyers of Jerusalem, these are the murderers
Of Jesus, who deny the Faith & mock at Eternal Life,
Who pretend to Poetry that they may destroy Imagination
By imitation of Nature's Images drawn from Remembrance.
These are the Sexual Garments, the Abomination of Desolation,
Hiding the Human Lineaments as with an Ark & Curtains
Which Jesus rent & now shall wholly purge away with Fire
Till Generation is swallow'd up in Regeneration."[21]

It is clear from this and many other equally fine passages what Blake understood, and wished and willed us to understand, by Jerusalem: a place where art is inspirational (as well as crafted) and the foundation of spiritual humanity, "Humanity Divine". In Blakean terms Christ, by his involvement in the dialogue of "Visionary forms dramatic", is the personal and poetic means to accomplish this creative design. The potent unity of Albion and Jerusalem is the source of all valuable human consciousness and knowledge. All their wars are "Wars of mutual Benevolence, Wars of Love" leading to mutual empathy, compassion and forbearance, in which "exemplars of Memory & of Intellect" are created, as we see in the magnificently stirring conclusion to Blake's *Jerusalem*:

"Awake, Awake, Jerusalem! O lovely Emanation of Albion,
Awake and overspread all Nations as in Ancient Time;
For lo! the Night of Death is past and the Eternal Day
Appears upon our Hills. Awake, Jerusalem, and come away!"

So spake the Vision of Albion, & in him so spake in my hearing
The Universal Father. Then Albion stretch'd his hand into Infinitude
And took his Bow. Fourfold the Vision; for bright beaming Urizen
Lay'd his hand on the South & took a breathing Bow of carved Gold:

---

[21] *Milton*, 40: 28-37 and 41: 1-28 (*Complete Writings*, 532-33).

Luvah his hand stretch'd to the East & bore a Silver Bow, bright shining:
Tharmas Westward a Bow of Brass, pure flaming, richly wrought:
Urthona Northward in thick storms a Bow of Iron, terrible thundering.

And the Bow is Male & Female, & the Quiver of the Arrows of Love
Are the Children of this Bow, a Bow of Mercy & Loving-kindness laying
Open the hidden Heart in Wars of mutual Benevolence, Wars of Love:
And the Hand of Man grasps firm between the Male & Female Loves.
....
And every Man stood Fourfold; each Four Faces had ....
....
The Four Living Creatures, Chariots of Humanity Divine Incomprehensible,
In beautiful Paradises expand. These are the Four Rivers of Paradise
And the Four Faces of Humanity, fronting the Four Cardinal Points
Of Heaven, going forward, forward irrestible from Eternity to Eternity.

And they conversed together in Visionary forms dramatic which bright
Redounded from their Tongues in thunderous majesty, in Visions
In new Expanses, creating exemplars of Memory & of Intellect,
Creating Space, Creating Time, according to the wonders Divine
Of Human Imagination throughout all the Three Regions immense
Of Childhood, Manhood & Old Age ....
                                               .... & they walked
To & fro in Eternity as One Man, reflecting each in each & clearly seen
And seeing, according to fitness & order ....
....
And from the Thirty-two Nations of the Earth among the Living Creatures.

All Human Forms identified, even Tree, Metal, Earth & Stone: all
Human Forms identified, living, going forth & returning wearied
Into the Planetary lives of Years, Months, Days & Hours; reposing,
And then Awaking into the Bosom of the Life of Immortality.

And I heard the Name of their Emanations: they are named Jerusalem.[22]

Clearly a world of commentary might still be spun around these lines, celebrating the resplendent creative paradox of the "Wars of mutual Benevolence, Wars of Love" in our own terms of psycho-babble and political faction, and some may feel that such a spin is required to draw this article to an appropriate academic close. But truly nothing further is to be said. After such music, after such vision, in which Blake's Jerusalem is finally and conclusively recognized for what she, for what it, is, the only proper response is silence.

---

[22] *Jerusalem*, 97: 1-15; 98: 12, 24-40, 55; and 99: 1-5 (*Complete Writings*, 744-47).

DICKENS AND THE BURIAL OF THE DEAD

ALAN SHELSTON

The title of this essay implies perhaps a connection between Dickens and T.S. Eliot: "The Burial of the Dead" is the title of the opening section of *The Waste Land*, and associations between Eliot's urban poetry and the city of Dickens are familiar ground. But Eliot, of course, took his title from the Anglican liturgy, where it appears as the title of the funeral service. Dickens, in Eliot's phrase, had a "love for death", in the pages of his fiction certainly: we think of the deaths of Smike in *Nicholas Nickleby*, of little Paul Dombey, of Jo in *Bleak House*, and most famously of Nell in *The Old Curiosity Shop*, all lovingly prepared for and ruthlessly executed. Furthermore, if Dickens had a vested interest in fictional deaths he rarely left the bodies unburied. One of the earliest memories of David Copperfield is of the preparations for his mother's funeral, with the tapping of the hammer of Mr Omer, "DRAPER, TAILOR, HABERDASHER, FUNERAL FURNISHER, &c" (125, ch. 9),[1] as he nails down her coffin – a sound that David only half understands, but whose portent he certainly fears – and Dickens himself was to become expert on funeral practices. From the pages of his early novels in particular we might write a history of the undertaking profession in the first half of the nineteenth century. In *Oliver Twist* we have Mr Sowerberry, blessed with a wife who "had a good deal of taste in the undertaking way" (33, ch. 5). Sowerberry, like Mr Omer, is a small town practitioner who is astutely aware of developments in his profession. In *Martin Chuzzlewit* there is Mr Mould, whose cheerfulness of manner belies his name. Mould, like Sowerberry, is driven by his consciousness of the relationship between bereavement and ceremonial, but his is a London practice and rather grander. Sowerberry's profits are small, but then, as Mr Bumble notices, so were his coffins. Mr Mould is introduced to the reader as a "professional person": he observes that "the laying-

---

[1] All page references to works by Dickens included in the text are to the relevant volume of the Oxford Illustrated Dickens, London, 1947-58. In this edition, separate volumes are devoted to *Master Humphrey's Clock* and *The Uncommercial Traveller* and page references to these works are to these volumes. For convenience of reference to other editions, chapter references, and in the case of *The Uncommercial Traveller* essay titles, are also given.

out of money with a well-conducted establishment, where the thing is performed upon the very best scale, binds the broken heart, and sheds balm on the wounded spirit" (321, ch. 19). In *Dombey and Son* the "grand funeral" of little Paul with its "feathers" which "wind their gloomy way along the streets" (240, ch. 18) is in sad contrast to the desolation of the occasion, and in *Bleak House* the contrast between high and low is never more starkly demonstrated than it is by the extremes of the mausoleum at Chesney Wold where Lady Dedlock is finally laid to rest and the burial-ground in Tom-all-Alone's where her lover lies in an unmarked grave. Two of the three final illustrations of *Bleak House* are of these locations: they remind us, finally and emphatically, that in their deaths the Victorians were very much divided (**figs 6, 7**).[2] Most famous of all of Dickens's deaths is that of Little Nell in *The Old Curiosity Shop*: not only does the novel conclude with her death and carefully described interment, but her progress in life reads at times like a guidebook to the graveyards of rural England. In this essay I shall disinter for one more time the corpse of Little Nell, and then suggest that Dickens's interest not only in death but in the burial that comes after it has a dimension that goes beyond the fictional, both for him and for his contemporaries. I shall argue in particular that the processes of urban burial focus anxieties for Dickens's generation and indeed for his successors on the London scene about what might really be involved in the passage from this life to the next.

To some extent Dickens's fascination not only with death, but with the apparatus that surrounds it, is a matter of personality. Not long before the death of Little Nell, Edgar Allen Poe was published for the first time in England, in *Bentley's Miscellany*, the periodical which Dickens had edited, and in which he published *Oliver Twist*.[3] Poe's fascination in particular with stories of being buried not dead but alive is something that we find in Dickens, too. The obsession with death and burial is a strange one for a young man still in his twenties – just how intense it was we can see from the circumstances surrounding the original publication of *The Old Curiosity Shop* which began in 1840. The first instalments of the novel appeared in the early numbers of Dickens's purpose-built periodical *Master Humphrey's Clock*. In fact, the novel soon took over the periodical completely, and the separate material from the early numbers is now largely forgotten. But if we go back to the stories which precede *The Old Curiosity Shop* in the opening pages of the *Clock* we find that they are all concerned with matters of death and burial. One of them, for example, is told by a narrator awaiting execution for the murder of his nephew, whom he has buried in his own garden. "'While I write this', he says, 'my grave is digging and my name is written in the black book of death'" (42). Another of

---

[2] All of the illustrations referred to in this paper are taken from the original editions of the works concerned. In the case of *Bleak House*, these were by Hablot K. Browne ("Phiz").

[3] *The Fall of the House of Usher* first appeared in England in *Bentley's Miscellany*, VIII, 1840. By this time, Harrison Ainsworth had taken over the editorship of the journal.

the stories, told somewhat improbably by Mr Pickwick who has been re-introduced for the occasion, describes the secret burial of a cavalier, an opponent of the state in the seventeenth century. The climax of the story is once again the subject of a very effective illustration (**fig. 8**).[4]

The story of Little Nell, therefore, has specific precedents in the fictional material that went before it. And indeed her own story is not simply climaxed in death; the paraphernalia of death is with her throughout the narrative. She emerges from the Curiosity Shop at the beginning of the novel as if from a kind of burial chamber furnished by the relics of antiquity. Again Cattermole's illustration reinforces the point (**fig. 9**). Her grandfather, we are told, "might have groped among old churches, and tombs, and deserted houses, and gathered all the spoils with his own hands" (5, ch. 1). Nell's progress through first industrial and then rural England after she and her grandfather have been evicted by Daniel Quilp is one that takes in graveyards and burial grounds at every turn. At one of these, the point is specifically made that graveyards have an instructional function: Nell learns her lesson well, and just before her death she is employed as a kind of guide for touring parties in an old church where she herself will ultimately be buried. In one of the most powerful of the illustrations to the novel, we see the sexton showing her an old well at the church itself: deliberately set into the text at the point where the sexton forewarns Nell of the fate that awaits us all, it is transformed into an emblem of mortality (**fig. 10**). "'It looks like a grave itself', said the old man. 'It does', replied the child" and the old man replies, "It's to be closed, and built over" (413, ch. 55).[5] The novel concludes with a sequence of illustrations in which the last stages of Nell's existence are graphically depicted. The last of these shows the old grandfather contemplating the stone under which she lies (**fig. 11**). Here, as in the case of *Bleak House*, the sense of an ending, in Frank Kermode's phrase, has a resonance that goes far beyond the merely textual.

As I suggested, to some extent this fascination with death originates in Dickens's own very morbid sensibility. But it has also a larger cultural

---

[4] This illustration is by George Cattermole, who shared the bulk of the illustration of the *Master Humphrey's Clock* project with Hablot Browne. Cattermole was a specialist in antiquarian and historical illustration, and he seems to be have been brought in especially to illustrate these particular elements. His illustrations to *The Great Civil War*, a work which he published in association with his brother Richard and the first part of which was published in 1841, reflect the currency of seventeenth-century subject-matter at this point in time.

[5] This powerful illustration is by Daniel Maclise; it is his single contribution to *Master Humphrey's Clock*, although he was later to contribute to the illustration of Dickens's Christmas Books. On the illustrations to *The Old Curiosity Shop*, see Joan Stevens, "'Wood-cuts dropped into the text': the Illustrations to *The Old Curiosity Shop* and *Barnaby Rudge*", *Studies in Bibliography*, 20, 1967, 113-33. Stevens emphasizes the effect for the reading experience of the illustrations having been set within the text itself, and not separately from it.

significance. As is well known, the death of the fictional Little Nell in *The Old Curiosity Shop* had behind it the very real death, in his own arms, of Dickens's seventeen year old sister-in-law in 1837, a death to which it has been argued that he over-reacted, just as he over exploited the death of his fictional character. The death of Mary Hogarth, transformed into fiction as the death of Little Nell, raises directly the question of what is involved in a confrontation on the author's part with the reality of death. It is a question that Wordsworth raised in his Lucy poem about the "Maid whom there were few to praise/And very few to love":

> She lived unknown, and few could know
>   When Lucy ceas'd to be
> But she is in her grave, and oh!
>   The difference to me.

Wordsworth's words apply precisely to Little Nell's death and both Wordsworth and Dickens are notorious for their apparent misapplication of pathetic sentiment. But not only did Mary Hogarth die in Dickens's arms, he was in charge of her funeral arrangements, and this gives us the opportunity to contextualize the death of Little Nell in the funerary culture of the 1840s.

As I have said, Dickens's morticians all appear in his earlier fiction, written in the decades of the Thirties and Forties. It was at precisely this time that, in England as elsewhere, practices of interment were a matter of urgent debate. In particular, it was a point in time at which the pressure on space in the old burial grounds of London and the other urban conurbations had intensified to the point of crisis. In 1843, the Parliamentary Commission appointed to enquire into "Interment in Towns" reported that "In all the practice of interment in towns the crowded state of the place of burial, the apparent want of seclusion and sanctity pollute the mental associations, and offend the sentiments of the population irrespective of public health".[6] By then, in fact, it was getting late: the problem had been acute since at least the beginning of the century. In a later essay, Dickens's Uncommercial Traveller reflects in a secularized vision of the last judgement that "it was a solemn consideration what enormous hosts of the dead belong to one old great city ... if they were raised while the living slept, there would not be the space of a pin's point in all the streets and ways for the living to come into" (375, "The City of the Absent"). The problem of numbers focuses the question of the impersonality of death which was to be reinforced by the findings of geology: the much mourned individual was not so much to be "blown about the desert dust,/Or sealed within the iron hills"[7] as lost in the anonymity of a burial ground in which corpse was piled upon corpse and all sense of identity extinguished.

By the 1840s – the very decade in which Dickens began his career as a

---

[6] Alan and Dorothy Shelston, *The Industrial City 1820-1870*, Basingstoke, 1990, 59-60.

[7] The lines are quoted from Tennyson's *In Memoriam*, LVI.

novelist – the problem of urban burial had reached a point where drastic measures were needed to ensure that those who could afford to do so could bury their dead with decency. As Jo tells the servant of Lady Dedlock in *Bleak House*, when they buried her lover at Tom-all-Alone's, "They put him wery nigh the top. They was obliged to stamp upon it to git it in" (225, ch. 16). The experience was a common one in city burial-grounds. Suggestions to solve the problem were as ingenious as they were desperate. In the 1820s, inspired by the current vogue for Egyptology, it was proposed to erect a London pyramid, four times as high as St Pauls and with a capacity for four million coffins.[8] The cost of freehold vaults in this edifice was to have ranged from £100 to £500: as with the garden cemeteries, these facilities were designed with a new middle class in mind. Philippe Ariès, in *In The Hour of Our Death*, reminds us that this was not simply an English problem: Père Lachaise, built in Paris in 1804, was soon to become the model for the new city cemeteries,[9] although Belfast had had its cemetery since 1797, while Manchester (1820), Liverpool (1825) and, most famously Glasgow (1831), were all in advance of London. In London the private cemetery movement got under way in the 1830s and it was at the first of the London cemeteries, Kensal Green, founded in 1832, that Dickens buried Mary Hogarth. The cemeteries were created for the new middle class, of whom Dickens was very much a member, and they were meant to mediate the grief of bereavement for those who could afford it. In particular they were to do so by providing a comforting environment, and this was to be done by appropriating the beauties of nature. The point was put explicitly in John Strang's *Necropolis Glasuegis* (1831) which included amongst the recommended features of a cemetery, "a little flower-garden surrounded by cedar, spruce, cypress and yew-trees, round which the rose and the honeysuckle were entwining".[10]

Many of Strang's ideas, and much of his language, are taken over in John Claudius Loudon's famous text-book *On the Laying-out, Planting and Managing of Cemeteries and on the Improvement of Churchyards* (1843). Loudon was a landscape gardener: he was also a man of his time. A properly appointed cemetery, according to Loudon, should be "free from all the horror of the old burying grounds" and both Strang and Loudon combine the language of

---

[8] My details of the development of the cemetery movement are take primarily from James Stevens Curl, *Celebration of Death*, rev. edn. London, 1993. See especially chs 6, 7, 8. See also Nicholas Penny, *Mourning*, London, 1981, and Hugh Meller, *London Cemeteries: An Illustrated Guide and Gazetteer*, Avebury, 1981.

[9] Ariès notes that the rural cemetery, founded on the example of Père-Lachaise, and which he describes as "a school of morality .... [which] will make everyone wiser and more serious especially the young" – exactly the effect of the graveyards on Nell – developed in particular in America and England, in contrast to "the new urban cemeteries of continental Europe" in which "nature lost all its impact, and all emotion was completely absorbed by the monument" (Phillipe Ariès, *The Hour of Our Death*, trans. Helen Weaver, Penguin, 1983, 531-34).

[10] Curl, 162.

sentiment with a new utilitarian emphasis on hygiene and efficiency. Loudon in particular was a modernizer who would not have been out of place in the California of *The Loved One*: he deplored the practice of "piling up musty vaults with coffins" as "quite unsuitable to the present age and practised by antiquated kings and nobles, fast dying off in every part of the world". Instead, "a church or churchyard in the country, or a general cemetery in the neighbourhood of a town, [should be] properly designed, laid out, ornamented with tombs, planted with trees, shrubs, and herbaceous plants". Such facilities, he argued, would be "the sworn foe to preternatural fear and superstition [and would be] calculated to *extend virtuous and generous feelings*" (Loudon's italics). In true utilitarian fashion, he paid great attention to detail: "The want of perpendicularity in the Monuments and Gravestones" he believed to be a consequence of not placing them on "secure foundations", and he gave precise instructions for systems of drainage to be organised in such a manner that they would inhibit the over-exuberant growth of grass and nettles by which existing graveyards were defiled. According to Loudon, "the grass should be kept very constantly very close cropped, by the scythe, the hedge-shears, and sheep-shears, or the hook".[11] Finally, dogs and smoking were expressly forbidden on cemetery grounds. Daniel Quilp, who in *The Old Curiostiy Shop* dies in torment and remains unburied (the ultimate Victorian horror) would never have been admitted, alive or dead.

I have gone into some detail here because Loudon's principles define precisely the spirit in which Nell's passage from this world is conducted in *The Old Curiosity Shop,* even to the point of the obsession with tidiness. Arriving at what is to be her final resting-place, she immediately sets about cleaning it up: "They plucked the long grass and nettles from the tombs, thinned the poor shrubs and roots, made the turf smooth, and cleared it of the leaves and weeds" (408; ch. 54). Her duties involve showing round "the parties who would come to see the church", much like the parties who apparently turned Kensal Green cemetery into a tourist attraction. True, she finally dies not in the city, but in the country, and she is buried not in the churchyard but in a vault, in a church which was in its own time known for its antiquarian associations. In 1845 *The Archaeological Journal* published an illustrated account of Tong church in Shropshire – by general agreement the model for Nell's last resting-place – which drew attention to its historical significance.[12] But gothic – or rather pseudo-gothic – architecture was an important feature of the new cemeteries: the original designs for the gateway, and in particular the chapel at Kensal Green, by H.E. Kendall, are exercises in antiquarian fantasy that compare very well with

---

[11] John Claudius Loudon, *On the Laying Out, Planting, and Managing of Cemeteries and on the Improvement of Churchyards*, 1843 facsimile edn, with "Introduction" by James Stevens Curl, Ilkley, Yorks, 1981, iv, 11-13 *passim*, 78-80 *passim*.

[12] "Tong Church Salop", *The Archaeological Journal*, 2 (1845), 1-13.

the landscapes and interiors devised by Cattermole for Dickens's novel.[13]
In *The Old Curiosity Shop* the antiquarian elements are in fact very much
sanitized: the novel endorses Loudon's rejection of the "fear and superstition"
attached to death and burial, transforming them by its appeal to the beneficent
effects of nature. Arriving at what is to be Nell's final resting-place,

> they [Nell and the grandfather] admired everything – the old grey porch, the
> mullioned windows, the venerable gravestones dotting the green churchyard, the
> ancient tower ... the brown thatched roofs of cottage, barn, and homestead,
> peeping from among the trees; the stream that rippled by the distant water-mill;
> the blue Welsh mountains far away. It was for such a spot the child had wearied in
> the dense, dark, miserable haunts of labour (347; ch. 46).

This is the countryside, and a country churchyard, not as it is but as the weary
Londoners need it to be. *Master Humphrey's Clock* is a project conceived not so
much in anticipation of T.S. Eliot as in the shadow of Charles Lamb: its London
is not in fact "new" but, as so often in Dickens, the London of a fantasized
antiquity, its streets the site of the lonely narrator's nocturnal wanderings. Nell
leaves the darkness of the city to engage with the modern world of industry and
theatre before ending her journey, if not in a new model cemetery, in a place
whose associations, in direct contrast to the city burial-grounds where Dickens
himself loved to linger, are those of cleanliness, sanctity and peace.

There is moreover a larger point to be made. The consolations of nature are
needed precisely because the traditional consolations of religion are at best only
tenuously available. Nell's burial, described in graphic detail from the tolling of
the bell to the closing of the grave, concludes with "the vault covered and the
stone fixed down" (543; ch 72). Those illustrations of the sexton at the well, and
of the grandfather at Nell's grave (oh!/The difference to him) are effectively
images of oblivion (**figs 10, 11**). At the point of the final illustration the text
refers to "the blank that follows death – the weary void – the sense of desolation
that will come upon the strongest minds, when something familiar and beloved is
missed at every turn" (545; ch. 72). In one of the essays in *The Uncommercial
Traveller*, Dickens describes an occasion when, at the Paris Morgue, he had
looked down upon a corpse: he describes his experience as "looking at
something *that could not return a look*" (192; "Some recollections of Mortality",
original italics). Here Dickens can be said to look forward to a later novelist of
London for whom the "sense of desolation" was to become little short of an
obsession, Henry James. James's most recent biographer, Fred Kaplan, devotes a
full chapter to James's experience of a sequence of deaths of intimate friends and
associates in the 1880s and 90s, culminating in the long drawn-out death of his

---

[13] Kendall's designs are reproduced in Curl, 216-17. In fact they were not used, neoclassical models being finally preferred, but neo-gothic has always remained as a popular
style for memorial architecture.

sister Alice in 1892. On more than one occasion during this period James found himself at Kensal Green.

Kermode, in the final chapter of *The Sense of an Ending,* writes about the impossibility of imagining one's own death. He cites the observations of a British agent in the war who had been captured and kept in solitary confinement by the Gestapo: "'Death' is a word that presents no real target to the mind's eye", and "If you imagine yourself being shot ... you are cheating yourself by substituting for your own body someone else".[14] In the 1890s James engaged with this problem in stories like "The Altar of the Dead" (published in a volume entitled *Terminations,* incidentally) and "The Beast in the Jungle" in which men whose lives are effectively concluded transform their own awareness of mortality into a fixation with the dying and the recently dead. At the climax of "The Beast in the Jungle", John Marcher visits the "plot of ground, the graven tablet, the tended flowers" where the woman he has failed lies. They are located in a suburban cemetery:

> Before he quitted London, however, he made a pilgrimage to May Bartram's grave, took his way to it through the endless avenues of the grim suburban necropolis, sought it out in the wilderness of tombs, and, though he had come but for the renewal of the act of farewell, found himself, when he had at last stood by it, beguiled into long intensities. He stood for an hour, powerless to turn away and yet powerless to penetrate the darkness of death; fixing with his eyes her inscribed name and date, beating his forehead against the fact of the secret they kept, drawing his breath, while he waited as if, in pity of him, some sense would rise from the stones. He kneeled on the stones, however, in vain; they kept what they concealed; and if the face of the tomb did become a face for him it was because the two names were like a pair of eyes that didn't know him. He gave them a last long look, but no palest light broke.[15]

The "pair of eyes that didn't know him" echoes Dickens's sense of "looking at something that could not return a look". The dead are irremediably absent from us, "other" in a way that allows for no mediation. As James put it in the "Preface" to "The Altar of the Dead" (the "New York" volume in which "The Beast of the Jungle" is included): "Brutal, more and more to wondering eyes, the great fact that the poor dead, all about one, were nowhere so dead as there." He goes on, quoting a visitor from France: "Mourir, à Londres, c'est être bien mort!" for

> London [is] a terrible place to die in; doubtless not so much ... by conscious cruelty or perversity as under the awful doom of general dishumanisation .... It takes space to feel, it takes time to know .... Monstrous masses are, by this truth,

---

[14] Frank Kermode, *The Sense of an Ending,* New York, 1967, 161.

[15] Henry James, *The Beast in the Jungle,* 1903, reprinted in *Tales of Henry James,* Norton Critical edition, selected and edited Christof Wegelin, 1984, 307.

so impervious to vibration ... that ... the very tradition of sensibility would perish if left only to their care.[16]

And here we can look forward to Eliot: "A crowd flowed over London bridge, so many/I had not thought death had undone so many." To revert to *The Old Curiosity Shop*, however, Nell is the last survivor of, if not the tradition, the cult of sensibility, not least because, as James says, "It takes space to feel, it takes time to know". What both illustration and text suggest at the conclusion of Dickens's novel is that, whatever the degree of sentimental excess, he is facing the reality of death not as passage to a new life, but as extinction: extinction, furthermore, within a city whose "monstrous masses" have destroyed the capacity to accommodate the experience of death in any meaningful way.

I referred earlier to the frailty of traditional religious consolations: this has to remain at the level of assertion rather than argument. James's characters die and are buried without benefit of clergy: in a memorable phrase he rejected the idea of the afterlife as "*all* mere wrath and yearning in the darkness!".[17] Dickens, whenever asked directly, would assert the conventionality of his Christian beliefs, including a specific belief in individual survival after death, and, to be strictly accurate, the last illustration of *The Old Curiosity Shop* is not the one of the grieving grandfather but a little emblem of a group of angels guiding Nell to her rest, which appears at the foot of the final page. But the inscriptions on English tombstones reveal a very distinct difference between those of the Victorian period, and those of earlier centuries. Whereas the earlier inscriptions express the certainties both of death, and of what follows it – "the resurrection and the life" – the Victorians refer to death by the kind of euphemisms with which we have all become familiar – "Fell asleep", "At rest", "Asleep in the arms of Jesus".

A Tale of Two Cities is a novel which makes great play with the symbolism of resurrection, and of restoration to life, but finally it is "a far far better rest" that

---

[16] Henry James, "Preface" to "The Altar of the Dead", reprinted in Henry James, *The Art of the Novel*, "Introduction" by R. P. Blackmur, London and New York, 1935, 244-45. The quotation from Eliot which follows is from the opening section of *The Waste Land*.

[17] Fred Kaplan, *Henry James: The Imagination of Genius,* London, 1992, 358. In an extremely complex late essay, "Is There a Life after Death?", James addresses the question directly, referring to it as "the most interesting question in the world". James concludes, "It isn't really a question of belief; it is on the other hand a question of desire ..." ("Is There a Life after Death?", reprinted in F.O. Matthiessen, *The James Family*, New York: Alfred A. Knopf, 1948, 602-14). In his commentary, Matthiessen identifies the influence of James's brother William on his thinking, but notes that "even less than WJ [William James] did he manifest an active participation in religious experience" (594). Richard A Hocks, however, makes a case for a more radical reading of James's essay, arguing that it reflects "those distant 'correspondences' with the traditional theological propositions" that are equally to be found in the late fiction (Richard A. Hocks, *Henry James and Pragmatistic Thought*, Chapel Hill, 1974, 217-25).

Sidney Carton looks forward to (406; ch. 54) not "the sure and certain hope of the resurrection" promised by the Service for the Burial of the Dead. For him the rest will certainly be silence. At the same time, while the tombstones of the eighteenth century invariably use what might be called the "Hic jacet" formula, the Victorian stones invariably replace it by "In memory of" – or, rather, "In Memoriam". And it is in memory, not in the afterlife, that Nell must hope to be enshrined. As the old schoolmaster tells her in response to her anxious questions:

> "There is nothing ... no nothing innocent or good that ever dies, and is forgotten. Let us hold to that faith or none .... There is not an angel added to the host of Heaven but does its blessed work on earth in those that loved it here" (406; ch 54).

The Victorians were not without religious faith, but they tended to find it, as Tennyson wrote, "in honest doubt", and they tended to express it through the cult of memory. But memory is at best vulnerable, as Nell's own anxious questions imply. In the very last words of *The Old Curiosity Shop*, Kit Nubbles returns much later in life to search for the house in which he had known Nell as a child: he cannot find it because "The old house had long ago been pulled down and a fine broad road was in its place ... he soon became uncertain of the spot" (555; ch 73). The urban reference is a significant one which we may legitimately read ironically. Here we have not simply the priority of memory, but the need to memorialize: Tennyson, grieving for Hallam "in the long unlovely street" where "the noise of life begins again",[18] writes a poem whose very title identifies the anxieties of his generation. The fear of death, the sense of loss, religious doubt, and half-acre tombs were hardly the exclusive property of the Victorians, but in the context of the expanding city they took on new meanings, and indeed a new threat.

---

[18] *In Memoriam*, VII.

Figure 6: *Bleak House*, ch. 49: "The Morning", by Hablot K. Browne ("Phiz")

Figure 7: *Bleak House*, ch. 56: "The Mausoleum at Chesney Wold", by Hablot K. Browne ("Phiz")

He followed the body into the church, and it was well he lost no time in doing so, for the door was immediately closed. There was no light in the building save that which came from a couple of torches borne by two men in cloaks who stood upon the brink of a vault. Each supported a female figure, and all observed a profound silence.

By this dim and solemn glare, which made Will feel as though light itself were dead, and its tomb the dreary arches that frowned above, they placed

Figure 8: Illustration to "Mr Pickwick's Tale", *Master Humphrey's Clock*, by George Cattermole

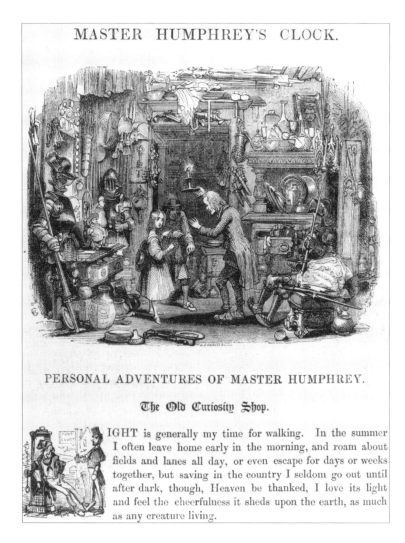

Figure 9: Opening illustration to *The Old Curiosity Shop*, by George Cattermole

108   MASTER HUMPHREY'S CLOCK.

" A black and dreadful place !" exclaimed the child.
" Look in," said the old man, pointing downward with his finger.
The child complied, and gazed down into the pit.

" It looks like a grave, itself," said the old man. ,
" It does," replied the child.
" I have often had the fancy," said the sexton, " that it might have been
dug at first to make the old place more gloomy, and the old monks more
religious. It's to be closed up, and built over."
The child still stood, looking thoughtfully into the vault.
" We shall see," said the sexton, " on what gay heads other earth will
have closed, when the light is shut out from here. God knows ! They'll
close it up, next spring."

Figure 10: Illustration to *The Old Curiosity Shop*, ch. 55, by Daniel Maclise

Figure 11: Concluding illustration to *The Old Curiosity Shop*, ch. 72, by George Cattermole

CHARTING THE GREAT WEN: CHARLES DICKENS, HENRY MAYHEW, CHARLES BOOTH

ROBERT DRUCE

... I wonder how much of the histories I invented ... hangs like a mist of fancy over well-remembered facts! When I tread the old ground, I do not wonder that I seem to see and pity, going on before me, an innocent romantic boy, making his imaginative world out of such strange experiences and sordid things.[1]

There are real people and places that we have never outgrown ... which we always regard with the eye and mind of childhood .... We have never outgrown the whole region of Covent Garden. We preserve it as a fine dissipated mystery.[2]

"But what is to be the fate of the great wen of all? The monster, called ...'the metropolis of the empire'?"[3] In the course of the tours through rural England which he undertook between 1821 and 1826 and reported in the pages of the *Political Register*, again and again William Cobbett returned to his favourite image of London as a "monstrous wen" – a disfiguring and ceaselessly-growing tumour, that is – which was deforming the body of England by sucking into itself and its corrupt and corrupting tissues the peoples and the prosperity of the country and her empire.

It was an enduring image, one closely related to Cowper's earlier vision of "proud and gay and gain-devoted cities":

> Thither flow,
> As to a common and most noisome sewer,
> The dregs and feculence of every land.
> In cities foul example on most minds
> Begets its likeness. Rank abundance breeds
> In gross and pampered cities sloth and lust,
> And wantonness and gluttonous excess.
> In cities vice is hidden with most ease,

---

[1] *David Copperfield*, 1849-50, closing paragraph of ch. XI; text as in Testimonial Edition, 18 vols, London, 1912, X, 169-70.

[2] "Where We Stopped Growing", *Household Words*, 1 January 1853 (rpt. in *Memories and Sketches*, Testimonial Edition, I, 79-80).

[3] *Rural Rides*, London, 1885, I, 52.

> Or seen with least reproach ....
> Such London is, by taste and wealth proclaimed
> The fairest capital of all the world.[4]

Along with the closely-related recognition that each teeming slum and rookery of the city was little better, literally and perhaps metaphorically, than a cesspool, that same image underlies the "phantasmagoria of poverty and crime" so frequently to be found in Dickens's novels;[5] as it does the four volumes of Henry Mayhew's *London Labour and the London Poor* of 1861 and 1862, and the three editions, and more than seventeen volumes, of Charles Booth's *Life and Labour of the People in London*, published between 1889 and 1902.

As for the image of London as a social and racial cesspool, we find it dear to the imaginations of generations of thriller writers, well into the present century. For such a vision of the metropolis is perfectly attuned to the essentially xenophobic giant-killer formula of spy and invasion story writers, for whom immigrants, and above all those from eastern Europe, are seen as scum or sewage, a dangerous source of infection. Thus, in 1887 we find Conan Doyle's Dr Watson pointing to London as "that great cesspool into which all the loungers of the Empire are irresistibly drained".[6] Twenty years later, E. Philips Oppenheim endorses his hero's view of the cause of political unrest: it is "what comes of making London the asylum of all the foreign scum of the earth ... half a million and more of scum eating their way into the entrails of this great city of ours".[7]

A further twenty years on, and four years after the First World War, "Sapper" (Lt.Col Herman McNeile) was still appealing to the same vision: "we can't go on as the cesspit of Europe, sheltering microbes who infect us as soon as they are here. We want disinfecting: we want it badly."[8]

Today that same sick image of London, and elsewhere of other great cities, is a commonplace of neo-Nazi rhetoric.

In their own century, Dickens, Mayhew, Booth, and their collaborators all set out to anatomize the city, to chart its relentless growth – Dickens, with imaginative freedom in his novels, and by way of more factual reportage in his sketches and occasional pieces; Mayhew both in dramatized interviews with the men and women he encountered on the streets and in their dwellings, and in almost obsessively compiled lists and statistical tables; Booth, and his assistant Beatrice Potter (later to marry Sidney Webb), in meticulous house-to-house and street-by-street enquiries across the city, and the unimpassioned reports of what they discovered there. All these authors in varying ways "charted" – and I would

---

[4] *The Task*, Book I, 1785; *Poems of Cowper*, intr. John Bailey, Nelson Classics, London, undated, 21-22.

[5] The phrase is Leslie Fiedler's; see *Love and Death in the American Novel*, New York, 1970, 446.

[6] *A Study in Scarlet* (1887), in *The Complete Sherlock Holmes*, Penguin, 1981, 15.

[7] *The Secret*, London, 1907, 32.

[8] *The Black Gang*, London, 1922, 178.

not want the distant half-echo of Blake's "chartered streets" and "chartered Thames" and the marks of weakness and woe that Blake saw there to be lost – all three charted "the Great Wen". Hence my title.

At the time of the Great Fire of 1666, the population of London numbered around 350,000, and was rising inexorably, doubling itself, according to Sir William Petty, every two generations. Within a hundred-and-thirty years, by the last decade of the eighteenth century, there were more than 800,000 souls living in the capital. A considerable part of that increase was due to the incoming tide of foreign migrants – Germans, Frenchmen, Danes and Swedes – as well as to the flood of negroes, Irishmen, Scotsmen and country people, all looking to find work and better wages in the city. The majority of the newcomers joined their fellow-countrymen in ever-increasingly cramped quarters in their own particular parts of the town – the French in Soho, Moorfields and Spitalfields; the Irish in the slums of St Giles and Covent Garden; the negroes, of whom, Christopher Hibbert suggests, "there may have been as many as 10,000 in the 1770s – mainly freed, escaped or absconded slaves" – crowding along the river east of the Tower.[9]

William Wordsworth, recollecting his stay in London at this time, claimed to have been well pleased by the ethnic variety he encountered in the streets in 1791. After wandering through Long Acre or Seven Dials – he does not name the area, but there are clues enough in his description of the giant-sized advertisements, and the long files of ballads dangling "from the dead walls" – the poet took his way homewards "through the thickening hubbub", accosted by a street-scavenger begging for money, and encountering Danes, Italians, Jews, and Turks carrying the tools or the products of their trades. "The mighty concourse I surveyed", he tells us:

> With no unthinking mind, well pleased to note
> Among the crowd all specimens of man,
> Through all the colours which the sun bestows,
> And every form of character and face:
> The Swede, the Russian; from the genial south,
> The Frenchman and the Spaniard; from remote
> America, the Hunter-Indian; Moors,
> Malays, Lascars, the Tartar, the Chinese,
> And Negro Ladies in white muslin gowns.[10]

The flow of British migrants and foreign immigrants did not slacken, and few who observed it would have endorsed Wordsworth's pleasure in ethnic diversity. Within nine years of Wordsworth's visit, the population of London had swollen by an additional 65,000, and one in ten of all the peoples of

---

[9] Christopher Hibbert, *London: The Biography of a City*, London, 1969, 178-79. I am indebted to Hibbert for further details in this paragraph.

[10] *The Prelude*, Bk VII, ll. 211-28; in Wordsworth, *Poetical Works*, ed. Thomas Hutchinson, London, 1905, 690.

England and Wales were living in the metropolis. Over the next decade, it increased by over twenty-one per cent, and at the time of George IV's coronation in 1821, stood at 1,378,947.

By 1830, soon after William Cobbett had gazed at the city and characterized it as a great, relentlessly growing tumour, a wen, London's population had risen to one and a half millions. In 1837 – the year which saw the publication of the first part of *Oliver Twist* and the final part of *The Pickwick Papers* – it was calculated that some 90,000 people were passing forth or back across London Bridge every day.

With the building of the railways the increase in population growth accelerated, and London expanded still further outwards. In 1834 Stephenson made the first excavations in Camden Town and Somers Town for the London and Birmingham Railway. Both were areas with which Dickens had been familiar since his childhood, and he presents a graphic account in the sixth chapter of *Dombey and Son*, of how Stephenson's workings "rent the whole neighbourhood to its centre" with "the first shock of a great earthquake". Constructed by an army of 20,000 labourers, the line was completed in the five years between 1833 and 1838.

In subsequent decades, the same seismic effect was to be felt across the whole metropolis and in the rapidly-expanding suburbs beyond. By 1875, there were thirteen main-line London termini in operation;[11] and the metropolitan railway had cut a swathe through central London, circling to link the City with Kings Cross, St Pancras and Baker Street and, via Gloucester Road, Earls Court, and the Hammersmith and City Line, with Westbourne Park and Paddington; Swiss Cottage was linked by the St John's Wood Line to Baker Street; the London Chatham and Dover Railway connected the Elephant and Castle with the Metropolitan line and the stations at Ludgate Hill, Holborn Viaduct and Farrington Street. The builders of railways and roadways, often driven through the most populous districts, were under no obligation to rehouse those whom they dispossessed. In London over 100,000 people were expelled from their homes by the coming of the railways, many of them crowding into those slums and rookeries which had not been swept away

In the decade between 1830 and 1840, when the railway mania first manifested itself, London's population rose by a further half-million, and the Registrar-General's 1841 Census figures for the Metropolis record a total of 1,948,369. A decade later, in 1851, the year of the Great Exhibition, the census

---

[11] The explosive growth of the railway network can be glimpsed from the completion dates of the main-line termini: London Bridge 1836, Euston 1837, Paddington 1838, Fenchurch Street 1841, Bricklayers Arms (close to the Old Kent Road) 1844, Kensington 1844, Shoreditch (later renamed "Bishopsgate") 1847, Waterloo 1848, Kings Cross 1852, Paddington New Station 1854, Victoria 1860, Charing Cross 1864, Broad Street 1865, Cannon Street 1866, St Pancras 1868, Liverpool Street (replacing Bishopsgate) 1874. Details in this footnote and the paragraph to which it refers are gleaned from maps to be found in Francis Sheppard, *London 1808-1870: The Infernal Wen*, London, 1971, 127 and 140.

figures revealed that the number had now risen to 2,361,640, and this at a time when the Metropolitan area officially covered some hundred-and-fifteen square miles.

From then on, close to half a million more people were shown to be living in or around the capital as each decade passed. In 1871, London's population numbered 3,254,260: nearly one in seven of the total population of England and Wales. In the years which immediately followed, at the time of the most severe depression in Britain's history, the situation grew worse. The United States and Germany were challenging the supremacy of Britain's markets; there was mass unemployment and millions of English and Irish farmers were migrating to the cities; waves of European Jews were fleeing persecution and streaming into the industrial centres and slums of England. By 1900, London could boast of some four and a half million inhabitants.

When Wordsworth contemplated the city and the river from Westminster bridge in 1802, his was a vision as romantic as had been his vision of the thronging streets eleven years earlier:

> This City now doth, like a garment, wear
> The beauty of the morning; silent, bare,
> Ships, towers, domes, theatres, and temples lie
> Open unto the fields, and to the sky;
> All bright and glittering in the smokeless air ....
> The river glideth at his own sweet will.
> Dear God! The very houses seem asleep;[12]

Anyone who stands by while iron-shod hoofs and the iron-tyred wheels of a card go grinding and clashing over cobblestones will be able to imagine something of the din of the city streets. Pausing at the centre of Westminster Bridge perhaps, Wordsworth might have been able to close his ears to the morning noise of Friday 3 September and see only a vision (or recall the vision of 31 July shared by Dorothy). But under that garment of apparent beauty lay squalor and corruption. The sweet-willed river was an open drain. Huddled among the towers and domes and temples were grossly overcrowded courts and alleys where no sunlight and little air could penetrate, where adults and children daily walked barefoot through filth, and where criminals had their bolt-holes.

---

[12] "Sonnet Composed Upon Westminster Bridge", in *Poetical Works*, London, 1905, 269. In her Journal for 1802, Dorothy refers not to the date given in the title of the poem, but to an earlier crossing of the bridge at 5 or 6 a.m. ("I have forgot which") on 31 July. They were on the Dover Coach, en route to Paris: "It was a beautiful morning. The City, St Paul's, with the River and a multitude of little boats made a most beautiful sight as we crossed Westminster Bridge. The houses were not overhung by their cloud of smoke and they were spread out endlessly, yet the sun shone so brightly with such a pure light that there was even something like the purity of one of nature's own grand spectacles" (*Journals of Dorothy Wordsworth*, ed. Mary Moorman, London, 1971, rpt. 1974, 150-51).

Justice of the Peace at Westminster as he was half a century earlier, Henry
Fielding had no illusions about the criminality:

> Whoever indeed considers the Cities of *London* and *Westminster*, with the late
> vast Addition of their Suburbs; the great Irregularity of their Buildings, the
> immense Number of Lanes, Alleys, Courts and Bye-places; must think, that, had
> they been intended for the very Purpose of Concealment, they could scarce have
> been better contrived. Upon such a View, the whole appears as a vast Wood or
> Forest, in which a Thief may harbour with as great Security, as wild Beasts do in
> the Desarts of *Africa* or *Arabia*.[13]

As the capital and its buildings sprawled ever wider, and the number of its
inhabitants daily grew, the evils, both physical and social, could only worsen.
For Shelley in 1819, "Hell [was] a city much like London – a populous and
smoky city".[14]

A year later, he came to see it as a "great sea":

> whose ebb and flow
> At once is deaf and loud, and on the shore
> vomits its wrecks, and still howls on for more.[15]

To the ebb and flow of noise and the smoke fumes, Shelley might have added
the unremitting stench of sewage.

Since at least the close of the seventeenth century, the city's streams and
ditches had drained – and the contents of her middens and cesspits increasingly
had found their way – into the Thames and its tributaries while, as late as the
mid-nineteenth century, more than seven-tenths of London's drinking water was
still being drawn from the Thames:

> ... polluted as it was by outfall from the sewers, ... by stable dung, rotten
> sprats, guano, and by quantities of solid rubbish and offal thrown into it even
> at this late period from slaughter-houses, knackers' yards, tanneries, and tar
> works. The colour of the river was a greeny black, its consistency so thick that
> each time the tide went down a greasy, foul-smelling scum was deposited over
> the mud. In the hot dry summer of 1858 it was impossible to cross
> Westminster Bridge without a handkerchief pressed closely over nose and
> mouth, impossible to take a trip on a river steamer without feeling sick,
> impossible to breathe in the House of Commons until the windows had been
> covered with curtains soaked in chloride of lime.[16]

---

[13] Henry Fielding, *An Enquiry into the Causes of the Late Increase of Robbers, &c.*
(1751), ed. M.R. Zirker, Middletown: Conn., 1988, 131.

[14] "Peter Bell the Third", 3 – Hell, in Shelley, *Poetical Works*, ed. Thomas
Hutchinson, Oxford Paperback, 1970, 350.

[15] "Letter to Maria Gisborne", ll.193-95, in *Poetical Works*, 367.

[16] Hibbert, 187.

Throughout the nineteenth century, as in earlier times, and along with tuberculosis and all the other bronchitic and infectious diseases, there were regular and often lethal plagues of typhus, the "Irish fever", carried by body-lice, fleas and bedbugs; and of cholera, carried by contaminated water. An unremitting flood of newcomers, crowding into an overcrowded city, made matters more and more desperate. Yet not until the end of the century was there any systematic control of drinking water and sanitation in London, or a public health system.

Some attempts were made to mitigate the danger. Under the Metropolitan Sewers Act of 1848, every house built or rebuilt had henceforth to be drained into a sewer – but only if one was to be found within a hundred feet of the premises. If not, it must be drained into a cesspool; where none existed, a cesspool must be constructed. The Act, concerned as it was with the disposal of sewage, did little or nothing towards ensuring a supply of clean water. And, of some effect as it might be in well-to-do neighbourhoods and in the sprawl of new housing in the suburbs, the Act did little or nothing for the increasingly-crowded slums, where night-soil was piled up in courtyards for weekly cartage, and where in heavy rain what cesspools there were, overflowed into the streets, and into ground-floor and basement rooms. It was not until 1888, when the population had reached a total of some four million inhabitants, that the London County Council was established, to assume overall responsibility for education, sanitation, housing, and hospitals in the metropolis.

In the middle years of the century, London epitomized the extraordinary contrasts that characterized nineteenth-century England. There was an affluent bourgeois London, the glittering London of towers, domes, theatres, temples, and broad thoroughfares which had caught Wordsworth's eye at the turn of the century; there was a *petit-bourgeois* and working-class London of city offices, counting-houses, shops and workplaces, of decent streets and house-proud homes, with its numerous music-halls, pubs and churches. And there were the ghettos and the rookeries of the slums, with their unpaved courts and alleys, their cramped and disease-ridden tenements, and their prostitution, drunkenness and violence. Slums like those of Westminster; of Drury Lane, St Giles, and Seven Dials; Clerkenwell and Saffron Hill; Wapping, Ratcliffe and Limehouse; and, facing Wapping across the Thames, Bermondsey and Jacob's Island. It is this third London, and images of it, that concern me here.

Images of London then, the capital of the empire: as a place of corruption, a tumour, a freakshow, the nightmare forest of a fairy tale, a cesspool, a boneyard, a dustheap, or, as Ruskin came to see it, "that great foul city of London there, – rattling, growling, smoking, stinking – a ghastly heap of fermenting brickwork, pouring out poison at every pore …".[17]

In this essay, I largely confine myself to the labyrinthine slums of Seven Dials and St Giles – "the Holy Land". Equally notorious slums and rookeries elsewhere in the capital can only be given a brief mention.

---

[17] *The Crown of Wild Olive*, I: "Work", 25; London, 1912, 32.

Thomas Neale, Master of the Mint from 1678 to 1699, began the star-shaped pattern of streets east of Wardour Street, which was rapidly to become the slum district known as Seven Dials. The adjacent district to the north was the equally notorious rookery of St Giles. Here "Rats' Castle" was to be found. It was "a large dirty building occupied by thieves and prostitutes, and boys who lived by plunder .... At this place criminals were allowed a bowl of ale on their way from Newgate to Tyburn."[18] With construction of New Oxford Street in 1845, Rats' Castle was swept away, but the name lingered on, referring to the district as a whole. For a while the demolitions laid the area partially open. What remained was

> like a honeycomb, perforated by a number of courts and blind alleys, *culs de sac*, without any outlet other than the entrance. Here were the lowest lodging houses in London, inhabited by the various classes of thieves common to large cities, – the housebreaker, who did not profess to have any other means of livelihood; the tramp and vagrant, whose assumed occupation was a cloak for roguery; the labourer who came to London to look for work; the hordes of Irish who annually seem to come and go with the flies and the fruit, – were here banded together .... The streets were narrow; the windows stuffed up with rags, or patched with paper; strings hung across from house to house, on which clothes were put out to dry; the gutters stagnant, choked up with filth; the pavement strewed with decayed cabbage stalks and other vegetables; the walls of the houses mouldy, discoloured, the whitewash peeling off from damp; the walls in parts bulging, in parts receding, – the floor covered with a coating of dirt.[19]

Seven years later, and a hundred yards distant from the crowded new thoroughfare, the inhabitants of St Giles had not changed:

> squalid children, haggard men, with long uncombed hair, in rags, most of them smoking, many speaking Irish; women without shoes or stockings – a babe perhaps at the breast, with a single garment, confined to the waist by a bit of string; wolfish-looking dogs .... Never was there so little connection between masses of living beings and their means of livelihood.[20]

The unsavoury reputation of the back streets and alleys in St Giles, Seven Dials, and the adjacent Soho was to linger on until the 1950s and later.

In "Gone Astray", Dickens describes how as a child he strayed away from an adult guide close to St Giles's church, and wandered on alone through Covent Garden and Seven Dials. The fascinated aversion which Dickens felt then never left him. "Most of all," as Forster tells us:

---

[18] Henry Mayhew, *London Labour and the London Poor* (1861-2), 4 vols; fac. edn, New York, 1968, IV, 301.

[19] Thomas Beames, *The Rookeries of London: Past, Present, and Perspective*, 2nd edn, 1852; new impression, London, 1970, 25-26.

[20] *Ibid.*, 30.

he had a profound attraction of repulsion to St. Giles's. If he could only induce whomsoever took him out to take him through Seven Dials, he was supremely happy. "Good heaven!" he would exclaim, "what wild visions of prodigies of wickedness, want, and beggary, arose in my mind out of that place!"[21]

Visions, Dickens might have added, which in memory almost invariably end in a moment of comedy: this is a point to which I shall return.

In a "Scene", first published on 27 September 1834 in *Bell's Life in London*, he describes the area as he saw it in 1834:

> The stranger who finds himself in "The Dials" for the first time and stands ... at the entrance of seven obscure passages, uncertain which to take, will see enough around him to keep his curiosity and attention awake for no inconsiderable time. From the irregular square into which he has plunged, the streets and courts dart in all directions, until they are lost in the unwholesome vapour which hangs over the house-tops, and renders the dirty perspective uncertain and confined.[22]

North and south of the Dials ran, as it still does, Monmouth Street. In another Scene, "Meditations in Monmouth-street", published two years later, in 1836, Dickens explains how "we have always entertained a particular attachment to Monmouth-street, as the only true and real emporium for second-hand wearing apparel ...".[23]

Shelton Street today still runs north-eastwards out of Monmouth Street, a hundred metres or so south of the intersection of streets which is Seven Dials. Before returning to Dickens's accounts of these places, it is interesting to read what Charles Booth had to say of Shelton Street as he saw it in 1889, at a time when wholesale demolitions carried out for the construction of New Oxford Street in 1847 and Shaftesbury Avenue in 1885 had cut a swathe through "the Holy Land". On Booth's poverty map, Shelton Street is coloured black, the colour he chose for the most squalid streets in London:

> Shelton Street was just wide enough for a vehicle to pass either way, with room between curb-stone and houses for one foot-passenger to walk; but vehicles would pass seldom, and foot-passengers would prefer the roadway to the risk of tearing their clothes against projecting nails. The houses, about forty in number, contained cellars, parlours, and first, second, and third floors, mostly two rooms to a floor, and few of the 200 families who lived here occupied more than one room. In little rooms no more than 8 ft. square, would be found living father, mother, and several children .... Most of the people described are Irish Roman Catholics getting a living as market porters, or by selling flowers, fruit, fowls, or vegetables in the streets, but as to not a few it is a mystery how they live. Drunkenness and dirt and bad language prevailed,

---

[21] John Forster, *The Life of Charles Dickens*, ed. A.J.Hoppé, London, 1969, I, 12.

[22] "Seven Dials", *Sketches by Boz* (1836), Testimonial Edition, I, 66.

[23] "Meditations in Monmouth Street", *Sketches by Boz*, 70.

and violence was common, reaching at times even to murder. Fifteen rooms out of twenty were filthy to the last degree .... Not a room would be free from vermin, and in many life at night was unbearable. Several occupants have said that in hot weather they don't go to bed, but sit in their clothes in the least infested part of the room. What good is it, they said, to go to bed when you can't get a wink of sleep for bugs and fleas? A visitor in these rooms was fortunate indeed if he carried nothing of the kind away with him. The passage from the street to the back door would be scarcely ever swept, to say nothing of being scrubbed. Most of the doors stood open all night as well as all day, and the passage and stairs gave shelter to many who were altogether homeless. Here the mother could stand with her baby, or sit with it on the stairs, or companions would huddle together in cold weather. The little yard at the back was only sufficient for dust – bin and closet and water – tap, serving for six or seven families. The water would be drawn from cisterns which were receptacles for refuse, and perhaps occasionally a dead cat ....[24]

Shelton Street was not unique, but typical. Six years earlier, in 1883, the story had been told of similar slums elsewhere in the city:

To get into them you have to penetrate courts reeking with poisonous and malodorous gases arising from accumulations of sewage and refuse scattered in all directions and often flowing beneath your feet; courts, many of them which the sun never penetrates, which are never visited by a breath of fresh air, and which rarely know the virtues of a drop of cleansing water. You have to ascend rotten staircases, which threaten to give way beneath every step, and which, in some places, have already broken down, leaving gaps that imperil the limbs and lives of the unwary. You have to grope your way along dark and filthy passages swarming with vermin. Then, if you are not driven back by the intolerable stench, you may gain admittance to the dens in which these thousands of beings ... herd together ....

In many cases matters are made worse by the unhealthy occupations followed by those who dwell in these habitations. Here you are choked as you enter by the air laden with particles of the superfluous fur pulled from the skins of rabbits, rats, dogs and other animals in their preparation for the furrier. Here the smell of paste and drying matchboxes, mingling with other sickly odours, overpowers you; or it may be the fragrance of stale fish or vegetables, not sold on the previous day, and kept in the room overnight.

Eight feet square – that is about the average size of very many of these rooms. Walls and ceiling are black with the accretions of filth which have gathered upon them through long years of neglect. It is exuding through cracks in the boards overhead; it is running down the walls; it is everywhere. What goes by the name of a window is half of it stuffed with rags or covered by boards to keep out wind and rain; the rest is so begrimed and obscured that scarcely can light enter or anything be seen outside ....[25]

[24] Cited in *Charles Booth's London: A Portrait of the Poor at the Turn of the Century*, eds Albert Fried and Richard M. Elman, Penguin, 1971, 108-10.

[25] William C. Preston, *The Bitter Cry of Outcast London: An Enquiry into the Condition of the Abject Poor*, London 1883, facs. edn, Portway, Bath, 1969, 5-6.

For a notion of the detritus resulting from this squalid over-crowding, we may turn to Mayhew's statistics of 1861; compiled three decades earlier and when the population of London was smaller by some one and a half millions.

Whether rich or poor, Londoners heated their houses and cooked their food with wood or coal and, at the time of Mayhew's survey, three-and-a-half million tons of coal were annually consumed in London. Mayhew quotes Dr Ure's evidence to a House of Commons Committee that "a column of smoke might be seen extending in different directions around London, according to the wind, for a distance of some 20 to 30 miles", and Dr Reid's report that on one occasion falling soot had deposited so complete and continuous a film at the Horseguards, that Reid could see the print of his foot as clearly as if in snow.[26] Mayhew adds that – compared with the variously "sulphurous" and "acid" smokes produced by chemical works, the "metallic" smokes that arose from the smelting of lead, arsenic and copper, and the "putrescent smokes" that evolved from drains – the opaque, soot-laden smoke is "least injurious to animal or vegetable health".[27] Unable to calculate how many tons of soot per year fell in this way on the city, Mayhew however notes that the soot swept from chimneys annually amounted to 1,100,810 bushels.[28]

The collection of night-soil, mostly carted away at night, was the perquisite of sweeps, bricklayers, and dust- and other contractors. Between them, these men emptied 50,692 cesspools annually, and in addition shovelled up 253,960 cartloads of nightsoil, at a cost paid to the Master nightsoil-men of £131,692 in a year.[29] To this human refuse, must be added the discarded waste and the effluvium of the various commercial enterprises scattered among the houses and tenements, and inevitably most thickly clustered in the slums. The parish of St James, Westminster, which included, alongside the Abbey and the establishments of the rich and powerful, a notorious slum, provides an example. In a pamphlet addressed to the inhabitants of the parish in 1847, the Hon. Frederick Byng lists "14 Cow-sheds, 2 Slaughter Houses, 3 Boiling Houses, 7 Bone Stores, and 1 Zincing Establishment".[30]

Mayhew presents a table in his second volume, of the quantities of refuse bought, sold, and collected in the city streets.[31] Along other statistics collected by Mayhew, it throws light on the commercial value of Noddy Boffin's dust-heaps in *Our Mutual Friend*. There were:

> 750,000 cartloads of soil, from cesspools (sold, like the soot, to farmers, graziers and gardeners for manure);

---

[26] Mayhew, II, 341.

[27] *Ibid.*, 339.

[28] *Ibid.*, 343. This amounts to rather more than 40,040 cubic metres; to visualize it, one might imagine a wall 100 metres long, 100 metres high, and 4 metres thick.

[29] *Ibid.*, 461.

[30] Cited in Beames, 214.

[31] Mayhew, II, 462-63.

900,000 cartloads of household dust, mainly coal-ash, cinders, etc.
(the coal fragments and cinders sold to brickmakers, and the ash to farmers).

143,983 cartloads of street sweepings (sold, like the nightsoil, for manure).

Here we might pause, alongside Jo, the crossing-sweeper, and contemplate the filth that he brushed away ahead of his clients' feet.

Mayhew has much to say about London's street dust and detritus in 1860, basing his calculations on such details as the number of horses – 24,214 – in the metropolis daily, the number of livestock led through the streets to Smithfield and other markets, and veterinary information about the average daily quantity of dung dropped by each species. Four-fifths of the street refuse, Mayhew concludes, was dung. The remaining fifth consisted of dust abraded from the stones of the street, soot, rotting fruit and vegetable matter, sewage swept or thrown from houses and, in wet weather, the surface water which turned the whole into mud.

Among the other items of refuse, so meticulously enumerated by Mayhew, we might notice the

3,494,400 lbs of bones, collected in the streets by bone-grubbers and sold at ¼d a lb for manure and knife-handles;

4,076,800 lbs of rags (collected by the rag-pickers and sold to the paper-makers at ½d a pound).

Mayhew interviewed a bone-grubber near to Rosemary-lane:

"I got so bad off, I didn't know what to do. But seeing a great many about here gathering bones and rags, I thought I'd do so too – a poor fellow must do something .... There's a great deal more than 100 bone-pickers about here, men, women, and children. The Jews in this Lane and up in Petticoat-lane give a good deal of victuals away on the Saturday. They sometimes call one of us in from the street to light the fire for them, or take off the kettle, for they musn't do anything on the Sabbath; and then they put some food on the footpath, and throw rags and bones into the street for us, because they must not hand anything to us."[32]

Mayhew lists, item by item, the discarded clothing, furs, boots and shoes sold to the old-clothes dealers of Monmouth-street and Petticoat-lane at an annual value, he computes, of £675,555 6s. 8d. Among the refuse simply picked up at random in the streets he lists the 52,000 pails of "pure", dogshit, sold at 1s per pail to tanners and leather-dressers, and the 2,240 pounds weight of cigar-ends at 8d per lb, sold, he says, to the Jews in Rosemary-Lane.

With Mayhew's calculations in mind, let us move forward again to Charles Booth and Shelton Street in 1889:

---

[32] *Ibid.*, 140.

The houses looked ready to fall, many of them being out of the perpendicular. Gambling was the amusement of the street. Sentries would be posted, and if the police made a rush the offenders would slip into the open houses and hide until danger was past. Sunday afternoon and evening was the hey-day time for this street. Every doorstep would be crowded by those who sat or stood with pipe and jug of beer, while lads lounged about, and the gutters would find amusement for not a few children with bare feet, their faces and hands besmeared, while the mud oozed through between their toes. Add to this a group of fifteen or twenty young men gambling in the middle of the street and you complete the general picture.[33]

Booth goes on to map the street room by room and house by house; there are thirty-nine six-roomed houses in Shelton Street – each with a two-roomed basement, and three floors above of two rooms each. Two hundred families, all Irish, live in them. Thus, calculating five members in an average family, a thousand souls live in this street alone.

Like Mayhew, Booth notes down what a few of them have to say; but in the third person, unemotionally, setting down facts. We must turn back to Mayhew's volumes to look at the statistics of their lives as jobbing workers, street sellers, street finders, street thieves and street women, and to hear them and their fellow slum-dwellers speak, if ventriloquially, and with much editing of their words.

In Dickens's account of a night-time visit to Rats' Castle, first published in *Household Words* on 14 June 1851, the poor rise up in their rags to speak:[34]

> How many people there may be in London, who, if we had brought them deviously and blindfold, to this street, fifty paces from the [Metropolitan Police] Station House, and within call of St Giles's church, would know it for a not remote part of the city in which their lives are passed? How many, who, amidst this compound of sickening smells, these heaps of filth, these tumbling houses, with all their vile contents, animate and inanimate, slimily overflowing into the black road, would believe that they breathe *this* air? How much Red Tape may there be, that could look round on the faces that now hem us in – for our appearance here has caused a rush from all points to a common centre – the lowering foreheads, the sallow cheeks, the brutal eyes, the matted hair, the infected, vermin-haunted heaps of rags – and say "I have thought of this. I have not dismissed the thing? ..."
>
> Ten, twenty, thirty – who can count them! Men, women, children, for the most part naked, heaped upon the floor like maggots in a cheese! Ho! In that dark corner yonder! Does anybody lie there? Me sir, Irish me, a widder, with six

---

[33] *Charles Booth's London*, 108-10.

[34] Dickens's account of his visit in 1851 refers to the *street*, rather than to the original building; as does Mayhew, who notes that, in 1851, rooms about twelve feet by ten commonly housed as many as sixteen people: "any lay on loose straw littered on the floor, their heads to the wall and their feet to the centre, and decency was entirely unknown among them" (Mayhew, IV, 301).

children. And yonder? Me sir, Irish me, with me wife and eight poor babes. And
to the left there? Me sir, Irish me, along with two more Irish boys as is me
friends. And to the right there? Me sir and the Murphy fam'ly, numbering five
blessed souls. And what's this, coiling, now, about my foot? Another Irish me,
pitifully in want of shaving, whom I have awakened from sleep – and across my
other foot lies his wife – and by the shoes of Inspector Field lie their three eldest –
and their three youngest are squeezed between the open door and the wall. And
why is there no one on that little mat before the sullen fire? Because O'Donovan,
with his wife and daughter, is not come in from selling Lucifers! Nor on the bit of
sacking in the nearest corner? Bad luck! Because that Irish family is late tonight,
a cadging in the streets!

They are all awake now, the children excepted, and most of them sit up, to
stare. Wheresoever Mr Rodgers turns the flaming eye [of his lantern], there is a
spectral figure rising, unshrouded, from a grave of rags.[35]

Dickens's tone at this point is very different from the accounts which he
wrote fifteen years earlier of Seven Dials, and Monmouth-street, the street from
which Shelton-street sprang:

Seven Dials! the region of song and poetry – first effusions, and last dying
speeches: hallowed by the names of Catnach and Pitts – names that will entwine
themselves with costermongers and barrel-organs, when penny magazines shall
have superseded penny yards of song, and capital punishment be unknown! ...

... what involutions can compare with those of Seven Dials? Where is there
such another maze of streets, courts, lanes, and alleys? Where such a pure
mixture of Englishmen and Irishmen, as in this complicated part of London? ...

The unexperienced wayfarer through "The Dials" ... traverses streets of dirty,
straggling houses, with now and then an unexpected court composed of buildings
as ill-proportioned and deformed as the half naked children that wallow in the
kennels. Here and there, a little dark chandler's shop, with a cracked bell hung up
behind the door to announce the entrance of a customer, or betray the presence of
some young gentleman in whom a passion for shop tills has developed itself at an
early age ... and shops for the purchase of rags, bones, old iron, and kitchen stuff,
vie in cleanliness with the bird-fanciers and rabbit-dealers, which one might
fancy so many arks, but for the irresistible conviction that no bird in its proper
senses, who was permitted to leave one of them, would ever come back again.
Brokers' shops, which would seem to have been established by humane
individuals, as refuges for destitute bugs, interspersed with announcements of
day-schools, penny theatres, petition-writers, mangles, and music for balls or
routs, complete the "still life" of the subject; and dirty men, filthy women, squalid
children, fluttering shuttlecocks, noisy battledores, reeking pipes, bad fruit, more
than doubtful oysters, attenuated cats, depressed dogs, and anatomical fowls, are
its cheerful accompaniments.[36]

---

[35] "On Duty with Inspector Field", *Household Words* (1851), Testimonial Edition,
XIV, 140-44.
[36] "Seven Dials", 67-68.

The inhabitants of Monmouth-street are a distinct class; a peaceable and retiring race, who immure themselves for the most part in deep cellars, or small back parlours, and who seldom come forth into the world, except in the dusk and coolness of evening, when they may be seen seated, in chairs on the pavement, smoking their pipes, or watching the gambols of their engaging children as they revel in the gutter, a happy troop of infantine scavengers. Their countenances bear a thoughtful and a dirty cast ..., and their habitations are distinguished by that disregard of outward appearance, and neglect of personal comfort, so common among people who are constantly immersed in profound speculations, and deeply engaged in sedentary pursuits.[37]

In streets somewhere to the west of Seven Dials lay "Tom-all-Alone's", where in *Bleak House*, the crossing-sweeper Jo lay down to sleep at night. Field-lane, a court off Saffron Hill, and the rookery of St Giles's have both been suggested as the original of Tom-all-Alone's. But the slum streets that centred on Drury-lane, Russell Court, and the burial ground of St Mary-le-Strand, are as likely a model. There is no comedy in Dickens's account of St Mary-le-Strand. Closed and grassed over in 1885 and so beyond the scope of Booth's researches, and since then absorbed into the new district formed by the making of Aldwych.[38] In Dickens's novel, it remains:

a hemmed-in churchyard, pestiferous and obscene, whence malignant diseases are communicated to the bodies of our dear brothers and sisters who have not departed .... With houses looking on, on every side, save where a reeking little tunnel of a court gives access to the iron gate – with every villainy of life in action close on death, and every poisonous element of death in action close on life .... [With its] flame of gas, burning so sullenly above the iron gate, on which the poisoned air deposits its witch-ointment slimy to the touch![39]

Mayhew's ninety-six and a half column inches on the city's smoke and effluvia, are anticipated and epitomized in Dickens's "poisoned air [that] deposits its witch-ointment slimy to the touch".

In his apostrophe on the death of Jo, Dickens's tone is as angry and engaged as it is possible for him to be:

Dead!
    Dead, your Majesty. Dead, my lords, and gentlemen. Dead, Right Reverends and Wrong Reverends of every order. Dead, men and women, born with heavenly compassion in your hearts. And dying thus around us, every day.[40]

---

[37] "Meditations in Monmouth-street", 70.

[38] Arthur L. Hayward, *The Dickens Encyclopaedia*, Routledge Paperback 1971, 155.

[39] *Bleak House* (1852), ch. XI; Testimonial Edition, XI, 152.

[40] *Bleak House*, ch. XLVII; *ibid.*, 655.

But more often and more typically, Dickens, with his habitual devices of reification, animation and word-play, contrives to escape – and his reader along with him – from the squalor that he is describing, into comic irony, and farce.

Catnach and Pitts of Long Acre were publishers of ballads and broadsides, often obscene, and spurious "last dying speeches" of those about to be hanged, peddled about the streets and at the gallows-foot before the condemned man or women had uttered a word. Seven Dials, Dickens tells us, is for him "hallowed" by their memory. A sneak-thief is a "young gentleman in whom a passion for shop tills has developed itself at an early age"; the broker's shops "would seem to have been established by humane individuals, as refuges for destitute bugs". Fowls, which being "anatomical", are reminiscent of the skeletal remains of the anatomized malefactors displayed at Surgeon's Hall, are the no less "cheerful accompaniments" of "attenuated cats", and "depressed dogs". Given the other adjectives nearby, we might conclude that it is not the passers-by so much as the "more than doubtful" oysters themselves who entertain doubts about the nature of their own existence. In Monmouth-street, Dickens continues to play the same game of comic irony. The children gambol and revel in the gutter, a "happy troop of infantine scavengers"; the exhausted, or drunken, parents sprawled on their chairs are "immersed in profound speculations, and deeply engaged in sedentary pursuits".

Nor was this descent from the horrors of squalor to the ridiculous a feature only of Dickens's earlier writing. His night on duty with Inspector Field, which began in Rats' Castle, led him, at two o'clock in the morning, to the Ratcliffe Highway and the river. As Christopher Hibberd points out:

> Dickens' fascination with the river, or more exactly with the river at night, was one almost of repulsion. He was drawn to it, and to crumbling buildings decaying by its shores, to places like Jacob's Island and Quilp's wharf, as he was drawn to the Paris morgue – he never wanted to go there, but he was always pulled there, "dragged by invisible forces". The riverside at Limehouse, below his godfather's house at 5 Church Row, was an early and significant stage in a reluctantly yet compulsively repeated journey.[41]

When Stowe recorded it in 1603, the Ratcliffe Highway was a "continual street, or filthy strait passage, with alleys of small tenements, or cottages ... inhabited by sailors' victuallers, along by the river of Thames, [leading] almost to Radcliff, a good mile from the Tower".[42] Untouched by the Great Fire, the Highway and the slums around it continued to engulf the wharfside and its marshy hinterland, sprawling eastward along the north bank of the river to beyond Limehouse.

A maze of dingy streets and narrow alleyways which led down to the wharves and the river, the area was in 1811 the scene of a notorious series of

[41] Christopher Hibbert, *London: The Biography of a City*, London, 1969, 44-45.
[42] *The Survey of London*, by John Stowe, Citizen of London, 2nd edn, 1603 (Everyman, London, undated, 375).

murders which, in "On Murder as One of the Fine Arts", De Quincey retailed with more exuberance than accuracy sixteen years later. In 1860, their investigations in Limehouse provided Henry Mayhew and Bracebridge Hemyng with the material for their accounts of thieves' kitchens and brothels recorded in volume four of *London Labour and the London Poor*. In May 1869, Dickens escorted a group of friends through the criminal quarters and lodging-kens of Limehouse and the Ratcliffe Highway. The scene which they witnessed in a riverside opium den that night, was to re-appear in 1870 in the opening pages of *The Mystery of Edwin Drood* where, as James Field reported later:

> The identical words which Dickens puts into the mouth of the wretched creature [the "hostess", Princess Puffer] in *Edwin Drood* we heard her croon as we leaned over the tattered bed on which she was lying. There was something hideous in the way the woman kept repeating, "Ye'll pay up according, deary, won't ye?" and the Chinamen and lascars made never-to be-forgotten pictures in the scene.[43]

In Jasper's drugged nightmare, "Princess Puffer" surfaces as an almost comic figure.

Coming to an end as it did in Ratcliffe, Dickens's night out with Inspector Field two decades earlier, which began in the squalor of Rats' Castle, collapses into farce with the party's encounter with Bark, a lodging-house keeper and receiver of stolen goods:

> Bark sleeps in an inner wooden hutch, near his street-door. As we parley on the step with Bark's deputy, Bark growls in his bed. We enter, and Bark flies out of bed. Bark is a red villain and a wrathful, with a sanguine throat that looks very much as if it were expressly made for hanging, as he stretches it out, in pale defiance, over the half-door of his hutch. Bark's parts of speech are of an awful sort – principally adjectives. I won't, says Bark, have no adjective police and adjective strangers in my adjective premises! I won't by adjective and substantive! Give me my trousers, and I'll send the whole adjective police to adjective and substantive! Give me, says Bark, my adjective trousers! I'll put an adjective knife in the whole bileing of 'em, I'll punch their adjective heads. I'll rip up their adjective substantives. Give me my adjective trousers! says Bark, and I'll spile the bileing of 'em ....
> We leave bully Bark to subside at leisure out of his passion and his trousers, and, I dare say, to be reminded of this little brush before long.[44]

In his account of Quilp's Wharf, probably Butler's Wharf, directly across the water from Wapping and a stone's throw from the rookery of Jacob's Island; in his description of Fagin's academy for thieves in a court in Field-lane off Saffron Hill; as with Squeers' *Dotheboys Hall*; as so often elsewhere; Dickens reveals the same fascinated aversion that he displays in his childhood reminiscences of London. For an instant, the squalid surroundings collapse into

---

[43] James T. Fields, *Yesterdays with Authors*, London, 1900, 202-203.
[44] "On Duty with Inspector Field", *Household Words* (1851), Testimonial Edition, XIV, 151-52.

pasteboard, and the menacing figures deflate into pantomime villains, as though the horror of reality can only be swept away by laughter.

After the volumes of unemotional statistics and clearly compassionate face-to-face interviews, Mayhew's final volume comes to an end in a sudden and remarkable warning against uncalculating charity. Mayhew concludes:

> It is the office of reason – reason improved by experience – to teach us not to waste our own interest and our resources on beings that will be content to live on our bounty, and will never return a moral profit to our charitable industry. The great opportunities or the mighty powers that heaven may have given us, it never meant to be lavished on mere human animals who eat, drink and sleep, and whose only instinct is to find a new caterer when the old one is exhausted.[45]

Wealthy ship-owner that he was, and "as a man of affairs ... an implacable conservative",[46] Charles Booth nevertheless concluded on the basis of information received from four thousand poor people, that some eighty-five per cent of the cases of poverty resulted either from lack of work or low pay, or from sickness or the need to support a large family. The idle, the drunken and the thriftless – contrary to the middle-class myth – made up only fifteen per cent of the indigent poor. Coming after the pages of coolly-noted detail, Booth's peroration is also remarkable for its sudden passion:

> The dry bones that lie scattered over the long valley that we have traversed together lie before my reader. May some great soul, master of a subtler and nobler alchemy than mine, disentangle the confused issues, reconcile the apparent contradictions in aim, melt and commingle the various influences for good into one divine uniformity of effort, and make these dry bones live so that the streets of our Jerusalem may sing with joy.[47]

Clearly, it is a political solution that Booth has in mind here. But phrases in Booth's closing sentence could be aptly applied to Dickens, and Dickens's success in bringing the squalor of unemployed and lower working-class London to the attention, and to the emotions, of a huge readership. These images of the city streets that he never ceased to explore with that "profound attraction of repulsion", as Forster reminds us, hit a public nerve. We delight in the sheer, hideous *verve* of Fagin, Quilp, Squeers, Krook, the Sampson Brasses, even of Bark, and all the other nightmare or pantomime villains, and even while we are itching to see them sent to jail or the gallows: both, as Dickens saw things, a fitting destiny for the incorrigibly vicious. We can recognize, and rejoice in, the humanity – and the comedy – to be discovered in a teeming slum, while we can't wait to see the foulness swept away.

---

[45] Mayhew, IV, 448.

[46] Albert Fried and Richard M. Elman, "Introduction", *Charles Booth's London*, 31.

[47] *Ibid.*, 437.

As years pass, the statisticians' precise figures and quantities are liable to become blurred, their exhortations – even their interviews, items in a catalogue rather than, as in Dickens, the dramatic elements of a larger gothic fabula – may fade and be forgotten, but Dickens's fascinated aversion remains. In the second paragraph of a description of Newgate, he defines his answerability to the truth of his own vision, and not in terms of statistics:

> we do not intend to fatigue the reader with any statistical accounts of the prison; they will be found at length in numerous reports of numerous committees, and a variety of authorities of equal weight. We took no notes, made no memoranda, measured none of the yards, ascertained the number of inches in no particular room; are unable even to report of how many apartments the gaol is composed.
>
> We saw the prison, and we saw the prisoners; and what we did see, and what we thought, we will tell at once in our own way.[48]

His visions of the city were made, as he tells us, "out of strange experiences and sordid things". They are angry, mocking, ironic, squalid, pitying, and comic. They are often all of those things in the same breath, and for that very reason we can't shake ourselves free of them.

This might sound like a paradox. I don't think it is.

---

[48] "A Visit to Newgate", *Sketches by Boz*, 190.

VICTORIAN POETRY OF THE CITY: ELIZABETH BARRETT BROWNING'S *AURORA LEIGH*

DANIEL KARLIN

This article forms part of a larger topic: the way Victorian poetry represents urban experience, and the special transformations and figurative re-shapings which are involved in adapting the rhetoric of the sublime, so vital to Romantic and post-Romantic aesthetics, to the life of the modern city. Along with this aesthetic issue, indeed inseparable from it, goes the issue of social responsibility – the extent to which poets, like novelists, felt an obligation to comment on contemporary life, to intervene in social and political questions, and to represent the city through images of its material and economic conditions. For Robert Browning, who was born in London and returned there after the death of his wife ended his long period of residence in Italy, the city meant modernity both of content and form, a multitude of competing voices and authorities whose interconnections make up the pattern of his urban masterpiece, *The Ring and the Book*, an epic in which late seventeenth-century Rome doubles as mid-nineteenth-century London. But for Elizabeth Barrett Browning, born and brought up in rural England, and for whom London meant estrangement and internal exile, the city posed a different challenge. It is her work, and especially her "novel poem" *Aurora Leigh*, published in 1856, that I have chosen to focus on here.[1]

The heroine of *Aurora Leigh* is born in Italy of an English father and Italian mother. Her mother dies in childbirth and her father when she is fourteen. Aurora is sent to England and brought up in the country by her aunt. She discovers her vocation as a poet. Her cousin, Romney Leigh, an ardent believer in social and political reform, falls in love with her and asks her to marry him. He does not share her belief in the redemptive power of art, and anyway he does not believe that women can be great artists. Aurora refuses to marry him, and a small legacy from her aunt means that she is able to go to London and try to establish herself as a professional writer. She becomes a journalist as well as a poet, and gains some success. Meanwhile

---

[1] All quotations from *Aurora Leigh* are from Margaret Reynolds's edition, Athens: Ohio, 1992; book and line references are given in the text.

Romney, who has inherited the lion's share of the Leigh fortune, pursues his notions of social philanthropy and reform. He rescues a young working-class woman, Marian Erle, from poverty and abuse and determines to marry her as a gesture of reconciliation between the higher and lower classes. Enter Lady Waldemar, a frivolous society beauty who is in love with Romney. She tries to thwart the match by getting Aurora to intervene. Aurora does go to visit Marian but realizes she is truly innocent and good and gives her high-minded approval to the marriage. However, Marian fails to turn up at the church and seemingly disappears without trace. This takes us up to the end of Book IV of the poem; the remaining five books reveal what has happened to Marian, and follow the story both of Aurora's life as a poet and her love for Romney, but these plot developments are not my concern here. I am interested in the image of the city, which becomes the scene both of Aurora's first steps as a writer and of the experiment in social philanthropy which Romney pursues.

Aurora Leigh is what you might call a quasi-autobiographical poem, in which various aspects of Elizabeth Barrett Browning's own life are dispersed among the various characters and events of the story. For my purpose only two of the many points of resemblance and difference really matter. The first concerns the outline of Aurora's career as a writer, and the second, which is of course linked to the first, concerns the nature of her direct experience of urban life. Aurora's determination to establish herself as an independent professional writer represents, to some extent, a fantasy on Barrett Browning's behalf. She never lived on her own in London, and never made her living by her pen. She lived in her father's house until her marriage at the age of forty, and was then enabled to defy Mr Barrett's authority because she had an income, not from her books but from a legacy left to her by her maternal grandfather. Aurora not only writes for the metropolitan reviews and turns her hand to all kinds of miscellaneous hack-work to support her vocation as a poet, she also attends London parties where she is lionized and meets other celebrities and people of fashion.

Barrett Browning was famous in London from the late 1830s to the date of her marriage with Robert Browning in 1846 not for social visibility but for seclusion, and though she did not object to making money from her poetry she was in no sense a professional writer – quite unlike her close friend Mary Russell Mitford, for example, or Harriet Martineau, or Anna Jameson. Aurora's presence at evening parties is in fact more reminiscent of how Barrett Browning saw her future husband, Robert Browning, "A guest for queens to social pageantries", as she describes him in one of the *Sonnets from the Portuguese*, while she calls herself "A poor, tired, wandering singer, singing through/The dark". The contrast is melodramatically phrased but perfectly accurate. The courtship correspondence of the two poets is filled with references to Browning going to evening parties, dances, the theatre, art exhibitions, public dinners, or even simply walking around the streets, giving a penny to the blind clarionet-player by the toll-gate of Waterloo Bridge, or "going about sight-seeing with a friend & his lady-cousins" and coming home "dead with intense boring".[2] For Barrett Browning a carriage drive to nearby Regent's Park, or a shopping trip to Bond Street, were epoch-making events in the recovery of her health and spirits in the period leading up to her marriage and elopement with Browning in 1846. She wrote to him with awe of her first sight of the Great Western at Paddington station, and even at the height of her recovery she shrank from attending a church service with her sister Arabel because the music of the organ overpowered her.

When Barrett Browning came to write of Aurora Leigh's decision to trust her genius, to reject becoming Romney Leigh's handmaiden and helpmeet and to launch herself on a literary career, she deliberately chose to link this decision with a journey to London. Since Aurora has a small financial independence, she could theoretically have stayed in the country and probably lived more cheaply – certainly more respectably. A middle-class spinster living on her own in genteel poverty in a village was not as unusual as a female author living on her own in London. But this question is never even canvassed. Announcing her determination to Romney at the end of Book II, Aurora says:

> I go hence
> To London, to the gathering-place of souls,
> To live mine straight out, vocally, in books ….
>
> (II 1181-83)

Although Romney is sceptical about Aurora's chances of success as a writer, he has nothing to say on this point; he simply accepts that London is where a literary vocation must be pursued. When Aurora describes what followed, at the outset of Book III, she gives a fairly detailed and specific account of what life in the "gathering-place of souls" involves:

> When Romney Leigh and I had parted thus,
> I took a chamber up three flights of stairs
> Not far from being as steep as some larks climb,
> And there, in a certain house in Kensington,
> Three years I lived and worked.
>
> (III 157-61)

Kensington at this date was not a particularly fashionable location, and when the fashionable Lady Waldemar visits Aurora in her lodgings she feelingly comments on the steep climb. Later on, when Aurora visits Marian Erle, she too will undertake a difficult social climb, in a location considerably less fashionable than Kensington. The opening of Book III presents Aurora

---

[2] Letter of 10 April 1846, in *The Brownings' Correspondence*, eds Philip Kelley and Scott Lewis, Winfield: Kan., 1994, XII, 234.

Leigh in her Kensington lodgings, scolding her maid and opening her day's correspondence. She has received fan letters from male and female admirers, about whom she is equally scornful, letters from critics and fellow-writers, and letters from friends, in particular the painter Vincent Carrington who writes to her with great freedom about a sexy sketch of a Greek nymph he wants her opinion of. Subsequent scenes in this book and in Book V will show Aurora attending London evening parties and meeting representative figures of current social and political trends. The impression might be that of a busy professional woman, immersed in literary life in a way quite foreign to Barrett Browning's own experience and therefore, possibly, a focus for imaginative desire. But the point of the poem is obviously not to promote the joys of life as a hard-working metropolitan literary hack. The city is where Aurora has gone to become a writer, but not just any kind of writer. The phrase which Aurora uses to describe London, the "gathering place of souls", corresponds to her ambition to live out her own soul; the question of what the city offers an independent woman writer overlaps with, but is not identical with, the question of what it offers a poet.

The economics of this issue are carefully laid out. "In England, no one lives by verse that lives", Aurora realizes:

> I was constrained, for life,
> To work with one hand for the booksellers
> While working with the other for myself
> And art ….

She has to have a supplementary source of income, so she "resolved by prose/To make a space to sphere my living verse" (III 307, 302-305, 308-10). The concentration of publishing houses in London, together with the rapid expansion of the periodical press in the first decades of the nineteenth century, driven both by increased literacy and developments in printing technology, means that there is a market to be supplied. Accordingly, we hear of Aurora writing "for cyclopaedias, magazines,/And weekly papers", of her learning "the use/Of the editorial 'we' in a review", of her writing short stories and frivolous articles "[carved] on cherry-stones/To suit light readers" (III 310-11, 311-12, 318-19). All the time, however, this professional activity is intended to subsidize a different kind of work, what Aurora calls the "veritable work" of poetry (III 328). The freedom and economic opportunity of the city are desirable only on these terms.

A picture begins to emerge of Aurora's life in London as a double existence, one which takes advantage of urban culture and economic conditions, but which is not in fact committed to urban identity. When she was still shut up, more or less, in Wimpole Street, Elizabeth Barrett wrote to Robert Browning that the social world he inhabited seemed to her "a strange husk of a world", which "looks to me like mandarin-life or something as remote";[3] this feeling persists in *Aurora Leigh*, for even though Aurora herself goes out into the social world, she portrays herself as alien to it, always on the edge of a conversation or reluctantly drawn in to the circuit of gossip, keener to observe than to take part. Her real self, her real life, lie elsewhere, in transcendent opposition to cyclopaedias and magazines, to the house in Kensington and to the minor celebrity she has attained.

I can best illustrate the nature of this opposition by a remarkable passage in which Aurora describes looking out from the windows of her lodging. These lines evoke the city as a source of visionary creative power, but they do so by figuring its dissolution:

> Serene and unafraid of solitude
> I worked the short days out, – and watched the sun
> On lurid morns or monstrous afternoons
> (Like some Druidic idol's fiery brass
> With fixed unflickering outline of dead heat,
> From which the blood of wretches pent inside
> Seems oozing forth to incarnadine the air)
> Push out through fog with his dilated disk,
> And startle the slant roofs and chimney-pots
> With splashes of fierce colour. Or I saw
> Fog only, the great tawny weltering fog,
> Involve the passive city, strangle it
> Alive, and draw it off into the void,
> Spires, bridges, streets, and squares, as if a spunge
> Had wiped out London, – or as noon and night
> Had clapped together and utterly struck out
> The intermediate time, undoing themselves
> In the act. Your city poets see such things
> Not despicable. Mountains of the south,
> When drunk and mad with elemental wines
> They rend the seamless mist and stand up bare,
> Make fewer singers, haply. No one sings,
> Descending Sinai: on Parnassus-mount
> You take a mule to climb and not a muse
> Except in fable and figure: forests chant
> Their anthems to themselves, and leave you dumb.
> But sit in London at the day's decline,
> And view the city perish in the mist
> Like Pharaoh's armaments in the deep Red Sea,
> The chariots, horsemen, footmen, all the host,
> Sucked down and choked to silence – then, surprised
> By a sudden sense of vision and of tune,
> You feel as conquerors though you did not fight,
> And you and Israel's other singing girls,

---

[3] Letter of 17 April 1845, in *The Brownings' Correspondence*, X, 170.

Ay, Miriam with them, sing the song you choose.

(III 169-203)

The density of figurative language in these lines makes them hard to follow, but it seems that a transfer of creative authority is taking place, from the natural to the urban sublime. The transfer is marked by images of terrible violence, with the sun as a "Druidic idol" inside which sacrificial victims are being burned alive, the "great tawny weltering fog" strangling the city alive, the fabric of London perishing in the mist "Like Pharaoh's armaments in the deep Red Sea"; this violence affects the very concept of time, so that "noon and night" collapse into each other, "undoing themselves/In the act". The "city poets" who "see such things" are "Israel's singing girls", and Aurora herself clearly identifies with Miriam, the first female poet in the Hebrew bible, who leads the Israelite women in a song of triumph over Egypt in Chapter 15 of Exodus. We are a long way from the rhapsodic contemplation of nature in Wordsworth – in *The Prelude*, for example, which had been published in 1850 as Barrett Browning began work on *Aurora Leigh* – but we are an even greater distance from another famous Wordsworth poem, the Westminster Bridge sonnet. For these apocalyptic images of loss and dissolution reverse those of clarity, stillness, and harmony which dominate the earlier poem, a rare example of Wordsworth's willingness to find in the city a locus of creative power:

> Earth has not anything to show more fair:
> Dull would he be of soul who could pass by
> A sight so touching in its majesty:
> This City now doth, like a garment, wear
> The beauty of the morning; silent, bare,
> Ships, towers, domes, theatres, and temples lie
> Open unto the fields, and to the sky;
> All bright and glittering in the smokeless air.
> Never did sun more beautifully steep
> In his first splendour, valley, rock, or hill;
> Ne'er saw I, never felt, a calm so deep!
> The river glideth at his own sweet will:
> Dear God! the very houses seem asleep;
> And all that mighty heart is lying still![4]

Wordsworth's title gives a specific place and date, the poem itself a particular time of day; the poet himself, like his own poem, is "composed upon Westminster Bridge", suffused with the calm of the majestic sight which he in turn majestically reflects. What he sees in the city, he feels in himself, a great poised moment of clarity. Since he is evidently not "dull of

---

[4] "Composed Upon Westminster Bridge, September 3, 1802", first published in *Poems*, London, 1807; in *Poetical Works*, London, 1905, 269.

soul", the "bright and glittering" vision corresponds to his own alertness, and is like a quality of his mind and art. Although there is a suggestion of precariousness, the sense that "This City now" will not endure in its beauty for more than a moment, that the air is not usually "smokeless" (otherwise why use that word?) and will soon be smoky again – despite this the poem rests with consummate assurance between heartbeats, impossibly suspended in the timeless moment of art.

For Barrett Browning, by contrast, the poet who "sit[s] in London at the day's decline" and "views the city perish in the mist" is not composed but *surprised* – "surprised/By a sudden sense of vision and of tune" – her voice released by the spectacle of something "choked to silence". Such creativity is vicarious – "You feel as conquerors though you did not fight" – but nonetheless authoritative and self-determining. Where nature "leave[s] you dumb", to identify with the force which erases London's identity gives you the power to "sing the song you choose".

Barrett Browning had planned *Aurora Leigh* from the mid-1840s as a "novel-poem", one which, as she told Robert Browning in a letter written early in their correspondence, would be

> completely modern ... running into the midst of our conventions, & rushing into drawing-rooms & the like 'where angels fear to tread'; – & so, meeting face to face & without mask, the Humanity of the age.[5]

In its accomplishment *Aurora Leigh* does indeed attempt this task, challenging the supremacy of the novel as a genre dealing with contemporary life, and especially urban experience; but passages such as the one I have quoted tell a different, and possibly incompatible story. Barrett Browning greatly admired Dickens, and envied him a little; certainly she wanted to emulate his popularity, but not by producing versified forms of *Dombey and Son* and *Bleak House* – two great London fictions published in the period she was writing her poem. Poetry implies something higher than prose, something which dissolves and remakes reality as much as it "re-presents" it.

I come now to the passages of *Aurora Leigh* which are not about writing poetry in the city, but about the city itself. When Aurora learns of Romney's involvement with the working-class Marian Erle, she goes to see her in her slum tenement in "St Margaret's Court", whose name probably derives from the parish of St Margaret's, Westminster, site of one of London's worst slums, known as "rookeries" because of their overcrowding. Here is Aurora's description of this visit:

> Within St Margaret's Court I stood alone,
> Close-veiled. A sick child, from an ague-fit,
> Whose wasted right hand gambled 'gainst his left

---

[5] Letter of 27 February 1845, in *The Brownings' Correspondence*, X, 101.

With an old brass button in a blot of sun,
Jeered weakly at me as I passed across
The uneven pavement; while a woman, rouged
Upon the angular cheek-bones, kerchief torn,
Thin dangling locks, and flat lascivious mouth,
Cursed at a window both ways, in and out,
By turns some bed-rid creature and myself, –
"Lie still there, mother! liker the dead dog
You'll be to-morrow. What, we pick our way,
Fine madam, with those damnable small feet!
We cover up our face from doing good,
As if it were our purse! What brings you here,
My lady? is't to find my gentleman
Who visits his tame pigeon in the eaves?
Our cholera catch you with its cramps and spasms,
And tumble up your good clothes, veil and all,
And turn your whiteness dead-blue." I looked up;
I think I could have walked through hell that day
And never flinched. "The dear Christ comfort you,"
I said, "you must have been most miserable,
To be so cruel," – and I emptied out
My purse upon the stones: when, as I had cast
The last charm in the cauldron, the whole court
Went boiling, bubbling up, from all its doors
And windows, with a hideous wail of laughs
And roar of oaths, and blows perhaps ... I passed
Too quickly for distinguishing ... and pushed
A little side-door hanging on a hinge,
And plunged into the dark, and groped and climbed
The long, steep, narrow stair 'twixt broken rail
And mildewed wall that let the plaster drop
To startle me in the blackness. Still up, up!
So high lived Romney's bride. I paused at last
Before a low door in the roof, and knocked;
There came an answer like a hurried dove –
"So soon? can that be Mister Leigh so soon?"
And, as I entered, an ineffable face
Met mine upon the threshold.

                                                          (III 759-99)

"Meeting face to face the Humanity of the age" is not quite the same as meeting this "ineffable face". The organizing intelligence which conducts Aurora to the "threshold" of her encounter with working-class innocence and purity also determines the details of squalor and vice which surround it. These details are like prose which "make[s] a space to sphere [the] living verse"; or, to put it another way, a negotiation with social and economic reality allows the poet to gain her real object by sleight of hand.

The description of St Margaret's Court itself is filled with standard images, familiar to middle-class readers who were shocked and thrilled by accounts of darkest London. Thomas Beames's book *The Rookeries of London* appeared in 1850, Henry Mayhew's *London Labour and the London Poor* in 1852, besides numerous articles, pamphlets and government reports, the kind of documents on which Romney Leigh wastes his energies – not to mention fictional slums such as Tom-all-Alone's in *Bleak House*. I would emphasize the intense literariness of the images, the way they conform to type and to expectation, because although they are "poetic" in expression, real poetry as Barrett Browning understands it has nothing to do with them, having its eyes fixed on a higher plane. Aurora passes through three ordeals on her way to Marian: the sick child who jeers at her "weakly", the bitter woman who misreads and misrepresents her, and the threat of the "whole court" which she placates, like Cerberus at the gates of the underworld, by throwing them the sop of her purse. Of these the second figure takes the most space and is given the most overdetermined rhetoric. She is marked as a consumptive, a prostitute, and a lost soul, incapable of understanding either Aurora or Marian. Her hostility to Aurora is both class-based and gender-based – she has a particular hostility to Aurora's small feet because this was a conventional attribute of gentility, and it is she who venomously characterizes Marian as Romney's "tame pigeon", one of many slang terms for a prostitute. The task of poetry is to pass by this apparition and convert the "tame pigeon" into the "hurried dove" whose voice Aurora hears cooing in the roof. When she actually sees Marian she wonders how this "daughter of the people" can be so lovely:

> Such soft flowers,
> From such rough roots? the people, under there,
> Can sin so, curse so, look so, smell so ... faugh!
> Yet have such daughters?

>   (III 806-809)

That exclamation graphically sums up a whole aspect of middle-class thinking about the urban poor, as does Aurora's gesture of emptying out her purse and the image of the slum-dwellers as an undifferentiated and dehumanized substance which boils and bubbles up through the doors and windows.[6]

In a later passage (IV 538-601), Aurora describes the scene in the fashionable church on the day of Romney's wedding to Marian Erle, half-filled with the fashionable guests from Romney's class, and half with representatives of Marian's. As in St Margaret's Court, not a single representative of the slums appears humanly distinct or self-possessed; it is

---

[6] There is also a strange echo of the gravediggers scene in *Hamlet*: "[Hamlet] Dost thou think Alexander look'd a this fashion i' th' earth? [Horatio] E'en so. [Hamlet] And smelt so? Pah!" (V.i).

as though the entire lower class of London except Marian Erle is ugly, diseased, deformed, and malignant. The poor are like pus oozing from the "social wound" (544) or like the walking corpses of plague-victims, they enter the church "In a dark slow stream, like blood" (554), and crawl down the aisle like "bruised snakes" (566). Confronted by the "crammed mass" of faces (571), Aurora again resorts to an exclamation to convey the depth of her revulsion:

> Faces? ... phew,
> We'll call them vices, festering to despairs,
> Or sorrows, petrifying to vices: not
> A finger-touch of God left whole on them,
> All ruined, lost ...
> Those, faces? 'twas as if you had stirred up hell
> To heave its lowest dreg-fiends uppermost
> In fiery swirls of slime ....
>
> (IV 579-83, 587-89)

In her vision of the disintegrating city, Aurora saw the material structures of London dissolving; in such passages it is the urban crowd which is ruined and lost, metamorphosed into "fiery swirls of slime". It is too easy, I think, simply to accuse the poet, or the heroine of the poem, of crass insensitivity, so that we end up reading these sections of *Aurora Leigh* with a liberal revulsion of our own. I doubt if Barrett Browning knew how priggish, condescending, and self-serving Aurora sounds when she blesses the prostitute in St Margaret's Court or wrinkles her nose at the smell of the wretched, but I also doubt whether she would have seen the point of the criticism. Romney Leigh, the representative of social responsibility and material progress, is left blinded and humble at the end of the poem; what remains is not the real city and the task of its representation, but an ideal city and the task of prophesying it. The path of the poem is ascending, not levelling; poetry itself does not struggle alongside the people, but exhorts them to rise – "crying from the top of souls", as Romney puts it,

> To souls, that, here assembled on earth's flats,
> They get them to some purer eminence ...
> What height we know not, – but the way we know,
> And how by mounting ever, we attain,
> And so climb on ....
>
> (IX 933-35, 937-39)

In the final lines of the poem, when Romney has declared his love for Aurora and his faith in the power of art to transform the world, Aurora herself seals up the sum by referring to the most visionary and apocalyptic city of them all:

He stood a moment with erected brows
In silence, as a creature might who gazed, –
Stood calm, and fed his blind, majestic eyes
Upon the thought of perfect noon: and when
I saw his soul saw, – "Jasper first," I said,
"And second, sapphire; third, chalcedony,
The rest in order, – last, an amethyst."

(IX 958-64)

These lines allude to the New Jerusalem, whose walls are set with twelve precious stones from jasper to chalcedony in the Book of Revelations.[7] In a daring image Romney is described standing "as a creature might who gazed", the point being that he has transcended his "creaturedom" and has reached the plane of spiritual vision. Still the last insight, and the last word, belong to the poet: when Aurora is sure of Romney's allegiance ("I saw his soul saw") she speaks of a city being built, not dissolved, and set in order, not disintegrated. Looking back over the whole poem it is clear that London functions as the anti-type of the New Jerusalem, and that when Aurora called herself a city poet she was being a little disingenuous. Her citizenship lies not in Kensington, let alone St Margaret's Court; she is a stranger and pilgrim, on her way to a heavenly city and – if I may allow myself a moment of unkindness – not much caring who she tramples on to get there.

---

[7] See Chapter 21, verses 19-20: "And the foundations of the wall of the city *were* garnished with all manner of precious stones. The first foundation *was* jasper; the second, sapphire; the third, a chalcedony; the fourth, an emerald; the fifth, sardonyx; the sixth, sardius; the seventh, chrysolite; the eighth, beryl; the ninth, a topaz; the tenth, a chrysoprasus; the eleventh, a jacinth; the twelfth, an amethyst."

"RUINS OF AN UNREMEMBERED PAST": POETIC STRATEGIES IN JAMES THOMSON'S *THE CITY OF DREADFUL NIGHT*

VALERIA TINKLER-VILLANI

It is the image of the city that contains and barely controls the many concepts and forms which lend power to much of James Thomson's poetry. It is true that urban settings, characters and language had become a strong force in much of the poetry of the second half of the nineteenth century, throughout Europe. But Thomson's work – and, in particular, his poem *The City of Dreadful Night* – occupies a unique position. Not only does it contain most of the motifs, themes and images connected with the concept of "the city in literature", as examined in many recent and less recent studies, it also forms the locus where other strands of analysis intersect. Quite apart from the useful function of illustrating the multiform perceptions of the city in literature, *The City of Dreadful Night* narrows the focus Thomson had already developed in his earlier poem, "The Doom of a City". In particular, his use of stone figures and monuments reveals a process of intensification in the development of Thomson's poetics and of the poetics of the period. An analysis of these monuments in the later poem highlights an important moment in the shift from Romantic to Modernist poetics. Moreover, an analysis of the formal aspect of the poem – the specific nature of the techniques used by Thomson – sheds some light on the dynamics of this intermediate stage.

James Thomson's *The City of Dreadful Night* is one of the texts in the English language in which a very large number of the various concepts involved in the trope of the city, or the "word-city", are most comprehensively developed and explored. At the beginning and end of the poem the description of a specific geographical layout suggests the possibility of an ordering view from above, whereas the body of the poem traces the labyrinthine routes by which the half-lost walker goes on his aimless quest. The city is a semi-generalized "Venice of the Black Sea", but it can also be viewed specifically as London; at the same time, however, like Italo Calvino's Venice, it also stands for any city. Indeed, rather than a real or even an "unreal city", it represents a vision of civilization and of the human life within it. This mythical four-gated or four-square city turns into its five-gated counterpart when, in the course of the poem, the cathedral becomes increasingly more prominent in the geography of the city.[1] Large buildings, squares and monuments – Christian and pagan – add their bulk to the "ruins of an unremembered past",[2] but also to the mental ruins of the half-remembered lives some of the characters recount for the benefit of the persona and the reader. Thus we find here a perfect illustration of Freud's use of the layered city as an image of the psyche in *Civilization and Its Discontents*. More aspects which make up the trope of the city in literature emerge in Thomson's poem. Along the network of interlocking streets the persona walks, a silent observer and spectator recording his personal viewings, but at important nodes we also hear the very different, public voice of a prophet addressing a mass of people. Yet to read the poem is to enter an inner space; from first to last the shapes and figures are shadows moving within the mind, and this holds the fragments together. All these elements – and this also gives the poem part of its cohesion – are explored in one direction only, that is, in terms of the demonic city. My main aim is to analyse how this text relies for its cohesion and significance on the idea of the City considered as the epitome of a man-made construction – the city as the book of man where nature is the book of God – and how the text's cohesion is created by means of various other man-made constructions, such as poetic techniques.

Lothar Hönnighausen has briefly discussed Thomson in the book translated into English in 1988 as *The Symbolist Tradition in English Literature*. Hönnighausen mentions Thomson's use of a "modified form of allegory" and states that "In this modified form of allegory, a stange oscillation between symbolic indefiniteness and allegorical definiteness arises". This, according to the critic, has been seen as contributing to the poem's "lack of coherence".[3] I want to show to what extent Thomson was systematically exploring and displaying in his city a view of allegory and symbolism which in itself communicates a view of civilization and human life. I do this by first extracting three specific examples of strategies – beginning with allegory – and then considering a feature central to the structure of the poem and the thematics of the city, that is, certain monuments or monumental figures which are described in the last two parts of the poem. I argue that it is Thomson's concern with literary strategies and their significance that gives the poem coherence, and that this coherence is due to

---

[1] See James Dougherty, *The Fivesquare City*, Notre Dame and London, 1980.

[2] James Thomson, *The City of Dreadful Night*, in *The Penguin Book of Victorian Verse*, ed. Daniel Karlin, 1997, 553. Further references in the text will be to the part number.

[3] Lothar Hönnighausen, *The Symbolist Tradition in English Literature: A Study of Pre-Raphaelitism and Fin de Siècle*, tr. Gisela Hönninghausen, Cambridge, 1988, 51.

his poem forming a link between Romantic and Modernist poetics, providing us with a unique opportunity to examine what Carol Christ sees as the mediative role of Victorian poetry.[4]

The City of Dreadful Night was first published in its entirety in 1874 in the *National Reformer* and then in 1880 in the volume *The City of Dreadful Night and Other Poems*. It consists of 1123 lines, divided into 21 sections, sometimes called "Cantos". There is a basic narrative: in many sections a protagonist speaks in the first person while walking through the city. These sections alternate with meditations, often in the third person. The narrative is deliberately fragmented, therefore, and we listen to a number of voices. Thomson, like Eliot, does, as it were, the city in different voices. These voices, however, are more disembodied than Eliot's because they do not have a local habitation and a name, but inhabit a city which is a purely mental and poetic space. Poetic strategies, one could say, assume a voice of their own, and the first of these strategies is allegory.

The whole poem presents vivid and detailed locations which are nevertheless suggestive of general concepts, and we are told that this city is "perchance of Death,/But certainly of Night", though it is not a city "of Sleep" (I). Such generalized phrases and capitalized nouns immediately suggest a reading in terms of allegory. Some of the figures that speak in the poem, such as the "wounded creature" from Part XVIII, come close to allegory because they could be animated representations of abstract ideas.

The poem is also closely linked, in various ways, to Dante's *Inferno* and some of its figurative narrative strategies. The encounters that the poem's traveller records are very Dantesque: as in Dante, we have an immediate retelling of the encounter (introduced simply by an "I saw"), a direct questioning which goes to the heart of the traveller's concern, and the revelation, by those addressed, of the most crucial episode or epiphanic moment in their lives – a combination, therefore, of personal experience and ideal, general significance. Very specifically, there are many echoes of phrases from *Inferno*: Thomson's "doleful city", for example, is clearly Dante's "città dolente".[5] More directly, twice we read a version of the phrase inscribed above hell's gate in *Inferno*: "leave all hope behind, you who enter here".

But Dante's allegory is not just retraced and alluded to, it undergoes a treatment which breaks it down as a strategy. The process is sustained over whole episodes, and is clearly deliberate. In Part VI, the persona overhears two figures speaking; one had previously left his or her companion, but has come back, and this is what he reports:

---

[4] See Carol Christ, *Victorian and Modern Poetics*, Chicago, 1984.

[5] See also Robert Crawford, *The Savage and the City in the Work of T.S. Eliot*, Oxford, 1987, 39, 42-43, and Ian Campbell, "'And I Burn Too': Thomson's *City of Dreadful Night*", *Victorian Poetry*, XVI/1 (1978), 127.

> I reached the portal common spirits fear,
> And read the words above it, dark yet clear,
> "Leave all hope behind, all ye who enter here";
> And would have passed in, gratified to gain
> That positive eternity of pain,
> Instead of this insufferable inane.
>
> A demon warder clutched me, Not so fast;
> First leave your hopes behind! – But years have passed
> Since I left all behind me, to the last:
>
> You cannot count for hope, with all your wit,
> This bleak despair that drives me to the Pit:
> How could I seek to enter void of it?
>
> He snarled, What thing is this which apes a soul,
> And would find entrance to our gulf of dole
> Without the payment of the settled toll?
>
> Outside the gate he showed an open chest:
> Here pay their entrance fee the souls unblest;
> Cast in some hope, you enter with the rest.

Much could be said about this episode. But note in particular the colloquial address uttered by the Devil ("Not so fast"), his urban rather than urbane speech, his civic rather than civil manner of speaking. But it is the twist in the allegory that is relevant to my argument here. Allegory is generally described as a sugared pill, where the narrative supplies the entertainment by which we are led to swallow the pill, or receive the hidden significance. Thomson, however, gives us the rather bitter covering of the pill, underneath which no meaning is hidden. In the phrase "leave all hope" the word "hope" is taken by the Devil quite literally to denote a solid object, a fee; the verb "leave", similarly, is not a metaphorical letting go of hope but a physical act. Indeed, in this world (in a small addition to Dante's) the candidates for hell are even provided with a container, "an open chest", to drop their fee in. So, in the world of the Devil the words are signs of matter and movement, and do not directly signal mental or spiritual reality.

Unlike most of the appearances of devils in Dante, in Thomson's city the speaker attempts to enter into a dialogue with the Devil, explaining his own system of meaning and questioning the Devil's. His attempt to explain the meaning he attributes to the words which refer to his feelings – "You cannot count for hope …/This bleak despair" – reveals not only that in the world of demonic signification words correspond to matter, but also that, in the world of the man, the Devil's hope signifies its very opposite: despair. The gap in signification is complete.

The second of the strategies I focus on is a complex metaphor occurring in Part II: the speaker has been following a quester, someone who "seemed to walk with an intent". Rather than following an aim, however, this quester is trapped in a vicious circle, repeatedly visiting three places in turn. The first location marks the place where "Faith died", the second where "Love died", and the third where "Hope died", as the quester himself is heard to mutter. Again the protagonist speaks, abandoning his role of stalker – of man of the crowd – and actively searching for meaning:

> I spoke, perplexed by something in the signs
> Of desolation I had seen and heard
> In this dread pilgrimage to ruined shrines:
> Where Faith and Love and Hope are dead indeed,
> Can Life still live? By what doth it proceed?
>
> As whom his one intense thought overpowers,
> He answered coldly, Take a watch, erase
> The signs and figures of the circling hours,
> Detach the hands, remove the dial face;
> The works proceed until run down; although
> Bereft of purpose, void of use, still go.

What is notable in the first stanza is that the various buildings the quester has just visited ("a tower that merged into the heavy sky", a "villa [which] gleamed beyond the foliage dense" and "a squalid house"), to which he attributed an allegorical meaning, are further interpreted by the protagonist. The latter is not satisfied with an allegorical level, but wants to probe further and identify the ultimate authority – call it a prime mover or a transcendental signifier – behind these "signs". The quester responds to the speaker's address with his version of the metaphor of the clock.

The metaphor of a clock to represent the system of nature seen as an instrument regulated by a clockwork movement is traditional. It was frightening to some, because it removed the personal presence of God and his providential scheme, but was consoling to others, who saw order, control and impartiality in a mechanical system. Thomson makes use of this traditional comparison only, once more, to do violence to it. If you "erase the signs and figures", "detach the hands" and "remove the dial-face", you also remove all signs which visibly announce the presence of some order, albeit mechanical. The relief offered by the clarity and impartiality of the system as it announces itself on the dial is removed, and the system becomes unreadable. Thomson is here engaged in the steady dismantling of a system of signification, particularly in terms of the written sign, and this demonstrates the deconstructive impulse at work in Thomson's poetry, since the process he is engaged in corroborates Derrida's "problematic of the trace".[6] Indeed, Thomson is creating a poetic system out of the corrosion of other signs. His use of the word "signs" and, elsewhere, its synonyms, indicates his focus on the most abstract concepts deriving from the interpretation of the sense perceptions ("I saw and heard"), by which the system might be expected to be revealed.

The third strategy is illustrated by Thomson's own footnote to the passage just quoted:

Life divided by that persistent three = LXX/333 = 210

The first passage I examined showed how Thomson's use of Dante modifies allegory. In the second, the blanked face of the clock removes the vehicle from the extended metaphor to which it belongs. In this citation we have a mathematical sign, like x or pi. This is a symbol which requires close analysis. Thomson conflates two systems: the semi-religious idea of man's allotted lifespan of three score years and ten (in Roman numbers: LXX) and a repetition of the numerological three, the number of the spirit. At the same time, there is the scientific concept of a formula. A formula is a mathematical relationship which has no resemblance to its referent and x is a non-representational symbol. What Thomson's footnote says is that a combination of the two systems of signification – religion and science – produces no comprehensible result, for the resulting number is either inherently meaningless, like 42 in *A Hitchhiker's Guide to the Galaxy*, or it scans a countdown which reduces numerology to zero, multiplicity to entropy.

In the *City of Dreadful Night*, allegory, metaphor and symbol do not function as these three strategies usually do, because they do not suggest, even in an indefinite manner, any thing. The signs are all there is. The three examples of poetic strategies are associated with the concept of the City in its most extended meaning. The city is the ultimate trope of man's life and human civilization, a man-made system like a text such as Dante's *Inferno*, or a clock as technological device, or mathematics are man-made systems. Thomson's poem is the epitome of a poem on the word-city because it includes a vision of other systems of words and signs.

I now move to the large monuments and figures described in Parts XX, XXI and XXII of the poem. Within the trope of the city, monuments form the element of stability and signal the survival of the past. The work which is usually mentioned in this context is Freud's *Civilization and Its Discontents*, with its use of the Eternal City, Rome, and its layers of ruins, visible and hidden, as an image of man's psyche. Freud was to create a complete version

---

[6] See Jacques Derrida, *Of Grammatology* [1976], trans. Gayatri Chakravorty Spivak, Baltimore and London, 1976, esp. 44-65.

of this trope, but Thomson contributed to its development, describing the city, in Part I, as "not ruinous, although/Great ruins of an unremembered past,/With others of a few short years ago,/More sad, are found within its precincts vast". In the course of the poem, when the protagonist or the third-person narrator recount various wanderings, the mention (or description) of many buildings sustains the thematics which link lack of memory with ruins and often form crucial nodes in the mental story being told, as in the first passage quoted. Buildings and ruins culminate in the cathedral, which appears with increasing importance starting from Part XII of the poem. Part XII takes us to "the great cathedral's cloistered square", from which we "then entered the cathedral.../Marked [by] the closing of the massive door". In Part XIV we listen to the preacher's sermon on the desirability of suicide. In Part XX we return to the cathedral square, where the protagonist describes a sphinx and an avenging angel which were "so mighty and magnificent of form/They weren't dwarfed beneath this mass enorm". Size is stressed repeatedly, as if the monumentality of the city has accumulated and is concentrated in these structures. In Thomson's earlier "The Doom of a City", sculpted figures were ubiquitous:

> What found I? – Dead stone sentries stony-eyed,
> Erect, steel-sworded, brass-defended all,
> Guarding the sombrous gateway deep and wide
> Hewn like a cavern through the mighty wall;
> Stone statues all throughout the streets and squares,
> Grouped as in social converse or alone;
> Dim stony merchants holding forth rich wares
> To catch the choice of purchasers of stone ....[7]

Stone well represents the passivity of the inhabitants of Cosmopolis, who have remained fixed in the conventional class and religious structure of their society. The city's Sage had dedicated the written statement of the result of his studies to the city's tyrant; and the sum of his wisdom is inscribed on a scroll, on which we read:

> "This glorious Universe shall live for ever;
> By all decay and death diminished never,
> Nor added to by constant birth and growth;
> But in the balanced interchange of both,
> Ascending slowly by successive stages
> Of nobler Good and Beauty through the Ages;
> Until its infinite Æther and the Whole
> Of stars and spheres that through it flashing roll
> Shall be informed with conscious Life and Soul:

---

[7] "The Doom of a City", in *The Poetical Works*, London, 1895 (VIII, 193-200), 33.

> The All, one perfect Sphere, breathing one breath
> Of cosmic Life too pure for birth or death ....
>
> Our Earth ....
>   .... openeth out her heart
> In throbs of passionate rapture, to impart
> The dearest secrets of her treasured beauty
> To Man, her Lord; ....
>
> O gracious Truth, divine and tranquil Truth,
> As I long years have worshipped only Thee,
> Thou hast at length unveiled Thy face to me,
> That I may ever of Thy priesthood be!"[8]

The vanity of this "Truth" is refuted by the Sage's metamorphosis into stone and the state of Cosmopolis. Still, the world of this city had been ruled by a tyrant and guided by this Sage, and is under the control of some external all-powerful force, some "dreadful God" (143) who punishes the city as a warning. The situation is completely different in the later poem. No centre of authority assumes responsibility for the individual. There is no written scroll; the only expression of authority is the speech in the cathedral, where the voice of the scholar/traveller publicly utters his entropic message: if you are sick with life, you can "end it when you will".

The narrative of the earlier poem becomes concentrated in the confrontation in the cathedral square between the two single statues of the sphynx and the avenging angel. While the sphinx remains unchanged, the other monument crumbles in front of the speaker's eyes, first losing its wings, then its sword – and finally completely breaking into fragments. The destruction of the entire population of the doomed city, in the earlier poem, become intensified into one single figure, and an event which had been due to a "judgement" of God is not attributed to any responsible agent. The two immobile structures enact a kind of allegorical play, representing not the passing of the Golden Age so much as an evolution in reverse. The collapse of the human figure is a monument to man's degeneration, or it is the collapse of the illusion of a belief in the divinity or power of man. Thomson works his horror by means of erosion. What interests me here, however, is Thomson's stress on words, symbols and their significance.

An avenging angel that at one point in time loses one of its attributes, its wings, is not described in the poem as a modified avenging angel, but turns into an essentially different object: when the "angel" loses its wings, it becomes a "warrior". Then, the sword breaks off:

---

[8] *Ibid.*, (XVII, 400-13, 416-18, 422-25) 143, 144.

> The warrior's sword lay broken at his feet:
>   An unarmed man with raised hands impotent
> Now stood before the sphinx ....

Merely the loss of an implement turns the "vigilant", "mighty" warrior into a pleading man. It is the representational value of the figure's appearance, rather than any intrinsic significance of the original statue, that is highlighted. The same immobile structure has changed its significance completely. Finally:

> The man had fallen forward, stone on stone,
>   And lay there shattered, with his trunkless head
> Between the monster's large quiescent paws

Angel has turned into warrior and then into man, and man has then turned into matter. In accelerated time-motion, we watch a process of evolution in reverse.

This backward journey is the culmination of other backward journeys in the poem, starting with the "pilgrimage to ruined shrines" analysed above. Most notable is the "something crawling" in Part XVIII, a "wounded creature" that, on closer observation, reveals "That he had been a man", though now he is "an infamy for mankind to behold". This figure journeys through the city, ready to "fling [a] phial" and kill whoever might approach him to steal his secret, "the sacred secret of the clue": the "long-lost golden thread/Which reunites my present with my past." Not unlike the Professor in what is perhaps Joseph Conrad's most ostensibly Modernist novel, *The Secret Agent*, this figure represents the city's immanent self-destructive power. The protagonist believes this creature should attempt to retrace his "antenatal night" and to "hide his elements in that large womb/Beyond the reach of man-evolving Doom". Evolution is Doom; it would be best to dissolve back into matter. Reverse evolution is one way out of the system. Whereas Part XVIII traces the reverse evolution of the "lifetrack" of one individual, in Part XX the angel's destruction illustrates mankind's course through time.

The confrontation between man and time in the angel and sphinx episode invites comparison with a key Romantic text, Shelley's "Ozymandias". As we know, Thomson greatly admired Shelley; still, it might seem pointless to compare the word-city in Thomson's poem with the word-city in "Ozymandias", since, obviously, there is no city in "Ozymandias". But that is precisely my point. The vision of the powerlessness of man and of civilization narrated in "Ozymandias" is just as bleak as in Thomson's poem – we are shown man's arrogant pride and the fragility of human constructions. However, although in the command "Look on my works, ye mighty, and despair" the words point to something absent, they actually invite us to imaginatively re-envision a grand and beautiful city of the past. For it must have been a wonderful marble city to contain a monument such as the statue of Ozymandias. The Romantic poet invites us to recreate, by means of a ruin, this unremembered past, or at least to realize its striking absence; this monument performs its function. Similarly, in "Ozymandias" the "lone and level sands" have solidity – they are there, we can picture them. The Romantic poet, that is, can still use words to trigger meaning and vision, and establish some relationship with the cosmos, with the universe of matter. If, furthermore, we consider that Shelley wrote the poem at the time of the exhibition of certain Egyptian findings in the British Museum, we realize that the poem becomes a link in a chain of conservation, and of the preservation of memories, of which a museum is the node, itself a monument to human memory and to the worth of past civilizations.

Thomson's statues point at a very different kind of absence – the absence of solidity in the world of meaning. What the poem gives us is an intensive use of symbolism, but a symbolism which is non-referential. The fragments in the poem are held together not by signification, but by the musical orchestration of the verse and the great variety of stanza forms, metres and rhythms used, of which the lines quoted here are but a small example. The distrust of the lyric mode, the lack of authority of the authoritative figures presented, the rhythms of the voices – it is these elements that knit the poem into one unit in the Modernist manner of T.S. Eliot's *The Waste Land*.

When we come to the final part of the poem and meet the City's "patroness or Queen", we find that she is not just melancholy, but Dürer's *Melancholia*, with all the accoutrements of the existing emblem, described in specific detail. Thus, in the world of the poem, rather than a God, or a generalized human passion, the one external, controlling authority or power is another man-made construct. Dürer's massive figure is lost in thought, and her vision is

> That all the oracles are dumb or cheat
>   Because they have no secret to express;
> That none can pierce the vast black veil uncertain
> Because there is no light beyond the curtain ….

This bleak philosophy is not difficult to understand; what is difficult, what makes the poem difficult is its use of poetic strategies in a High Modernist manner. Moreover, we do not need scholars and commentators to point out the indefiniteness of the symbols, as if this was an occasional or unintended effect of the poetry, or indeed a failure of imagination; Thomson himself states in so many words that "the vast black veil" is "uncertain".

The text is not unstable because it lacks coherence, but because it mediates between Romantic and Modernist poetics; the gulf between science, religion and lived life, and between nature and poetics explains the necessity for a cosmic vision which cannot but inhabit the City.

ARTHUR SYMONS'S NIGHT LIFE

KARLIEN VAN DEN BEUKEL

Arthur Symons's nightly haunt was Leicester Square – in the 1890s, a gaudy entertainment centre where youths watched shows and became drunk. There, the Alhambra Theatre, with its Moorish façade and three thousand five hundred audience capacity, and its rival, the Empire Theatre, staged ballet spectacles as part of their music-hall repertoire.[1] Arthur Symons's contemporary and friend, Yeats, wrote of him:

> There is Arthur Symons, who has made the music-halls of London and Paris his peculiar study, and set forth their gaieties and tragedies in even, deftest verse .... He has studied them for purposes of literature and remained himself, if I understand him rightly, quite apart from their glitter and din.[2]

Through his music-hall studies, the fin-de-siècle poet and critic Arthur Symons introduced into Anglo-American literature the Baudelairean image of the female dancer and also the Symbolist ideas on dance aesthetics. Symons wrote four books on Baudelaire, whilst his critical study *The Symbolist Movement in Literature* (1899) introduced writers such as Mallarmé, Laforgue, Verlaine, and Huysmans to the Anglo-American public. T.S. Eliot wrote that "Arthur Symons' book on the French Symbolists was of more importance for my development than any other book".[3] Modernists such as Yeats, Pound and Joyce express a similar cognizance of his influence. Symons also wrote on art, music and cities, and wrote poems. His poems are not very much read today, but Eliot notes that "Symons is himself, we must not remember, no mean poet; he is typical of the 'nineties; this influence of Baudelaire upon Mr. Symons was manifestly genuine

---

[1] See Ivor Guest, *Ballet in Leicester Square: The Alhambra and the Empire 1860-1915*, London, 1992.

[2] W.B. Yeats, *Letters to the New Island*, Oxford, 1934, 144.

[3] T.S. Eliot, "Tradition and the Practice of Poetry" (Lecture 1936), in *Inventions of the March Hare: Poems 1909-1917*, ed. and selected by Christopher Ricks, London, 1996, 395.

and profound".[4]

As a Baudelairean, it was important to acquaint oneself with all aspects of urban modernity, particularly nightlife, but as a Symbolist it was important to apprehend the dance as a form of symbolic production. Hence the music halls held a special attraction to Symons. Yeats was at pains to point out that Symons "remained himself", "quite apart from their glitter and din", because the Empire, and even more so the Alhambra, were well-known haunts of prostitutes. The wide promenades around the theatres' central area were used as *flâneusing* catwalks, and afforded such attraction that it was believed no music hall could survive commercially without them. Symons himself, in his capacity as music-hall critic, wrote a public response of reasoned protest to Mrs Sheldon Amos of the National Vigilance Association, who, in 1894, had called for the removal of the Empire's promenade in order to eradicate the "known evil".[5] On the stage itself, performances were not exactly prim and proper. The Empire and Alhambra ballet spectacles had no dramatic plot, and indeed, that, combined with technological ingenuity and a large corps de ballet, made for great Victorian, male, working-class, erotic entertainment. The absence of narrative plot meant that the Lord Chamberlain's theatre licensing laws did not apply (and therefore neither did censorship),[6] and allowed plenty of emphasis to be placed on the display of female legs – for example, in "the first-aid dance of the Red Cross Nurses" celebrating the Boer War victory, the Viennese doll dances, and the Turkish harem dances, all with sophisticated lighting effects. Though some music-hall ballets did have dramatic plots (in which the male roles were danced in travesty), it is important to note that the balletic chorus-line spectacle – that is, substitutable female dancers performing a series of repeated operations within a scenic display of the latest technology – was particular to, and continued to be the popular staple fare of, the music hall. In 1867, Ruskin wrote in "The Corruption of Modern Pleasure – (Covent Garden Pantomime)" of the "novel elements" of the chorus line-up in *Ali Baba and the Forty Thieves*:

> The forty thieves were girls. The forty thieves had forty companions, who were girls. The forty thieves and their forty companions were in some way mixed up with about four hundred and forty fairies, who were girls. There was an Oxford and Cambridge boat-race, in which the Oxford and Cambridge men were girls. There was a transformation scene, with a forest, in which the flowers were girls, and a chandelier, in which the lamps were girls, and a great rainbow, which was all of girls.[7]

---

[4] "Baudelaire in Our Time" (1927), *ibid.*, 395.

[5] Letter to the *Pall Mall Gazette*, 15 October 1894, in *Arthur Symons: Selected Letters, 1880-1935*, eds Karl Beckson and John M. Munro, Basingstoke, 1989, 107.

[6] John Johnston, "Indecency on the Stage", in *The Chamberlain's Blue Pencil*, London, 1990, 126-39.

[7] John Ruskin, "Letter V: The Corruption of Modern Pleasure – (Covent Garden Pantomime)", in *Time and Tide and Miscellanies*, London, 1910, 20.

By the 1890s, the English ballet was performed only at the Leicester Square music halls and then mainly as this kind of burlesque erotic spectacle. Hence the ballet was considered a theatre form that was beyond the pale. Lilly Grove notes that this extravaganza spectacle was the only form of ballet in Britain at her time of writing, and criticizes it on aesthetic grounds:

> Efforts are being made to-day towards a revival of the ballet, which forms such a large element in the entertainment at music halls. Thousands of pounds are spent on these shows, whole battalions of girls are enrolled and are made to pass before the public in kaleidoscopic way under limelight flashes and with everything that can enhance the scenic effect. These ballets, however, are pageants, and have little in them of the dance in its more artistic form.[8]

Symons, however, was so serious about its repertoire that he had been appointed critic of music hall and ballet on the *Star* in 1892. Friends spoke of his "long symbolistic studies at the Empire" – a little ironically, perhaps, for Symons was unhappily enamoured of a member of the Empire corps de ballet, Lydia,[9] who was the inspiration for many of his poems. Symons was, however, quite clear on its aesthetic attractions:

> I found the beauty, the poetry that I wanted only in two theatres!: the Alhambra, and the Empire. The ballet seemed to me the subtlest of the visible arts, and dancing a more significant speech than words. I could have said as Verlaine said to me, in jest, coming away from the Alhambra, "J'aime Shakespeare, mais – j'aime mieux le ballet"; A ballet is simply a picture in movement. It is a picture where the imitation of nature is given by nature itself; where the figures of the composition are real, and yet, by a very paradox of travesty, have a delightful, deliberate air of unreality.[10]

For all its marginality in relation to high culture, the dance spectacle was a principal tenet in Symons's aesthetic philosophy. This is most notably articulated in the concluding essay of his *Studies of the Seven Arts*, from which I have just quoted, "The World as Ballet". This essay, on the dancer as symbol, is a representative elaboration on Mallarmé's views in "Crayonné au Théâtre",[11] although informed, of course, by Symons's own music-hall scholarship:

> And something in the particular elegance of the dance, the scenery; the avoidance of emphasis, the evasive, winding turn of things; and above all, the intellectual as

---

[8] Lilly Grove, *Dancing*, London, 1895, 380.

[9] Her surname has been lost (see Roger Lhombreaud, *Arthur Symons: A Critical Biography*, London, 1963, 115).

[10] Arthur Symons, "The World as Ballet" (1898), in *Studies in the Seven Arts*, London, 1906, 391.

[11] Cf. Stéphane Mallarmé, "Ballets", in *Oeuvres Complètes,* 303-307.

well as sensuous appeal of a living symbol, which can but reach the brain through the eyes, in the visual, concrete, imaginative way; has seemed to make the ballet concentrate in itself a good deal of the modern ideal in matters of artistic expression. Nothing is stated, there is no intrusion of words used for the irrelevant purpose of describing; a world rises before one, the picture lasts only long enough to have been there: and the dancer, with her gesture, all pure symbol, evokes, from her mere beautiful motion, idea, sensation, all that one need ever know of event. There, before you, she exists, in harmonious life; and her rhythm reveals to you the soul of her imagined being.[12]

Yeats abstracted his own image of the dancer from Symons's mediating work, but without the overt indication that the urban theatre is the necessary condition of the Symbolist aesthetic. Yet Yeats, more true to the Symbolist aesthetic, writes poems which position the dancer within the abstract sphere that is produced through agency of the dance. Simply, the dancer produces "with her gesture" a durational aesthetic "event": her gestures are such that "a world rises before one". But Yeats was slow on the uptake (he wrote his dancer poems twenty years after Symons was writing on the Symbolist dance aesthetic) precisely because he could not separate the Symbolist aesthetic from the music-hall milieu of the ballet.

After the Ballets Russes Season of 1910-11 it was acceptable to write on dancers, of course. For reasons of his own, Symons would not separate the Symbolist aesthetic from the urban music hall in his poems. Thus Symons frames his dancers with devices similar to the ones found in the 1890s paintings of dancers, or in Baudelaire's description of the *flâneusing* prostitute type who roved around the dance music halls such as "the Tivoli, the Idalie, the Folies and the Paphos":

> Against a background of hellish light, or if you prefer, an *aurora borealis* – red, orange, sulphur-yellow, pink (to express an idea of ecstasy amid frivolity), and sometimes purple (the favourite colour of canonesses, like dying embers seen through a blue curtain) – against magical backgrounds such as these, which remind one of variegated Bengal lights, there arises the Protean image of wanton beauty.[13]

The gaslights are the framework of the dancer image in the urban nocturne. In "To a Dancer", "the footlights" are a barrier between the subjective ego and the object of his desire. The "Décor de Théâtre" cycle, five poems set in different music halls, refers to gaslights dozens of times. Symons frames even gypsy dance, the *sine qua non* of the free Romantic spirit, in urban space. In the poem "Spain", the gypsy dancer is explicitly situated in the metropolitan theatre:

---

[12] "The World as Ballet", 391.

[13] Charles Baudelaire, "The Painter of Modern Life", in *The Painter of Modern Life and Other Essays*, trans. and ed. Jonathan Mayne, London, 1995, 36.

> The footlights flicker and spire
> In tongues of flame before your tiny feet,
> My warm-eyed gipsy, higher,
> And in your eyes they meet
> More than their light, more than their golden heat.

Yeats or Rilke concentrate incandescence in the dancer (Rilke has his Spanish Dancer stamp out a flaming match dead on the beat) and that makes their poems fantastic. Symons's cadence does approximate a rise in the excitement, but something about those "footlights" restricts him to the language of the banal. In some poems by Symons, such as "To a Gitana Dancing", the textual framing device ("Seville") indicating its urban situation is so light (indeed extraneous to the poem itself), that the dancer, as a subject, can work clear of it. But usually in Symons, the subject is restricted to the dance spectacle within the music hall itself. Those poems reveal that fine line between social reality and the illusion produced for pleasure. In other words, in Symons, the dancer is inextricable from the urban nocturne, the leisure zone of the city.

The nocturnal metropolis, with all its variegated attractions, features throughout Symons's poetry, but his collection of poems *London Nights* (1895) is of most relevance. The structure of *London Nights* reflects the music-hall variety programme: the three "London Nights" sections are interspersed with "Intermezzo: Pastoral" and "Intermezzo: Venetian Nights". Its opening poem is "Prologue: My life is like a music-hall".[14] The aesthete becomes the architect of the nocturnal pleasures. We have to recall, of course, that women did not take their leisure in public night-spaces until the 1910s;[15] before, they functioned in it primarily as workers. Thus, the initiating perspective of *London Nights* is the late-Victorian male idea of self-expression through the night-time sensations to be found in this music-hall space, where the women in it are leisure industrial workers that produce the illusion.

There are some prostitutes in *London Nights*, such as in "Stella Maris" and "To One in Alienation", but most of the leisure industrial workers are the corps de ballet dancers. "Prologue" is an exemplary poem on the alienated labour process of the chorus-line dance in the music hall:

> My life is like a music-hall,
>   Where, in the impotence of rage,
> Chained by enchantment to my stall,
>   I see myself upon the stage
> Dance to amuse a music-hall.

---

[14] Arthur Symons, *London Nights* (1895), 2nd rev. edn, London, 1897, 3. All references by page number are to this second edition.
[15] See Lewis A. Erenberg, *Steppin' Out: New York Nightlife and the Transformation of American Culture, 1890-1930*, Westport: Conn., 1981.

'Tis I that smoke this cigarette,
    Lounge here, and laugh for vacancy,
And watch the dancers turn; and yet
        It is my very self I see
Across the cloudy cigarette.

My very self that turns and trips,
    Painted, pathetically gay
An empty song upon the lips
    In make-believe of holiday:
I, I, this thing that turns and trips!

The light flares in the music-hall,
    The light, the sound, that weary us;
Hour follows hour, I count them all,
    Lagging, and loud, and riotous:
My life is like a music-hall.

This is the anthem of the leisure industrial worker, the bacchanalian chain-gang song. "Make-believe of holiday" is what is produced, whilst "the light, the sound, that weary us" emphasizes the exhaustion, if not the wear and tear, of working in this distraction factory. The hours are counted, because the identity, "I", is in fact a personification of labour time, and the hour that follows hour add up to "all". The remarkable thing about "My Life is like a Music-Hall" is the poet's total identification with a chorus-line dancer.

Siegfried Kracauer notes in his essay "The Mass Ornament" (1927) that The Tiller Girls, the London chorus line fêted for their precision dancing, "are no longer individual girls but indissoluble girl clusters whose movements are demonstrations of mathematics": "The bearer of the ornaments is the *mass*."[16] Kracauer perceives that the gaiety chorus girls come to resemble the modern Fordist production line:

> When they formed an undulating snake, they radiantly illustrated the virtues of the conveyor belt; when they tapped their feet in vast tempo, it sounded like *business, business, business*; when they kicked their legs high with mathematical precision, they joyously affirmed the progress of rationalisation; and when they kept repeating the same movements without ever interrupting their routine, one envisaged an uninterrupted chain of motor cars gliding from the factories into the world, and believed that the blessing of prosperity had no end.[17]

---

[16] Siegfried Kracauer, "The Mass Ornament", in *The Mass Ornament: Weimar Essays*, trans., ed. and intr. Thomas Y. Levin, Cambridge: Mass., 1995, 76.

[17] Kracauer, quoted in David Frisby, *Fragments of Modernity: Theories of Modernity in the Work of Simmel, Kracauer and Benjamin*, Oxford, 1988, 194. Cf. Kracauer, 79.

This task line manages to produce another modern desirable symbol of freedom: the motor car. The idea is that the chorus line is an incipient product of mass culture, which repeats, in its products of amusement, the mechanized labour the spectating individual seeks fruitlessly to escape from in his leisure time. Thus the "I" in "My Life is like a Music-Hall" is also an identification with the daytime identity of the proletarian audience. It also seems an anthem for workers in the queue when labour supply exceeds demand: "lounge here and laugh for vacancy." This is a shocking poem for a 1890s aesthete to write, not least because it links the rhymed metric form to the music-hall song. The dissociation of sensibility, where the self becomes a dancing, singing and cosmeticized "thing" within an abject female mass that must produce an ambience of "holiday", somewhat ironizes the lyric subject. The impersonality of the chorus can be read as the feminine cosmetic mask. So whose "empty song upon the lips/In make-believe of holiday" are we singing next? We could sequence into the second set, say Wordsworth's "She Was A Phantom of Delight", without so much as a batted eyelid or a missed beat. Hence Symons's image of the Dancer – "chained", "painted", "lagging" – is also a fundamental precursive component to the modernist ironic lyric.

In Symons, urban modernity is the frame that reveals the reified icon – the image of the dancer – as the commodity, whilst the variations in focal perspectives allow for the movements of the chorus – as the serial reproduction of reified icons – to be analogous to that of the urban crowd. We can compare some Symons poems with the following description of a dancer in Gautier's novel *Jettatura*:

> In London he often went to Her Majesty's Theatre, where *the grace of a young English dancer had particularly impressed* him. Without being taken with her any more than one is by a graceful figure in a painting or an engraving, his eyes followed *her among her companions of the corps de ballet* in the swirl of the choreography. He loved her sweet, melancholy features, her delicate pallor that the animation of the dance never caused to flush, her beautiful blonde hair, silky and lustrous, crowned, according to the part, with stars or flowers, her *long look lost in space*, her shoulders of virginal chastity that he could see *trembling* through his eye-glass, her *legs reluctantly raising* their gauzy cloud and gleaming through the silk like the marble of an antique statue; each time she came before the footlights he greeted her with a little sign of furtive imagination or levelled his opera-glass to see her better.[18] [My italics]

The crown of stars, the "gauzy cloud", her legs – in tights – "like the marble of an antique statue", and "virginal chastity": this is Baudelaire's "Woman". Yet she is one appearance amongst a series of similar appearances, for there is an entire corps de ballet of them. In Gautier's novel, the protagonist has singled out one appearance with his binoculars. Her aura appears to be the direct result of his

---

[18] In *Gautier on Dance*, sel., trans. and ann. by Ivor Guest, London, 1986, 153.

own cogent aesthetic discrimination of her costume, but whom the voyeur has sighted is the absent-minded one, the vulnerable one in the pack. Where Gautier shows himself to be the predatory voyeur, Symons identifies with the one caught off-guard: "I, I this thing that turns and trips." In other poems, the focus remains entirely on the appearance of the corps de ballet. In "Behind the Scenes: Empire":

> The little painted angels flit,
>   See, down the narrow staircase, where
> The pink legs flicker over it!
>
> Blonde, and bewigged, and winged with gold,
>   The shining creatures of the air
> Troop sadly, shivering with cold.
>
> The gusty gaslight shoots a thin
>   Sharp finger over cheeks and nose
> Rouged to the colour of the rose.
>
> All wigs and paint, they hurry in:
>   Then, bid their radiant moment be
> The footlights' immortality![19]

The corps de ballet is a serial representation of ethereal femininity, its supposedly unique qualities repeated over and over again, an effect emphasized by the repeated sound pattern in the costume evocation in the second stanza. The imperative "See" views it from the audience's perspective (pink tights and blonde wigs), whilst the title, assuming the reverse perspective, leads to the backstage observation "troop sadly, shivering with cold". This erotic pathos is only observable, of course, to the privileged backstage observer. Yet the entire perspective remains at the level of the general assemblage throughout the poem. The poem represents the impersonal collective of the beautiful appearances and their erotic pathos at the Empire Theatre. To refuse a choice that would have taken place on the false supposition of an ability to discriminate, on appearance, one appearance from all the appearances precisely like it, is a good choice. In the synaesthetic poem "On the Stage", from the "Lilian" cycle, a comparison is made between the general audience's view in the first stanza, and the subjective ego's process of visual identification of the beloved amongst the corps de ballet in the second. The "multi-coloured lights" blend in with, and summarize, the entire spectacle. The corps de ballet consists not so much of women, as of a series of cosmetically emphasized body parts, "eyes and rouge", "tights, and wigs, and tights", acknowledging the commodification of the chorus-line

---

[19] *London Nights*, 21.

spectacle. He looks for the face he knows personally amongst all the appearances – an impossible task. In "At the Stage-Door", also from the "Lilian" cycle:

> Kicking my heels in the street,
>   Here at the edge of the pavement I wait for you, sweet,
> Here in the crowd, the blent noises, blurred lights, of the street.
>
> Under the archway sheer,
>   Sudden and black as a hole in the placarded wall,
> Faces flicker and veer,
>   Wavering out of the darkness into the light,
> Wavering back into the night;
>   Under the archway, suddenly seen, the curls
> And thin, bright faces of girls,
>   Roving eyes, and smiling lips, and the glance
> Seeking, finding perchance,
>   Here at the edge of the pavement, there by the wall,
> One face, out of them all.
>
> Steadily, face after face,
>   Cheeks with the blush of the paint yet lingering, eyes
> Still with their circle of black ...
>   But hers, but hers?[20]

The search for her face amongst the corps de ballet is repeated outside on the street, after the ballet is over. If the "lingering, eyes" are offering him something, it is just for a moment, because he is the faithful type of stage-door Johnny. Looking for a particular face amongst the swirl of the dancers corresponds, then, to urban scanning, that intent looking for the face amongst the faces of the crowds that pour out of a public building. Every face is a mystery, but the one looked for – familiar to the person – is not there until the final: "her eyes to my eyes."

The poem "Impression", from *Silhouettes*, seems particularly suffused with pathos:

> The pink and black of silk and lace
> Flushed in the rosy-golden glow
> Of lamplight on her lifted face;
> Powder and wig, and pink and lace,
>
> And those pathetic eyes of hers;
> But all the London footlights know
> The little plaintive smile that stirs
> The shadow in those eyes of hers.[21]

---

[20] *Ibid.*, 16.

[21] Arthur Symons, *Silhouettes* (1892), 2nd edn, revised and enlarged, London, 1896, 15.

Yet "the pink and black" is an allusion to Baudelaire's notorious quatrain on a Spanish dancer, eponymously titled "Lola de Valence", in which the final phrase, "un bijou rose et noir", was considered by an outraged public in 1863 as having "pudendal overtones".[22] In "Impression" the lights personify, perhaps, the punters, and evidently a libidinal currency is released by that hint of a smile, which, by seeming to recall past pleasure, is also a request for it.

The dancer, who may or may not be on stage, is erotic, teasingly unobtainable; her appearance, not least as evoked by the allusion to a scandalous poem, is deeply complicit with the repression that invented it. And yet, when "Impression" starts describing that dancer's face, the reader's focus changes too and engages in reading its complex affective signs. "Impression" juxtaposes the dancer's erotic stage appearance as an angel with its final lines:

> Outside, the dreary church-bell tolled,
> The London Sunday faded slow;
> Ah, what is this? what wings unfolds
> In this miraculous rose of gold?

The analogy between the dancer's angel costume and the "rose of gold" of the dusk and the lighting of street lamps now takes the material into a spiritual economy. When Symons implies that chorus girls in the ballet are the angels of the house, this is not just some Baudelairean comment on Victorian mores. Those "imbued with raptures for Bacchus, Terpsichore and the Church" understand the dance as a holy-day rite, a mass. It is a mystery ritual. The dance expresses the ineffable transcendence of the human being, soul.

II

In 1890s London, a project which was supposed to transform the places of spiritual worship forever was unfolding: Headlam's Church and Stage Guild project. Whilst Symons's dancer poems may be formally identified as a product of the Symbolist aesthetic, it is in historical reference to the work of Rev. Stewart Headlam that the lustre of their social commentary becomes apparent. Members of the Rhymers Club – Ernest Dowson, Selwyn Image, Victor Plarr, W.B. Yeats, and Symons – became acquainted with the Rev. Stewart Headlam (1847-1924), a London-based Anglican clergyman, around the 1890s. Headlam's insouciant Church and Stage Guild parties, "for uplift" as Pound has it, were considered by Victor Plarr "a brilliant and picturesque episode in the artistic life of the early nineties".[23] This frivolity was inextricable from social idealism. Headlam's Christian Socialist principles were combined with a critical attitude toward the

---

[22] Charles Baudelaire, *The Flowers of Evil and Paris Spleen*, trans. William H. Crosby, Rochester, 1991, 478. Cf. Symons's poem "Mauve, Black, and Rose" in *London Nights*.

[23] As recalled by Victor Plarr in his *Ernest Dowson* (1914). Quoted in John J. Espey, *Ezra Pound's* Mauberley: *A Study in Composition*, London, 1955, 95.

prevailing repressive sexual mores. This attitude was given comprehensive expression, for example, during Oscar Wilde's trial. Together with Selwyn Image, Headlam formed the Anti-Puritan League in response to Wilde's arrest, and stood bail for Wilde. Such an active commitment to personal liberty was not incidental. His sustained campaign to rehabilitate the music-hall ballet presented a similar challenge to the mores of the establishment. It was this ballet campaign, "imbued with raptures for Bacchus, Terpsichore and the Church", that both attracted the society and drew upon the aesthetic work of the fin-de-siècle poets.

The initial impetus for Headlam's campaign may be said to have arisen from social rather than aesthetic considerations. Headlam had first come into contact with music-hall dancers when he was appointed curate at St John's, Drury Lane (1870-1873). There he had observed that dancers were "the victims of prejudice" and liable to be "cold-shouldered" by the other local parishioners.[24] As ballet was known as "pornographic", it followed that its practitioners were that by association. As George Bernard Shaw wrote in a letter to Headlam in 1922:

> You were making efforts in the Church and Stage Guild and at every other opportunity to make people understand that this kind of dancing is a fine art; but until the Russian Ballet arrived, long after Pertoldi was superannuated and forgotten, there were practically no converts; and the Alhambra ballets ranked with the other Leicester Square entertainments as pornographic and outside criticism.[25]

If ballet were to become known as "a fine art", its practitioners would be those who, in Valéry's words, are "in another world ... one that she weaves with her steps and builds with her gestures",[26] or, in Symons's words, who inscribe space "with glittering lines that link and interlace" – that is, artists.

Headlam recognized that the social acceptance of the dance profession was conditional on fostering wider public appreciation of the ballet as an autonomous aesthetic form. His strategy was threefold: he emphasized the aesthetics of the ballet through authoritative exposition of the dance technique itself; he set up the Church and Stage Guild, which aimed to bring together members of all the theatre professions on an equal footing; and he formulated a theological position

---

[24] "One evening Headlam recognised on the stage a couple of girls who were communicants, and he spoke of his discovery that they were dancers when he met them subsequently. They implored him not to let other church attendants know how they made their living, because if the nature of their work were once known they would be cold-shouldered in the church. This little incident made a great impression on the young curate. It determined him to see more of the art these victims of prejudice practised, and to frequent the theatre generally more" (F.G. Bettany, *Stewart Headlam: A Biography*, London, 1926, 78).

[25] Letter G.B. Shaw to Headlam, Dec. 26, 1922 (quoted in Bettany, 127).

[26] Paul Valéry, "Philosophy of Dance", trans. Ralph Manheim, 55-65, in *What is Dance?: Readings in Theory and Criticism*, eds Roger Copeland and Marshall Cohen, Oxford, 61.

on the dance, informed by the Symbolist aesthetic mediated through Symons and other poets and, possibly, by the lectures on the role of dance in the early Christian Church, by G.R.S. Mead. Another source might have been Ruskin's "Letter IX: The Use of Music and Dancing Under the Jewish Theocracy, Compared with Their Use by the Modern French", which was written after attending *Ali Baba and the Forty Thieves*:

> And that very theatrical entertainment at which I sate thinking over these things for you – that pantomime, which depended throughout for its success on an appeal to the vices of the lower London populace, was in itself nothing but a corrupt remnant of the religious ceremonies which guided the most serious faiths of the Greek mind, and laid the foundation of their gravest moral and didactic – more forcibly so because at the same time dramatic – literature.[27]

Having made the point that the chorus line retains vestiges, if "corrupt", of the choric dithyramb in Greek tragedy, Ruskin proceeds to cite passages from both the Old and New Testament in which dance is a form of religious thanksgiving. Then he argues that:

> Supposing the Bible inspired, in any of the senses above defined, you have in these passages a positively Divine authority for the use of song and dance, as a means of religious service, and expression of national thanksgiving.[28]

To Headlam, ballet, rather than being "an appeal to the vices of the lower London populace", indeed itself represented spiritual grace. Headlam's authoritative exposition on the dance technique was extensively based on Carlo Blasis' *Code of Terpsichore*, which advocated the rigorous homogenization of dancing bodies, to which end classical and neoclassical sculptures functioned as a model. The republication of this Code would have legitimized the erotic element in ballet through its relationship to the elevated glories of neoclassicism, whilst the emphasis on dance technique would enable the appreciation of virtuoso accomplishments. Headlam's work as a music-hall ballet propagandist was directed to the London working classes. As a prominent member of the Guild of St Matthew, which aimed to further the welfare of workers, Headlam gave lectures on the music-hall ballet in working-men's clubs. The unauthorized printing of one of these popular lectures, "Lecture on Theatres and Music-Halls", given on 7 October 1877, was brought to the attention of his superiors in the Church. The direct result was his enforced resignation of his Bethnal Green curacy in 1878, leading to his eighteen-year exclusion as a practising clergyman from the Church of England. His licence was regranted in 1896.

Undeterred by the institutional castigation, Headlam founded the Church and

---

[27] John Ruskin, "Letter IX: The Use of Music and Dancing Under the Jewish Theocracy, Compared with Their Use by the Modern French", *Time and Tide*, 32.
[28] Ruskin, "Letter IX", 33.

Stage Guild in 1879, which was initially to be called the "Guild of Christ at Cana". The name was later dismissed as "too fanciful".[29] The Guild was aimed at all the theatrical professions and the clergy, and organized talks, debates and social events. Both George Bernard Shaw and Ruskin were supporters. Within a year, the Guild had 470 members, including 172 theatrical members and 91 clergymen. Dancers were also free to become Guild members. When it proved, however, that Headlam "did not carry on a more religious mission amongst such chorus-girls and members of the ballet as joined the Guild",[30] actor membership rapidly diminished. Over the years, the Guild became synonymous with the Leicester Square corps de ballet members, and started representing the interests of these members in a semi-official trade union capacity. The Church and Stage Guild parties were held each January in Headlam's "beautiful drawing-rooms", whilst the Rose & Crown was the habitual social meeting place for Empire and Alhambra dancers, poets and artists.

Headlam continued in his practical attempts to gain some form of Church sanction for the music-hall ballet. To this end, a meeting with the then Bishop of London, Bishop Temple, was arranged in July 1885 at Fulham Palace. The deputation included two dancers. Bishop Temple's opening gambit that the ballet was intrinsically immoral and "caused terrible harm to many good young men; such had been his experience at Rugby, Oxford, Exeter and London",[31] came out as a most shameless insult in the presence of these young women. The Bishop attempted to make up for this by stating that he did not include the present company in the category "dancers", which caused the real indignation. The Bishop thereafter was drawn into a divertissement, considering whether the legs of fairies were best represented with pink or blue tights. The delegation remembered the meeting with much amusement, but it was also clear that the Bishop was set to reinforce the hegemonic interests of "Rugby, Oxford, Exeter and London", a hegemony which not only disenfranchised dancers from public respect, but disenfranchised entire categories of people from partaking in the democratic process.

Headlam's apologia for the dance published in the *Church Reformer* (1884) proceeded from the phenomenology of dance as an expression of the "vital flame". Dance was apprehended by the hedonist as the transient fulfilment of the sensuous desires it elicited, and remained no more than a libidinal construct to the logical positivist, but to the true believer, dance – as an outward sign of the inner spirit – revealed the sanctity of the human soul:

> Your Manichean Protestant, and your superfine rationalist, reject the Dance as worldly, frivolous, sensual, and so forth; and your dull, stupid Sensualist sees legs, and grunts with some satisfaction: but your Sacramentalist knows something

---

[29] Bettany, 99.

[30] *Ibid.*, 103.

[31] *Ibid.*, 66.

worth more than both of these. He knows what perhaps the dancer herself may be partially unconscious of, that we live now by faith and not by sight, and that the poetry of dance is the expression of unseen spiritual grace.[32]

According to Havelock Ellis, Symons's father was "a Puritanic Wesleyan minister",[33] adding even more piquancy to Headlam's very "High" pulpit-thundering on the inclusion of dance within the formal liturgy of the Mass. Frank Kermode argues that "the liturgical ingredient [of dancing] developed luxuriously in the border country of Anglo-Catholicism".[34]

Luxurious as they are, some of these border developments lead back to the heretical sects stamped out by the Early Church Fathers and are thus theologically most unorthodox. The New Testament apocryphal scripture, "The Hymn of Jesus", which had been circulating via G.R.S. Mead amongst the Symons coterie, was one of those unorthodox "liturgical ingredients", and is called by Havelock Ellis "the earliest known Christian ritual".[35] This was to support the argument that theatre dance had been originally part of Christian church worship, where the Eucharist itself is a "divine pantomime". Yet the hymn is, in fact, not so much a hand-me-down early Church notation for dance worship as an apocryphal scripture from the Acts of St John, which attributes the danced verse to Christ Himself, the hymn mentioned in the Gospels too, as sung before his crucifixion.[36] Mead quotes salient passages in English translation from this "priceless fragment" in his essay "The Sacred Dance of Jesus",[37] published in *The Quest*, whilst the English composer Gustav Holst set the text "Hymn of Jesus" to music in 1917.

The Acts of St John[38] – said to be the earliest of the apocryphal texts and written around the second Century in Gnostic circles with knowledge of Hellenistic culture – include the miracles of St John the Divine, "The Hymn of Jesus" (that is, the secret initiation round dance danced by Christ and his disciples) and the "Revelation of the Mystery of the Cross" (the scripture on Christ's revelation to John after the round dance). This St John the Divine was Christ's favoured disciple, who wrote on Patmos the Book of Revelations and was so memorably assimilated in an early Eliot poem "The Descent from the Cross":

---

[32] Headlam quoted. in Frank Kermode, "Poet and Dancer before Diaghilev", in *What is Dance?*, 148.

[33] Ellis, quoted in Lhombreaud, 64.

[34] Kermode, "Poet and Dancer", 149.

[35] Havelock Ellis, *The Dance of Life*, London, 1923, 39.

[36] Cf. Mark 14:26.

[37] G.R.S. Mead, "The Sacred Dance of Jesus", *The Quest*, I/2 (Oct 1910), 45-67.

[38] The Acts of St John, *New Testament Apocrypha*, ed. Wilhelm Schneemelcher, English trans. and ed. R. McL. Wilson, Louisville: KY, 1992, II, 180-207.

Let us go to the masquerade and dance!
I am going as St John among the Rocks
Attired in my underwear and socks ....[39]

If dance rituals modelled on "the round dance of Jesus" did take place in the early Church, the practice would have been related to the gnostic sects. The "Hymn of Jesus" is associated with those Christian teachings that were suppressed by the early Patriarchs in the effort to consolidate the Pauline doctrine.[40] St Augustine, in his letter to Ceretius, quotes ten lines from the "Hymn of Jesus" and condemns those who "impute the hymn of praise to our Lord Jesus Christ", the Priscillianists, and "members of various other sects [who use it] with infamous vanity",[41] including the Manicheans. According to the Acts of St John, Christ had revealed the mysteries of the Logos to His disciples in a secret initiation ritual, the round dance:

> Now if you follow
>   my dance,
> see yourself
>   in Me who am speaking,
> and when you have seen what I do,
>   keep silence about my mysteries.
> You who dance, consider
>   what I do, for yours is
> this passion of Man
>   which I am to suffer.[42]

In these apocrypha, the Dance of the mysteries, rather than the Eucharist of the Last Supper is the central symbolic ritual in the divine drama. Max Pulver writes that the Acts of St John are "the ancient mysteries ... presented with a Christian coating".[43] In Symons, the doctrine would indicate that a mission to redeem the soul of the ballet girl is Pharisaical, for it is she, in dancing, who reveals herself to be the true follower of Christ.

---

[39] Unfinished poem, in a letter to Conrad Aiken, dated 25 July 1914, in *The Letters of T.S. Eliot*, ed. Valerie Eliot, I, London, 1988, 44.

[40] The Pauline doctrine and its repercussions on women in the Early Church are discussed in Stevan L. Davies, *The Revolt of the Widows: The Social World of the Apocryphal Acts*, Carbondale: Ill., 1980.

[41] Quoted in Max Pulver, "Jesus' Round Dance and Crucifixion According to the Acts of St. John", *The Mysteries: Papers from the Eranos Yearbooks*, London, 1955, 172.

[42] Acts of St John, 183.

[43] Pulver, 175. The Mithras mysteries are the particular point for comparison.

III

In "La Mélinite: Moulin Rouge", we find this mystico-religious choric description of the dance:

> The orange-rosy lamps are trembling
> Between the robes that turn;
> In ruddy flowers of flame that burn
> The lights are trembling:
> The shadows and the dancers turn.[44]

In this typically diffuse stanza, the full-rhyme line endings, with the emphasis on "burn" and "turn", suggest the solar cycle, but through the twice repeated "trembling" there is also a tension implied between "the robes that turn", and "the "flame[s] that burn". On an abstract level, transformation – "turn" – through sacrifice – "burn" – is an operative theme. The incandescent dancer is a great modernist image. We find the image in Yeats's "Byzantium", but also in Pound's "Pisan Cantos" and in the early T.S. Eliot. To assume some material relation between that cogent spiritual image and the world of the gaslights and the leisure-industrial worker might seem banal. Yet Adorno believes that the "approved broad-mindedness" with which Goethe's poem "The God and the Bayadère", an earlier precursor, has been received "is not to be trusted". The image of the incandescent dancer is always suspect:

> The bourgeois needs the bayadere, not merely for pleasure, which he grudges her, but to feel himself a god. The nearer he gets to the edge of his domain and the more he forgets his dignity, the more blatant becomes the ritual of power. The night has its joy, but the whore is burned notwithstanding. The rest is the Idea.[45]

Can the "Idea" separate itself from social history? Let us return to that passage from Gautier's *Jettatura*, about that foolish virgin ballerina who could not get her act together and spelt prey to the one with the binoculars:

> One evening, carried away by the circular flight of a waltz, the dancer brushed that row of fire which in the theatre separates the ideal world from the real; her light sylphide costume fluttered like the wings of a dove about to take flight. A gas-jet shot out its blue and white tongue and touched the flimsy material. In a moment the girl was enveloped in flame; for a few seconds she danced like a firefly in a red glow, and then darted towards the wings, frantic, crazy with terror, consumed alive by her burning costume.

---

[44] *London Nights*, 24.

[45] Theodor Adorno, "112. Et dona ferentes", in, *Minima Moralia: Reflections from Damaged Life*, trans. E.F.N. Jephcott, 173-74.

Paul had been very painfully affected by this accident .... Now he was convinced that his persistence in following her with his eyes had not been unconnected with the death of that charming creature. He looked on himself as her murderer; he felt a self-loathing, and wished he had never been born.

The fantastical creature, touched by the flame from a gas jet, turns from "Woman", back into "a girl", an ordinary mortal, who suffers being burnt alive. The protagonist links the fatal accident to the gaze, his own, which had voraciously consumed her. Yet the description is not only, as may be supposed, a metaphorical elaboration on the male gaze, nor does it only refer to the self-absorbed guilt attendant on the return to the reality principle. The nineteenth-century metropolitan theatre, whilst presenting illusions of Arcadia, was fraught with an industrial hazard which directly affected the female dancer – fire.

Théophile Gautier himself was moved to write a small tribute to the ballerina Clara Webster, who was burned during an 1844 London performance of *The Revolt of the Harem,* and died three days later:

> Let us spare a tear for poor Clara Webster who has just been burned alive in her gauze costume. The English, who were so proud at having a ballerina in their midst, applauded furiously and made her repeat every one of her *pas.* It was said she would recover, but her beautiful hair had blazed about her red cheeks, and her pure profile had been disfigured. So it was for the best that she died.[46]

Common sense regarding the damaged fetish commodity prevailed. In Gautier's tribute to the French ballerina Emma Livry,[47] who died in similar circumstances in 1863, literary pieties could make up for the absence of nationalistic *Schadenfreude.* Noted for her title role in *Le Papillon,* Gautier remarks on Livry's burial that, "two white butterflies hovered ceaselessly over her white coffin". "This detail", Gautier informs us, "the Greeks would have seen as a poetic symbol". Of course, any accident with fire and dance may be read as a "poetic symbol". Huizinga's *The Waning of the Middle Ages* notes that Jean Petit's plea of 1408 argues that the "bal des ardents" disaster (involving dance, fire, costumes and the King of France[48]) was a portentous symbolic sacrifice. Yet the incandescent dancer is urban modernity's banal poetic symbol, for nineteenth-century female ballet dancers were necessarily, indeed literally, enmeshed in the cause of their potential destruction. The Romantic ballet, like Gautier's *Giselle,* for example, with its dusks, moons, and dawns (all requiring "coloured fire" or "Bengal lights"), with its scores of Wilis (all in tulle costumes) and its pastoralism (plenty of garland-throwing in Act I), was an industrial disaster waiting to happen. Net skirts were found to shimmer ethereally behind

---

[46] "The Death of Clara Webster", in *Gautier on Dance*, 153-54.

[47] "Tribute to Emma Livry", in *Gautier on Dance*, 295-96.

[48] Johan Huizinga, *The Waning of the Middle Ages*, trans. F. Hopman, Penguin, 1990, 220.

the footlights, emphasizing the dancer's appearance as the archetypal Romantic "Woman". In fact, the very fabric of the dress, combined with the stage lights, was lethal. Dancers flicking their skirts against the open gas flames of the float, wings, battens, ground rows, lengths and standards, or crossing the sparks of coloured fire, could be immolated in seconds. It was one of the principal causes of fire accidents at theatres. According to Terence Rees in *Theatre Lighting in the Age of Gas*: "They were the victims of a mixture of indifference and incompetence at both administrative and managerial levels."[49] He also points out that whilst the Clara Webster incident, which evidently inspired Gautier, received much sentimental publicity, those involving corps de ballet dancers or, indeed, over time, a "small army of theatrical personnel" went unreported.

In Symons's poems, certainly, the gaslights are still marked as a threat: in "Behind the Scenes: Empire", "the gusty gaslight shoots a thin/Sharp finger over cheeks and nose". In "At the Foresters", the poet is standing "in the wings" next to "Flo", "a principal boy" as the travesty dancers were called.[50] She is about to go onstage:

> The shadow of the gaslit wings
>   Come softly crawling down our way;
> Before the curtain someone sings,
>   The music sounds from far away;
> I stand beside you in the wings.
>
> Prying and indiscreet, the lights
>   Illumine, if you chance to move,
> The prince's dress, the yellow tights,
>   That fit your figure like a glove:
> You shrink a little from the lights.[51]

On a metaphorical level, these are variations on the "fire is desire" theme, all emphasizing the sense of violation of the body exposed to view in the music halls. In "At the Lyceum":

> Her eyes are brands that keep the angry heat
>   Of fire that crawls and leaves an ashen path.
> The dust of this devouring flame she hath
>   Upon her cheeks and eyelids.[52]

The "ashen path" may refer to the soot from gas lamps on her face, but since the fire is linked to the woman's eyes, that "angry heat" also suggests quite

---

[49] Rees, 157.
[50] Ellen Terry, *The Russian Ballet*, London, 1913, 10.
[51] *London Nights*, 23.
[52] *Silhouettes*, 37.

contradictory tear stains. The consistent personification of gaslights as the agents of violation would imply that the violation is regarded as systemic and impersonal. The initiating point about what gaslights can do might be lost on the contemporary reader, but one understands that the crisis is not the madonna/whore dichotomy in the Decadent Symbol, as his contemporary detractors argued, but in the social system which leaves so much to be desired.

The socio-historical pressures on Symons's dancers are considerable; equally, the immediate material manifestations of those pressures would disappear by the 1910s. Electric lighting had replaced gas lighting, ballet had become an elite form of entertainment, and it had become acceptable, indeed fashionable, for women to go out in public spaces at night. The social space of the nocturnal metropolis had irrevocably changed. Accordingly, the idea of the incandescent dancer could separate itself from social history, and in itself symbolize, as Frank Kermode has argued, the aesthetic work. Symons had a mental breakdown in 1908, and so did not develop his poetry and critical writing into the Modernist period. He did still go to Leicester Square, however. There is that poem of Betjeman's about Symons turning up at the Café Royal in the 1940s, looking for his friends. By then, the Empire Theatre had become a movie theatre, as it still is today, and the dancers were gone.

THE *"PASSANTE"* AS *"FLÂNEUSE"* IN DOROTHY RICHARDSON'S *PILGRIMAGE*

DEBORAH L. PARSONS

The trope of the male flâneur can encompass an urban cultural field, populated with figures that vary from the literary Bohemian, the tourist, the exile and the ragpicker to the institutions of state power.[1] The stretched boundaries of this cultural space are permeable, and thus exploitable by women and by feminist critics. The city of spectacle and consumption patrolled by the male flâneur also provided the necessary conditions for women's greater access to public urban space. Adrian Rifkin notes of the years after the First World War that "a new stratum of single women, who learn their own circuits in the rounds of work and pleasure" enter the city and "hide, so to speak, in this man-made space, while their pleasures represent a real displacement of its values".[2] I would locate the timing of this phenomenon earlier than Rifkin, however, beginning in the late nineteenth century with the rise of the New Woman.

In social terms, a new female lifestyle became evident in the last decades of the nineteenth century as the marriage age increased and middle-class women began to gain entry into the universities and the workplace and to live, therefore, away from the family home. Moreover, they were increasingly prominent in the city streets as the commercialized metropolis opened up to them as consumers and workers. Although the numbers of such women were relatively low, their position and ambitions were sufficiently unorthodox to provoke widespread debate and criticism. As a result, the New Woman, a social phenomenon and a literary type of the 1880s and 90s, became a dominant preoccupation for writers of novels, essays and popular journalism, propounded in her stereotypical form by satirical publications such as *Punch*. As both social figure and literary caricature, she was a specifically urban character, the result of the circumstances and qualities of a growing metropolitan society. The single woman seeking independence in late nineteenth-century London marks the beginning of a sustained female presence and observance of the urban environment.

---

[1] Part of this present essay has been revised for publication in Deborah Parsons, *Streetwalking the Metropolis: Women, the City and Modernity*, Oxford, 2000.

[2] Adrian Rifkin, *Street Noises: Parisian Pleasure, 1900-40*, Manchester, 1993, 9.

Furthermore, this "new woman", "educated working woman", "professional woman" or "odd woman", as she was variously labelled, was to remain a spectral presence for the aesthetic self-consciousness of urban-based writers such as Dorothy Richardson and Virginia Woolf in their writing about the city two decades later.

Travel and the journey are common literary metaphors for a search for identity or self-discovery, and *Pilgrimage* can be regarded as a reworking of the traditional male Bildungsroman. Up to this point, the concept of "woman" and "search/voyage/pilgrimage" had been largely incompatible, the Bildungsroman being an exclusively male activity. In the modern urban environment, however, the Bildungsroman shifted from its traditional form of exotic travel or the Grand Tour to a journey in microcosm, the walk within the city itself. Here the journey is oriented inwards as a searching of the consciousness and self. From the complex associations of woman and city (the streetwalker as prostitute/shopper /tourist), a female Bildungsroman could be conceived – an exploration of the female consciousness based in the urban environment. The Romanticist, male Bildungsroman or "voyage out" is paralleled in the twentieth century with a voyage in, in which the protagonist journeys to or in confined spaces rather than vast, natural landscapes. The city provides a spatial manifestation of this journey, the mind or consciousness a psychological one. Moreover, the city is not only aesthetically but also structurally a different environment from the open landscape. Crucially, it is labyrinthine, and, although mappable, is a place of numerous trajectories, along which one can wander. An extension of this city/consciousness metaphor is to imply that the mind is also a place where one wanders, perhaps that the consciousness shaped by modernity has a particular structure – a relational, socially defined, changing identity rather than a fixed, constant one.

Richardson's work is a constant wandering of memory, at once autobiographical and fictional, as the author attempts to establish her identity both in the past and the present. Living and walking in London at the turn of the century, the young Richardson sought a coherent self-identity; retracing her past and her steps in the persona of Miriam Henderson in *Pilgrimage* she sought to express and thus define and confirm this identity; remembering both the 1890s and her fictional reworking of that period, her writing in the late 1930s is a conscious and self-reflexive analysis that establishes the identity of the past from the authority of the present, whilst simultaneously using that identity as the basis of the self-knowledge of the present itself. Richardson's oeuvre is thus palimpsestic. The time periods of the 1890s, 1910s/20s, and late 1930s are layered, connected by the thread of imaginative and physical wanderings through the same mental and urban space. In the "Foreword" to *Pilgrimage* written in 1938 and the article of the following year "Yeats of Bloomsbury", Richardson both describes and displays her identity as an urban and specifically female writer through the metaphor of walking and its cultural associations with the alien outsider and the transgressive female.[3]

The "psychological novel" has been defined by Leon Edel as characterized by an attempt to express rather then describe the activity of the subjective consciousness, achieved through a narrative style that renders thought in terms of movement and flux. Positing Proust, Dorothy Richardson and James Joyce as its leading proponents, Edel notes the common trope of the urban walk in their work, stating that their works exhibit "a curious kinship of search, voyage, pilgrimage" and that "all were voyages through consciousness".[4] This connection of perceptual consciousness and movement is manifest in the Baudelairean act of flânerie. The formative function of walking for the urban writer is registered, for example, by Virginia Woolf in *The Years*, when Eleanor Pargiter walks for "relief" through a foreign quarter of eighteenth-century London houses. Replicating the constructive effect of Bloomsbury walks on Woolf and Richardson, Eleanor's thoughts suggest the creative influence of street walking that they experienced:

> Her mind was full; her being brimmed populous with sights, with sounds, with half realized ideas .... She had been bringing things together; building up new combinations as she walked; adding fresh to old ones.[5]

Despite the persistent tendency to interpret the flâneur as a metaphor for the male artist, the aleatory perspective, often represented by styles of writing termed "stream of consciousness", is frequently described as a particularly feminine characteristic. Coined by William James as a model of inner mental activity, the term was appropriated for literary criticism by May Sinclair to describe Richardson's techniques in *Pilgrimage*. The urban environment becomes an active presence rather than a situational backdrop in Richardson's text. Exterior and interior life interact as metaphors of the urban scene are used to describe the structure and workings of the consciousness, just as the city is frequently personified and takes on the characteristics of the consciousness. Consciousness and the city are thus mutually interactive and expressive. Although Richardson rejected the "stream of consciousness" label, her long psychological narrative does stem from an effort to create a new literary style that will accommodate the experiences of the female consciousness, in contrast to the conventions of technique and subject of the traditional English novel, which she regards as masculine and alienating to female understanding.

The distinction Richardson makes between the traditional realist novel and the new style she attempts to forge, is one of masculinity and femininity rather than male writing and female writing. In her retrospective "Foreword" to the 1938 publication of *Pilgrimage*, she describes both her endeavour, an attempt

---

[3] Dorothy Richardson, "Yeats of Bloomsbury", *Life and Letters Today*, April 1939, 60-66.

[4] Leon Edel, *The Psychological Novel, 1900-1950*, New York, 1955, 16.

[5] "Appendix" to Virginia Woolf, *The Years*, Oxford, 1992, 454.

"to produce a feminine equivalent of the current masculine realism", and her technique in terms of journeying, specifically walking, evoking a literary "pathway", a "lonely track" that becomes "a populous highway" (*P*, I, 9, 10).[6] With the benefit of hindsight, she perceives the laying put and treading of this path as a collective activity that includes male as well as female writers (Henry James, Marcel Proust, James Joyce and Virginia Woolf). By attributing to Henry James the role of path-finder, she at once reasserts the idea of the walking artist as male yet also characterizes his perspective as feminine. For Richardson, James and Proust are path-finders of a style that is concerned with, and represents, a mode of consciousness that has been consistently set up as "feminine" within a dichotomous gender structure.

I want to suggest that walking as a literary metaphor is not so much parallel to thinking and writing but rather extends into thinking and writing in terms of aesthetic engagement with its spatial, situational surroundings. My argument is that this interaction differs from the traditional masculine perspective of detached urban observation. The viewpoint of the flâneur can be described by two dominant structures of vision in modernity: one, a static panorama/panopticon model; the other, a moving, shifting model of flux. Yet the two cannot easily be set up as a dichotomy for reasons that are significant for the positing of a female flânerie. In actuality, the male flâneur as conventionally defined still exists within the controlling discourse of the panorama. Although he epitomizes the idea of the artist-observer in motion, able to see and represent the fluid nature of modernity, he is yet threatened by this moving flux that ultimately denies his pretension to omniscient vision. The urban characters evoked in the work of Charles Baudelaire, which, along with Edgar Allan Poe's "The Man of the Crowd", have become metatexts for the discussion of flânerie, exhibit this paradox of the visually authoritative yet wandering and placeless flâneur, whose habits result from a mixture of reaction against, dependency on, and anxiety in, bourgeois culture.[7] Poe's story provides a paradigm for the experience of the detached, observing and categorizing male figure in the city. Walter Benjamin's essay "The Flâneur", and its revised version, "On Some Motifs on Baudelaire", however, illustrate the condition of the male urban observer as a figure of visual authority that is threatened by the modernizing environment of turn-of-the-century modernity. In "On Some Motifs in Baudelaire", Benjamin states that the flâneur (and bear in mind that Benjamin's flâneur is always male) enjoyed his leisured superiority in the world of the Parisian arcades, and became "out of place" and disoriented once these arcades were destroyed and he was forced out into the streets as a "man of the crowd" – "what had to become of the flâneur

---

[6] References after quotation are to the four-volume Virago Modern Classics edition of Dorothy Richardson's *Pilgrimage* (1979, rpt. 1982).

[7] See Charles Baudelaire, *The Flowers of Evil*, trans. James McGowan, Oxford, 1993, and *Parisian Prowler*, trans. Edward K. Kaplan, Athens: Ga., 1989; Edgar Allan Poe, *The Portable Poe*, ed. Philip Van Doren Stern, Viking, 1945.

once he was deprived of the milieu to which he belonged".[8] In Benjamin's revised description, the flâneur thus increasingly retreats away from the crowd, in an attempt to retain a certain individual control and self-order over the chaos of the city street. The moving perspective of the walking urban observer, physically within the city street, is exchanged in this act for the panoramic perspective of a static urban observer, who can gain gendered power and authority only in a position of superior detachment.

The act of walking, therefore, seems incompatible with a totalizing, panoramic and authoritative viewpoint. But, significantly, the very environment that Benjamin sees as necessitating the detachment of the leisured, male flâneur was, at the same time, creating public interiors geared towards women (such as the department store), which promoted their access to the city streets and consequently encouraged a fresh perspective on the urban experience. The *passante*, the female counterpart to the flâneur in Baudelaire's oeuvre, suddenly becomes important as a walking figure, whose position in the city streets, moreover, cannot be easily denigrated by objectification. Being an enigma, like the man in the crowd, she cannot be placed by the categorizing perspective of the male flâneur. She is also a mirror image of the male observer, her height and confidence implying a masculinity that parallels the femininity of the dandy-flâneur, and as such she is a plausible metaphor for women as artist-observers of the city.

Baudelaire's "A une passante" appears in *Tableaux Parisiens*, a collection of poems on the marginal, enigmatic inhabitants of the city. Standing in the street, the narrator is passed by a woman whose grace and figure attract him. Whilst in the process of objectifying her as type (mourner) and erotic object (he notes the line of her leg through the hem of her skirt), she returns his look and he experiences the shock of the mutual encounter. This experience is particular to the modern city – a sudden collision with the unknown, a transient moment of communication and then a move away back into anonymity. He is disturbed by the returned glance, which is unusual to the urban condition of isolation, and the shock brings him "suddenly to life again". Like the artist, the woman walks the night city, yet she cannot be denigrated in sexual or moral terms, since her status and actions are ambiguous and defy interpretation. Janet Wolff, by contrast, has argued that "There is no question of inventing the *flâneuse*: the essential point is that such a character was rendered impossible by the sexual divisions of the nineteenth century", and suggested that, as a respectable woman of the time would not have met the male gaze, the *passante* of Baudelaire's poem is herself still a prostitute.[9] For Wolff, the marginalized social outcast of the prostitute cannot participate in the authoritative gaze of the bourgeois flâneur. However,

---

[8] Walter Benjamin, "On Some Motifs in Baudelaire", in *Illuminations*, ed. Hannah Arendt, trans. Harry Zohn, London, 1970, 174.

[9] Janet Wolff, "The Invisible *Flâneuse*: Women and the Literature of Modernity", *Theory, Culture and Society*, II/3 (1985), 45.

Baudelaire rarely misses an opportunity to damn the prostitute or lesbian (even when also admiring them) and the extreme shock the narrator experiences seems at odds with the common sight of the prostitute. Indeed, the woman's dark mourning attire prevents the identification of her as a prostitute in terms of outward appearance and subverts the implications of a woman looking at a man in the night street – two categorizing motifs contradict. Crucial to the idea of the *passante* is precisely the fact that it is impossible to define her as a type and that, as a result, she is the most perfect reflection of the characteristics of the urban narrator-observer.

By manipulating the idea of the *passante*, early twentieth-century women writers pose a challenge to the exclusivity of the male artist-personas in the city of canonical Modernism. The concept of the Baudelairean artist-observer, for example, is most directly continued in the urban poems of T.S. Eliot, in which modern women are safely categorized as superficial, neurotic or of unequal class status. However, the visibility of the woman as object/invisibility of the woman as subject in Eliot's work is countered by women writers in explicit examples of the middle class woman's urban experience. One contrast to Eliot's urban women is the observant, peripatetic Miriam Henderson in *Pilgrimage*, and in the following part of this paper I shall discuss book seven, *Revolving Lights*, as an explicit critique of the depiction of the woman in the city in terms of the concept of the *passante*, and a concentrated delineation of a female alternative to the public urban observer of the flâneur. In *Pilgrimage*, Dorothy Richardson reverses the conventional structure of the male/female urban encounter by revealing it from the angle of the *passante*. Given her own visual perspective, the *passante* becomes a *flâneuse*.

At the beginning of *Revolving Lights*, the protagonist Miriam Henderson takes a fifty-page walk in the London streets from the City to her room in Bloomsbury. Much of this is taken up with her solitary movement along fairly deserted streets whilst she ponders on the movements of her life itself and the position of independence she has developed. It is a fascinating evocation in writing of a city and psyche explored in walking. It seems to me to directly answer Wolff's call for a description of the experience of the *passante*, and yet also to offer a detailed indication of the duality of the flâneur and *passante* roles. I shall, therefore, study it at some length. Twice in her journey home Miriam briefly passes people who prompt shocked recognition: a man standing alone amidst the rush of Piccadilly, and an old woman stooping in the gutter at Cambridge Circus. In Miriam's walk through London, therefore, the reader is offered the experience of the *passante* herself as *flâneuse*.

Miriam's marginality is emphasized as she starts on her walk. Throughout *Pilgrimage* to this point she has struggled to identify herself with a particular place or social group – as a middle-class woman in the city, she has had no such place open to her. Richardson vividly evokes Miriam's isolation from the different worlds in her life by emphasizing their separateness and the boundary spaces between them that Miriam is constantly traversing – roads, rail tracks, stairs. The walk home occurs in just such a vacuum. On the threshold of "the busy planning world of socialism", the Lycurgan meeting she has been attending, Miriam observes the vistas of her present life:

> Far away in tomorrow, stood the established, unchanging world of Wimpole Street, linked helpfully to the lives of the prosperous classes. Just ahead, at the end of the walk home, the small isolated Tansley Street world, full of secretive people drifting about on the edge of catastrophe .... In the space between these surrounding worlds was the everlasting solitude (*P*, III, 233).

The solitude in the streets relieves her from the associations of these classified areas of politics, work and domesticity. It is almost as if the night streets, even though sites of movement and flux, halt time and hold her suspended, away from the daily pressures of work and the steady progression of days in her meagre room. As with the flâneur, who makes a home of the boulevard, for Miriam the street is a natural habitat, soothing and welcoming: "She went out into its shelter" (235). The androgynous implications of the *passante*, within whom the Baudelairean narrator finds self-recognition, are also present in Miriam, who continually reflects on her sense of masculinity. Here, for example, she sees this masculine quality ("she had a masculine mind") as being responsible for her life's path and her active perception, as well as for her present enjoyment of her walk and visual appreciation of the city:

> all the things of the mind that had come her way had come unsought; yet finding her prepared; so that they seemed not only her rightful property, but also in some way, herself. The proof was that they had passed her sisters by, finding no response; but herself they had drawn, often reluctant ... to a path that it sometimes seemed she must explore to the exclusion of everything else in life, exhaustively, the long way round, the masculine way (236).

However, Miriam's masculinity is not reaffirming of the inherent maleness of the urban observer, as she often vehemently condemns both the masculine and feminine mind. Rather, her masculinity refers to androgyny, to a maleness that combines with femaleness to cancel the excesses of each.

Finding herself in the West End, Miriam observes

> [the] wide, leisurely shop-fronts displaying in a restrained profusion, comfortably within reach of the experienced eye half turned to glance from a passing vehicle, all the belongings of West End life; on the pavements, the trooping succession of masked life-moulded forms, their unobservant eyes, aware of the resources all about them, at gaze upon their continuous adventure (240).

This is the city much as Benjamin and other urban theorists describe it, populated by absent-minded spectators, trained to register its myriad sights unthinkingly, and a faceless crowd propelled by purpose. Moreover, like the flâneur, Miriam feels an affinity with the crowd and understands the reason for its guarded anonymity:

> There was something here that offered her again and again a solution of the problem of social life, a safe-guard of individuality .... Always to be solid and resistant; unmoved. Having no opinions and only one enthusiasm – to be unmoved (241).

Miriam values the crowd's social method of detachment as a form of self-protection. Yet, at the same time, the crowd implies the disturbing uniformity that results from the widespread adoption of this act and Miriam revolts from it to the more privileged social position of her youth.

Thus, in *Revolving Lights* Miriam is still aware of a certain instability of self. The viewpoint she takes, and the aesthetic perspective that Richardson develops in relation to it, is ultimately impressionistically mobile, shifting and transgressive, but at the same time remains somewhat isolated. She paradoxically retains an attraction to the stylishness and assurance of the upper classes, whilst feeling associated with the lower classes. Making herself an anonymous figure that belongs to neither category, she takes up a position of detached observation: "She, with no resources at all, had dropped to easy irresponsible labour to avoid being shaped and branded, to keep her untouched strength free for a wider contemplation, ... a *plebeian* dilettantism" (245). This desire for freedom from responsibility in order to enjoy almost Epicurean observation is reminiscent of the flâneur. Miriam's struggle to find an identity and define herself objectively is expressed through linguistic shifts in Richardson's text. Miriam's self-reflection moves back and forth between possessives as Richardson changes from third person to first person narration and back again. As well as registering Miriam's self quest, however, these shifts also emphasize the double role of the *passante* as both object and subject in the city.

Sexualization is an important factor in the Parisian flâneur's relationship to the urban street, as he eroticizes and fetishizes both woman and city. In the tradition of male urban literature in England, the explicit equation of London/woman is more rare. However, women writers apply a gender to the city more frequently. There are certainly sexual connotations attached to Miriam's response to the London streets, and, upturning the topological image of city/woman/prostitute, Richardson depicts London as Miriam's "mighty lover". Recalling returning to London, Miriam describes the city as welcoming and enclosing her:

> No one in the world would oust this mighty lover, always receiving her back without words, engulfing and leaving her untouched, liberated and expanding to the whole range of her being .... She would travel further than the longest journey, swifter than the most rapid flight, down and down into an oblivion deeper than sleep ... tingling to the spread of London all about her, herself one with it, feeling her life flow outwards, north, south, east and west, to all its margins (272-73).

Richardson thus reverses the tendency to feminize cities and the image of the artist-flâneur traversing the city landscape as metaphorical female body. In such analogies the male observer can be regarded as cutting up the body of the city by categorizing it along social distinctions. Miriam's journey decategorizes the city and herself, as she moves and flows through the border areas and streets that are rather the arterial images of the cityscape.

It is immediately after this image of the sexualized city that Miriam reaches the centre of the West End at Piccadilly. The side streets are full of solitary old men "still circulating, like the well preserved coins of a past reign" (273), themselves figures in passing and in the last stages of their transitory existence. The only other women are prostitutes in the shadows, and Miriam herself is approached by a prowling man, evidence that at least at night the woman in public is still deemed an immoral figure. Modernity is heralded by the Circus itself and the noise and hansoms of young people of both sexes. Miriam still belongs nowhere and feels "the need for thoughtless hurrying across its open spaces", regretting that she has no place, no metaphorical interior or club, "a neutral territory where she could finish her thought undisturbed" (274).[10] This desire for a version of the private home in the public-private club parallels the flâneur's public-private interior of the arcade. Indeed, the woman developing her independence in the city was negotiating both her own private and public space. Yet, actually, at the centre of the Piccadilly island, Miriam feels in a place of "central freedom" and it is at this point that she sees a man, also "a watchful habitué" (276), and they come together in a moment of shared recognition, interchanging the roles of observer/observed, flâneur/*passante*.

The moment of recognition is emphasized by being literal as well as psychological – the man is Tommy Babington, an ex-suitor. He preserves aspects of the flâneur, dandiacal in his "dapper" dress and "pince-nez", and standing in solitude. As Miriam observes him, he is "expressionless" and anonymous. His face is "unawakened" and merely the reflection of the people he observes, similar to the way the narrator of "The Man of the Crowd" realizes he appears to others. The act of passing takes place:

> He had glanced .... Going on, she must sweep right across his path .... She rushed on, passing him with a swift salute, saw him raise his hat with mechanical promptitude as she stepped from the kerb and forward, pausing an instant for a passing hansom.

Miriam is the active, moving figure, Babington the passive one. Her look is one of challenge, the *passante* defying the male onlooker to objectify her and celebrating her ability to shock him out of his masculine stability. She rejoices in denying his possession of her; on the streets, of which they are both "habitués", "They had met equally at last" (277). Yet, despite achieving her own right to the

---

[10] By the next volume of *Pilgrimage, The Trap*, Miriam has joined a female club, "The Belmont" which provides her with such a place of neutral public territory in the city.

night streets, Miriam realizes that Babington's reaction will be to reassert his male, bourgeois authority and emphasize her position as an unmarried woman out at night alone: "Already in his mind was one of those formulas that echoed about in enclosed life .... 'Oui, ma chère, little Mirry *Henderson*, strolling, at midnight, across Piccadilly Circus'" (278).

Although Miriam displays many of the characteristics of the flâneur, she also criticizes him. She derides Tommy Babington's aura of freedom, when in fact he is ultimately conventional and dependent on his home life. In Michael Shatov, the exotic Russian, she criticizes another aspect of the flâneur, horrified at his self-assured categorizing of people in terms of physiognomy: "You don't *see* them; they are not *there* in what you see." Yet Miriam finds herself adopting a masculine mode of vision, realizing that "now she herself was interested; had attained unawares a sort of connoisseurship, taking in, at a glance, nationality, type, status, the difference between inclination and misfortune" and questions whether "this [was] contamination or illumination" (279). Having placed herself as subject in the city, she now realizes that she can also act as the flâneur and appropriate for herself the masculine gaze. Whether this identification with the male should be the aim of the independent woman, is an essential part of Miriam's "pilgrimage" of self-discovery.[11] She tends towards a rejection of a male position, however, and certainly Richardson's literary style can be interpreted as a new form of flânerie, which she regards as particularly female and in which "all the practical facts, the tragedies and comedies and events, are but ripples on a stream" (280).

At one point in Miriam's walk, for example, in the commercially developed streets of the West End, the conditions that eradicated the original flâneur are brought into focus. Benjamin describes how the building of the grand Haussmann boulevards in Paris, which aided large volumes of traffic moving quickly through the city, ultimately led to an environment unsympathetic to the strolling observer. The opening up of Paris thus reasserted the public space of the city streets that had been metaphorically privatized in the spaces of the arcades and older boulevards. In London, Miriam contrasts late Victorian Oxford Street with Georgian Bond Street in the same way. Oxford Street is unsafe for the walker and constantly bombards the senses in a way that allows no pause for reflection:

> Even at night it seemed to echo with the harsh sounds of its obvious conglomerate traffic ... there was nothing to obliterate the permanent sense of two monstrous streams flowing all day, fierce and shattering, east and west. Oxford Street, unless she were sailing through it perched in sun-light on the top of an omnibus lumbering steadily towards the graven stone of the City, always wrought destruction.

---

[11] An example of the familiar liberal/cultural feminist dilemma of whether woman should assert her place within the traditionally male order, denying her femininity, or oppose that order, emphasizing her female difference.

Faced with a choice between turning into the wide, constantly moving road or the "sacred pavements ... the winding lane" (246) of Bond Street, Miriam chooses the latter. It is in the image of the physically as well as mentally detached observer, positioned on the rooftop of a bus, that the decline of the flâneur is evident. As Miriam's allusion to the bus-top observer illustrates, the urban observer as a walking agent and flâneur makes way for the urban observer as a static, high-level spectator, whose moving perspective has no agency because it results from moving transport. A removal from human interaction, therefore, takes place as the flâneur withdraws mentally and physically (onto the rooftop, bus or balcony common to the new apartments of Haussmann's Paris) from the tumult of the street. Miriam declares that the fate of the flâneur, protecting himself by choosing "to live outside the world of happenings, always to forget and escape ... was certainly wrong". The narrative style that Richardson develops can perhaps be regarded as a negotiation away from this objective detachment. Through it she connects the immediacy of the experience of spectacle with a rendering of the enduring essence of self, combining an aesthetic, impressionistic structure of perception with a concern for human subjectivity.

As she approaches home, Miriam experiences the second encounter. Paralleling her meeting with Babington in Piccadilly Circus, she crosses paths with a grotesque woman in Cambridge Circus, yet the experience is now not so much that of the *passante* as of the "man of the crowd". In this passage, Richardson evokes a suspended moment in a misty, lamp-lit atmosphere when an almost mystical encounter of doubles occurs. The poetic rhythm and imagery recalls the intensity of Poe's story and Baudelaire's prose poems, the imagination taking over from reason in perceiving the relations of self and world. The woman stooping in the gutter, illuminated by the lamplight is the "last, hidden truth of London, spoiling the night" (288). Miriam meets her glance and experiences "naked recognition .... It was herself, set in her path and waiting through all the years", as if the walk up Shaftesbury Avenue has been an avenue of time between illuminated pools of present and future. In an almost direct female reworking of Poe's tale, the old crone is a stealthy, evil figure (her reddish, knobbled skull is not dissimilar to conventional images of the devil), a lone woman in the city without the fetishizable features of youth or beauty. Yet she is also pathetically forgotten, pushed into a dark passage by the bourgeois world that ignores "the awful face above the outstretched bare arm". Miriam is shocked into self-recognition by this confrontation with her "reflection". Her youth, job and room allow her to construct an image of conformity, yet this is really only a pretence, "a semblance that was nothing but a screen set up, hiding what she was in the depths of her being" (289). Richardson indicates here the precariousness of woman's position in the city and the fear that she will end up as both alienated and alien, a forgotten, unwanted London "secret".

In Baudelaire's poem, the *passante* is arguably a metaphor for what can be glimpsed within the urban crowd – the "feminine" muse embodying what is beautiful, fleeting and inspiring. Yet she is also a mirror image of the poet-narrator himself, anonymous and with the freedom of the city streets. The *passante* thus seems a female parallel to the flâneur. Richardson's depiction of Miriam Henderson's walk through the night streets of London offers the perspective of a female urban walker. Miriam's awareness of being viewed as morally transgressive, her questioning of her identification with a male point of view, and her assertion of her distinct femaleness point up issues to be addressed in any discussion of the definition of a female flâneur or separate category of *flâneuse*.

Richardson provides an anecdotal account of her own role as at once both *passante* and *flâneuse* in her essay "Yeats of Bloomsbury". As the title suggests, the essay situates the poet firmly within an urban milieu that Richardson also sees as her own home territory, and she devotes as much space to her perceptions of the area as she does to Yeats. Bloomsbury, an "oasis to the north of the British Museum" (60), was a perfect site for the modern woman defining her independent identity and the female writer defining her creativity, since it provided both street and room in a central urban area that was nevertheless conducively peaceful. Edwardian Bloomsbury, as Richardson describes, was "comfortably modest", its eighteenth-century buildings having been turned into apartments and boarding houses offering "a noble heritage for those of the inhabitants who in square, or in street linking square with square, for a modest outlay could enjoy their exceptional surroundings". For Richardson, Bloomsbury was a place of stability amidst the tumult of the capital, one that reconciled "London's exhausted prisoners" to its daily grind by its cool stillness at night. The city does not seem external and indifferent in Richardson's essay, even when she is inside, as "Soon after sunset a message would reach even the most stifling attic, brought by the evening air stealing in at its open window" (61). Her room above the city is open to the air and noise of the streets, unlike a detached ivory tower. The female writer does not mourn for a rural simplicity, but, in contrast, thrives on "the familiar, inorganic air of London" (62). Indeed, Richardson implies, the occasional fresh breath of trees is to be appreciated more in the middle of London's humidity, and, reversing Simmel's concept of the blasé metropolitan, she argues that it is, instead, the rural dweller who has only "a habitual or a deliberate receptivity" to his surroundings, accepting trees just as a matter of course.

Retracing the steps of a night walk in which a passing stranger (the iconographic "urban encounter") turns out to be Yeats himself, Richardson creates a symbolic metaphor for the relationship of male and female writer with the city and each other. Returning home after an evening of discussion with friends (possibly Elsie Schleussner and her flatmate, the originals of Jan and Mag in *Pilgrimage*), Richardson goes out of her way to extend her walk and aesthetic enjoyment of Bloomsbury:

The surrounding buildings became mere reflectors of moonlight, infinitely far away. The giant trees mingled their breath with mine, their being with my own.

These are the words of an urban artist, wandering and perceiving the night city. In a pool of light, that urban phenomenon that is so frequent in Richardson and Woolf's writing, she comes face to face with an urban *doppelgänger*, "a fellow-lover of nocturnal solitude", distinguished from him by gender and his status as a famous poet compared to hers as a developing writer of the "feminine consciousness". Yet both are city dwellers, and walkers who perceive "Bloomsbury's deepest enchantment". How are they to relate in the city? The immediate reaction is one of confrontation: "It was *my* chosen path. It was *his.*" Richardson as walker holds her ground, refusing "skipping into the gutter to make way for men" (the gutter, of course, being the place of the traditional female "streetwalker"), but is unable to move anyway, recognizing the famous presence and wanting to "acknowledge [her] debt" to this fellow-worshipper of the city (63). Richardson as woman writer is in a similar position of confrontation with a masculine literary tradition, refusing to deny her own literary ability yet remaining in respectful awe of the male urban writers before her.

Although Richardson and Yeats as walkers presumably passed somehow in the street, the female writer remained struggling with the obstruction in her path and Richardson notes that "For memory, we stand permanently confronted on either side of that lake of moonlight" (64). Yet ultimately it is not a position of subservience or confrontation that Richardson takes in relation to Yeats, but one of identification. For in this essay, which in its subject, setting and even its language (the first paragraphs replicating passages from *The Tunnel*) exemplifies the continuity Richardson emphasizes between the stages of her urban and literary life, she notes that, later in life, Yeats repudiated the results of this period of his creativity, in direct contrast to her own practice. But she hopes that, "despite his protests" against the "Bloomsbury solitary" of the past, he secretly regarded him as "not a regrettable wanderer in a self-made darkness, but the hesitant younger brother of the author of *Michael Robartes*" (66), just as the Richardson portrayed in the character of Miriam Henderson was a younger sister of the author of *Pilgrimage*.

PARIS OF MAXIME DU CAMP:
THE WRITER-PRIEST BECOMES REPORTER

PHILIP RAND

In the 1840s, it seemed hardly likely that Maxime Du Camp, who professed, like his friend Gustave Flaubert, to worship art and to despise the bourgeoisie, would come to sing the praises of capital and technology as saviours of the city and humanity itself. Indeed, Du Camp insisted, in his unpublished notes, that he had never seriously considered any vocation but that of the literary artist. Yet in 1867, he undertook a study of the material functioning of the city of Paris, which led to a six-volume description of the capital and the life of its inhabitants, as observed through the activities of the city's administration. *Paris: ses organes, ses fonctions et sa vie dans la seconde moitié du XIXe siècle* is a highly ambitious and original study of the Paris of the Second Empire. In *Paris*, capital and technology play a major role.

This apparent about-face of Du Camp is not, however, as surprising as it may first seem. Flaubert and Du Camp would soon come to recognize their differences in outlook. Du Camp was always most interested in the matters of this world, downright ambitious according to not a few critics and too impatient to create through painstaking efforts the perfect work of art.[1] He was inclined to produce volumes of factual descriptions, of *choses vues*, especially from accounts of his travels to the Middle East, notable for the meticulous nature of their descriptions of what he had seen. The best known of these was *Le Nil, Egypte et Nubie* published in 1851, describing a trip to Egypt with Flaubert. The practical-minded Du Camp had, in fact, made the trip possible, as a fact-finding archaeological mission, thanks to his connections with government authorities who subsidized the mission.[2] The study of cities, at that point, did not seem to interest the author. His travel accounts were recollections of adventures, scenes of local colour and catalogue-like descriptions of monuments. While Du Camp busied himself

---

[1] Maxime Du Camp, *Lettres inédites à Gustave Flaubert*, eds Giovanni Bonaccorso and Rosa Maria Di Stefano, Messina, 1978, 349.

[2] J.M. Carré, *Voyageurs et écrivains français en Egypte*, Le Caire, 1832, 83-84.

with compiling his factual material, Flaubert absorbed atmosphere and impressions that could be put to aesthetic use in his novels and short stories.

Le Nil is purportedly the first printed volume to be accompanied with photographs and Du Camp's interest in photography would be important in his formation as a writer. Here we already find something to differentiate him from the advocates of pure art and from Baudelaire, who perceived in the new photography a threat to artistic creativity.[3]

An event which, in my view, was of primary importance in the works of Du Camp, was his meeting with an engineer named Charles Lambert, which took place during this trip to the Middle East. A follower of the Saint-Simonian movement, Lambert was instrumental in converting Du Camp to the Socialist ideas that would influence him deeply at least up to the advent of the Paris *Commune* of 1870.[4]

Saint-Simonianism was a curious mixture of transcendental and materialistic values. Its followers performed rituals, wore particular garments, worshipped the powers of the hereafter, and possessed many other characteristics of the devotees of a religious cult. Yet they believed that salvation would be attained mainly through the proper use of science, technology and capital. Indeed, many Saint-Simonians were engineers, trained at the Ecole Polytechnique in Paris.[5]

According to Saint-Simonian doctrine, human life was at present out of harmony with the transcendental order, but action by intelligent human beings could transform the social order of the entire world so that men and women could live productive and harmonious lives. Crucial to the achievement of this new order was the breaking down of traditional but irrational ideas and practices, such as social distinctions based on class and sex, and such as belief in the justice of waging war. As in all the versions of socialism that proliferated in the first part of the century, Saint-Simonianism held, too, that each member of a society must find a role consonant with his or her talents and abilities. Education was of primary importance in preparing

---

[3] Charles Baudelaire, "Le Public moderne et la photographie", in "Salon de 1859", *Curiosités esthétiques: L'Art romantique et autres Oevres critiques de Baudelaire*, Paris, 1962, 313-20. Baudelaire criticizes the contemporary fashion of admiring art as "la reproduction exacte de la nature", associating this form of realism with the "irruption" of industry in art. Industry in turn being associated with ideas of progress, the poet comments, "la poésie et le progrés sont deux ambitieux qui se haïssent d'une haine instinctive" (192). This is not to say that the poet objects to *Le Nil*, since he acknowledges the contribution of photography to sciences such as archaeology. On the other hand, aware of Du Camp's enthusiasm for progress, he dedicates his poem *Le Voyage* to Du Camp and ironically comments in a letter that it is "à faire frémir les amateurs du progrès" (see note to *Le Voyage* in Charles Baudelaire, *Les Fleurs du mal*, Paris, 1961, 429).

[4] Pierre Bonnefon, "Maxime Du Camp et les Saint-Simoniens", *Revue d'histoire Littérarie de la France*, 17 (1910), 710.

[5] Sébastien Charléty, *Histoire du saint-Simonisme* (1825-1864), Paris, 1931.

people for the New Order. Artists had a particular role to play in the process. Since they were gifted with exceptional intuitions and sensitivity, they would be the priests who would spread the gospel of Saint-Simon.

The Saint-Simonians devised utopian schemes for the city of the future, and for them the physical transformation of Paris would lead towards the creation of the new society towards which they aspired. The utopia of one follower, Duveyrier, for example, involved a totally new urban scheme for the capital whose individual functions would be laid out in perfect analogy with the human body. They, too, would then function in perfect harmony. Moreover, Paris was destined, in his opinion, to lead the rest of the world towards perfection.[6]

For over twenty years, Du Camp evidently fancied himself as one of the writer-priests devoting their talents to propagating Saint-Simonian ideas. We may observe briefly the relevance of these ideas to some of his novels, short stories, and poetry.

His novels deal with what he views as the ills afflicting Paris in particular, and French society as a whole. They are case histories of heroes, or rather anti-heroes, living in Paris, who, as their narrators tell us, are afflicted with the *mal du siècle*. Their idleness, their failure to follow the oft-repeated principle, *il faut travailler*, and the pernicious influences of a frivolous Parisian society combine to ensure their downfall.

The first novel, *Le Livre posthume, mémoires d'un suicidé* (1853), suggestive as a study in the psychology of an adolescent, offers an account of how the early loss of parents, a hedonistic social environment like that of Paris and an archaic educational system (one that emphasizes the study of classical antiquity at the expense of, presumably, mathematics, science and technology) can lead to the depraved behaviour and eventual despair of the hero. The psychological degeneration occurs, largely as a result of influences coming from the external environment. Had he been able to embrace a work ethic – to reject the frivolity characteristic of Parisian existence – he would have avoided the anguish that, in this case, led to suicide. But it is apparently appropriate that such youths should die. The writer/narrator tells his readers that he himself once met the hero and has come to recognize the futility of that person's life. He is actually satisfied that this generation, inspired by the despairing heroes of Chateaubriand, should be disappearing. The great defect of the personage was that of being "useless", *un homme inutile*.

Les Forces perdues, the second of Du Camp's novels, received some praise from Flaubert, who had harshly criticized the *Livre posthume*. As in the earlier novel, the hero's defect is that of failing to recognize the falsity of the values implied in the facile pleasures offered by Parisian society. The protagonist has devoted himself entirely to the amorous intrigues that are typical, as we are given to understand, of a class of well-to-do young

---

[6] Quoted in *Oeuvres de Saint-Simon et d'Enfantin*, I, Aalen, 1963, 72-93.

Parisians. The opportunity arises to marry a woman educated outside of France, and such a marriage could have saved him from self-destruction. This person was brought up *not* to be an ornament, a love object, as, we are told, is the case for women of respectable Parisian society, who spend their lives being sociable and seductive. She has been trained to manage a small commercial enterprise on a perfectly equal basis with men.

But the frivolous young man, attracted to the excitement Paris offers – it was a commonplace that Paris was the pleasure capital of the world – does not take advantage of the opportunity. Later the hero returns on a visit to this woman and finds her happily married to another man. The scene of felicity he witnesses is that of a man and woman working together as equals, in perfect bliss, in the management of a productive, socially useful enterprise. Having departed for the Middle East to escape the anguish that Paris has represented, he becomes involved in another disappointing love affair. When his partner runs off with another man, he disappears into the wilderness, knowingly exposing himself to great danger, and dies – once again, a suicide.

Short stories written between 1857 and 1862 pursue a highly idealistic goal. They recount the adventures of single-minded, self-sacrificing heroes, who can be considered the positively useful counterparts to the useless anti-heroes portrayed in his novels. Devoted to causes such as Polish, Hungarian and Italian freedom from foreign oppressors, they are also fully conscious that their missions may be rewarded only generations later, when they will not be around personally to reap the rewards.

As for the poetry of Du Camp, this appeals not to a distant future but shows how contemporary attitudes may be reformed. The first of two volumes, *Les Chants modernes* (1857),[7] contains an introduction that severely criticizes the antiquated ideas prevalent in his view, among contemporary writers and thinkers. Du Camp spares neither the members of the *Académie française* nor the exponents of pure art, all too inclined, in his view, to worship classical antiquity, and to ignore that which is modern.

A section of this volume, called *Les Chants de la Matière* consists of series of allegorical poems that present the basic achievements of nineteenth-century technology. Each of these speaks to us in the first person. For example, "I shall build a new world" (this is Steam, *La Vapeur*, talking), or "I shall relieve pain" (now it is Chloroform). Electricity, Gas, Photography and a Locomotive present themselves one by one to explain how they will transform peoples' lives. Finally, a bag of money speaks to explain that although it is maligned by many as an evil corrupter, it need not be devoted to the purpose of accumulating fortunes in the hands of the few. It has the potential to relieve people in distress, to subsidize inventors and to build roads instead of weapons. In other words, capital can be put to use for the benefit of mankind as a whole.

---

[7] Maxime Du Camp, *Les Chants modernes*, Paris, 1857.

Clearly the prose and poetry of Du Camp, while not without literary merit, suffer from the oppression of ideology, and the confusion of the material and the spiritual. In the *Livre posthume*, for example, various narrators, friends of the hero, launch on long-winded tirades against the ill effects of romanticism and on behalf of the work ethic that dilute the otherwise promising passages of psychological analysis. The poetry, too, as the critic Sainte Beuve observed, leaves room for improvement.[8] The task of creating convincing allegories of locomotives and money bags, in which such material objects are convincingly reconciled with transcendental values, has proven too difficult for Du Camp. It might also be observed that metre and rhyme suffered at times from the zeal of the young poet. Indeed, as he later points out in his memoirs, in 1867, the writer himself came to the realization that, "je n'étais ni poète ni romancier".[9] Instead of believing in his own fiction, he adds, "J'ai été discipliné par la vérité" and by "la vérité" he means precisely that which is tangible, concrete, that which can be directly observed. The writer has, in my view, come to recognize his impatience with abstractions; he will hereafter return to the literature of description of *choses vues*.

Yet his *vérité* involves more than the viewing of surfaces; it is a truth that must also be intuited. Du Camp tells us in his memoirs that the decision to undertake the Paris project was the fruit of a sudden inspiration, a vision, as he viewed the central city from the Pont Neuf, and watched the feverish activity going on. A statement of his suggests that he aspired to find a deeper truth in Paris:

> Je me suis demandé comment vivait ce peuple, par quels miracles de prévoyance on subvenait à ses besoins, à ses exigences, à ses fantaisies, et combien de serviteurs inconnus s'empressaient autour de lui pour le surveiller, le diriger, l'aider, le secourir, écarter de lui tout danger et le faire vivre sans même qu'il s'en aperçut![10]

The remarks imply the awareness that a wholeness, an organic or mechanical wholeness in this city can be identified and characterized. He set out to explore every angle of the city and describe the life of its inhabitants, presumably in hopes of revealing this unity.[11]

The Paris Du Camp set out to portray had the reputation of being a capital of *corruption*, the *bourbier* described in the novels of Balzac, the place

---

[8] Sainte-Beuve, "Les Chants modernes de Maxime Du Camp", *Causeries du lundi*, Paris, 1857, 17.

[9] Maxime du Camp, *Souvenirs Littéraires*, Paris, 1994, 554.

[10] Du Camp, *Paris: ses organes, ses fonctions et sa vie dans la seconde moitié du XIXe siècle*, Paris, 1869-1875, I, 4-5.

[11] Daniel Oster speaks in terms of the writer's conversion (see Daniel Oster, "Le Paris de Maxime Du Camp", *Corps Ecrit*, March-October 1989, 88).

where ambitions are cynically fulfilled or frustrated, the capital of sin and, as was certainly the case, the pleasure capital of the world. But having experienced three major revolutions in a little over half a century, Paris, as Christopher Prendergast reminds us, also had the reputation of being a centre of revolutionary activity – another reputation that was well deserved.[12]

Du Camp undertakes his research as a massive project of urban renewal is going forward. It is being performed under the supervision of the Baron Haussmann, the Prefect of the Seine in the government of Napoleon III. As is well known, this project involved, among other things, the highly controversial destruction of poor tenement housing with the consequent dislocation of less well-to-do inhabitants, the revamping of sanitary facilities and the construction of major arteries that cut through neighbourhood units. Many disciples of Saint-Simon co-operated with Napoleon's government in this reconstruction, believing, as did the Emperor, that a healthy physical context was the key to a positive moral environment.[13] Du Camp's enthusiasm, as he conceives the well-run, smoothly functioning city of the future is evident throughout his work.

Knowing important government figures, occasionally attending social functions of the Empress Eugénie, Du Camp had no difficulty in being introduced to any administrator that might be of use to him in carrying out his research. Thus he was able to observe all the activities of the postal service and the railways, to learn how telegraphs worked, to visit police stations, prisons, homes for invalids and the elderly, schools, brothels, the general market, the morgue or whatever place that involved, in some way, the city administration.[14]

Each chapter of *Paris* begins with an historical account of the administrative department under study. In the presentation of the telegraph, for example, the author describes the history of long-distance communication from the earliest signals to the telegraph itself. Throughout the work, great attention is devoted to how machines function. The Second Empire's fascination with efficiency as noted by Prendergast (189-90), and its belief in the superiority of present-day services to those of the past are supremely evident in Du Camp's study. Efficiency is evoked time and time again. For example, Du Camp describes with admiration the split-second timing of the workers who sort the mail, the speed and precision involved in slaughtering an animal, or the work of the police as they control fraud and ensure the smooth functioning of entities such as the central food market. *Paris* echoes the spirit strongly evident in Second Empire France: fascination for the operation of machines and for the efficiency implied in technological innovations. It is significant that Du Camp's original inspiration to

---

[12] Christopher Prendergast, *Paris and the Nineteenth Century*, Oxford, 1995, 79.

[13] See Prendergast, ch. 5

[14] For Du Camp's own view of his activities, see *Souvenirs littéraires*, 555.

investigate the functioning of Paris came to him in the year that witnessed one of a series of great expositions, that of 1867, in which science and technology played a large role.

Another theme that runs through *Paris* is that of disease and the treatment of disease, which is generally a metaphor for all anti-social behaviour such as theft, fraud and prostitution. City officials are portrayed as constantly engaged in combating these "diseases", these forms of deviant behaviour. Two types of metaphor thus prevail in Du Camp's narrative: that of machines, and that of organisms, the latter recalling perhaps Duveyrier's utopian vision of a city that resembles a healthy human body.

This is a further example of something which is of particular interest in this work, that is, that Du Camp, in his celebration of that which is material, has developed highly effective literary techniques to portray the city. To some degree the *poète* and *romancier* are still present. The sheer quantity of detail, such as the array of food products in the central market, or the activities of the people involved, artfully arranged by the narrator so that these details speak for themselves without interference on his part, gives the reader a sense of authenticity and of presence in the scene. Interestingly enough, Zola consulted Du Camp as he prepared his own book that seeks to bring the Halles to life in print, *Le Ventre de Paris*.[15] While Du Camp's *Paris* is not without pedantic and tedious moments, there emerge scenes of life which are striking and effective because the rich assortment of visual impressions enable the reader to reconstruct Paris in his or her own imagination.

An episode that demonstrates the curing of disease, the excision of a cancer in the body politic, is that of the execution of a prisoner. However grotesque the subject may seem, it exemplifies especially well the techniques that enable Du Camp to heighten the sense of drama of the scene. There is first a description of the physical setting: the prisoner's quarters, then the place where the execution will take place. These broad perspectives are interspersed with close-ups and private details such as the prisoner's face as he expresses the wish to have a lock of his hair sent to his brother; contrasting with the private details, never over-dramatized, are the cryptic comments, culled from assorted members of the crowd, that summarize with apparent objectivity the attitudes of the public. The actual procession from the cell to the guillotine is narrated with a masterful sense of timing, worthy of certain scenes in novels such as Flaubert's *Education sentimentale*. In this case, the rapidity of the actual execution is skilfully conveyed in the use of verb tenses and contrasts with the slowness of the procession. The modulation of time, as well as the technique of spot lighting in scenes such as the execution make one think of the devices used in cinema and television

---

[15] See notes to *Ventre de Paris* in Emile Zola, *Les Rougons-Macquart*, I, Paris, 1963, 1616.

reportage. Most important of all, the details generally speak for themselves since the overbearing narrators of the novels have all but disappeared.

Such moments in *Paris* confirm Du Camp's own judgment: that his writing is most convincing when he observes his material and describes what he sees. He is not alone, to be sure. The popular press, commercially motivated, is full of descriptions of Paris life, as Walter Benjamin has shown. Newspapers and magazines delve into every aspect of city life that can possibly be of interest to all sorts of readers, including even the *voyeur*. A magazine such as *L'Illustration*, with engraved illustrations of the scenes described in the articles, doubtless whetted the nineteenth-century reader's appetite for pictorial representation of reality. *Paris* possesses multiplicity of appeal, too, as it offers the "inside story". In a sense, the work offers the services of a department store (a burgeoning institution during the Second Empire) or the arcades described by Benjamin, insofar as it sets forth products, in this case descriptions, to suit every taste and is therefore not an attempt to present a dispassionately complete and rigorously documented report on Paris life.[16] The reader has access to the thrills of the forbidden or the inaccessible: insane asylums, women's prisons, places and machinery usually not visible to the public. Not many readers would otherwise have had the chance to witness in close-up that the now decapitated prisoner's body still wriggles as it falls into a waiting basket (although whether or not this should be considered a good thing is a different matter). The comment of the usually silent narrator, "C'est terrible!" seems incongruous, after the description that satisfies the reader's possibly prurient or sadistic interest in a forbidden activity, as if the writer needed to reassure the reader that he did not intend to appeal to such instincts. *Paris* is, in any case, designed not only for the serious, socially conscious reader, but also for the flâneur, the aimless wanderer and for the *voyeur* that Benjamin writes about.

The alienation of the writer from the city is, of course, one prominent theme in nineteenth-century France, as Jean-Calude Susini's interesting analysis of Baudelaire's "Je n'ai pas oublié" reminds us.[17] Du Camp seems diametrically opposed, however, to this tendency towards alienation, as he both rejoices in the sensations offered by the city and celebrates the benefits of the efficient functioning. Du Camp's masterwork successfully combines two governing conceptions. One is that of the regenerated city – Paris as the new Athens, or the city of light. The other, which becomes especially prominent towards the end of the long work, is that of the city as threatened still by degeneration. The capital could even disintegrate and die one day. The fear of such an outcome derives from the outbreak, at a certain point, of the Franco-Prussian War and then from the constitution of the *Commune*,

---

[16] Walter Benjamin, *Das Passages – Werk*, 2 vols, Frankfurt am Main, 1982.

[17] Jean-Claude Susini, "'Voisin de la ville': Baudelaire et l'espace suburbain", in *French Literature in/and the City*, ed. Norman Buford, Amsterdam/Atlanta: GA, 1997, 129-40.

which, incidentally, caused the destruction of much of the documentation that Du Camp needed for his study. But the social fabric of his city had already been torn apart by the massive destruction and reconstruction of old districts, and, as Du Camp suggests, by new workers brought in to accomplish this task as well as with the arrival of other outsiders.

Our final impression, though, is of an ongoing tension between the creative and the destructive forces, still kept under control by the selfless, even heroic civil servants, who make up the Paris bureaucracy. The freedom fighters celebrated in the short stories of Du Camp have given way to city officials, never named, never given a recognizable physiognomy, whose task is basically that of managing the city's affairs and keeping discipline. The governing principle of *Paris* seems no longer to be the Saint-Simonian one, associated with the mission of enlightening all of humanity – indeed Du Camp dissociated himself from Saint-Simonianism[18] – but rather the principle that everyone must work to ensure the smooth functioning of an administrative machine or maintain the threatened health of the urban body politic. Absolute imperatives and transcendent conceptions of good and evil, implied in the religious origins of nineteenth-century social thought have been redefined in *Paris*. We are now offered the value of efficiency and order as opposed to the disorder represented by deviant social behaviour. The evolution in the thought of Du Camp seems characteristic of that of nineteenth-century France: from the metaphysically inspired social aspirations of the first part of the century to the more practical possibilities of the technological and capitalistic order envisaged during the Second Empire.

Du Camp seems thus to have discovered that the writer, as Benjamin suggests, can no longer interact with a city as representative of a transcending Saint-Simonian-inspired truth or even unity. But he does not merely "reduce the city to what we can comprehend within our field of vision", to borrow the phrase of Priscilla Ferguson referring to nineteenth-century portrayals of the French capital.[19] Paris remains somewhere in between a visionary location and a purely physical presence. So, too, does Du Camp as a writer bring some of the zeal of the Saint-Simonian priest and the skills of the artist into his rediscovered role of reporter. Because of the tensions both within the city as the object observed and within the author as a subject observing, the six-volume study gains its own vitality as possibly one of the most ambitious and vivid delineations that we have of the urban material during the Second Empire.

---

[18] Maxime Du Camp, *Souvenirs littéraires*, Paris, 1994, 408-26. In this work, first published in 1882-83, Du Camp describes some of the extreme aspects of the behaviour of the Saint-Simonians, denies that he was ever a disciple of their leader, Prosper Enfantin, but admits that he had been fascinated with their ideas.

[19] Priscilla Parkhurst Ferguson, "You'll never be French, but you *can* be Parisian: Fashion and Food in Proust's Paris", *French Literature Series: French Literature and the City*, XXIV (1997), 112.

FACING THE TRUTH: TWO BELFAST NOVELS

WIM TIGGES

The attitude expressed by twentieth-century Irish writers towards their cities seems to be predominantly a mixture of love and hatred; phrases like James Joyce's "dear dirty Dublin" or James Plunkett's "strumpet city" give expression to an ironizing attitude also found in Frank McCourt's recent, best-selling *Angela's Ashes* (1996) – acclaimed for doing for Limerick what Joyce did for Dublin – when the narrator is repeatedly aware of the clearly ironical notion that "everyone knows Limerick is the holiest city in Ireland".[1] More than anything else, the Irish city appears to feature as a myth, the myth of what Frank O'Connor has called the "submerged population group",[2] whose less submerged heroes of the past are now petrified in the names of the streets and squares they pass daily – Wolfe Tone Street, O'Connell Street, Parnell Square, Pearse Street – stony as Cuchulain in the Dublin Central Post Office.

Indeed, the streets and squares, statues and public buildings in a city are a constant reminder of the past, to those that have to live in the present, and to survive into the future. In some cities, however, this is obviously more self-evident than in others. Even in a time of tenuous peace, Belfast can never, since the division of Ireland, have been an easy place to live in – for thousands of people it has been only too easy a place in which to die, or get maimed for life. In this essay, I will discuss two recent novels by Northern Irish writers, in which the city of Belfast plays a major role: Mary Beckett's *Give Them Stones* (1988) and Robert McLiam Wilson's *Eureka Street* (1996).[3] Written respectively by a Belfast-born woman and man who belong to different generations, these novels are also complementary in structure, style, and tone. Mary Beckett's first person narrator, Roman Catholic Martha Murtagh, born like her author in 1926,

---

[1] Frank McCourt, *Angela's Ashes: A Memoir of a Childhood*, London, 1996, rpt. 1997, 163.

[2] Frank O'Connor, *The Lonely Voice: A Study of the Short Story*, London, 1965 (orig. 1962), 18.

[3] Page references to these novels will be given between brackets in the main text. For *Give Them Stones* the references are to the Bloomsbury paperback edition, for *Eureka Street* to the Minerva paperback edition.

presents a restrained but incisive chronological account of her life on the outskirts of Belfast, that includes the vicissitudes of four generations of her relatives against the background of the often violent history of her city. In this largely monotopic but diachronic novel, domestic "troubles" are weighed against public Troubles. During the process, Martha learns to "face the truth" (152) about herself, her family, her status (or rather lack of one) as a woman (daughter, wife and mother), a Catholic, a representative of the working class, and an inhabitant of that city that is her only familiar home.

Wilson's *Eureka Street*, on the other hand, is polytopic (although firmly anchored in Belfast) and synchronic, covering only some six months just before and after the August 1994 ceasefire. Eight of its nineteen chapters are narrated by seedy man-about-town Jake Jackson, Catholic, born, like his author, in 1964. The other chapters are a third-person narration, most of them centring around Jake's Protestant chum, fat and fame-seeking Charles ("Chuckie") Lurgan, who lives with his mother Peggy in a flat in Eureka Street. In contrast to the resigned and dignified realistic style of *Give Them Stones*, the style of *Eureka Street* is mainly demotic, and the novel breathes a postmodern flair and occasionally super-realistic atmosphere.

It is hard to believe that the writing of these novels is only eight years apart. But from both novels, albeit in very different ways, it becomes clear that the beauty of Belfast is in the eye of the beholder, and also that there are two basically simple solutions to its brutality (in terms of learning to live with): love and labour. An illustrative reading of both books may serve to demonstrate in particular how an imaginative sense of the city's identity can enable its inhabitants to face its truths, and to survive its traumas.

It is the knee-capping of a boy by two Provisional IRA-men, soon after the Long Kesh hunger strikes, that triggers Martha Murtagh's account of her life in Belfast, starting off with her childhood in her grandmother's house on the city's north-western boundaries. "At home", she begins the second chapter, "we were reared very gently. I had heard children talking about being beaten. I had seen women pulling at their children and slapping bare legs with their hands. It never happened to us." Violence seems remote, in both space and time. Her grandfather had left for America "in 1921 when the Protestants chased all the Catholics out of the Island" (11) and has not been heard from since, and her grandmother and mother have to work in the nearby linen mill. Significantly, Martha will never learn to do needlework, although she has to work in the same mill and in a textile factory during her teens and early twenties.

At primary school, where she witnesses the unjust violent punishment of a schoolmate by a hysterical head teacher (a memory which flashes into her mind like an epiphany when she lies sleepless in bed after the knee-capping event), she becomes shamefully aware of her Belfast accent, thinking she can get rid of it (14). She observes political squabbles going on between her maternal uncles. Uncle Joe, a socialist, who dates her birth to the General Strike of January 1926, is willing to overlook the difference between Irish and English workers, but Uncle Jimmy, a nationalist, argues that the English should run their own country, and that "We should be in the Free State" (16). Her father, who started out as a barman in a Belfast pub which "was burnt out by the Protestants in the Troubles" is put in gaol for being in the IRA, but he "certainly never belonged to any organisation" after Martha was born (17).

Cave Hill, whose top was really called MacArt's Fort, where Wolfe Tone had addressed a meeting of United Irishmen, announcing the freedom of Ireland, is a favourite place for outings, and her father and two cousins are there, looking for bilberries, when the Troubles of 1935 break out on 12 July:

> ... it was a place with a great view that could let people long, long ago see for miles if an enemy or invader was coming .... I didn't like the stories about tribes attacking or being besieged but I loved listening to how Ireland was going to be free. I'd look off down Belfast Lough with the ships in it and the shipyard ... and I'd think wouldn't it be lovely if it was really our own country that we could be proud in, instead of being kept in cramped little streets with no jobs for the men and sneered at by the people who deprived us. It was as if we were all in prison looking out at a beautiful world we'd never walk free in (18).

But in Belfast there have been shootings that day, and Uncle Jimmy is arrested by the RUC. The shootings continue all summer. "In some districts the houses were burnt and people moved with a few sticks of furniture they could salvage to an airy new estate where each house had a garden, between our street and the mountains", and men are shot standing at street corners (20):

> On the opposite side of the road were Protestant streets – not very different from ours except there were not as many children and the doors and windows were more often shut, and better painted (21).

In the composition she writes for her scholarship examination (a scholarship which she has to refuse because her wages will be needed at home), Martha reminisces about her excursion to the labourers' cottages just below Cave Hill, about "looking down on Belfast with all its lights as if it was a Christmas tree" (27). Martha's younger sister Mary Brigid is allowed to go on to secondary school, but Martha has to start work in the linen mill. Her father, meanwhile, has been interned and will remain in prison all through the Second World War. New violence hits the area in the Blitz of Easter 1941, and her brother Danny comes home

> telling us that houses were wrecked two streets away and people killed and whole blocks of houses down on the Protestant side of the road. He said he'd heard the Protestants saying that the Pope was in the first plane to show the Germans not to bomb Catholic streets (30).

Her mother takes the three children to two sisters of her grandfather, who live in the countryside near Lough Neagh. Significantly, Martha finds the country "threatening" (34), but she will stay with her great-aunts for five years, her mother, Mary Brigid and Danny returning to Belfast after a short while. It is during her lengthy stay with her great-aunts Maggie and Bessie that Martha learns to bake soda bread, which will become a life-fulfilling occupation for her until the time of writing. She is surprised to learn from Maggie that "there's nothing wrong with Protestants here" (40). However, "In spite of learning in the catechism that the Church was universal", Martha always feels

> that Catholics were only fit for backstreets and boglands and if by any chance you penetrated into the Protestant world they would no more mention your strange religion than you would draw attention to a disfiguring birthmark. I didn't think we were inferior except in wealth and opportunity but to the world I glimpsed in books we were invisible (46).

Martha is yearning to go back to Belfast, "just to run away like the coward I was" (54), but she stays on until both her great-aunts have died. She returns to her parents' house in October 1946, having inherited her great-aunts' farm, which she has sold without her parents' knowledge. Back in Belfast, she works in a textile factory without much success, and bakes the bread for her mother, while her father, now removed from prison to hospital with tuberculosis, lies dying. She takes Irish lessons and meets Dermot Hughes. When she sees the oven at Dermot's mother's house, she knows she wants to marry him, and so she does, moving in with the Hugheses, who according to Dermot have owned their house "for hundreds of years" (76) – an apparent lie, in fact, a myth of possession.

The point to be made at this stage is that the narrator is not made to look back from "these terrible times" to a careless, happy youth and early married life. Martha feels neglected by her mother, ignored and forgotten by her dying father, passed over by her ambitious younger sister and her sullen brother, tolerated by her great-aunts, terrorized at school, uncouth at work, too shy to make love – and yearning for love and fulfilment all the time. But she does not complain: "I never was any good at asking for things", she remarks almost exactly halfway through the book (82). Her husband is kind but spoilt and selfish, and she has to earn her own housekeeping money. Envying her sister the birth of a daughter, she bears four sons within six years, and after that refrains from sexual intercourse. She is treated spitefully by her sister-in-law Theresa, but never complains, because she "just never answered back" (94). It is, of course, highly ironical that this otherwise strong-minded woman, in her thirties like Ireland and Northern Ireland, refuses to play the possession game, to fight the battle of "asking for things" and answering back – a battle which continues around her until the time of writing, when she decides at last to let them know what she thinks (10).

After the death of her mother-in-law, Martha decides to start selling bread rather than give it away, and she begins trading with the local community. In order to be able to have an extension built to their house, a move which Dermot does not really approve of but tolerates, she travels by train to see the solicitor who has taken care of the money she has received from selling her great-aunts' farm. It is as if Belfast, her anchor, is only really there when she is travelling away from it:

> The train left the old railway station in Great Victoria Street and chugged past the back of blackened brick houses much the same as ours except that there were things written up like "Prepare to meet thy God" and "The Wages of sin is death". It was a cold day with frost and near Lisburn there was a fog so that the view disappeared and trees were only darker shapes in the gloom. After that when the sun came out my heart lifted and I thought maybe it was a good sign. But even in the broad sunshine the frost on the fields didn't melt and the twigs on the bushes in the hedges stayed white like Christmas decorations. There wasn't a soul stirring. The big houses were planted on the tops of round hills with a view right down the valleys harking back to our ancestors on the Cave Hill. I saw very few wee houses like the ones round Maggie's and Bessie's. This was country for big farmers with houses far apart. I was glad that I was back living in Belfast with rows of houses and the smoke tugging parallel black out of all the chimneys and everybody keeping everybody else warm (103-104).

It is a picture of Belfast literally in black and white, with a notable return to the Christmas tree motif we saw earlier on, and an emphasis on the sense of sight. To Martha, Belfast is essentially a view from Cave Hill, but also a sense of closeness, of warmth.

The floods that hit Belfast that same year are considered a punishment by Martha, but they also trigger political awareness. Needing to replace her spoilt flour she exchanges views with a local shopkeeper, who complains to her about his ruined stocks:

> "Did you ever go to the City Hall and tell them to do something about it?" I asked and he leaned across, tapping on the counter. "Every time it happens I go and every time I get fobbed off. I write letters to the Corporation and I get no answer."
> "We must have an MP?" I said because I couldn't remember voting. There was hardly ever a contest in our constituency or if there was it was between a Unionist and a bitter Unionist.
> "That oul' Unionist! What does he care about us? A major in the British army. What would he know about a dirty flood disrupting our lives? We're just like the natives in India – we should get used to it." (109)

But life goes on, even in Belfast. Mention is made of unemployment in the Sixties, the closing down of factories, the civil rights movement of 1968, the beginning, or rather renewal, of the Troubles in Belfast.

One day, when I bought jerseys for the boys "made in the Republic of Ireland"
and just afterwards saw a big ice-cream lorry up from Dublin, I said to Mary
Brigid optimistically, "Maybe the border will just fade away with people wearing
clothes and eating food from one part to the other."
All Mary Brigid said was, "You and your united Ireland! Are you always thinking
about it?"
"No," I said, "I'm always thinking of baking bread and selling it and feeding my
family and what they'll be when they grow up but the thought of the border's like
a nail sticking up in my shoe. I've got used to it but it's never comfortable."
    She just laughed.
It was great excitement that year. Some people got fed up with it but it was like
drink to me – the meetings and the interviews day after day at tea-time when I had
the shop closed. Dermot wasn't really interested but he pretended to be to humour
me. I had the constant feeling that Stormont was on the edge of the cliff on Cave
Hill and something would topple it over.
That was all very well until some of the people in our parish who lived in
Protestant streets were ordered out of their houses. I tried not to believe it. I said it
was only a carried story. I said maybe they wanted to get into new houses in
Ballymurphy and used this as a reason. I talked like a Unionist because I couldn't
bear to think of it happening. Then we saw the fighting in Derry and had to
believe it but we weren't in any way prepared for it in Belfast and we had no
defence when Protestant mobs set fire to all the streets that led off the main road.
They couldn't get in as far as us but when I saw all those wee houses going up in
blazes and children crying and women screaming and the men in desperation
because they weren't able to do anything, I was in a rage. The next day they built
barricades across the streets and the young lads were ready with stones and lumps
of piping. None of them had guns.
"Where's the IRA now when we need them?" the women said when they came in
for their bread, terrified (118-19).

Then the British army move in, and British soldiers become her customers,
as the situation becomes more and more grim. After the Falls Road curfew of
July 1970, "There were plenty of rough things" and "Riots kept happening" and
"people living away from their own had to leave or be burnt out" (124). Soon
afterwards, her brother Danny, who has joined the IRA, is shot dead, and Martha
is questioned by the British military, but she defends herself like a man. Life in
Belfast becomes a history of explosions and bomb scares, and Martha is shocked
by the loss of dignity of terrified hotel workers at the Europa Hotel, which also
features prominently in Wilson's *Eureka Street*. After Bloody Sunday in Derry,
we are told how local society becomes demoralized: "All my lovely escape
world disappeared but nobody else had any escape so why should I?" (134). Her
two elder sons move out – Patrick, the eldest, with a degree in Queen's
University, as a translator in Strasburg; the second, Declan, as a mechanic in
Dublin. The two youngest, Owen and Eamon, enlist in the Irish army and "they
liked it well, especially when they were sent a couple of times to the Lebanon"
(136):

Another thing was happening. Streets were knocked down and new houses were
built – very pretty wee houses with trees in front. Even in our street where there
was no word of that, people were leaving, and empty houses had their windows
filled with concrete blocks.

"We'll never leave, sure we won't, Martha?" Dermot said to me, like a child,
and I just shrugged.

"Where would we go?" (137)

Returning from Declan's wedding in Dublin, Martha muses: "I just feel a terrible
deep sadness that there is no life in Belfast for our children" (138). This is the
"lost generation" that features so largely in *Eureka Street*.

Having expressed her appalled concern about Patrick's loss of faith, Martha
is surprised to hear her eldest son retort: "You never had time for us all our lives,
not one of us. All you cared about was your baking and your shop" (139).
Shortly afterwards, the knee-capping of the boy at the wall of her shop by
"order-keeping" Provos occurs, and Martha decides to stop her small weekly
contribution to their fund for relatives, refusing to support cruelty. In retaliation,
the couple are burnt out of their house, and Dermot moves in temporarily with
his sister, shocked at the loss of his parental home, while Martha is taken in by
Mary Brigid. Soon afterwards, they move into a new house, and Martha thinks
of opening a bakery in an old shop close by, refusing to give in: "If I am not
baking bread I am nobody and nothing" (147). She has faced the truth of life in
Belfast and of her marital life, and, in spite of her disappointment about her
husband's motives in marrying her, as she perceives them, she realizes that
Dermot's helpful words ("I'll do anything at all for you") may be true from his
point of view. In the final sentence of the novel she admits that "maybe I don't
always face the truth about myself either" (152).

Some questions to be posed if not answered here are: is this woman's life
spoiled by her living in Belfast, or by her being who she is? Or is her life not
really spoiled at all? Is *Give Them Stones* (a title Mary Beckett has derived from
a passage in Nathanael West's novella *Miss Lonelyhearts*, which serves as the
novel's epigraph but which itself, of course, carries the Biblical references of
man not living by bread alone and being given stones for bread) a novel about
Martha Murtagh, or about Belfast? Perhaps the difficulty of answering yes to the
first two questions depends on one's giving an unconditional affirmative answer
to the final option. In *Give Them Stones* the city is, in my view, more than a mere
setting, although perhaps not so prominently as in *Eureka Street*. Lovingly
viewed from Cave Hill, from a departing train, the stones and lights of Belfast
are the stones Martha cannot live without. But neither, of course, can Belfast
continue to exist without inhabitants like Martha.

Eureka Street starts off in the early spring of 1994. Jake Jackson, a Roman
Catholic repossession worker, whose job requires occasional violence when
unpaid goods have to be reclaimed (indiscriminate violence, like so much other
Northern violence, rendered to Protestant and Catholic alike), has lost his

English girlfriend Sarah six months earlier. England has "repossessed" Sarah
from him, he feels later on (72). In fact, she has left because, as a broadsheet
journalist having to report Northern Irish violence, she does not want to live in
Belfast any more, hating her job (as Jake hates his) after two years of killings.
Jake has bought the flat they shared on Poetry Street near Adelaide Halt
(Railway Station) in south-west Belfast, not very far away from Eureka Street
near Sandy Row, where Jake's chum Chuckie Lurgan shares a flat with his
mother.

   More than is the case in *Give Them Stones*, the physique of the city is
vitalized in *Eureka Street* by the mention of street names, for instance when
following in some detail the trajectories of car drives or long walks made by its
major characters, somewhat in the manner of James Joyce's *Ulysses*. Poetry
Street, which is in "bourgeois Belfast" (13) and which always disappointed
Sarah's English friends and family "by the lack of burnt-out cars or foot patrols"
(14), may well be fictional, but there is a Eureka Drive near where Eureka Street
is said to be situated, and most (if not all) of the sixty-odd names of streets,
avenues, roads, squares, and so on can easily be traced on a map of Belfast.[4] As
was pointed out at the start of this essay, city street names carry memories of the
past. They can be reassuring as well as, one supposes, offensive (depending on
one's creed or political conviction), inoffensively neutral, and highly ironical.
Many Belfast street names would remind the passer-by of the colonial past –
and, in the eyes of many, desirable or undesirable present. Royal Avenue,
Victoria Street and Great Victoria Street, Albert Square, Queen's Square,

---

[4] The following names feature in *Eureka Street*, in order of appearance (the names of
locations that have not been retrieved in the 1994 edition of the Ordnance Survey of
Northern Ireland *Greater Belfast Street Map* are given in italics): Hope Street (2, 212,
215); Lisburn Road (3, 170, 284, 288); *Poetry Street* (3 and *passim*); Delhi Street (16);
Shaftesbury Square (19, 170, 358); Governor's Bridge (19); Ormeau Bridge (23);
Agincourt Avenue (23); *Democracy Street* (24); Damascus Street (24), Jerusalem Street
(24); *Constitution Street* (25); Palestine Street (26); Botanic Avenue (35); Donegall Place
(26, 235); College Street (27); Cairo Street (32); Pacific Avenue (35); *Eureka Street* (36
and *passim*); Chemical Street (36); Sandy Row (47, 158, 267, 284); Bradbury Place (61,
203); Ottawa Street (62); Shore Road (65, 105); *Peace Street* (65); *Parliament Street* (65);
Iris Drive (65); *Bosnia Street* (75); Arthur Street (82); Abyssinia Street (91); Antrim Road
(103); Bedford Street (132, 201, 235, 348); Great Victoria Street (132, 358); Lower
Crescent (137); Donegall Road (143); Cornmarket (166); Falls Road (168, 300); Elmwood
Avenue (170); Dublin Road (171); Century Street (197); Grosvenor Road (203); Clifton
Street (204); Carmel Street (212); Cedar Avenue (212); Arizona Street (212); *Sixth Street*
(212); *Electric Street* (212); Brunswick Street (213); *Chapel Street* (215); Chichester
Street (213); Chief Street (215); *Cable Street* (215); Royal Avenue (218, 233); Queen's
Arcade (221, 226); *Fountain Place* (222); Fountain Street (223 and *passim*); Castle Street
(227, 233); Donegall Square (235); the Westlink (299, 359); Glengall Street (358); Divis
Street (360); Leeson Street (362); Templemore Avenue (370); Newtownards Road (371).
Give Them Stones has references to: Hightown Road (18); York Street (20); Falls Road
(22, 71); Royal Avenue (71); Great Victoria Street (103); Crumlin Road (110).

Wellington Place, Albion Street and Union Street would, one expects, be reassuring to the Loyalist citizen, whereas one doubts how many Catholics would feel comfortable in Cromwell Street or Ireton Street. Protestants might feel themselves more at home in the "Holy Land", with names like Damascus Street, Jerusalem Street, Palestine Street. The names in the area west of Ormeau Road with its Elm Street, Oak Way and Pine Way would reassure not only the tree lover; but names such as Hope Street, Joy Street, Friendly Street, Peace Street and Pacific Avenue are, of course, highly ironic in view of the Troubles. Falls Road and Shankill Road have sadly become notorious names the world over.

In what follows I would like to concentrate on the way in which Wilson recreates the city of Belfast as the true protagonist of his novel, its material plot being largely the interweaving of Jake's search for a meaningful love relationship and more purposeful work, and Chuckie's clever rise from bum to millionaire by means of outrageous manipulation of the credulity of his fellow citizens and inspired by the love for his new American girlfriend Max, who has "fled" to Belfast (where her father, a diplomat, had been shot on arrival) after a very turbulent life. There are subplots as well, concerning Chuckie's growing appreciation of his mother and the changes that suddenly come into her personal life with the ceasefires (she ends up in a Lesbian relationship with a caring neighbour), and Jake's commiseration with Roche, a twelve-year old boy from Falls, who is neglected by his mother and regularly beaten up by his father. What is most directly relevant is that all these and other characters are seen as individual and unique protagonists in the novel which is Belfast. In the novel's central Chapter 10, from which I will quote in more detail later on, because it is in effect a paean to the city of Belfast, the third-person narrator establishes that "The city is a novel" (215), and its citizens "epic", "tender" and, tragically, "murderable" (217).

After affirming, more generally even, "All stories are love stories" (1), the narrator shifts into first person, as Jake, sitting in a bar chatting up a waitress, has to be careful in order not to say "something too Catholic" as the big Protestant bouncer flashes his UVF tattoos (8) – the next night he will be "scared of not seeming Catholic enough" when a different bouncer wears Republican tattoos (18). It is by means of such witty echoes that Wilson establishes the schizophrenic atmosphere pervading this divisive city which shares "the status of the battlefield", well-known to all the world:

> The place-names of the city and country had taken on the resonance and hard beauty of all history's slaughter venues. The Bogside, Crossmaglen, The Falls, The Shankill and Andersonstown. In the mental maps of those who had never been in Ireland, these places had tiny crossed swords after their names. People thought them deathfields – remote, televised knackers' yards. Belfast was only big because Belfast was bad.

As if in direct rapport with Martha Murtagh from *Give Them Stones*, the narrator continues:

> And who would have thought it thirty years before? Little Belfast could be such a beautiful city. Squatting flat in the oxter of Belfast Lough, hazily level with the water, the city was ringed with mountains and nudged by the sea. When you looked up the length of most Belfast streets, there was some kind of mountain or hill staring back at you (14).

Whereas Martha observes the city from Cave Hill, from outside and above, Jake has a complementary view from inside, from the streets up to the hills. Everyday he cleans the windows of his otherwise dilapidated and "shitty" car ("the Wreck") "so that I could see my city when I drove" (16). Walking after closing time with Mary, the waitress, he dodges "the chuck-out crowds in Shaftesbury Square, with all their shouts and pukes and fights" and chooses "a more lyrical path ... by the river where everything could feel briefly eighteenth century" (19), a pointed reference to Belfast's peaceful and civilized origins.

Coming home to Poetry Street, Jake notices a new graffito: OTG. As one of Jake's friends will remark towards the end of the novel, Belfast is "the city of the three-letter initial written on walls" (356), and it turns out that "OTG", which is never explained, may mean anything, and may indeed be a satire on the "ritual" of writing on the walls: "IRA, INLA, UVF, UFF, UDA, IPLO, FTP (Fuck the Pope), FTQ (Fuck the Queen), and once (hilariously) FTNP (Fuck the Next Pope)" (22). The new and unexplained graffito OTG will run like a thread through the novel, speedily seen as a serious threat by the RUC, and at some stage even claimed by Chuckie Lurgan as the initials of a new political movement he is going to co-operate with.

Beautiful as he finds his city, with "its citizens ... mild and lovable as children", Jake longs to leave Belfast whenever he "inadvertently" hears a news story, a feeling he gets "twice a week every week of the year": "When the bad things happened, I always wanted to leave and let Belfast rot", but that, he muses, is "what living in this place was all about" (61). He realizes that his own aggression (he gets into a fight on several occasions during the novel) is due to his lack of imagination (62) – a lack of imagination which also, paradoxically, allows decent people such as his foster-parents Matt and Mamie to see the world as a "loving world", failing to "understand shabbiness or harm" (111).

While Jake Jackson is making these discoveries and exchanges his job for a more peaceful one as a "construction worker" or "brickie" (an interesting version of the "give them stones" motif), Chuckie Lurgan builds his own future, getting his starting capital by means of a hilarious "Giant Dildo Offer" scheme. Advertising a mail order for this *risqué* "love tool" at "a sensational £9.99", which one would have thought quite out of place in a Puritan city, he offers a refund when his "stock" (which really consists of a single item) runs out. Of course, very few of his potential buyers care to cash a refund cheque stamped "GIANT DILDO REFUND". Chuckie legitimately cashes several thousand pounds within a few days, and starts to apply for business project grants on behalf of enterprises such as "genuine Irish leprechaun walking sticks" (156), consisting of ten thousand twigs collected by local boys from the foot of the hills, varnished by a furniture restorer and exported wholesale to the United States at a net profit of $ 40,000.

By the end of the novel Chuckie will be a millionaire, fêted by American tycoons and literally taking the mickey out of the Republican movement. A Methodist by origin, Chuckie has a strong ecumenical bias, and most of his fanciful enterprises carry that label. Belfast becomes a city where everything is possible. Towards the end of the novel, Jake admiringly informs us that

> Chuckie's rapid accruing of wealth had not been without its amorally democratic grandeur. He had ripped off and duped Protestants and Catholics with egalitarian zeal. He was a pan-cultural exploiter. I had discovered that he had bought a controlling share in a regalia company that supplied the Orange lodges and Loyalist bands that marched so Protestantly on the Twelfth of July. He had just negotiated a contract for this company to supply the Vatican with various regalia and uniforms. If anyone heard about this, Chuckie would be hung upside down from some street-lamp in East Belfast (307-308).

Meanwhile, mostly drugged by nitrazepam, Chuckie's mother knows "how this small city in which they lived could expand or contract at will, leaving them feeling claustrophobic or agoraphobic as paranoid circumstance demanded" (136-37), reflecting another familiar city motif, that of the city as literally a living organism. Jake, on the other hand, working in a team including a racist Protestant and a Muslim, has a Pisgah view of Belfast from the roof of the Europa Hotel, repeatedly bombed and repeatedly under repair:

> ... I loved this roof. It was the only good thing about working there. Failure always has some upside. The hotel was one of the tallest buildings in this flat, flat town and I could see all Belfast from up there. I could see the City Hospital like a biscuit box with orange trim. I could see the bruised, carious Falls. I could see the breezeblock rubble and trubble of Rathcoole, fat and ominous in the thinned distance. I could even see the Holy Land. I could see all the police stations, I could see all the Army forts, I could see all the helicopters. But, from up there, the streets smelled sweet and Belfast was made of cardboard in the mild and cooling air (160).

In close contact with sectarian workmates as well as with the cultural crowd of Republican hangers-on headed by the "inappropriately famous" (173) poet Shague Ghinthoss and fanatically supported by Max's friend Aoirghe (with the inappropriate surname of Jenkins), Jake gets a proper taste of the "Belfast hatred ... a lumbering hatred that could survive comfortably on the memories of things that never existed in the first place" (164). His concern for young Roche, moreover, takes him out to West Belfast, where he himself was born, with its distinctive cityscape:

Beechmount looked like Beechmount always looked – small, unprosperous. Little terraced houses with little terraced people standing on the doorsteps. Some kids ran about the pavement as they always did and some broken glass lay around as was habitual. The walls were painted with a variety of crude scenes depicting how much nicer Catholics were than Protestants and a series of inventive tableaux in which large numbers of British soldiers were maimed and killed.

These were the Belfast mean streets, the internationally famous and dreaded West Side jungle. It was no big deal. The scorbutic children and big mamas were stock stuff. You could see worse in any city. Even as nearby as Dublin and London you could find more dramatic poverty, more profound deracination. You mightn't come across the same quality of Armalites but everything else would look much the same (205).

Returning home after delivering Roche at his doorstep, Jake feels the boy has been "enough to make Belfast seem like a washed-out mouth", and through his "clean, clean windscreen the city look[s] dirty suddenly" (207).

The five pages of text that constitute Chapter 10, printed without marginal justification, are very powerful in their evocation of Belfast by night when, "With so many of its people asleep, Belfast lay like an unlit room. The city rises and falls like music, like breathing" (212). After a bird's-eye view of some nightwalkers, graffiti, posters, billboards, flags ("There are a thousand flags, but five mere colours and only two designs. Green, white, gold, red and blue. The two three-coloured emblems of difference") and bunches of flowers commemorating the dead, the narrative continues:

> It is only late at night, if you stand up high, that you can see the city as one thing, as a single phenomenon. While all sleep, the daytime jumble is unified and, geographically at any rate, the city seems a single thing. You can see it ringed by its circles of black basalt, mountains, cliffs and plateaux. You can see the dark sea in the wide bay lapping right up to the foot of the metropolis, wetting its very heart.
>
> You can see that Belfast is, quite literally, a dump. Its core is built on level land that simply wasn't there two hundred years before. Earth was dumped into the sea and Belfast was built there. Slob land, reclamation. The city is a raised beach, an abutment. The townsfolk say it rose from the water like some god but the truth is that it was dumped in the sea but didn't sink.
>
> Belfast is Rome with more hills; it is Atlantis raised from the sea. And from anywhere you look, the streets glitter like jewels, like small strings of stars (213-14).

This city of "279,000 people ... squashed into 11,489 hectares" is "magical", but it is also a city "where people are prepared to kill and die for a few pieces of coloured cloth" (214). Its "most reliable" division, however, is money: "Belfast is a city that has lost its heart", having lost its shipbuilding, rope-making, linen-weaving: "A city can't survive without something to do with itself" (215). It is as if Wilson here applies Mary Beckett's epigraphic title to the city itself.

Cities are simple things. They are conglomerations of people. Cities are complex things. They are the geographical and emotional distillations of whole nations. What makes a place a city has little to do with size. It has to do with the speed at which its citizens walk, the cut of their clothes, the sound of their shouts.

But most of all, cities are the meeting places of stories. The men and women there are narratives, endlessly complex and intriguing. The most humdrum of them constitutes a narrative that would defeat Tolstoy at his best and most voluminous. The merest hour of the merest day of the merest of Belfast's citizens would be impossible to render in all its grandeur and beauty. In cities the stories are jumbled and jangled. They clash, they converge or convert. They are a Babel of prose.

And in the end, after generations and generations of the thousands and hundreds of thousands, the city itself begins to absorb narrative like a sponge, like paper absorbs ink. The past and the present is written here. The citizenry cannot fail to write there. Their testimony is involuntary and complete (215-16).

In the chapter that follows, one of these stories is brought up to the present and brought shatteringly to a halt, ironizing the concluding sentence of Chapter 10: "In Belfast, in all cities, it is always present tense and all the streets are Poetry Streets" (217). It is July 1994, shortly before the IRA ceasefire. Office worker Rosemary Daye walks through the centre of town in her luncheon break, revelling in the memories of her recent night spent with a new boyfriend, revelling in the joys of the flesh. She has "a map of the city whose milestones were places where she might look at herself" (219). She buys an expensive green skirt, finding the narrow Queen's Arcade "transfigured and glamorous", feeling "wrapped and snug in her skin", thinking "she would never be cold again" (221). She enters a small sandwich shop in Fountain Street – and ceases to exist. Seventeen people are killed and eleven seriously injured in the Fountain Street bombing, which Jake observes from the roof of the Europa Hotel. Details about some of these aborted "stories" are given factually, ironically. A "simple event" has happened:

> Some stories had been shortened. Some stories had been ended. A confident editorial decision had been taken (231).

After this *tour de force* of indictment, the novel moves back to the stories of Jake and Chuckie. The latter, charging Jake to take care of his shocked mother, who had been close to the bombing and forced to witness its gruesome results, travels off to America to trace Max, who has run off without notice – later we are informed why she has run off: she is pregnant by Chuckie and earlier had had a handicapped child. Walking the streets of Manhattan on the day of his arrival, Chuckie Lurgan is far more terrified than in violent Belfast:

> He expected every face he saw or could not see to do him some form of big-city harm. He waited for someone to pull a gun or a blade. The constant sirens made him walk twitchily, with the delicacy and strangeness of a soldier patrolling no man's land. He was used to the traditions of Belfast brutality and gunplay but

New Yorkers looked like they would all do it to you. They'd do it casually, quickly, and they'd enjoy it (257).

Later on the same day, he and the New York Irish detective he has hired to trace Max's whereabouts are mugged twice, first by two polite coloured men, then by three more threatening white men. Chuckie scares them off by doing an impersonation of the Rev. Ian Paisley.

He travels to San Diego, where Max's mother lives, and from there to Kansas, where her grandmother lives and where he retrieves her. Wilson uses these American scenes to relativize the perceptions of violence. Observing a series of nightly brawls in San Diego, Chuckie longs "for the comforts of familiar Belfast and the understandably butch and brutal Sandy Row. He longed for the safety of some terrorism, some civil war" (267-68).

Meanwhile, life in Belfast, where people are shattered by the Fountain Street bombing, goes on just the same. Driving up and down the city, Jake observes:

> It was like the seventies: a time when rubble scars marked the city like a good set of fingerprints. But as I drove street to street, I felt sorry for Belfast. It had a guilty, sheepish air, as though it knew it had blundered again, made its name sound dark in the world's mouth again. It was uniquely endearing to me and it chose to look its prettiest in recompense .... The evening was light, fragrant, the air was clear. Look at all my good points, the city seemed to say.
> There were many. For all my big talk, this was still a city I loved .... It never mattered what happened (283-84).

Then the ceasefire is announced, and again Jake's perception of the city is modified:

> First of all, I felt as though Belfast had finally given up smoking. A twenty-five-year-old habit had just stopped. I dreaded the withdrawal. What were we supposed to do with our afternoons now? How were we going to look cool?
> Then I felt fury. Nothing had changed. The boys in the ski-masks had called it a victory but their situation was exactly the same as it had been a quarter of a century before. Three thousand people had died, countless thousands had had bits blown or beaten or shot off, and all of the rest of us had been scared shitless for a significant proportion of the time. What had this been for? What had been achieved?
> Additionally, I couldn't help thinking that if I was husband, wife, father, mother, daughter or son to any of the twenty-seven who'd died in the last eight days I'd have been highly fucking miffed at the timing of this old armistice (313).

Observing a trio of skinheads, who seem to be frightening a girl but are in fact handing her something she dropped, Jake concludes that "suddenly Belfast seemed again a place to be" (314). And indeed, Belfast has overnight become "the city of love" (345): Chuckie and Max are going to get married and start a family, Peggy Lurgan has found a lover and discovered the delights of lesbian sex, Jake's Muslim workmate Rajinder is going out with a Jewish girl:

> Yeah, Belfast felt like a city of love that night. A city of sex. It felt strange. It felt uncharacteristic. It felt slightly illegal and it felt like I hadn't been invited (358).

But that will change, too, as Jake himself ends up in bed with Aoirghe, who has annoyed and frustrated him throughout the book.

Chuckie Lurgan will "bring back work to the city single-handed". Having witnessed a riot in the Falls shortly after his return from the United States, he has realized that "Belfast people had amounts of energy they didn't know what to do with" (381). In a TV interview he divulges his entrepreneurial plans, flooring the inapt Jimmy Eve, the leader of Just Us (rather than We Ourselves!) and announcing a new political party in cooperation with the imaginary OTG movement.

The novel ends with Jake waking up beside sleeping Aoirghe. But it is Belfast he loves:

> The mountain looks flat and grand. In the greyness, it is stupidly green. It looks like all cities this morning, Belfast. It's a tender frail thing, composite of houses, roads and car parks. Where are the people? They are waking or failing to wake. Tender is a small word for what I feel for this town. I think of my city's conglomerate of bodies. A Belfastful of spines, kidneys, hearts, livers and lungs. Sometimes, this frail cityful of organs makes me seethe and boil with tenderness. They seem so unmurderable and, because I think of them, they belong to me.
> Belfast – only a jumble of streets and a few big bumps in the ground, only a whisper of God (396).

Eureka Street is a powerful novel, both funny and moving. In terms of its plot, no matter how flippant in places, its main characters, Jake Jackson from Poetry Street and Chuckie Lurgan from Eureka Street, Catholic and Protestant, maker and finder, have faced the truth about human existence, about life in a violent city in a more violent world in a most violent universe. More importantly, the reader has faced these truths as well. Man (and woman) passes, the city remains.

THE HORN OF BABYLON: JAZZ AND THE
INVOLUTION AND EVOLUTION OF THE SPIRIT
IN JOHN CELLON HOLMES'S *THE HORN*

DOC ROSSI

In an earlier article called "The Devil's Music", I discussed John Cellon Holmes's use of jazz and the life it demands in his novel *The Horn* as a representation of an aggressive, avaricious parasite that cuts all competitors to the quick, a violent, urban existence that manifests itself as a destructive sickness of body, mind and attitude, a fatal obsession with a way of life that ultimately sterilizes or destroys natural potency.[1] Although jazz is supposed to be a music of celebration, this reading places *The Horn* firmly in Babylon rather than Jerusalem. There is, however, more to this association than that implied by the decadent, corrupt nature of the novel's characters. The aspect of *The Horn* that I am concerned with in this article is similar to the transmutation undergone by the city of Babylon as cultural symbol. Here I look at Holmes's expression of Beat philosophy in *The Horn* as an attempt to rehabilitate Babylon by placing what we call corruption or degradation in a new light. Rather than relishing in the attraction of repulsion or the sanctuary of alienation, *The Horn* arrives at a different understanding of what lies behind degeneration, of the uses to which the process itself might be put..

In his disclaimer at the beginning of *The Horn* (1958) Holmes says his book, "like the music that it celebrates, is a collective improvisation on an

---

[1] Doc Rossi, "The Devil's Music: Jazz in *The Horn*", in *Città reali e immaginarie del continente americano*, eds Cristina Giorcelli, Camilla Cattrulla and Anna Scacchi, Rome, 1998, 347-59. For other works that discuss jazz and literature, see Richard N. Albert (Compiler), *Annotated Bibliography of Jazz Fiction and Jazz Fiction Criticism* (*Bibliographies and Indexes in World Literature, 52*), Westport: CT, 1996; for jazz and culture, see Jon Panish, *The Color of Jazz: Race and Representation in Postwar American Culture*, Chicago, 1997; Burton W. Peretti, *The Creation of Jazz: Music, Race and Culture in Urban America (Music in American Life)*, Chicago, 1992; Chip Rhodes, *Structures of the Jazz Age: Mass Culture, Progressive Education, and Racial Discourse in American Modernism*, New York, 1998.

American theme; and if there are truths here, they are poetic truths".[2] As he points out in the "Preface" to the second edition, he had dealt himself a tough hand, reworking the lives of famous jazz men and women into a celebration of the fruits of outrage, of a good that had grown out of evil. This paradox operates as a *verfremdungseffekt* which forces the reader to question not only celebration itself but what is celebrated and why. When Brecht had reworked John Gay's *The Beggar's Opera* into his own "Gangsterspiel" *The Threepenny Opera*, he hoped he would be presenting his bourgeois Berlin audience with a grotesque, disgusting, embarrassing portrait of itself, much as he had attempted with the more obviously grotesque *Baal*. Unfortunately, the joke the audience understood was quite different from the one intended, and Brecht's thieves, prostitutes and murderers became celebrated heroes. Instead of educating his audience through the shock of ridicule, he had entertained them by holding a mirror up to them in which they could bask in their own reflections, and they did so; they went home whistling the tunes, and continued whistling right through 1928, into 1929 and the disasters that followed. Holmes faces quite the opposite problem in *The Horn*. He has not put a negative character in the role of the hero in the hope that such a *verfremdungseffekt* would startle readers into reform; rather, the hero at the centre of the celebration represents a vile, repulsive life that infects or violates everyone who comes into contact with it. The truth is that the celebration is a condemnation as well, but one that is absolutely necessary.

This play between celebration and condemnation illustrates how the novel turns the bleak, violent, inhuman world of the modern American city, represented by the almost fiercely urban music of modern jazz, into an opportunity for spiritual growth. The city of Babylon as cultural symbol has undergone a similar transmutation. Although once celebrated as the most splendid city in the world, Babylon is remembered in the Old Testament only for its persecution of Israel; the biblical whore of Babylon is the opulent oppressor, first Nebuchadnezzar, then, after the Israelites' liberation by the Persians, Rome, an association the Eternal City retained during the Reformation. In *The Horn*, jazz has already undergone a comparable defamation, developing from its roots in New Orleans to bebop in New York,[3] from a communal celebration expressed in collective improvisation to a form dominated by the solo, a virtuoso display supported by an accompaniment which is all but ignored. The popular view of jazz as a collective improvisation is thus transmuted, like the city of Babylon, from hallowed rite to harlot.

Just what jazz means in *The Horn* is succinctly stated by one of the two men who rape the fourteen-year-old Geordie Dickson: "Hey, Austin boy-ee-ee, let's

---

[2] John Cellon Holmes, *The Horn* (1958), New York, 1988, no page number. All subsequent quotations will be followed in the text by page number in parentheses.

[3] Recent works on jazz history include Scott Deveaux, *The Birth of Bebop: A Social and Musical History*, Los Angeles, 1999, and Ted Gioia, *The History of Jazz*, Oxford, 1997.

jazz her" (110).[4] Jazz is rape, a brutal act where, in this case, two human beings improvise solos on the body of another. The communal aspect of this inverted celebration is emphasized further in Geordie's complicity in her own rape, standing "docile, under a sweaty hand", asking the men to leave her alone, but neither struggling nor calling for help, then drinking the whiskey one of them had offered so that they could somehow all "celebrate" together. That act of giving – she remembers the rapist had even drawn back on the bottle when she choked – had "blurred her hatred ever since then ... and taken some of the outrage out of it" (111). Significantly, the men who rape Geordie are from the city, and there is more to this metaphor than the city's violation of the country or the journey jazz made from country to city, from south to north, for jazz is not only a representation of corrupt, violent urban existence: like the ancient city of Babylon, it is also a vehicle for spiritual growth.

Although Babylon is now a symbol of fallen or corrupt existence, esoterically it represents the solid or material world in which the involution and evolution of the spirit can occur, as its name "gate of the gods" implies. Babylon is the space and time where spirit can turn in on itself, enduring abuse so that it may evolve to a higher level. In *The Horn*, jazz, especially bebop, along with the life it entails, is the dark side of music, the passage through the underworld that must be risked in order to attain enlightenment, represented by what Holmes calls pure song. He portrays the life of the modern jazz musician as a decadent, almost disgusting state of existence; some characters are able to develop through their experience in that world and find a purer music, even if it remains jazz, in a life outside the tight circle of modern New York jazz, while others become stuck and are unable to rise above or out of it. For Geordie the results of the rape are a stillborn child, sterility and reform school, but this was only her first opportunity to transmute jazz into pure song, to use involution as an impetus to evolution; the next came when she met Edgar Pool, the Horn of the title.

Edgar Pool, "everybody's evil worldly father" (35), is at once an image of involution *par excellence*, a satanic figure of heroic proportions, and the oppressor who must be overcome. As the man who invented bop, who invented modern jazz, he has profoundly touched all those "who came later and blew more"; like Wing Redburn, each bop originator has found that he or she is still irked by Horn because his "dark, sour look" was in their own hearts all the time (47). But it is not just Horn's look that is dark, not just his skin that is black: he is "all turned in upon himself, all dark" (10); his whole demeanour and appearance is "inexplicably suggestive of night" (23). If the rapists had jazzed Geordie in one way, he jazzed her in another, physically rather than metaphorically taking

---

[4] Scott Fitzgerald has written that "The word jazz in its progress towards respectability has meant first sex, then dancing, then music. It is associated with a state of nervous stimulation, not unlike that of big cities behind the lines of a war" (F. Scott Fitzgerald, "Echoes of the Jazz Age", in *The Fitzgerald Reader*, ed. Arthur Mizener, New York, 1963, 325).

her to the city, making her into a star while developing his "nightmare music" during the extra jobs they played during the war years. A child of war, bebop was liberated from its prison in the formal constraints and uses of traditional jazz and swing just as the world had been liberated from fascism, or the Israelites from Babylon. As Babylon changed from holy city into whore, jazz went from swing to Horn's nightmare music, thus providing the darkness necessary for achieving enlightenment. The members of the original bebop family, those who have followed in Horn's footsteps, have either transmuted the jazz life by using the outrage of Horn's dark world, or remained stuck in the debauched circle of modern New York jazz. Although her sources for renewal seem endless, Geordie has been unable to evolve from her part in the creation of Horn's nightmare music, netting only a dead love and aborted career that is never reborn. Her journey into the underworld ends with her trapped inside the world of modern jazz. Unlike Horn, who keeps outrage inside himself, deriding it, using it, never wearying of it, unable to "see it as the biggest drag of all" (111), she seems to have reached some kind of agreement with outrage. But the single wet, just-budded rose that symbolizes her life, that is plucked in all its fresh infancy and stuck into the sterile habitat of her smartly lacquered hair each night, only to be thrown away and replaced each day, confirms that she has not moved from that shadeless road in the country. Her sterility is only the physical, outward sign of her stunted development.

If Horn is the point on which the plot turns, and Geordie the most graphic example of the failure to evolve, the focus is on Walden Blue, one of the new generation of bop stylists, who is at a point where he will either transmute the opulent trappings of the jazz world and reach a new balance, or be seduced by and entrapped within Horn's nightmare. Walden provides the impetus for the main action of the novel by taking a step into the future of his own evolution. While Horn is the devil incarnate overcome by irony, and Geordie a sterilized Ishtar, the fertility goddess of Babylon, Walden is Lucifer, not the devil Isaiah had associated with the king of Babylon and who later became Satan himself, but simply Lucifer the light giver, the very role he plays in the act that changes his life forever:

> If he had better understood himself and the inconsolable ambiguity of men's aspirations, the unforgivable thing he did then might not have stunned him so. But he did not understand, and knew little of the concepts upon which men struggle to define their existence (although down in his heart waited a single note of music that he felt would shatter all discord into harmony), and so when he found himself suddenly beside Edgar, his horn clipped to its swing around his neck, and heard himself break into the pedestrian chorus of "Out of Nowhere" that Edgar was blowing, he was filled with the same sense of terror that had swept over him ten years before, the first time he had stood up before live, ominous drums and cut out a piece for himself. Only it was worse, because there was a complex protocol to "after hours", unwritten, inarticulate, but accepted ... and it did not countenance an uninvited intrusion from the watchers, no matter who. On top of that, Walden

(thought of among musicians as a "good, cool tenor," reliable, with sweet ideas and a feel for riffs, but one who had not yet found his way) was presuming upon Edgar Pool, revered from a distance by everyone who came later and blew more, whose eccentricities were accorded the tolerance due to anyone embittered by neglect, and whose lonely eminence as "the Horn" was beyond challenge, a matter of sentimental history. What Walden did, then, was unheard of (16-17).

But do it he does. In a neat variation on Lucifer's challenge to God, which ends with the archangel being banished to Hell, his own kingdom, Walden rebels against the devil himself, coming from "out of nowhere" into "a new moral position to everything around him" (21). What had inspired Walden into action was his "sudden thought" that Horn was a "Black Angel", an incarnation from a world where "Satan carried a razor and Babylon was a place in midnight Georgia ... and even Jehovah wore a Kluxer's sheet". Walden recalls in the same instant that "sometimes when he played ... he thought about some possible heaven, some decent kind of life" (16), so he challenges the Horn, "loving him even in all his savage, smearing mockery, battling not him but the dark side of that Black-angel soul; bringing light". Walden experiences "a moment of incredible, hairbreadth joy" when, in the heat of the duel, he blows "four bars of ringing melody, so compelling" that the Horn stumbles; Walden then comes back in so clear that he almost falters himself, understanding beyond doubt "that his was the warmer tone, that this was what he had always *meant*" (18). The rebellion over and his battle won, Walden stands "alone in the light, isolated in his achievement, and by it breathless and transformed" as one who has, "on an impulse coming up from far down in his soul, totally altered his life all in a moment" (20-21). Walden's unwelcome and unheard of step into the Babylonian spotlight of the New York jazz scene, bringing light to Horn's black soul, is his first step towards transmuting the material world and moving on to a new level.

It is at this moment of "dazzling isolation" that Geordie approaches him, "coming so close her fragrance swirled thickly through his head". But instead of being overwhelmed by the myth, he sees that Horn's former lover, the sensual, fleshly goddess of jazz, is "exhausted, sobered, and somehow resigned" (21). If Walden can already see through the trappings of Horn's world, however, his new moral position has given him more than a new perspective:

> He had brought the light all right, but the conflicts in a man's nature were not to be resolved by light alone. Edgar had fled in disgust and despair at what it had revealed, fled from the light because it was not for him any more. Walden was frozen ... by the power one man had over another; it sickened something trusting in him, even though he could not disbelieve the clear impulse that had prodded him to stand up. He had ... for once and for all, damned himself to going his way. (21-22)

Having taken the first step, Walden is now at a point where either a path must be taken or he will remain frozen where he stands. Like Lucifer, he too has been banished to his own kingdom, but it is still internal, having not yet been, like Horn's, projected externally onto Geordie and countless others, including Walden himself. Although music is his business, and Holmes hints that "business" has a more profound meaning for Walden, he is not yet completely immersed in the jazz life – it is music itself that occupies him, love of music that has kept him alive (4); his relationship to his sax and what he can pull from it are his concerns, not Horn's ironic, tragic hipness. Before cutting Horn, Walden had seen himself as "a saxophone, as bright and shiny and potential as that, and the night and his life would play on him" (6); now, with "the quiet loneliness of self-knowledge descended over him like a prophetic hint of the shroud toward which all lives irrevocably progress" (22) he is poised to turn the outrage into spiritual enlightenment.

Walden has yet to find his way, his place, having taken only the first step into Babylon, but the prospect of hoped-for celebration is contained in the imagery Holmes uses to describe his first day in this new world, the possibility of achieving and maintaining the balance the Horn and most of those who followed him have somehow lost. The book opens with Walden being gently nudged awake by "the wizened October sun" stretching "its old finger" to touch his eyes, which he opens only to see the "water-cracked ceiling" that has always reminded him of the first time the city touched him, when "a great lumbering bullock" careening toward him became "a Cadillac-full of wild, zoot-suited city boys", leaving him agape on the roadside (3-4). In his "first moment of waking reflection … which in its limpid, almost idiotic clarity is nearly the closest human beings come to glimpsing the dimensions of their consciousness" (4), he contemplates his sax, the emblem of his inner life, "the key to the world in which he found himself" (5); and although ensconced at Fifty-third and Eighth for the past decade, he is still able to dangle "his feet in an imaginary brook". A source of renewal for Walden, moving water is anathema to Kansas City-born Horn, whose own image of security, of "the end of struggle", is the "land-locked spaces of his youth, where the Great Unknown [somehow always associated with the river in his head] was held to its proscribed channel by the jealous land, and not, as ... on [the] doomed and blasphemous island, lapping malignly [*sic*] at the end of every street" (211-12). Horn only vomits blood and bile into the river, for the river cannot be a symbol of fertility and progression for one whose name – Edgar Pool – suggests at once rich reserves and stagnation in an all-consuming material, superficial world. Walden – an as yet uncorrupted blue pond in the New World – is still at least partly in the stream, fed by it, still in a position to cleanse himself and move on.

It is to bebop icon Wing Redburn that Walden turns when he fully wakes and realizes that his first act in his new world must be to make peace with Horn – as Cleo had said, to "Catch him before he dies!" (22). Disgusted for the last time by Horn and his audacious arrogance, Wing had sought "moving water because it went somewhere, and all complexities and attitudes and wraths were swept before it" (41); his journey into Babylon took him down the Mississippi in search of a truth he found through loss rather than transgression. Although still in New York and still playing music, he has evolved out of the modern jazz scene.

Walden catches Wing in "the hushed cream-white lobby of the W E L L Studios" where the legendary alto saxophonist "had just wedged himself into a slot in the revolving door", and hearing Walden's "Hey, there, man", turned around just "where the neutral odor of air-conditioning was always the strongest". The revolving door ejects Walden, as if from one world into another, and the two men stand in an incongruous Garden of Eden "by an ash stand whose bowl of fine white sand had yet to know a butt" (31). Walden has entered one possible place in his new world – the safe regularity of a studio gig, a "non-jazz job" (33). Wing, on the other hand, is pulled back toward his former, irregular life in which Horn had played such an important part, to remember how he got to where he is now, both physically and with his music. Wing had once followed the river to Babylon, fought against his demons, and come out somewhere beyond the city's seductions. No longer part of the jazz world, he represents an achievable balance between the spiritual and material, for despite the middle-class trappings which seem so sterile when juxtaposed to the excitement of the jazz life, Wing has overcome Horn, gone beyond him, and is now able to take his reed between workmanlike jaws and blow pure music,

> … taking up the particular chords into his horn and forgetting them, his mind clear … except for the feeling ... that at the bottom somewhere there was song, the same song, the one song – to know which ... was worth more to him whatever life might take away (47).

Wing has transmuted the material world into a quiet fulfilment; the juxtaposition of the jazz life to his own, of kicks to satisfaction and enlightenment, emphasizes its seeming squareness only to belie outward appearances.

The other bebop originators who are still involved in the jazz life – Junius Priest and Curny Finnley – remain trapped within Horn's world, unable to progress beyond it. Like Geordie, these men are consistently identified and associated with Horn. Junius, who is never without his dark glasses, even at breakfast with his mother, and who had idolized Horn more than anyone else had, has not been able to face the light since his one and only recording session with his source of inspiration. Showing up to the session twenty minutes late and shamelessly drunk, Horn stumbles through the A-side, a standard. During the flip side, "Junius Sees Her", Junius is so overwhelmed by Horn's drunkenness that when the time comes for him to solo on his own tune he helplessly and unconsciously falls into "a literal extension of Edgar's last idea", something that so shocks Horn that he tells Junius "'Hey, boy, Ah'm not me ... *You're* me,' just as he pitche[s] forward, with a shameless, capitulant uproll of doused eyes, onto his face" (71). The recording becomes legendary, but for Junius it is the end: just as the rape had completed something for Geordie, "something had told him that if all *this* could lead to all *that* – the simple, feckless resonance of the right chord lead to the winced eye and the shrewdly supplied bottle to keep it open – it was not for him" (72). His infatuation, even worship of Geordie is a further sign of his stagnation; a larger-than-life poster of her hangs over his bed in the only room in the world where he removes his dark glasses. He spends the rest of his days living with his mother in Harlem, only seldom venturing out to play his "gooney-bird" piano tunes, and then only with raw, inept side men.

Curny's sidemen are anything but inept, but his arrangements are so cerebral, so full of the little musical jokes he alone understands, that he is thought of as

> one of that introverted group of rash experimentalists who had created, in Bop, a music that few could play and to which only the equally rash would listen .... Curny simply loved big, complex, *funny* arrangements, dense with conflicting section work, buoyed by relentless driving rhythm, but (above all) *loud* (130-31).

When his exasperated manager reminds his band at a rehearsal that "Young America likes to dance", one of the sidemen quips, "not to this band they don't" (124). Although still very much a part of the modern jazz scene, Curny is all but out of touch with his audience; his bands never stay together for more than a few weeks, and his life is an endless repetition of hope and failure.

Walden has contact with neither Junius nor Curny – they come into the tale only because Horn contacts them himself to hit them up for the cash he needs to return to Kansas City. Walden's seeking help only from those removed from the current New York jazz scene separates him further from Horn's dark influence. Besides Wing, the only other person Walden looks to in his quest to make peace with Horn is Metro Myland, the man who new Horn first; like Wing, he presents another example of growth. Although not one of the bebop originators and never part of the New York jazz scene, he had only taken up tenor sax because of Horn. He then immediately went his own way, working Harlem dance halls rather than downtown clubs, now driving his working-class audience into ecstatic contortions, howling the "idiot truths" of "zonky! zonky! zonky! zonky! zonk!". From his short time with Horn, Metro had learned that simple song could stand in defiance of the bleak, barren and desolate (164). Surrounded by the windswept desert of the winter Midwest on a train seemingly headed straight through hell, Metro saw that images of hope and tenderness existed not in the real world but in his mind, the outcome of his own perspective (171-73). This thought never leaves him, reflected persistently in the wild, unsophisticated music he plays in the unfashionable neighbourhoods, transmuting the wild and senseless longing he shares with his audience into pure celebration.

"Celebrate" is Horn's last word. Cleo, the pianist who is still young and inexperienced enough to side always with innocence, who has stuck to Horn all day and alone hears his final words, cannot understand what this notorious icon could have meant. After reading about the squalid, decadent, sterile and always unfulfilling lives of the characters in this novel, the reader can also be forgiven for not understanding what the dying Horn could possibly have meant. Not only that: Holmes's homily on America that spells out just what Horn *had* meant by

"Celebrate", or what Cleo had eventually understood, is too saccharine to be taken seriously, although the words "Jazz was as much a celebration of ... American reality as a protest against it" (241) does suggest a worthwhile direction to follow. Holmes's own version of Beat philosophy would seem to be that the modern American city, with all its outrage and sickness, its desecration of democratic ideals with an ill-fated and out-dated "survival of the fittest" reading of evolution, is after all the best place to pick up the song and create it anew. In *The Horn* the key to spiritual evolution comes from the involution of the spirit that can only take place in Babylon.

THE SQUARE CIRCLE IN THE CITY:
THE BOXING TALE AS URBAN GENRE

KASIA BODDY

The reliance of turn-of-the-century naturalism on the Darwinian-inspired metaphor of the city as jungle is well known. A related metaphor is drawn from the boxing world. The ring, or the square circle, has frequently been evoked as an urban microcosm; in particular a microcosm of urban competition and corruption. But drawing on the boxing world enables a writer to explore many aspects of urban life other than simply corruption. Questions about performance and spectatorship, suffering and redemption, and what being or behaving, as a man (or a woman), might entail are at the heart of modern representations of this world. The symbolic impact of the boxing ring is never straightforward. Indeed it resonates with many other urban spaces of enclosure and struggle: the factory, the home, the brothel, the jail, and the neighbourhood. The boxer's body itself is also a microcosm of these wider structures, the ultimate space in which one is imprisoned and within which all fights begin and end.

Most commentators on modern boxing divide its history into two distinct periods, the first associated with bare-knuckle fighting and pre-industrial rural life and the second with increasing regulation and industrial urban structures. Although it has its origins in ancient Greece, by medieval times boxing had become associated less with classical competition than with other rowdy rural pastimes such as cockfighting and bull-baiting, and, like these, it was outlawed under the Puritan government of Cromwell. The Restoration brought a relaxation of popular morality and, as historian Elliott Gorn notes, boxing quickly became "an urban phenomenon, supported by city nobles, local squires migrating to the commercial centers, and growing numbers of working-class men".[1] By the end

---

[1] Elliott J. Gorn, *The Manly Art: Bare-Knuckle Prize Fighting in America*, Ithaca: NY, 1986, 23-24. The first boxing match recorded in a newspaper (*The Protestant Mercury*) took place in 1681 in the presence of the Duke of Albemarle. James Figg, generally thought of as the first boxing champion, opened his academy (or, as he called it, "amphitheatre") in London's Tottenham Court Road in 1719. In 1723 a boxing ring was erected in Hyde Park "by order of His Majesty". It remained there until 1820; see H.D. Miles, *Pugilistica: A History of British Boxing* (1866), Edinburgh, 1906, I, vii, 9, 10.

of the eighteenth century, Gorn argues, partly due to "a larger flowering of commercialized leisure and popular recreations" and partly to the English gentry's rediscovery of Greek and Roman culture, boxing had become so popular as to be deemed the national sport.[2] Academies teaching "the manly art of self defence" to young aristocrats (such as Lord Byron) sprang up in the major cities, and the self-styled "new Corinthians" displayed their skills whenever they could.[3] The sport's classic chronicler, Pierce Egan, published his *Boxiana* in three volumes in 1812, 1818 and 1824, but by the 1820s the golden age was already over. Scandals dogged the boxing world and works of the early 1820s such as Egan's picaresque tale of the original Tome and Jerry, *Life in London*, John Reynold's exuberant The Fancy, or William Hazlitt's essay of the same year, "The Fight", which evokes an Arcadian moment saturated in classical allusion and stable feudal relations, already have an air of nostalgia about them.[4]

By the middle of the nineteenth century, prizefighting fell out of favour and was largely driven underground by the middle-class "rise of respectable society".[5] The Marquis of Queensbury Rules – introduced in Britain in 1865, and the United States in the 1880s – were an attempt to remove the sport's associations with street fighting, and so make it more appealing to the middle classes. The rules encouraged a more upright contest, disallowing all the holds now associated with wrestling, stated that gloves must be worn, and introduced three-minute rounds with one-minute rest periods and a ten-second recovery period. Ironically, Gorn argues, these rules made things more dangerous – not only did boxers wearing gloves hit their opponents (in particular their

[2] Gorn, 24. G.M. Trevelyan describes "scientific pugilism" as "the chief national interest in the Regency period" (*English Social History* [1944], London, 1973, 503). The best account of boxing in this period is John Ford's *Prizefighting: The Age of Regency Boximania*, Newton Abbot, 1971. See also Donald A. Law, *Thieves' Kitchen: The Regency Underworld*, Gloucester, 1987.

[3] The opening of John Jackson's academy at 13 Bond Street in 1798 initiated "an era in the gymnastic education of the aristocracy. Not to have had lessons of Jackson was a reproach. To attempt a list of his pupils would be to copy one-third of the then peerage" (Miles, I, 97).

[4] See John Hamilton Reynolds, *The Fancy: A Selection from the Poetical Remains of the Late Peter Corcoran, of Gray's Inn, Student of Law, with a Brief Memoir of His Life*, London, 1820; Pierce Egan, *Life in London; Or the Day and Night Scenes of Jerry Hawthorn Esq. And his elegant friend Corintian Tom accompanied by Bob Logic the Oxonian in their Rambles and Sprees Through the Metropolis*, London, 1821; extracts of William Hazlitt's "The Fight" (first published in *New Monthly Magazine*, February 1822) are included in *Selected Writings*, Oxford, 1991, 117-27. See also R.C. Reid, *Bucks and Bruisers: Pierce Egan and Regency England*, London, 1971, and Gregory Dart, "'Flash Style': Pierce Egan and Literary London, 1820-1828", *History Workshop Journal*, 51 (2001), 181-205.

[5] I borrow the phrase from F.M.L. Thompson's *The Rise of Respectable Society: A Social History of Victorian Britain, 1830-1900*, London, 1988.

opponents' heads) harder, "the Queensbury rules took control over the pace of action away from the fighters. Like factory workers, boxing's new rhythms mandated regular periods of work and rest."[6]

Gorn's comparison of boxers with factory workers is not accidental. Within a century boxing had been transformed from a "noble art" with classical, amateur and rural associations, into an urban, working-class and professional sport. But at the same time that novels such as Arthur Conan Doyle's *Rodney Stone* (1896) and Jeffrey Farnol's *The Amateur Gentleman* (1894) nostalgically evoked a rural and gentlemanly Regency past, an art of urban boxing was being created by painters such as George Bellows and writers such as Jack London and Arthur Morrison. It is the twentieth-century Anglo-American urban story that I want to consider here, in particular the two most common (and seemingly contradictory) ways boxing metaphors operate within it. First, I will consider how boxing is used to represent the persistence of non-urban values in the city and to suggest a "way out" of the city; secondly, how the "square circle" comes to represent something absolutely urban, a microcosm of city life itself.

The Way Out: Getting "rid of the devil"

If respectable Victorian society disapproved of professional boxing, it largely supported the amateur sport in the context of what became known as the Muscular Christian doctrine of *mens sana in corpore sano*. A pivotal chapter in Thomas Hughes's public school classic, *Tom Brown's Schooldays* (1857) describes an exemplary fight of honour, and Hughes concludes, "Fighting is the natural and English way for English boys to settle their quarrels".[7] The Amateur Boxing Association was set up in London in 1880 to encourage schoolboy contests with the maxim "box, don't fight", and, with this in mind, social and religious reformers encouraged the setting up of gyms in working-class areas. The violence of the street, it was thought, could be redirected into the gym. In his 1899 study of East London, for example, Walter Besant wrote of the importance of bringing the aristocratic amateur public school ideal into poor neighbourhoods:

---

[6] Gorn, 205.
[7] Thomas Hughes, *Tom Brown's Schooldays*, Penguin, 1994, 246. See Jeffrey Richards, *Happiest Days: The Public Schools in English Fiction*, Manchester, 1988, chapters 2 and 5, and Dennis W. Allen, "Young England" Muscular Christianity and the Politics of the Body in *Tom Brown's Schooldays*", in *Muscular Christianity*, ed. Donald E. Hall, Cambridge 1994, 114-32. Victorian fiction, and Dickens's novels in particular, abound in honourable fisticuffs. See James E. Marlow, "Popular Culture, Pugilism, and Pickwick", *Popular Culture*, XV/4 (1982), 16-30, and David Faulkner, "The Confidence Man: Empire, and the Deconstruction of Muscular Christianity in *The Mystery of Edwin Drood*", in *Muscular Christianity*, 175-93. See also George Bernard Shaw's denunciation of "the abominable vein of retaliatory violence" in nineteenth-century literature in the "Preface" to *Cashel Byron's Profession* (1886), London, 1925, xvii.

[They] get rid of the devil in the gymnasium with the boxing-gloves and with single stick; they contract habits of order and discipline; they become infected with some of the upper-class ideals, especially as regards honour and honesty, purity and temperance.[8]

The language Besant uses here is suffused with, and indeed confuses, religious and medical imagery. Boxing would not only enact a kind of exorcism, he suggests, but would also become a kind of beneficial contagion. Indeed, believing in the therapeutic quality of boxing led many churches to set up gymnasiums and support fighters.[9] The close involvement of the Church – usually the Catholic Church – in amateur boxing forms the basis of many fictional, as well as true, boxing stories. In the 1938 MGM film, *Boys Town*, for example, Father Flanagan (Spencer Tracey) urges the juvenile delinquents in his school to settle their conflicts in the ring.[10] Meanwhile, Arthur Morrison's 1896 novel of London's East End, *A Child of the Jago*, presents Father Sturt who tries to "wipe out the blackest spot in the Jago" by creating a lodging-house, a night-shelter, washhouses and a club where "he gathered the men of the Jago indiscriminately, with sole condition of good behaviour on the premises":

---

[8] Walter Besant, *East London* (1899), London, 1903, 172.

[9] See *ibid.*, 330-31. In some cases, the boxing club was only available to boys who also attended Church and Bible Class. See Stan Shipley, "Tom Causer of Bermondsey", *History Workshop Journal*, 15 (1983), 28-59 (42). See also John Springhall, "Building Character in the British Boy: The Attempt to Extend Christian Manliness to Working-Class Adolescents, 1880-1914", in *Manliness and Morality*, eds J.A. Mangan and James Walvin, Manchester, 1987, 52-74, and Gerard R. Gems, "Selling Sport and Religion in American Society: Bishop Sheil and the Catholic Youth Organization", in *The New American Sport History*, ed. S. W. Pope, Urbana, 1997, 300-11.

[10] Here follow some other examples. *On the Waterfront* (scr. Budd Schulberg; dir. Elia Kazan, 1954) presents the parallel crises of conscience of ex-pug Terry Malloy (Marlon Brando) and priest ("and something of an amateur boxer in his college days") Father Barry (Karl Malden) (Budd Schulberg, *On the Waterfront* [1955], London, 1988, 43). Schulberg says that he wrote the novel after the film was made in order more fully to explore "the spiritual and social development of Father Barry" ("Introduction", ix). In *The Leather Saint* (dir. Norman Retchin, 1955), John Derek plays a priest who fights to get medical supplies for the parish hospital; as an Episcopalian, he is fortunately able to marry the film's love interest. Bing Crosby, meanwhile, plays the pugilistic Father O'Malley in the hugely successful Catholic school drama, *The Bells of St Mary's* (dir. Leo McCarey, 1945); in *The Big Punch* (dir. Shelley Shourds, 1948), Wayne Morris leaves the ring in order to enter the church. "The-boxer-and-the priest" movie is one of the many genres parodically referred to by Nabokov in *Lolita*. The plot of one, told to Humbert by Charlotte Haze, is typical: "The boxer had fallen extremely low when he met the good old priest (who had been a boxer himself in his robust youth and could still slug a sinner)" (*The Annotated Lolita*, Penguin, 1980, 45).

And there they smoked, jumped, swung on horizontal bars, boxed, played at cards and bagatelle, free from interference save when interference became necessary.[11]

Needless to stay, Hollywood not withstanding, boxing did not always succeed in ridding the streets of the devil. In his book on the Kray twins, John Pearson describes their early, highly successful, boxing careers. Their father, he writes, "thought that boxing would be the making of the twins, give them the discipline they needed, take them off the streets and give them something other than mischief to occupy their minds". As amateurs, the twins won every bout they fought, and at the age of sixteen, they turned professional. But soon afterwards, Pearson notes, "the street violence they were involved in mysteriously increased as well".[12] I will consider the relationship between the violence and discipline of the streets and the ring more fully, in relation to Morrison's novel and others, later.

"The old, primitive, royal, animal way"

The amateur ideal of Muscular Christianity was also imported into America (and became increasingly important during the antebellum period when professional boxing began to develop). As well as a means of channelling the energies of working-class men, boxing was seen as a way of restoring vigour to middle-class men. Indeed, reformers such as Thomas Wentworth Higginson and William Ellery Channing believed that only vigorous exercise such as boxing could counteract the inherently emasculating effects of city life.[13] By the turn of the century, Theodore Roosevelt wrote directly of the nationalistic imperative behind "the strenuous life": "There is no place in the world for nations who have become enervated by the soft and easy life, or who have lost their fibre of vigorous hardness and masculinity."[14] For Roosevelt, boxing was an ideal sport for city dwellers. He writes in his *Autobiography* that "When obliged to live in cities, I for a long time found that boxing and wrestling enabled me to get a good

---

[11] Arthur Morrison, *A Child of the Jago*, London, 1996, 80. Morrison notes that Father Sturt's efforts are opposed by "the Sentimental-Cocksure" who find the thought of a club involving boxing and dominoes to be "flat ungodliness". See J.S. Reed, "Ritualism Rampant in East London: Anglo-Catholicism and the Urban Poor", *Victorian Studies*, XXXI/3 (1988), 375-403.

[12] John Pearson, *The Profession of Violence: The Rise and Fall of the Kray Twins*, revised edition, London, 1984, 41, 43.

[13] Extracts of the Rev. Higginson's 1858 essay "Saints and Their Bodies" are included in *Major Problems in American Sport History*, ed. Steven A. Riess, Boston, 1997, 83-85. See also Gorn, 130, 160.

[14] "The Strenuous Life" (1900), in *The Works of Theodore Roosevelt*, New York, 1926, XIII, 319. See also Gail Bederman, *Manliness and Civilization*, Chicago, 1995, chapter 5, "Theodore Roosevelt: Manhood, Nation, and 'Civilization'". On masculinity and "enervation", see Tom Lutz, *American Nervousness, 1903: An Anecdotal History*, Ithaca: NY, 1991.

deal of exercise in condensed and attractive form". But it was not only the
limited space needed for such a vigorous workout that appealed to him.
"Powerful, vigorous men of strong animal development", he maintained, "must
have some way in which their animal spirits can find vent".[15]

Roosevelt's contemporary, Jack London, also attempts to present boxing as
an activity that gives "vent" to animal spirit and is quite distinct from, and indeed
opposed to, the drudgeries and indignities of urban working life. In his essay
"The Somnambulists", for example, he writes that it is

> Far better to have the front of one's face pushed in by the fist of an honest prize-
> fighter than to have the lining of one's stomach corroded by the embalmed beef of
> a dishonest manufacturer.[16]

In the context of a discussion of corrupt meat production (which Upton Sinclair
also targeted in *The Jungle*), the prizefighter and his activities are seen as
"honest". Once again London is echoed by Roosevelt: "Certainly", wrote the
President, "prize-fighting is not half as brutalizing or demoralizing as many
forms of big business and of the legal work carried on in connection with big
business".[17]

Meat and honesty are also central to London's 1909 short story, "A Piece of
Steak", where he describes his has-been boxer-protagonist, Tom King, "leaving
to go out into the night" into the jungle "to get meat for his mate and cubs – not
like the modern working-man going to his machine grind, but in the old,
primitive, royal, animal way, by fighting for it".[18]

Shortly I will consider how far the rest of London's story undermines this
primitivist position, but the endurance of the urban desire for "the old, primitive,
royal, animal way" in more recent fiction is also worth observing. Chuck
Palahniuk's 1996 novel, *Fight Club* presents fighting as a way of restoring
strenuously masculine values to decadent, feminized city dwellers locked into
the late twentieth-century version of "the machine grind". "In the real world",
the novel's narrator is "a recall campaign coordinator in a shirt and tie ...
changing the overheads and slides as my boss tells Microsoft how he chose a

---

[15] Theodore Roosevelt, *An Autobiography* (1913), New York, 1985, 42.

[16] Jack London, "The Somnambulists", in *Revolution and Other Essays*, New York, 1910.

[17] Roosevelt, 43. In his report on the Britt-Nelson fight London expresses similar
sentiments: "... all hail to both of them! They play the clean game of life. And I, for one,
would rather be either of them this day at Colma than a man who took no exercise with his
body to-day but instead waxed physically gross in the course of gathering to himself a few
dollars in the commercial game" (*Jack London Reports*, eds King Hendricks and Irving
Shepard, New York, 1971).

[18] Jack London, "A Piece of Steak" (1909), in *The Portable Jack London*, ed. Earle Labo,
Penguin, 1994, 232-48. A story similarly concerned with food as fuel for the boxer's
labour is Arthur Morrison's "Three Rounds", in *Tales of Mean Streets* (1894), London,
1927, 85-96.

particular shade of pale cornflower blue for an icon".[19] But while other men go to the gym in order to "look like men, as if being a man means looking the way a sculptor or an art director says", the narrator goes to the secret fight club to actually become a real man.[20] While the followers of works such as Robert Bly's *Iron John* need to relinquish the city and go into the woods to regain their masculinity, the denizens of Fight Club can forgo urban values without leaving the city's confines.

But bringing the instincts of the jungle or the woods into the city streets is no more straightforward than channelling the energies of the street into the gym. If, in "A Piece of Steak", Tom King is presented as a "fighting animal", he is also, and perhaps more fundamentally, a modern urban worker, trying to scrape together a living. The language London uses to describe the fight continually confuses the primitive with the professional. "Sheer animal" that he is, fighting is nevertheless "a plain business proposition" to King. In boxing terms at least, he is "old", and so he must fight with a "policy of economy" – in a way that is "parsimonious of effort", showing little "expenditure of effort". His experience is described as his "chief asset". The story revolves around the "piece of steak" which he could not afford to have before the fight, and which, he thinks, would have enabled him to win:

> A great and terrible hatred rose up in him for the butchers who would not give him credit .... A piece of steak was such a little thing, a few pennies at best; yet it meant thirty quid to him (206).

On one level, the meaty imagery that pervades this and other boxing stories (think of Rocky training by punching a side of beef) evokes a world in which the "old, primitive, royal, animal" ways still operate. On another level, however, it is clear that in the urban jungle steak is simply what the modern worker requires to turn himself into the piece of meat that the urban capitalist "machine" itself requires.[21] The "pure" fight between dogs that London describes in *The Call of the Wild* is not possible in the city, where primitive animal instincts are always corrupted by the complexities of modern human life.[22] The "fight game", Midge

---

[19] Chuck Palahniuk, *Fight Club*, London, 1997, 49. In 1999 the novel was adapted into a film directed by David Fincher. See Kasia Boddy, "Franchising *Fight Club*", *Berliner Debatte Initial*, XII/1 (2001), 110-20.

[20] Palahniuk, 50.

[21] London was very aware of "muscle" as a commodity in capitalist society and wrote often of his decision "to sell no more muscle, and to become a vendor of brains": "What Life Means to Me" (1905), in *The Portable Jack London*, 478.

[22] See Jacqueline Tavernier-Courbin, "*The Call of the Wild* and *The Jungle*: Jack London's and Upton Sinclair's Animal and Human Jungles", in *The Cambridge Companion to American Realism and Naturalism*, ed. Donald Pizer, Cambridge, 1995, 236-62.

Kelly tells his brother in the classic film noir, *Champion*, is "like any other business – only the blood shows".[23]

Not "just another bum from the neighborhood"

If fighting did not always provide a way to leave the city in metaphorical ways, it was sometimes more successful in literal ways. Indeed the classic popular boxing story is one of escape: the poor boy from the neighbourhood who "makes it" and leaves the neighbourhood for the wider city, the wider world. A recent variation on this theme is Karen Kusama's film *Girlfight* (2000). Diana Guzman (Michele Rodriguez) and her boyfriend Adrian (Santiago Douglas) both want to box their way out of the Brooklyn housing projects. "I'm gonna turn pro and I'm gonna move far away from here, to a place where I'm not gonna get killed doing my laundry", he tells her. By the end of the film, and not only because she has beaten him in the ring, we realize that it is she who will manage to escape.

The story of the sportsman who escapes from the ghetto provides a particular spin on the perennial American myth of reinvention, epitomized in the nineteenth century by Horatio Alger's *Ragged Dick, Or, Street Life in New York with the Boot Blacks* (1868). Early in the book, Alger makes plain how indebted he is to fairy tales of transformation such as Dick Whittington or Cinderella. When Dick is given a new set of clothes by his benefactor, he looks in the mirror and exclaims, "that isn't me, is it? .... It reminds me of Cinderella, when she was changed into a fairy princess."[24] Reinvention starts by changing one's appearance by changing one's clothes. Cinderella needed a new dress before she could leave the kitchen and go to the ball. Dressed in his new suit, Dick can move in very different circles than he could in his rags. For the boxer, however, physical transformation must take place at a more fundamental level – that of the body itself. *Rocky* (1976) is a pure example of such a fairy tale.

Rocky Balboa (Sylvester Stallone) is "just another bum from the neighborhood", but, unlike all the others, he is given the fairy-tale chance of fighting the World Heavyweight Champion, Apollo Creed (played by Carl Weathers in a thinly disguised caricature of Muhammad Ali). Most of the film focuses on the training process, on Rocky's willing effort to transform his body. Crucially, this is not confined to the gym, and we see him running through the streets of Philadelphia, being offered fruit from market stalls, the local Italian community obviously behind him. Presumably Apollo Creed has the backing of the black community, but we never see any local popular support for him – he is presented simply as the product of corporate (that is, false) America.

Boxing dramas frequently enact a tension between local (ethnic and racial) identities and "Americanness" itself. *Rocky* presents this as unproblematic.

---

[23] *Champion* (dir. Stanley Kramer, 1949) starred Kirk Douglas as Midge. The film was based on Ring Lardner's short story of the same title.

[24] Horatio Alger, Jr, *Ragged Dick, Or, Street Life in New York with the Boot Blacks*, Signet Books, 1990, 24.

Apollo Creed's great crime, the film suggests, is assuming that he represents America – he enters the title fight dressed as Uncle Sam. But he is an illegitimate Uncle Sam, not only because he is black, but also because he represents the savvy and articulate (for which we are encouraged to read glib) values of the counterculture. Rocky – an inarticulate boy from "the neighborhood" – is really what "the land of opportunity" wants to be all about. He is both white ethnic – the "Italian Stallion" – and American; indeed, while Creed's race excludes him from "true" Americanness, Rocky's foreign ethnicity uniquely qualifies him. A self-conscious bicentennial fantasy, the film is set in the city of the Founding Fathers, Philadelphia. In the uneasy America of the mid-Seventies, though, Rocky's great test is not whether he can beat Creed – the film suggests that that is too much to hope for – but simply whether he can regain his pride, and the pride of the neighbourhood, by "going the distance".[25]

In *Rocky* it is significantly the neighbourhood rather than the city that is a synecdoche for the country itself. The film is deeply nostalgic for a national spirit based around the enduring allegiance to, rather than the transcendence of, neighbourhood loyalties and values. As in the boxing films of the Thirties and Forties, those values are embodied in the fighter's neighbourhood girlfriend. Unconcerned that he has not won, Rocky's only impulse at the end of the fight is to call out "Adrian". In the darker and more complex films of the Forties, the local girl (representing the neighbourhood) often has to put up a fight against the temptations of the femme fatale (the city). Robert Rossen's *Body and Soul* (1947), for example, is the story of a man seduced away from the values of the Jewish neighbourhood by the corrupt capitalism of the city, the neighbourhood and the city being each represented by a different woman. But in the final scene, although Charley (John Garfield) has taken money to throw the fight, his conscience overcomes him and he fights to win. His victory, however, affirms more than his own integrity. He regains his sweetheart, and the film ends with "the neighborhood swallow[ing] Charley up".[26]

---

[25] In *Rocky II*, Creed loses his title, and by III and IV the two men become friends, "a fantasy", as Tim O'Brien notes, "that implies that interracial harmony only blossoms as soon as the white man wins" (*The Screening of America*, New York, 1990, 87). See also Leonard Quart and Albert Auster, "The Working Class Goes to Hollywood", in *Cinema, Politics and Society in America*, eds Philip Davies and Brian Neve, Manchester, 1981, 163-75, and Daniel J. Leab, "The Blue Collar Ethic in Bicentennial America: *Rocky* (1976)", in *American History/American Film: Interpreting the Hollywood Image*, eds John E. O'Connor and Martin A. Jackson, New York, 1988, 257-72. *Rocky* is often compared to Robert Wise's 1956 biopic *Somebody Up There Likes Me* (where Paul Newman stars as Rocky Graziano), one of the few other boxing movies to affirm upward mobility in a straightforwardly optimistic way. See also Harold Robbins's 1955 novel *A Stone for Danny Fisher*, in which Danny fights in order that he can move back to the middle-class neighbourhood his family were forced to leave during the Depression.

[26] Brain Neve is quoting Abraham Polonsky's shooting script for *Body and Soul* (dir. Robert Rossen, 1947) in *Film and Politics in America: A Social Tradition*, London, 1992, 133.

"Are there no other Christians than *fighters* in America?"
Although films such as *Rocky* and *Body and Soul* suggest that the
neighbourhood represents a moral purity unavailable beyond its confines, neither
of these denies that success is nevertheless always measured by outside
recognition. In his memoir, *Manchild in the Promised Land*, Claude Brown
writes of his friend, Turk:

> Whenever I went up to Harlem and saw somebody like Turk, I knew that all the
> junkies admired him, and all the kids and the older generation too. Here was a
> neighborhood boy who had really made good. Turk had become quite a reputable
> boxer now. Just about everybody in the neighborhood watched him on TV when
> he had a fight. Many, including me, had even gone down to watch a couple of his
> fights down at the Garden. I guess it was a symbol of achievement that was
> possible in the community. Damn, somebody from Eighth Avenue could make
> it.[27]

Turk is a "symbol of achievement" for "the community" not only because he can
leave it behind but also because his success is recognized far beyond Eighth
Avenue. He now performs under the wider gaze of "the city" – in Madison
Square Garden – and indeed the country – through TV. Those forced to remain in
the neighbourhood (the vast majority) can "make good" vicariously through
their representative. In this case, Turk literally was "a neighborhood boy". Often,
though, the processes of symbolic identification are less direct.

The development of sports in the late nineteenth and early twentieth
centuries, it has been argued, is closely linked to questions of national identity –
what it meant to be an American, and, more critically for the new immigrant
populations, what was needed to become an American.[28] In Abraham Cahan's
1896 novel, *Yekl: A Tale of the New York Ghetto* (filmed in 1974 as *Hester
Street*), Yekl Podkovnik's metamorphosis into Jake, "an American feller, a
Yankee", begins when he starts following the fights and identifying with the
Boston-Irish fighter John Sullivan. He gives his fellow sweatshop workers a
detailed account of the exploits of Sullivan, Corbett and others – proudly
displaying his grasp of the correct idiom:

> "Say, Dzake," the presser broke in, "John Sullivan is *tzampion* no longer, is
> he?"

---

[27] Claude Brown, *Manchild in the Promised Land*, Signet Books, 1965, 368 (see also
Carlo Rotello, *October Cities*, Berkeley, 1998, chapter 11).
[28] On the development of an American national ethos in this period, see Alan
Trachtenberg, *The Incorporation of America*, New York, 1982, 179-81; Philip Gleason,
"American Identity and Americanization", in *Harvard Encyclopedia of American Ethnic
Groups*, ed. Stephan Thernstrom, Cambridge: Mass, 1980, 31-58, and most relevantly
S.W. Pope, *Patriotic Games: Sporting Traditions in the American Imagination, 1876-
1926*, Oxford, 1997.

"Oh no! Not always is it holiday!" Jake responded, with what he considered a Yankee jerk of his head. "Why don't you know? Jimmie Corbett *leaked* him, and Jimmie *leaked* Cholly Meetchel, too. *You can betch you' bootsh!* Johnnie could not leak Chollie, *becaush* he is a big *bluffer*, Chollie is," he pursued, his clean-shaven florid face beaming with enthusiasm for his subject, and with pride in the diminutive proper nouns he flaunted.[29]

For Yekl/Jake, following boxing not only provides an excuse to show off his new mastery of American colloquialisms, but offers also a means of asserting what he sees as a particularly American kind of masculinity

> "Let it be as you say," said the leader of the minority, withdrawing from the contest to resume his newspaper. "My grandma's last care it is who can fight best."
> "Nice pleasure, *anyhull*," remarked the widow. "*Never min'*, we shall see how it will lie in his head when he has a wife and children to *support*."
> .... "Don't you like it? I do," Jake declared tartly. "Once I live in America," he pursued, on the defensive, "I want to know that I live in America. *Dot'sh a kin' a man I am!* One must not be a *greenhorn*. Here a Jew is as good as a Gentile. How then would you have it? The way it is in Russia, where a Jew is afraid to stand within four ells of a Christian?"
> "Are there no other Christians than *fighters* in America?" Bernstein objected with an amused smile.[30]

Jake identifies here with the Irish-Boston fighter John Sullivan, and indeed many of the early Jewish fighters adopted Irish aliases because the Irish were considered the toughest.[31] In James T. Farrell's 1932 novel *Young Lonigan*, set in 1916, Old Man O'Brien remembers the good old days, "when most of them [the boxers] were real Irish, lads who'd bless themselves before they fought: they weren't fake Irish like most of the present-day dagoes and wops and

---

[29] *Gentleman Jim* (dir. Robert Buckner, 1942) tells the story of the man who took Sullivan's title, San Francisco Irish fighter Jim Corbett (Errol Flynn), and how he earns enough to move his family from the South Side to Nob Hill. For a discussion of *Yekl*'s relationship to the vaudeville tradition, see Sabine Haenni, "Visual and Theatrical Culture, Tenement Fiction, and the Immigrant Subject in Abraham Cahan's *Yekl*", *American Literature*, LXXI/3 (1999), 493-527.
[30] Abraham Cahan, *Yekl: A Tale of the New York Ghetto* (1896), in *The Imported Bridegroom and Other Stories*, Signet Books, 1996, 170-71. Negative attitudes to sports among Jews of Cahan's generation are also apparent in Irving Howe's *The World of Our Fathers*, New York, 1976.
[31] Vachel Lindsay also presents Sullivan as a masculine role model in his celebratory poem, "John L. Sullivan, The Strong Boy of Boston". Until he heard "the battle trumpet sound" of Sullivan, he writes, he was under the influence of "the cult of Tennyson's Elaine" with Louisa Alcott as his "gentle guide" (*Collected Poems*, New York, 1925, 93).

sheenies who took Hibernian names".[32] Meanwhile, Jewish boy, Davey Cohen, sees "all the Irish race personified in the face of Studs Lonigan" and imagines himself "punching that face, cutting it, bloodying the nose, blackening the eyes, mashing it". He dreams of becoming "a great fighter like Benny Leonard, who was one smart hebe that could beat the Irish at their own game".[33]

Nelson Algren's *Never Come Morning* (1942) is another story which uses attitudes towards boxing to represent the clash between ethnicities, generations, and Old and New World values. Set in Chicago's "Little Polonia", an area bounded triangularly by three streets (Chicago, Ashland, and Milwaukee Avenues), the novel tells the story of Bruno Bicek and his dream to be a boxing champion, and how, instead, he ends up in jail on a murder charge. "If they had stayed in the Old World", Mama Bicek thinks, "her son would have been a good son. There a boy had to behave himself or be put in the army."[34] The neighbourhood barer, and prime villain, Bonifacy, is reminiscent of the grandmother in *Yekl* in his incomprehension of "young Poles with a purely amateur enthusiasm for a wop outfielder or a Jew welterweight .... Life in the old world had been too hard to permit young men to play games."[35] (What he can appreciate – and herein lies the novel's tragedy – is the value of boxing, and gambling, as a way of making money.) The boys of "the Triangle" also follow Yekl in compulsively adding American nicknames to their Polish surnames – Bruno (aka "Lefty", "Biceps", "Powerhouse", "Iron-Man", "Killer") – more compulsively than anyone. When arrested on a murder charge, he proudly tells the police that he is "a citizen", "a Polish-American citizen" and distinguishes himself from greenhorns who do not speak English properly.[36] Nevertheless, all

---

[32] James T. Farrell, *Young Lonigan*, in *Studs Lonigan*, New York, 1977, 82.

[33] *Ibid.*, 143, 145. The first Jewish American champions were bantamweight Harry Harris, who won his crown in 1900, and featherweight Abe Attell, who held the title from 1904 to 1912. In the 1910s there were four Jewish champions, including lightweight Benny Leonard, and by World War I more contenders were Jewish than of any other ethnic group. Many faced disapproval from their families and the Jewish community. Benny Leonard, for example, adopted that name (he was really Benjamin Leiner) to hide his career from his parents (see Steven Riess, "The Jewish American Boxing Experience, 1890-1940", *American-Jewish History*, 56 [1985], 223-54, and Peter Levine, "'Oy Such Fighter!': Boxing and the American Jewish Experience", in *The New American Sport History*, 251-83).

[34] Nelson Algren, *Never Come Morning*, New York, 1987, 16.

[35] *Ibid.*, 3.

[36] *Ibid.*, 111, 122. Officer Adamovitch decides he does not like Bruno because "This was a low-class Polack. He himself was a high-class Polack because his name was Adamovitch and not Adamowski. This sort of kid kept spoiling things for the high-class Polacks by always showing off instead of just being good citizens like the Irish. That's why the Irish ran City Hall and the Police Department and the Board of Education and the Post Office while the Polacks lived off relief and got drunk and never got anywhere and had everybody down on them, even their own priests. All they could do like the Irish, Old Adamovitch reflected bitterly, was to fight under Irish names at the City Garden" (127-

the enmities in the novel are expressed in terms of their Old World nationalities and loyalties – we do not know names, just the Jew, the Mex, the Polack, the Litvak and the Greek. Only the idea of the Great White Hope overrides ethnic identity. In the fight that closes the book, Bruno is aware that the crowd are applauding him simply for "being white".[37]

Versions of Poisonville

"The only objection I have to the prize ring", maintained Roosevelt, "is the crookedness that has attended its commercial development". Crookedness has never strayed far from the prize ring, whose activities were linked with gambling, prostitution and other urban "underworld" activities from its very beginning.[38] Indeed, arguments about making (or keeping) boxing illegal have traditionally focused on its associations with crime rather than its inherent physically or morally damaging features.

In Upton Sinclair's novel of the Chicago stockyards, *The Jungle* (1906), prizefighting is illegal, but, like many other things, it continues for a price. The Democratic Party's "War-Whoop League" runs a clubhouse just outside the stockyards – "they had prize fights every now and then, and cock fights and even dog fights. The policemen in the district all belonged to the league, and, instead of suppressing the fights, they sold tickets for them":[39]

> The law forbade Sunday drinking; and this had delivered the saloon-keepers into the hands of the police, and made an alliance between them necessary .... It was the same with ... any other man or woman who had a means of getting "graft", and was willing to pay over a share of it: the green-goods man and the highwayman, the pickpocket and the sneak thief ... the prize-fighter and the professional slugger, the race-track "tout", the procurer, the white-slave agent, and the expert seducer of young girls. All these agencies of corruption were banded together, and leagued in blood brotherhood with the politician and the police; more often than not they were one and the same person – the police captain would own the brothel he pretended to raid .... "Hinkydink" or "Bath-house John" or others of that ilk, were proprietors of the most notorious dives in Chicago, and also the "gray wolves" of the city council, who gave away the streets of the city to the business men; and those who patronized their places were the gamblers and the prize-fighters who set the law at defiance, and the burglars and hold-up men who kept the whole city in terror. On election day all those powers of vice and corruption were one power; they could tell within one per cent what the vote of their district would be, and they could change it at an hour's notice.[40]

---

28).
[37] *Ibid.*, 261.
[38] Roosevelt, 44 (see Kellow Chesney, *The Victorian Underworld*, London, 1970, ch. 9, "The sporting underworld").
[39] Upton Sinclair, *The Jungle* (1906), Signet Books, 1960, 96.
[40] *Ibid.*, 250.

Following the introduction of the Marquis of Queensbury Rules in the 1880s, boxing became increasingly popular in the major American cities, and, depending on the political complexion of the state government, moved in and out of legality. As Sinclair indicates, even when technically illegal, prizefighting always continued for a price. One scam was to stage "exhibitions" or operate politically linked "membership clubs" – anyone who paid a dollar could join the club and watch the fight. George Bellows's 1909 painting "Both Members of This Club" presents such a fight. The setting is dark and the figures are grotesques; the boxers' bodies blend in a smear of white and brown (bodies) and red (blood). Looking at the painting we are placed in the audience, and ourselves become members of the club.[41]

In 1920, the sport assumed permanent legitimacy, but the interlinked corruption of prizefighting, police and politics that Sinclair presented in 1906 has remained a staple of urban storytelling ever since.[42] A cursory glance at two recent films indicates that it is still a powerfully available metaphor. In order to grasp the full devilry of Al Pacino as Satan-as-lawyer in Taylor Hackford's *The Devil's Advocate* (1997), we see him taking his innocent out-of-towner prey (Keanu Reeves) to a boxing match in one of America's last symbols of old-style urban sleaze, Atlantic City. Atlantic City is also the setting of Brian de Palma's 1998 *Snake Eyes*, where a political assassination takes place under cover of a corrupt championship bout. These examples draw on a deep-rooted image of professional boxing as corrupt to its core, an image that is perhaps most powerfully expressed in mid-century film noir and roman noir.[43]

In Dashiell Hammett's *Red Harvest*, for example, one of the crimes of

---

[41] See Marianne Dowzema's excellent *George Bellows and Urban America*, New Haven, 1992.

[42] One can, however, see an enormous difference in the treatment of boxing after legalization by comparing Bellows's "club paintings", "Both Members" and "Stag at Sharkey's" (1907), with his paintings of legitimate, high-profile boxing, "Ringside Seats" (1924) and "Dempsey and Firpo" (1924). As part of the process of making boxing respectable, women were encouraged to attend fights. We might compare Jack London's 1905 novella *The Game*, in which his heroine is forced to disguise herself as a man in order to watch her lover fight, with Djuna Barnes's 1914 essay "My Sister and I at a New York Prizefight", which begins by noting the new phenomenon of women attending boxing matches and concludes by asking "Was it, after all, the men in the audience who had been careless and indifferent to pain?" (*New York*, ed. Alyce Barry, Los Angeles, 1989, 173). By 1921, when she interviewed Jack Dempsey, Barnes no longer found it remarkable that women should be interested in boxing. Dempsey acknowledges that "The old days of cheating and cursing have passed …. I suppose it's due to women." Moreover, "it's no longer enough to have speed and a good right arm to be the favourite. You have to be good-looking, too, now that the ladies go to fights"("Dempsey Welcomes Women Fans", in *I Could Never Be Lonely without a Husband*, ed. Alyce Barry, London, 1987, 284). See also *The Game*, ch. 3, Lincoln: Nebr., 2001.

[43] A lighter treatment of this theme can be found in the Spider McCoy stories of Damon Runyon's *On Broadway*, 1950.

Poisonville is its crooked prizefighting. An operative from the Continental Detective Agency, San Francisco branch, is sent to investigate:

> We talked about the fights. Nothing more was said about me versus Poisonville .... [The gambler] even gave me what seemed to be a straight tip on the fights – telling me any bet on the main event would be good if its maker remembered that Kid Cooper would probably knock Ike Bush out in the sixth round. He seemed to know what he was talking about, and it didn't seem to be news to the others.[44]

At the fight, however, Cooper is unable to do what he had agreed to, and finally the referee is forced to acknowledge Bush's victory:

> When the referee had finally stalled through the count, he raised Bush's hand. Neither of them looked happy.
> A high twinkle of light caught my eye. A short silvery streak slanted down from one of the small balconies.
> A woman screamed.
> The silvery streak ended its flashing slant in the ring with a sound that was partly a thud, partly a snap.
> Ike Bush took his arm out of the referee's hand and pitched down on top of Kid Cooper. A black knife-handle stuck out of the nape of Bush's neck.[45]

In stories like these, the heroism of the boxer lies less in his ability to beat his opponent than in his attempt to resist the racket, to refuse to comply with the gangster's wishes. Perhaps the supreme example of such redemptive resistance is Robert Wise's highly allegorical film, *The Set Up* (1949). A third-rate boxer and his wife go to the ironically named Paradise City for one last fight. (Paradise City AC is next to a dance hall called Dreamland, and across the street from the Hotel Cozy.) Stoker Thompson (Robert Ryan) is fighting a much younger, stronger man, and everyone but he is aware that the fight is fixed. Everyone, including he himself, will gain if he loses. In the classic film noir gesture of integrity and futile defiance, when Stocker finds out about the set up, he fights so hard that he wins. But his victory is limited to the confines of the square circle. After he leaves the gym, the gangsters work him over in the grim alleyway. No matter how Christ-like Stoker is – and this is something we are not allowed to forget – Paradise City is really just another name for Poisonville.

Recent works have revisited and revised these *noir* settings. Tarantino's *Pulp Fiction* (1994) and James Ellroy's *The Black Dahlia* (1987) both provide an ironic twist on the "set up" theme. In Ellroy's novel, Blanchard and Bleichert are boxers turned LAPD-cops: they have "continued fighting out of the ring – this time in the war against crime". Recruitment into the force is down and in a ploy to "attract better men", a fight is planned between the old rivals. In the traditional

---

[44] Dashiell Hammett, *Red Harvest*, Pan Books, 1974, 63.

[45] *Red Harvest*, 72.

manner, Bleichert decides to take a dive and bets against himself in order to get enough money to put his father into "a class rest home".[46] During the fight, however, when he hears the crowd calling his name, he "knew that all bets were off" and fights to win. But as this is postmodern *noir*, he loses anyway, and so gets his money. "And when it all sank in", Bleichert confesses, "I laughed…".[47]

No Way Out

In the "social problem" discourse of the late nineteenth century, an often-repeated phrase was "the way out". What possible "way out" could there be for the urban poor, asked reformers such as William Booth (in England) and Jacob Riis (in the United States).[48] In Arthur Morrison's *A Child of the Jago*, despite the best efforts of Father Sturt, the violence of the streets is never channelled. A novel full of street battles, it ends with a fight in which the protagonist, Dicky, is killed. With his dying breath, he asks Father Sturt to "Tell Mist' Beveridge there's 'nother way out – better".[49]

If the classic naturalist fictions of the turn of the century tend to suggest death as the only way out, later twentieth-century works focus instead on exploring what happens when even that escape is denied. In *Never Come Morning*, for example, each of the spaces of the neighbourhood – the brothel, the jail, the beer flat, the gang clubhouse, the poolroom, the barber shop (and the bird cage within it), the police station, the amusement park, and the boxing ring – simply repeats the enclosure of the others. Indeed, Algren uses these places to create an insistently interlocking or interchangeable network of symbols. "The Triangle's my territory", boasts Bruno, and there is very little sense of the existence of a world, indeed of a city, beyond the boundaries of its three streets.[50] Identities are so local that characters introduce each other by their street names ("Catfood N. from Fry St", "Bruno B. from Potomac and Paulina", "Steffi R. from by the poolroom").[51] When, under police interrogation, Bruno brags about trips to St Paul and St Louis, a police officer interrupts:

> "He's just tryin' to throw you off, Scully – you ain't seen this Polack no place excep' between that poolroom 'n that barber shop. He was in trouble when he was in short pants 'n he ain't been out of the Triangle since him 'n a couple others like

---

[46] James Ellroy, *The Black Dahlia*, Arrow Books, 1993, 28, 36.

[47] *Ibid.*, 49, 51.

[48] William Booth, *In Darkest England and the Way Out*, London: Salvation Army, 1890. Jacob Riis wrote in *How the Other Half Lives* (1890): "The one way out [that the sanitarian of the last generation] saw – rapid transit to the suburbs – has brought no relief. We know now that there is no way out."

[49] *The Child of the Jago*, 173 (see Peter Keating, *The Haunted Study: A Social History of the English Novel 1875-1914* [1989], Fontana, 1991, 307-308; 313-15).

[50] *Never Come Morning*, 87.

[51] *Ibid.*, 59, 60.

him stole a W.P.A. check 'n cashed it. I don't ferget nothin', Lefthander. You don't even get as far south as Lake Street 'cause you're scared one of them Lake Street boogies 'll take after you with a shiv'." He confided earnestly to Scully: "These Polacks figure the South-side is out of town."[52]

The wider world, the wider city even, only really exists for Bruno and his friends in the magazines and movies that they consume. Chicago is indeed, as Algren puts it, a "city of [the] mind".[53]

The book is framed by two fight scenes. In the opening sequence, Casey Benkowski dutifully takes a dive and returns to the barber's shop. The final chapter rests on whether Bruno "Biceps" Bicek will do the same. He does not but, as was the case with Stoker Thompson, his gesture of existentialist heroism proves futile. The police are waiting to take him to prison, just one more "ropeless ring".[54]

If the dream embodied in boxing fiction is one of escape through the transformation (and sale) of one's body, the nightmare is one in which selling the body keeps you trapped forever in the same place. Boxing stories, and not only those of a *noir* type, frequently draw an analogy between boxing and prostitution – both the boxer and the prostitute sell their bodies and both are manipulated by their pimp managers. Perhaps the first writer to make this connection was George Bernard Shaw, whose fourth novel *Cashel Byron's Profession* (1886) was an immensely successful boxing story. Shaw was distressed that his readers did not fully apprehend his criticisms of the sport and in 1901 attached an "Afterword" to explain himself:

> As long as society is so organized that the destitute athlete and the destitute beauty are forced to choose between underpaid drudgery as industrial producers, and comparative self-respect, plenty, and popularity as prize-fighters and mercenary brides, licit or illicit, it is idle to affect virtuous indignation at their expense. The word prostitution should either not be used at all, or else applied impartially to all persons who do things for money that they would not do if they had other assured means of livelihood.[55]

---

[52] *Ibid.*, 105.

[53] *Ibid.*, 19. While popular culture encourages dreams of escape, Algren never lets us forget how illusory these are. In this, and other aspects, *Never Come Morning* owes a lot to Richard Wright's *Native Son* (1940) (see Ross Pudaloff, "Celebrity as Identity: *Native Son* and Mass Culture", in *Richard Wright: Critical Perspectives Past and Present*, eds Henry Louis Gates Jr and K.A. Appiah, New York, 1993, 156-70).

[54] *Ibid.*, 118.

[55] George Bernard Shaw, "Afterword", in *Cashel Byron's Profession* (1901), London, 1925, 345-46.

Shaw presents the parallel professions of Cashel Byron and Mrs Warren as rational career choices in an unjust world.[56] Algren is less sanguine. For Bruno and his girlfriend Steffi, the fact that they inhabit a "ropeless ring" and a "curtained brothel" is truly terrible. For both of them, "there is no outside world".[57]

"Dream on for yourself"

In his report on Joe Louis's victory over Max Schmeling, Richard Wright noted the political potential of the "High Tide in Harlem" that Louis's victory inspired:

> Carry the dream on for yourself; lift it out of the trifling guise of a prizefight celebration and supply the social and economic details and you have the secret dynamics of proletarian aspiration. The eyes of these people were bold that night. Their fear of property, of the armed police fell away. There was in their chant a hunger deeper than that for bread as they marched along .... They wanted to feel that their expanding feelings were not limited; that the earth was theirs as much as anybody else's; that they did not have to live by proscription in one corner of it ....[58]

For the communist Wright, this is a moment of potentially revolutionary significance – "the eyes of these people were bold that night". Through Louis's victory, he suggests, the proletariat broke out of the confines of their own square circle and recognized "that the earth was theirs ... that they did not have to live by proscription in one corner of it".[59]

More generally, it is hard to co-opt the boxing narrative for a revolutionary story. Boxing stories – "deghettoization narratives", in Carlo Rotella's terminology – rarely question the existence of the ghetto itself or why its boundaries should be so firmly drawn.[60] Indeed, the boxing tale (like boxing

---

[56] Shaw's play *Mrs Warren's Profession* (1893) was originally subtitled "A tragic variation on the theme of *Cashel Byron's Profession*". On Shaw's interest in boxing more generally, see Benny Green, *Shaw's Champions*, London, 1978. The sense that these are the inevitable violent professions of the city is memorably explored in Stanley Kubrick's *Killer's Kiss* (1955), which presents a triangle of sexual obsession between a gangster, a dance-hall girl and a prizefighter.

[57] *Never Come Morning*, 208. For a discussion of *Never Come Morning* as "a captivity tale set in the modern city", and, more generally, a consideration of the novel's debts to Chicago sociology, see Carla Cappetti, *Writing Chicago: Modernism, Ethnography and the Novel*, New York, 1993, 171.

[58] Richard Wright, "High Tide in Harlem", *New Masses*, 5 July 1938, reprinted in *Speech and Power*, ed. Gerald Early, Hopewell: NJ, 1992, I, 157.

[59] Earlier in the essay he describes Harlem as "that area of a few small blocks in upper Manhattan where a quarter of a million Negroes are forced to live through an elaborate connivance among landlords, merchants, and politicians ...." (*ibid.*, 156).

[60] *October Cities*, 279.

itself), whether it ends in victory or failure, is an inherently individualistic drama. Finding "a way out" is seen as an exceptional achievement, bordering in many cases on the miraculous. This insistent individualism distinguishes the boxing story from that other popular American sports genre, the baseball story. The mythology of baseball is one of community-driven teamwork and its dramas are enacted in sunlit pastoral oases rather than small dark corners of the city. Bruno is good at both sports, but finally he opts for boxing, partly because the money is better, but largely, he says, because, however futile it might be, "I feel more like sluggin' somebody these days than tryin' t' throw a ball past his knees".[61]

---

[61] *Never Come Morning*, 117. I would like to thank my father for his help with this article, and for suggesting I read Claude Brown.

THE LITERARY CITY:
BETWEEN SYSTEM AND SENSATION

FREDERIK TYGSTRUP

Representing the city or urban representation?
Questions concerning literary cities not only arise when the object of study is the impact of modern urban culture on the human intellectual and sensory apparatus and the various literary representations of this impact. You do not have to focus directly on problems related to the study of modern urban life to realize how greatly the modern city has influenced twentieth-century literature. Even the most cursory examination of the early twentieth-century novel shows that an astonishing number of the great works from this period are intimately linked to the image of the city; we all possess an imaginary literary Baedecker with reminiscences of Marcel Proust's Paris, James Joyce's Dublin, Robert Musil's Vienna, Franz Kafka's Prague, Alfred Döblin's Berlin, Virginia Woolf's London, John Dos Passos's New York, Alexander Bely's Petersburg, and so on.

Franco Moretti has observed that the image of the novel in the nineteenth century was closely related to the idea of the nation state, and that it was the nation state that formed the proper space of the novel, materially as well as mentally.[1] This space included the city as an element, and often as a crucial one, but still only as one of many interrelated parts, as we see it indicated in the metaphorical image of the capital as the head of the national organism. The protagonists of the nineteenth-century novels were French, Russians, English, and so forth. By contrast, their heirs in the twentieth-century novel do not live in national capitals, but in metropolizes in a radicalized and far more isolated sense. These metropolizes are no longer quintessential representatives of national organisms, but organisms in their own right, integral universes, which, furthermore, seem less characteristic by being specific cities rather than cities in a somewhat more general sense (as Musil puts it, "… one always wants to know quite exactly what particular town it is. This distracts attention from more important things. No special significance should be attached to the name of the

---

[1] Franco Moretti, *Atlas of the European Literature 1800-1900*, London, 1998, 17.

city").[2] Through this new relation to the phenomenon of the city, the novel ceases to be national literature and becomes world literature. The literary world map no longer consists of nation states, each characterized by a certain relationship between city and country, centre and periphery, but of a system of metropolizes. These metropolizes seem to have a closer relationship to each other than to their respective national contexts, and the non-urbanized regions are similarly reduced from being vital contexts to being mere residual left-over spaces, something not yet urbanized – reduced from a positive to a negative definition. In Balzac you can still find images of rural production as a fundamental prerequisite for urban circulation, while rural environments in the twentieth-century novel are more likely to signal regression than production.

But this still does not amount to literary history; it is only history, a heavily stylized version of the history of how the relationship between country and city was conceived throughout the nineteenth century. There are, however, two more specific literary historical points that could be made within the framework of this general historical survey. The first point concerns the nature of the conspicuously massive thematic use of the city in the novel of the 1920s and 30s, which has not been superseded either earlier or later. The second point concerns some quite technical aspects of the representation of the city in the modern novel, which in turn involves the interrelation between the representation of the city and the formal development of the novel.

It is tempting to impute a certain, mutual fund of experience to the great generation of Modernist novelists as a historical basis for the more or less common use of the city as a theme, as if the city or life in the city had suddenly demanded a concentrated attention. But it would surely be fallacious to link this experience directly to the phenomenon of urbanization as such, to a violent expansion of the cities and of the characteristics of urban life in this specific period. Such a procedure would blind us to local differences, as well as to the longer historical perspective – that is, to the common experience, not of a single generation, but of an entire epoch – that "the form of the city changes faster ... than the heart of a mortal being", to quote Baudelaire's famous poem.[3] The specific generational experience should rather be identified as a historical reorganization of the ways of thinking of the urban phenomenon than related to directly measurable changes: an "archeological" change in the ways of thinking of the city, thinking of urban life, and thinking of the relationship between the city and its environments. In 1973, Raymond Williams remarked that "the common image of the country is now an image of the past, and the common image of the city an image of the future".[4] Throughout *The Country and the*

---

[2] Robert Musil, *The Man Without Qualities*, trans. Eithne Wilkins and Ernst Kaiser, New York, 1953, I, 4.

[3] "(la forme d'une ville/ Change plus vite, hélas! que le cœur d'un mortel)", "Le Cygne", in *Œuvres complètes*, Paris, 1975, 85.

[4] Raymond Williams, *The Country and the City*, London, 1973, 356 ff.

City, Williams diagnoses an ongoing modification of our mental geography – a modification towards which he himself takes a critical stand, because he finds that the new mental geography blinds itself to the perspective of development in the interrelation of city and country, but also a modification that, however one evaluates it, succinctly points out the attitude towards the city expressed by the Modernist generation, for whom the city is not an integral part of a coherent universe where one can actually conceive of a perspective of development in the interrelation of country and city. After World War I, after the breakdown of "the world of yesterday" and the feeling of bearing witness to the history not of any individual nation state but of the entire world, this generation seems to have the feeling of waking up to a future that has already begun. They find themselves stumbling unprepared into the twentieth century. And when they try to find their own feet in this new and uncertain situation they do not hesitate to plant them in the universe of the city. This gesture is not primarily aimed at finding a place in space; it expresses the urgency of finding a place in time. The novelists unanimously focus on the metropolizes as the only possible locations for an exploration of the future, in which they feel they already live. This does not imply, however, that the cities they confront and struggle to represent have undergone any profound transformation at this specific time, only that they no longer feel able to merge the cities into the mental geography they inherited from the nineteenth century of their adolescence. When the city becomes the favourite and central motive for an entire generation of writers, it might not be because they are suddenly recognizing and experiencing an entirely new mode of urban life, nor because they have discovered the city, but rather because they have lost the inherited image of the city embedded in a national and urban environment. They have lost the ancient mental map and are left as orphans in an intimate and strange city with which they no longer know what to do.

Raymond Williams puts this very well; after having diagnosed the new ways of plotting the country and the city in the mental universe as representatives of the past and the future, he continues: "That leaves, if we isolate them, an undefined present." The Modernist novelists' confrontation with the city is an attempt to think and to represent the urban reality that surrounds them through a new set of ideas and techniques – that is, to establish a new sensuous and intellectual determination of the city's "undefined present". In order to intervene in this undefined present, they have to invent new techniques of thinking of the city through the practice of writing. This problem raises the second discussion I mentioned earlier – the technical aspects of the relation between urban representation and the formal and aesthetic evolution of the novel in the Modernist tradition.

In an important book published in 1969, *Die erzählte Stadt*, the German literary historian Volker Klotz examines a number of urban images in the novel from the early eighteenth century to the early twentieth on the basis of the hypothesis that the loose and horizontal aesthetic structure of the novel, which allows it to examine several parallel or juxtaposed temporal, spatial, or mental universes within the same framework, has its ideal object in the image of the city. Thus, according to Klotz, there is a profound communication between the structure of the city and the structure of the novel; they are both, he asserts, "not only an expression, but also, due to their system-like organization, a form-giving organization of the prosaic world".[5] Within the confines of this very broadly conceived familiarity, Volker Klotz is able to point out a number of historical differentiations and lines of evolution, different ways of organizing novelistic cities.

In a critical comment to Klotz, Klaus Scherpe, another historian of urban literature, proposes making a historical distinction that remains unmentioned within Klotz's framework, but which is, nonetheless, crucial for our understanding of the modern literary representation of the city, namely, the distinction between what he calls the "narrated cities" of the eighteenth and nineteenth centuries and the "urban narratives" of the twentieth century.[6] In brief, this distinction draws on the ways in which the representation of the city is mediated in the narrative strategies of the individual works. In a traditional novelistic narrative, the city is presented within the confines of a plot that is centred on a subjective destiny and unfolded in a continuous spatio-temporal universe through a series of interconnected events, where the city forms the context of some of the events linked up in the plot line, or, more often, where the city is the place where converging plot lines, ambitions, and individual projects are brutally subdued. The narrated city is a complex topography where plot-sequences cross, or where the individual characters' existential projects are wrecked in the heteronomous system of antagonistic projects – you can find both in Balzac.

If the novel and the city are consubstantial, as Klotz asserts, this consubstantiality also seems to embrace a fundamental antagonism between the ideal linearity of narrative and the labyrinth-like complexity of the city. The novel can contain and express this antagonism, but it also, particularly when we consider the novel of the nineteenth century, bears witness to a kind of ideological tension between linearity and complexity that is deposited in the form and transforms the urban novels into novels of disillusion and the city into a locus of disillusion: the place where the illusions of the young man – the constituents for the outline of the plot-structure – are wrecked. In this respect, the narrated city seems to be a temporary phenomenon in the fiction of the nineteenth century, an anomaly in the universe conjectured by the narrative gesture.

Therefore the transition from the narrated city to an urban narrative thus

---

[5] "nicht bloß Ausdruck, sondern auch, dank ihrem systemcharacter, formende Organisation der prosaischen Welt" (Volker Klotz, *Die erzählte Stadt*, München, 1969, 439).

[6] See Klaus R. Scherpe, "Von der erzählten Stadt zur Stadterzählung", in *Diskurstheorien und Literaturwissenschaft*, eds Jürgen Fohrmann and Harro Müller, Frankfurt am Main, 1988, 421 ff.

takes place where the city, to put it somewhat briefly, is no longer represented by pre-urban narrative devices, but where elements of an urban experience are instead incorporated directly into the technique of representation, where discontinuity, accelerated velocity, de-individualization, chance and abrupt collisions, complex interactions between different and juxtaposed discursive and physical systems, and so on, serve as guidelines for the formal organization of the narrative.

Therefore, in a certain sense, the historical point of departure for the Modernist urban narratives is derived from the idea that the reality of the city can no longer be represented at all, because it defies the inherited principles of representation. The city as an "undefined present" implies a double challenge: a challenge to the literary technique, an impetus to invent new modes of representation able to convey the essentially urban-like, and at the same time – and this is a corollary to the first – a challenge to our thinking: how to think of the city in the first place, how to extract patterns from its abundant impulses to the senses and to the intellect, in order to establish an idea and a mental representation of the city and of what urban life does to human life.

The phenomenological horizon
This extremely ambitious programme for a contemporary literary representation of the metropolis – that it should invent techniques of rendering urban reality and in the same manoeuvre establish ways of thinking of the "undefined present" of the city for the first time – stems from the novels themselves. In a more or less explicit way, they all share the common basic assumption that we do not know how to cope with urban reality. Therefore, any representation of the city necessarily also becomes an epistemological task. The novels read the city and thus make specific demands on our reading of them. We will have to understand representation as something different from, and more complex than, a matter of simple reference, which would still confine us to the framework of the narrated city (and, furthermore, blind us to the fact that even the seemingly natural representational schemes in traditional narratives are themselves a manifestation of a certain epistemological structure of pre-judgement). We do not simply confront a rendition of the city, but its veritable construction, an invention of a specific fictional order – the urban narrative – that is consciously designed to think of and to represent the city in the same movement.

Following this line of reflection, the central task in the study of literary representations of the city would be to establish strategies of reading able to grasp this double aspect of urban narrative. The greatest peril for such a project would be to reduce the literary works to simple indices of a historical change of urban life. The sociological annotation of the modernist urban narratives is an obvious temptation: here we get a direct formal expression of the individual urban being made anonymous (one thinks of the narrator in Rilke's *Malte Laurids Brigge*), the fragmentation of sensation (Franz Biberkopf in tram 41 on its way to central Berlin on the first page of Döblin's *Berlin Alexanderplatz*), the abstraction of social relations, the development of mass society and the substitution of substitution of individual agencies for collective ones (the super-individual patterns of commuting in Musil's *The Man Without Qualities*), the abrupt and fragmented modes of communication (the newspaper headlines and advertising signs in Dos Passos), and so on.

All these traditional insights are true enough (or, rather, it is an obvious task to examine their truth value); the novels constitute, as Michel de Certeau has noticed, a veritable zoo of modes of experiencing and using the city.[7] But, to keep up with the artistic ambition of these novels, we also have to consider how their modes of experiencing and using the city can teach us how to think about the city – to know that we have not finished thinking about the city when we have made this annotation, but that we are then first starting to appreciate the ways in which the experience and the use of it, as they are acted out in the texts, are modes of thinking.

This approach to the epistemological content of the urban narrative might be clarified by adopting a phenomenological vocabulary – that is, by paying attention to the ways in which the specific urban experience and sensation are objectified in the literary form. In his famous essay of 1947, "What is Literature?", Jean-Paul Sartre schematized the phenomenological aspects of literary representation in a very instructive way by splitting it up into two procedures. The first step towards representation is a simple perception, my confrontation with a world of objects, where I synthesize the sensory impressions in an inner image – "un objet fait âme". The second step is a construction where, by means of the literary technique, I reconstruct not the reality I first met but the intentional image I established through the faculty of imagination – "une âme faite objet".[8]

The literary work is a symbolization of a symbolization of a given world of experience. Thus, the two phenomenological steps really distinguish between three successive layers of representation. This is, of course, in itself fairly banal. As far as concerns the first step, by today it has probably become a completely uncontroversial insight that the literary form contains no simple reference and that representation does not unproblematically reveal a finite state of facts. But in this specific case, the representation of the city, it is worthwhile to consider the problem of intentional constitution rather carefully, given what kind of object representation is dealing with. After all, the city is no simple phenomenological apple tree – I shall return to this later.

Concerning the second step, the mediation of the intentional imagery in the literary objectification, it might be helpful again to insist on the discontinuity involved in the act of representation, that the phenomenological "rêverie" unfolded in the literary text does not signify a given perception but objectifies it. The artistic work might start out from a sensational content, but what is hereby

---

[7] Michel de Certeau, *L'invention du quotidien* (1980), I, *Arts de faire*, Paris, 1990, ch. 9.

[8] Jean-Paul Sartre, *Situations*, Paris, 1948, II, 89 ff.

created is no signification of this content. Gilles Deleuze and Félix Guattari have proposed a conceptual framework that emphasizes this moment of phenomenological reflection: what art creates, they assert, are percepts: art may start out from a sensation and might create sensations, but only sensations that are exteriorized as objective percepts in the artistic material: "the aim of art is through the aesthetic material to extract a percept from the perception of an object and from the state of the perceiving subject."[9] Artistic creativity has to free itself from the specific objects and subjects of sensation in order to create an aesthetic image through the invention of percepts and, as Deleuze puts it, affects, objectified sensations and states of mind.

So we do not read about real sensations and emotions. Rather, art invents possible sensations and emotions through the construction of percepts and affects. And this is what we should look for in the urban narratives: configurations of possible sensations and emotions through which they contribute to thinking of the city. The urban narratives give us a variety of aspects and models, variations on the experience of the city: Rilke's and Joyce's sound percepts, Musil's percepts of movement, Proust's fetishized and synecdochical percepts (the pavement in the Guermantes backyard ...). All of this is registered and combined with characteristic affects, a certain silence associated with the sound percept, an immobility associated with the percept of movement, and so on – a series of objectified mental situations that arise from urban life.

System and sensation
This understanding of the literary construction of sensory and emotional qualities gives us a first idea of the character of the order of fiction in which urban narratives are thinking of the city. Admittedly, these concepts remain very general, as they cover a wide variety of aesthetic products; in order to focus on the specificity of Modernist urban narrative, we should return to the question raised earlier concerning the city as a phenomenological object. What is striking here is that there does not exist any natural intentional level for the elucidation and representation of an urban universe. The constitution of the intentional object is already – we know that from Merleau-Ponty – an extremely complex procedure when the object considered is the Montagne Ste Victoire. It is considerably more complicated when the object is Paris. The city is a form, but it also embraces a forming activity, as it gives form to the objects as well as to the subjects of urban sensation.[10] Thus, it should be considered not only as an objective thing, but also as a practice; that is, it should be considered as both at the same time – hardware and software. This is probably the reason why the majority of recent descriptions of the city tend towards the systemic, to picture

---

[9] Gilles Deleuze and Félix Guattari, *Qu'est-ce que la philosophie?*, Paris, 1991, 158.

[10] See Alain Lhomme, "La fabrique de la ville", in *Les cahiers de la philosophie*, 17 [Le philosophe dans la cité], Paris, 1993.

the city as a functional nexus where it does not make any sense to distinguish too rigidly between the aspects of objectivity and practice. The systemic pictures are legion: the city as a cybernetic system, as a factory, as an organism, as a machine. Considered as a phenomenological object, the city emerges in the guise of a system that organizes the stable and the variable, the manifest and the virtual in such a way that these modes of existence, that in a normal approach to representation are seen as distinct, merge in a new kind of objectivity. And it is precisely this layer of description that Musil is tracking down when, in *The Man Without Qualities*, he compares the city to "a seething, bubbling fluid in a vessel consisting of the solid material of buildings, laws, regulations, and historical traditions".[11]

In general, it is a distinctive feature in Modernist urban literature that it involves an acute consciousness of the phenomenological unrepresentability of the city. The impetus to avoid the inherited schemes of perception and representation in order to get back to the phenomenological object itself (the Husserlian "zu den Sachen") has not, however, unveiled the object itself, but only, and in a sense more fundamentally, the extreme difficulty of determining and delineating the object in the first place. And this has initiated a variety of experimental openings towards the construction of techniques and perspectives of representation in order to grasp different aspects of urban reality.

This might be one of the reasons why the fictional universes of modern urban narratives tend to include some of the systemic-functional nexuses peculiar to the city. An important part of the indisputable strangeness in their aesthetic expression that keeps striking us as readers, often too hastily dismissed or left unexplained as Modernist formalism, is intimately linked to this ambition, precisely because such functions serve to break down the automatized schemata of representation. Devices that appear "paralogical" – when Musil carefully neglects the difference between *res extensa* and *res cogitans* by putting rules and traditions on the same level as houses and streets, when Joyce combines the most intimate stream of consciousness with ruthless polyphony, when Dos Passos makes personal motives interchangeable between his characters, when Virginia Woolf pans the streets of London, not mediated through one character that moves about, but through different characters at different locations, and so on – all such devices signal that the focus of representation, what is intended, is not to be found on a level of intimacy that corresponds immediately to our usual expectations. The intended objects are to be found, instead, on a systemic level that is not necessarily abstract or intellectual due to their lack of immediate evidence – only, they are pieces of objectivity that do not correspond to any of the common forms of representation. The unfamiliar patterns of composition contained in these works, patterns that the interpretive tradition has not yet ceased to work through – parallelisms, repetitions, counterpoints, inversions – can all, I think, be read as

---

[11] Musil, 4.

contributions to such a systemic-functional strategy of description that is coined in the fictional universes.

This way of reading might at first sight appear to contradict the Deleuzian reading introduced above, focusing on the literal construction of sensation: an abstract system versus an objectified sensation. This contradiction is, however, only apparent, and the tension between the two sides should be understood not as an inconsistency but as the precise place where the Modernist urban narrative has its greatest power of articulation, where it contributes most convincingly to thinking of the city by aesthetic means. The relation between the two sides is already emphasized in Sartre's phenomenological model, where the first relation – the establishment of the intentional image – involves the problematic that leads on to the making of systemic images, while the other relation – the question of inscribing the sensory stimulus and/or reaction into the aesthetic material, of constructing a percept or an affect – is not something completely different, but the very condition that makes possible the transformation of the systemic phenomenological image of the city into an aesthetic expression. To substantialize this thesis, I would like to end by sketching one of the ways in which the relation between the two sides – the systemic and the sensational – is carried out in the urban narrative.

In general it will probably not seem too controversial to assert that the two most conspicuous features in modern urban narratives are the weight assigned to the conveying of immediate sensation and the complex formal designs. Following Walter Benjamin's remarks on the shock-defence there is an obvious connection between urban life with its surplus of sensory stimuli and a representational form that mimes the way in which any individual consciousness (and any representation) is struggling to keep up with the pace of an accelerated rhythm of sensations; this principle is already unveiled on the first page of Döblin's *Berlin Alexanderplatz*:

> How people swarmed in the streets. How they moved. My brain gave up thinking, it had dried up completely. Wonder what it all was. Shoe shops, hat shops, light bulbs, pubs. People really need shoes when they hurry around like that – we also used to make shoes, I must try to remember that. Hundreds of shiny window panes, let them shine, they won't scare you anyway, you can break them to pieces, yes you can, now what's that all about, they have just only been polished.[12]

---

[12] "Gewimmel, welch Gewimmel. Wie sich das bewegte. Mein brägen hat wohl kein Schmalz mehr, der ist wohl ganz ausgetrocknet. Was war das alles. Schuhgeschäfte, Hutgeschäfte, Glühlampen, Destillen. Die Menschen müssen doch Schuhen haben, wenn sie so viel rumlaufen, wir hatten ja auch ein Schusterei, wollen das mal festhalten. Hundert blanke Scheiben, lass die doch blitzern, die werden dir noch niche bange machen, kannst sie ja kaputt schlagen, was ist denn mit dir, sine eben blankgeputzt" (Alfred Döblin, *Berlin Alexanderplatz*, Frankfurt am Main, 1999, 14-15).

Or take Musil's description of Count Leinsdorff's horse carriage on its way through Vienna:

> Pepi and Hans were quiet horses, well used to running in harness. They pulled eagerly, their hooves beating on the sunny street with its tall hedges of houses. The people for them were a grey swarming, a cause neither of joy nor of fear. The variegated displays in the shop-windows, the women gay in brilliant colours, were no more than patches of meadow no good for grazing; the hats, ties, books, diamonds along the street – a dessert. Only the two dream-islands of stable and trotting loomed out of it all and at times, as though in dream or play, Pepi and Hans shied at a shadow, thrust against the shafts, were freshened again by a flat flick of the whip and leaned thankfully into the curb.[13]

One of the most striking constant features in these novels is the interest in patterns of perception and the difficulties in making the urban perceptual patterns converge with the traditional modes of mental representation and cognition, and a predominant part of the novels' artistic mastery is invested in the construction of adequate percepts.

At the same time they also reveal a tendency towards what is usually called "abstraction", a tendency which, I have argued, should be considered not really as an abstraction at all but as an attempt to tune in on new types of phenomenality, the city's systemic phenomenology. But the most important contribution to the project of thinking of the city through the aesthetic form does not reside in one of these two tendencies viewed separately, but in the attempt to make sensation and "abstraction" (to keep this really unsatisfactory traditional term) converge. Each of them can be considered apart as efficient strategies of representation, but the most interesting attempts to convey a new and intelligent image of the city emerge most clearly when the sensation is grafted directly onto the systemic, that is, where a given systemic aspect present in a formal model is crystallized in a sensation, in what one might call a systemic percept.

Musil reveals this ambition in the famous first chapter of *The Man Without Qualities* – a handful of pages whose eminent exposition of the problems involved in urban narrative could be unfolded at length – in the system-dynamic presentation of the city's characteristic pace:

> Motor-cars came shooting out of the deep, narrow steets into the shallows of bright squares. Dark patches of pedestrian bustle formed into cloudy steams. Where longer lines of speed transected their loose-woven hurrying, they clotted up – only to trickle on all the faster then and after a few ripples regain their regular pulse-beat. Hundreds of sounds were intertwined into a coil of wiry noise, with single barbs projecting, sharp

---

[13] Musil, 206.

edges running along it and submerging again, and clear notes splintering off – flying and scattering .... Like all big cities, it consisted of irregularity, change, sliding forward, not keeping in step, collisions of things and affairs, and fathomless points of silence in between, of paved ways and wilderness, of one great rhythmic throb and the perpetual discord and dislocation of all opposing rhythms.[14]

But Musil also insists on examining the sensuous impact implied by such systemic images by changing their objectivity back to a sensory image; here, as often, this ambition is articulated in an ironic manner through the inevitable discrepancy between this systemic image and the subsequently described perceptive and affective effects of this system on a couple passing through all this:

> The two people who were walking up the wide, busy thoroughfare in the midst of it all were, of course, far from having such an impression. They obviously belonged to a privileged section of society, their good breeding being apparent in their clothes, their bearing and their manner of conversing. They had their initials significantly embroidered on their underclothing. And likewise – that is to say, not outwardly displayed, but as it were, in the exquisite underlinen of their minds – they knew who they were and that they were in their proper place in a capital city that was also an imperial residence.[15]

At the beginning of Chapter Seven of James Joyce's *Ulysses* (see Appendix), you find a similar list of characteristics belonging to the systemic order. Systemic elements are emphasized in a provocative manner through the abrupt listing of names of locations, elements from the city and world map of urban transportation and mail circulation; the locations themselves are totally absent, reduced to nodal points in different systematizations that subsume them without qualifying them; what is left of sensuous content is the slightly fetishizing – almost Proustian – infatuation with such a collection of names of places gathered in one location as catalysts for undetermined daydreaming.

The first attempt to establish a sensuous appropriation of this systemic inventory that dislocates the immediate topographical environments in an abstract map is established through the formal reference to the medium that effectively juxtaposes a dislocated map and the sensuous presence: the newspaper. The newspaper, which serves as an obvious formal foil for this chapter, is in fact one big dislocated map of world news, a collage of unrelated discursive facts that are placed – due to the continuous reading – in a sensuous, metonymical relation of contiguity. The implicit thematic of the newspaper is

---

[14] *Ibid.*, 3.
[15] *Ibid.*, 4.

reinforced by the fact that the chapter seems to be partly about "the gentlemen of the press"; thus, the convergence between system and sensation is established by the partly illogical pairing of the dislocated map and the dislocating medium on the one hand and the sensuous face of the medium and the sensuous immediacy of the action on the other. The central image operating this juxtaposition of the two aspects of system and sensation is probably Joyce's musically "dullthudding barrels" (see Appendix, 237); again, on the one hand they connote transportation, distribution of merchandise according to the lineage of the abstract map, on the other hand there is their present noise. The noise polyphonically accompanies the action in the passage, as it is repeatedly reinserted as a kind of background sonority and is, furthermore, evocatively varied through the rhythmic and senseless repetitions of sound patterns in the text, which might again connote reminiscences of the printing press. This central motive, or whatever one should call it, is apparently reiterated as a formal matrix for the image of Brayden coming up the stairs: the automaton-like back, maybe an evocation of the working draymen, and the "fat folds of neck, fat, neck, fat, neck". The presentation of Brayden's appearance, which in a conventional novel would have been reported sufficiently by affirming "at this moment, Brayden came up the stairs" or something to that effect, is schematized through a mode of representation where sensation is filtered through the presence of the systemic order. In a brief glimpse, we get an image of a commonplace sensation that has been modified by the means of the systemic order in which it takes place. It is as if Joyce wants to underscore the fragility and instantaneity of this sensation; it is present for a short while, before the passage ends by dissolving this unique percept through a sentence that is itself dissolved in the wind and general activity: "for the wind to. Way in. Way out."

A last example of such converging system-percepts could be the stately veiled motor car that passes through the streets of London while Clarissa Dalloway is buying flowers for her party. After the car's first appearance, the narrative voice follows it through the streets for the next five or six pages in an almost Flaubertian "survol" that occasionally descends into the impressions and hypotheses and associations it arouses at different places in different characters, all of which is condensed in a collective percept, a ripple in the texture of the city, maybe one of those shadows, "as though in dreams or play", from which the horses in Musil were thankfully freed:

> The car had gone, but it had left a slight ripple which flowed through glove shops and hat shops and tailors' shops on both sides of Bond Street. For thirty seconds all heads were inclined the same way – to the window. Choosing a pair of gloves – should they be to the elbow or above it, lemon or pale grey? – ladies stopped; when the sentence was finished something had happened. Something so trifling in single instances that no mathematical instrument, though capable of transmitting shocks in China, could register the vibration; yet in its

fullness rather formidable and in its common appeal emotional; for in all the hat shops and tailors' shops strangers looked at each other and thought of the dead; of the flag; of the Empire. In a public house in a back street a Colonial insulted the House of Windsor, which led to words, broken beer glasses, and a general shindy, which echoed strangely across the way in the ears of girls buying white underlinen threaded with pure white ribbon for their weddings. For the surface agitation of the passing car as it sunk grazed something very profound.[16]

APPENDIX

James Joyce, *Ulysses*, London, 1994, 122-24.

In the Heart of the Hibernian Metropolis

Before Nelson's pillar trams slowed, shunted, changed trolley, started for Blackrock, Kingstown and Dalkey, Clonskea, Rathgar and Terenure, Palmerston park and upper Rathmines, Sandymount Green, Rathmines, Ringsend and Sandymount Tower, Harold's Cross. The hoarse Dublin United Tramway Company's timekeeper bawled them off:

– Rathgar and Terenure!

– Come on, Sandymount Green!

Right and left parallel clanging ringing a doubledecker and a singledeck moved from their railheads, swerved to the down line, glided parallel.

– Start, Palmerston park!

The Wearer of the Crown

Under the porch of the general post office shoeblacks called and polished. Parked in North Prince's street His Majesty's vermilion mailcars, bearing on their sides the royal initials, E. R., received loudly flung sacks of letters, postcards, lettercards, parcels, insured and paid, for local, provincial, British and overseas delivery.

Gentlemen of the Press

Grossbooted draymen rolled barrels dullthudding out of Prince's stores and bumped them up on the brewery float. On the brewery float bumped dullthudding barrels rolled by grossbooted draymen out of Prince's stores.

– There it is Red Murray said. Alexander Keyes.

---

[16] Virginia Woolf, *Mrs Dalloway*, London, 1976, 22.

– Just cut it out, will you? Mr Bloom said, and I'll take it round to the *Telegraph* office.

The door of Ruttledge's office creaked again. Davy Stephens, minute in a large capecoat, a small felt hat crowning his ringlets, passed out with a roll of papers under his cape, a king's courier.

Red Murray's long shears sliced out the advertisment from the newspaper in four clean strokes. Scissors and paste.

– I'll go through the printing works, Mr Bloom said, taking the cut square.

– Of course, if he wants a par, Red Murray said earnestly, a pen behind his ear, we can do him one.

– Right, Mr Bloom said with a nod. I'll rub that in.

We.

Wiliam Brayden, Esquire, of Oaklands, Sandymount

Red Murray touched Mr. Bloom's arm with the shears ans whispered:

– Baryden.

Mr Bloom turned and saw the liveried porter raise his lettered cap as a stately figure entered between the newsboards of the *Weekly Freeman and National Press* and the *Freeman's Journal and National Press.* Dullthudding Guinness's barrels. It passed stately up the staircase steered by an umbrella, a solemn beardframed face. The broadcloth back ascended each step: back. All his brains are in the nape of his neck, Simon Dedalus said. Welts of flesh behind on him. Fat folds of neck, fat, neck, fat, neck.

– Don't you think his face is like Our Saviour? Red Murray whispered.

The door of Ruttledge's office whispered: eee: cree. They always build one door opposite the other for the wind to. Way in. Way out.[17]

---

[17] James Joyce, *Ulysses*, London, 1994, 122-24.

CITY AND MEMORY

ANNELISE BALLEGAARD PETERSEN

"My memory is the thing I forget with."[1]

"Hätte man doch wenigstens seine Erinnerungen. Aber wer hat die?" – "If only one had one's memories! But who has them?" – the eponimous first-person narrator in Rainer Maria Rilke's *Die Aufzeichnungen des Malte Laurids Brigge* (1910) writes in one of his first entries. What lies in the expression "to have one's memories"?[2] Naturally, Malte has his memories stored in his consciousness, or subconsciousness; but he does not have access to them, he cannot remember them, cannot recall them. This becomes clear if we include the sentence that follows as well, which is also formulated as a wish: "Wäre die Kindheit da, sie ist wie vergraben" ("If one could bring one's childhood to mind – but it is as though it had been buried"). Like other relics of the past, childhood lies buried under that which has subsequently taken place and, to retain the image, archaeological excavation is necessary if it is to be brought to light again.

Malte, the last descendant of an old Danish aristocratic family, writes his "notebooks" in Paris. Why he has chosen the French capital as his place of residence we are not told. In fact, throughout the novel the name of the city is never mentioned. Rilke himself lived in Paris while writing the *Aufzeichnungen*, and many reflections from the letters to his wife, Clara Westhoff-Rilke, have gone almost unchanged into the novel. More important, however, in relation to the subject of this article is the historico-cultural significance of Paris as the prototype of the modern metropolis. I want to analyse the role of the large city in Malte's attempts to get access to his memories and to the way he narrates them.[3]

---

[1] André Brink, *The Novel: Language and Narrative from Cervantes to Calvino*, 1998, 4, quoting a child's description of remembering.

[2] Rainer Maria Rilke, *Die Aufzeichnungen des Malte Laurids Brigge* (1910), Frankfurt am Main, 1981, 19; *The Notebook of Malte Laurids Brigge*, Oxford, 1984, 16. After quotations, the page number of the English translation will be given, followed by the page number of the German edition.

[3] The novel comprises entries of different kinds: in the first part most of them have to

The choice of the subjects "one" and "who" in the first quotation indicates that Malte feels that he is expressing a common experience. "One" includes both oneself and others, and "who" is an indefinite interrogative, meaning "who on earth/who among us". The general nature implied, however, is time-bound. My assertion is that the insight to which Malte gives expression belongs to modernity. If we look at one of the earliest autobiographies in the western tradition, Augustine's *Confessions*, we see that Augustine has no problems with memory. In Book 10, that is, after he has told of his childhood, his "wicked and disgraceful youth" and his conversion, he reflects on "the fields and spacious palaces of memory" to which the subject has unlimited access:

> When I enter there, I require instantly what I will to be brought forth, and something instantly comes; others must be longer sought after, which are fetched, as it were out of some inner receptacle; others rush out in troops .... Other things come up readily, in unbroken order, as they are called for; those in front making way for the following; and as they make way, they are hidden from sight, ready to come when I will.[4]

Why do Malte's memories not come "when I will"? This has a great deal to do with the fact that, according to his own self-portrayal, he is "a homeless person"[5] who, tired of life ("ohne Neugierde", without curiosity, is the expression he uses) travels round the world "with a trunk and a case of books". He is a person leading a life that basically is no life at all, as Malte sees it, because it is being lived "without a house, without inherited possessions, without dogs" (16/19). It is immediately after this self-portrayal that Malte enquires about the memories he does not have. In a slightly later entry, "to have" is used in a corresponding way, although reversed, positively, for here Malte relates that he has a poet, and, what is more, a happy poet, who lives in a quiet house in the mountains, who can stand in front of his bookcase, who is surrounded by "calm, sedentary things"(40/38) – a poet such as Malte would like to be himself, and perhaps could also have become, if only certain conditions had been different – perhaps if a location such as Malte's poet lives in had also existed as a opportunity for him.

However, it does not. His childhood home, the country manor of Ulsgaard, is in other people's hands, "strangers live in the old, long manor-house" (16/19), both his parents are dead, his father "in the town, in a flat

---

do with Malte's present state of mind, his impressions of Paris and his childhood. In part two we find both impressions of Paris – autobiographical narrations and Malte's stories about other persons, fictive as well as non-fictive.

[4] Quoted in Frances A. Yates, *The Art of Memory* (1966), Chicago and London, 1974, 46.

[5] In German, "ein Unbeauster", a word that alludes to Goethe's *Faust*, l. 3348: "Bin ich der Flüchting nicht? Der Unbehauste?"

that seemed alien and almost hostile to me" (127/124). Malte himself sees to the carrying out of "den Herzstich", the running through his father's heart to make sure he is indeed dead, thus following an old tradition of the aristocracy. And not only that, for thereby the family's heart has also been run through: "'Today Brigge and nevermore,' something said within me." For Malte's own heart is only "ein einzelnes Herz", an individual heart (151/128). He does not see his own existence as a continuation of that of the family, perceiving himself, as I have already implied, as an isolated, alienated individual: the definition of the modern individual in the metropolis.

This way of seeing himself represents both the loss which Malte regrets, despite the "Herzstich" executed in accordance with his father's will and his own full approval – and an opportunity, artistic creation. It presupposes, however, experiences and memories.[6] Memories are something "One must be able to forget ... when they are many and one must have the immense patience to wait until they come again" (19-20/22). The insight that Malte articulates (that it is necessary to forget in order to recall, intuitively sensed by the child that André Brink quotes) is a main point in Friedrich Nietzsche's "Vom Nutzen und Nachteil der Historie für das Leben", the second of his *Unzeitgemässe Betrachtungen* (1873-76). Here Nietzsche stresses that history, the collective as well as the individual, has to be acquired selectively and actively if it is to be of any "use for life".

In the linking together of "experiences" and "memories", Malte's reflections are reminiscent of those formulated about twenty years later by Walter Benjamin in various essays, such as "Der Erzähler": the myriad impressions which constantly bombard the modern individual are stored (if consciousness "in the interest of the stimulation barrier"[7] is successfully able to sort them) as "Erlebnisse" in the memory.[8] If, however, the impressions slip through the stimulation barrier of consciousness, they are stored as "Erfahrungen", in the memory of the subconscious,[9] and these the individual is not in a position to recall. A catalyst of some sort is required for recall to take place.

The metropolis can assume such a catalytic function. In the "Postscript" to his friend Franz Hessel's *Spazieren in Berlin* (1929), Walter Benjamin writes about the city as mnemotechnical aid: lounging about in the city-streets the "native" ("der Einheimische") can get access not only to the city itself, but first and foremost to his own childhood and youth. Therefore,

---

[6] "Erfahrungen" and "Erinnerungen" are the words used in the German text.

[7] "im Interesse des Reizschutzes"; Walter Benjamin, "Über einige Motive bei Baudelaire", in *Gesammelte Schriften*, I/ 2, Frankfurt am Main, 1980, 615.

[8] I have kept the words "Erinnerung" and "Erlebnisse" in my references to Benjamin, because English uses the same word for both: "experience(s)."

[9] Benjamin uses the words "Erinnerung" and "Gedächtnis" to distinguish between the two kinds of memory. The first refers to consciousness, the second to the subconscious.

Benjamin says, "the city-book of the native will have affinity to memoirs".[10]
In using the metaphors "fields and spacious palaces" and "receptacle",
Augustine had already pointed at a connection between memory, both in the
sense of "memories" and the process "to remember", and space. In fact, the
spacial imagery is found in works about "the art of memory" (see, for
example, the title of Frances A. Yates's work) or mnemonics as well as in
philosophical reflections on memory from antiquity (Aristotle, Cicero,
Quintilian, the anonymous *Rhetorica ad Herennium*) via John Locke to
Sigmund Freud. Quintilian, for example, suggests"in going through a city"
one should train the memory (quoted in Yates, 22). The classic example of
linking the spatial and the ability to remember is the anecdote about the
Greek writer Simonides, related by Cicero in the second book of *De oratore*:
Simonides is asked to identify the people who, during a banquet where he
has performed, were crushed beneath a roof that collapsed, for otherwise the
dead cannot be buried. And he is able to point them out "unius cuiusque",
each and everyone, because he can remember where each of them was sitting
when he sang his song. The moral is that it is a good idea to form images,
"effigies", and to place them spatially if one wishes to recall something. In
that way one creates order and clarity. For that which we remember best is
that which has been communicated to us via the senses, and since the sense
of sight is the keenest, we are best able to retain something we have heard or
experienced by visualizing it.

This linking of sight, the effigy, space and the ability to remember is of
interest in relation to the way in which the memory process and its function
are presented in Rilke's novel. The novel's present space and writing space is
Paris, indicated not by the name of the city itself, but by the place names
which especially occur in the first part of the notebooks. It is here that Malte
sits enquiring about the childhood that is "vergraben", buried like the dead in
the Simonides anecdote. Can the urban space help Malte to grasp, to gain
possession of his early experiences, his "Erlebnisse" and "Erfahrungen" –
experiences which belong to a completely different space than that of the
metropolis, that is, to a premodern, rural space?

Order and clarity were what Simonides advanced as prerequisites for
being able to remember, and order and clarity are what Malte is seeking to
achieve via the process he refers to as "sehen lernen". But, paradoxically
enough, it seems as if his memory process is activated by the opposite –
confusion and chaos. After representing what he sees in the first, famous
entry, one which both objectively registers and subjectively interprets the
visual impressions, Malte is quite literally invaded by the cacophony of the
metropolis:

[10] Walter Benjamin, "Die Wiederkehr des Flaneurs", quoted in Franz Hessel, *Ein
Flaneur in Berlin*, Berlin, 1984, 277.

The electric street-cars rage through my room with ringing fury. Automobiles race over me. A door slams. Somewhere a window-pane falls clattering. I can hear the big splinters laughing and the smaller ones sniggering (4/9).

Malte is mentally defenceless in the face of this invasion: "everything penetrates more deeply within me", he notes (5/10). To take up Walter Benjamin's distinction, he lacks the necessary mental filter, the "stimulation barrier", and the impressions of the city, therefore, are stored as experiences in the "Gedächtnis" of the subconscious, where, however, they activate a process of associations: barking dogs and crowing cocks suddenly appear in the city's jumble of sounds, reminding Malte of the space of childhood and enabling him, at last, to fall asleep. Whether the dogs and cocks belong to the "inventory" of the large city like the automobiles and trams is unimportant. To Malte they are associated with childhood, and this is the main thing here. Not least "the dog" plays a prominent and recurring role in relation to the remembered childhood, and so the entry can be read as the first stage in the process of remembering and writing initiated by the metropolis.

Just as he feels he is run over by the sounds of motor cars, Malte is also in danger of being run over by the many vehicles that rush as quickly as possible towards Hôtel-Dieu, where those in the vehicles can be allowed to die a modern, impersonal "fabrikmäßige" (12) – mass death. Once again, memory is triggered by confusion and by feeling overwhelmed; here, the memory is of the violent, terrifying and highly personal death of the grandfather, the old chamberlain Christoph Detlev Brigge (with dogs constantly present). The description of this death is remembered by the reader for its visual power: "Only the stiff-haired pointer with the surly face sat beside his master, and one of his broad, shaggy forepaws lay on Christoph Ditlev's big, grey hand" (12/16). In the context of the novel this is an example of the fact that Malte's "sehen lernen" extends from the urban space to that of childhood. It comes as no surprise that the narrative of the grandfather's "hard death" (15/18) is spatially structured and abounds in spatial imagery: people carry their death inside them "as a fruit bears its kernel" (9/14), the women in the womb, the men in the chest. The old chamberlain's death is so large that not only his body, but even the manor-house is too small for it and "It seemed as if additional wings would have to be built on it" (10/14). While he is dying, the chamberlain is carried from one room to another, because his death "demanded the blue chamber, demanded the little drawing-room, demanded the large reception-room" (13/16). The voice of his death reaches the remotest parts of the neighbourhood.

Another example of how the chaos of the metropolis, and not its order, which is the alternative aspect of urban space, functions as a "mnemo-technical aid" in recalling childhood is Malte's visit to la Salpêtrière hospital. When Malte, without knowing how, has fled from the almost surrealist scenes in the hospital, he has the typical city experience of getting lost in the labyrinthine maze of the streets, where the electric trams (which already

occurred in his second entry) once more rush towards him and graze past
him: "I did not know in what city I was, or whether I had a lodging
anywhere, or what I ought to do in order not to have to go on walking"
(59/54). The maze experience is immediately followed by illness, during
which the forgotten fears of childhood break out. The childhood anxieties
have literally been incorporated in Malte: they have been buried and
forgotten. They are awakened and remembered after another body
experience: getting lost and overwhelmed in the large city. And now Malte is
able to translate the language of the body into words. He lists the anxieties in
a series of parallel statements all of which begin with the words, "die Angst,
daß ..." (55 ff). The entry is rounded off by a direct reference to the passage I
quoted in my first paragraph:

> I prayed for my childhood and it has come back to me, and I feel that it is just
> as burdensome as it was before, and that I have grown older to no purpose
> (61/54).

Malte has had his wish fulfilled; indeed now he has his childhood – but he
does not have any direct influence on when and how he comes into contact
with it. The memories come to him without any chronological order, in
scraps and fragments, evoked by the city's chaos of impressions. He also has
his childhood memories in the sense that he can present them, talk about
them in an ordered sequence, whether it be a narrative, as in the story of the
grandfather's "hard death", or a rhetorical sequence, as in the listing of
childhood's many "dreads".

What he is unable to do, however, is to tell of his childhood in the way in
which "one" usually relates one's memories. The norm for relating memories
in a German literary context was established by Goethe in *Dichtung und
Wahrheit* (1811-33), where it was not, as in *Die Aufzeichnungen des Malte
Laurids Brigge,* a question of a first-person narrator in search of his
memories, but of a first-person narrator who, in sovereign fashion, recalls,
owns, contains and masters his memories, which he has access to via his will
and his consciousness, who has an overview of them and is therefore able to
present his story as a well-ordered, teleological sequence. Goethe's memories
are underpinned by a belief in the homogeneity and wholeness of the self.[11]
This conception is not shared by the modern first-person narrator which
Malte represents – a key word in his self-image is "zerbrochen", broken. The
word occurs in the entry about "the dreads", and its content is fleshed out,
among other things, in Malte's masquerade memory: as a child, like
thousands of children before and after him in the world of reality, he has
dressed up and looked at his disguised self in a mirror, while pretending to be
the person he has transformed himself into. Malte writes first about these

---

[11] Theodor W. Adorno, "Kleine Proust-Kommentare" (1958), in *Noten zur Literatur*,
Frankfurt am Main, 1961, II, 99.

masquerades that they "never, indeed, went so far as to make me feel a stranger to myself: on the contrary, the more varied my transformations, the more assured I was of my own identity" (97/86).

The masquerades serve as a confirmation and consolidation of the personality. One day, however, everything goes wrong. Malte disguises himself to such an extent that he does not know and, even with the aid of the mirror, is unable to find out "was ich eigentlich sei", "what I actually was" (98/87). On the contrary, his mirror image assumes control: "I simply ceased to exist. For one second I had an unutterable, sad, and futile longing for myself, then there was only he ... I had no longer any voice." (101/89).

"He" – the stranger in the mirror – has taken over, the "I" has disappeared. The boy Malte loses consciousness and falls down like just a bundle of something ("wie ein Stück, rein wie ein Stück" [102]) the remembering Malte tells us, thus again, as the comparison shows, underlining that memory is not only a mental but also a bodily process (90). The episode also shows that Malte's uncertainty about, and loss of, identity are based on the pre-modern space of childhood and are thus not produced by the encounter with the metropolis. But the metropolis repeats and reinforces this experience. The metropolis means a change to the "Bedeutungen", that is, the contexts of understanding in which Malte once lived and with which he felt familiar. He has left them behind after the dissolution of his childhood home and the death of his parents, and he feels that he cannot get up again "because I am broken" (50/47) – "broken" like the panes of glass in the second entry.

If Malte is to be able to put together his fragmented personality and become whole, just like the poet he has, he must try to become the one who does the writing, instead of the one who is written. The urban space offers Malte mnemotechnical aid in this process, since it teaches him to see and then to order both his concrete observations and the glimpses of memory which "pop up" in the form of "freisteigende Vorstellungen" – the characterization of our way of remembering given by the Austrian physicist and philosopher Ernst Mach (*Erkenntnis und Interesse*, 1905).

The approach I have chosen to link the metropolis and memory in Rilke's *Aufzeichnungen des Malte Laurids Brigge* makes it possible to pave the way for a more nuanced evaluation of the function of the metropolis than that found in the majority of the books and articles that have dealt with this aspect of the novel. It is not just a question of "Leiden an der Stadt" (see Andreas Freisfeld's book by this title) or of a description of "the terrors of Paris", as Naomi Segal writes in her psychoanalytically inspired article "Rilke's Paris – 'cité plein de rêves'". Malte's Paris, as I would want to call it, rather than "Rilke's Paris", is not only "childhood corrupted into adult nightmare".[12] It

---

[12] Naomi Segal, "Rilke's Paris – 'cite plein de rêves'", in *Unreal City: Urban Experience in Modern European Literature and Art*, eds Edward Timms and David Kelley, Manchester, 1985, 106.

also contains experiences of beauty that are depicted in a flickering, impressionist colour idiom, and where memory is not associated with heaviness but
with lightness, as in the image of the tall, slim man who no longer uses his
crutch in the way for which it was designed, but holds it out in front of him
like a herald's rod, who smiles at everything and everyone and moves shyly,
"unusually light, charged with memories of earlier walking days" (17/20).

With the urban space as "mnemotechnischer Behelf", as Benjamin puts it, it
is not only the childhood experiences stored in Malte's "Gedächtnis" that
"pop up". The metropolis also releases Malte's artistic abilities, sharpens his
sensitivity towards other people and towards impressions which he already
had as a child, and teaches him to see and observe, so that he can write about
it, not, like childhood, as a causal sequence in traditional autobiographical or
semi-autobiographical writing – for it is not possible to "reconstruct" Malte's
childhood on the basis of the sketched memories – but rather in a way
analogical to the labyrinthine doubleness of order and disorder of the metropolis. The separate childhood memories are presented in a rhetorical order, or
they are told as rounded short stories, like the narration of Christoph Detlev
Brigge's long and difficult dying, or the tales of other family members,
Maman, Abelone, Erik Malte relates both his own experiences and parts of
the family biography which have been told him. From there he moves on to
what you might call collective memories: he retells stories he has read about
historical characters such as Karl der Kühne, Duke of Burgundy (1433-57),
the French king Charles le Fou (1368-1422) and "the Portuguese", the poet
Marianna Alcoforado (1640-1723). Malte concludes his entries with a new
deeply personal version of the parable of "The Prodigal Son":

> Above all he thought of his childhood, which, the calmer his reflection,
> seemed to him more and more to have been unfulfilled; all its memories had
> about them the vagueness of premonitions, and that they were reckoned as
> past, made them almost part of the future. And to take all this once more, and
> this time in reality, upon himself – this was the reason he, estranged, turned
> home (241/200).

This passage emphasizes that remembering not only means excavating
occurrences and sensations incorporated in the self but is also, and maybe
foremost, a way of organizing the present and open up to the future.[13] Malte
cannot return home in the literal sense; but in taking on his memories like the
prodigal son, and in writing them down, he may emerge out of his alienation
and gain a future. In this process the large city functions as a
"mnemotechnical aid".

---

[13] Svend Erik Larsen, "Glemmer du, så husker jeg ...", in *Litteratur og erindring som
aktuel betydningsproces*, Working Papers from the Institute of Literary History,
Aarhus University, Aarhus, 1998, 2.

EUGÈNE SUE, G.W.M. REYNOLDS, AND THE REPRESENTATION OF THE CITY AS "MYSTERY"

SARA JAMES

In June 1842, the Parisian reading public witnessed the start of what was to be the publishing phenomenon of the century. Less than a week after the first instalment of Eugène Sue's new serial in *Le Journal des Débats*, a paper known for its conservative views, a critic for the Fourierist newspaper, *La Phalange*, hailed the work as a milestone for the socialist cause.[1] The novel in question, *Les Mystères de Paris*, was so popular with readers that it was extended from four volumes to ten; the circulation of *Le Journal des Débats* rocketed, rescuing the paper's financial situation and ensuring the continuation of the serial, despite its increasing distance from the editorial stance. According to contemporary reports, the novel's success reached epic proportions. Subscribers to public reading rooms faced queues of several hours for a half-hour consultation of the day's instalment. Less than a decade after the first edition in volume form, 60,000 copies of the work had been sold. Within a year, rival newspapers and authors were cashing in on this enormous publishing success in a way that was to prefigure the mass commercialism of the bestseller in the twentieth century, unleashing a flood of copycat "mysteries". The work was imitated, plagiarized, pirated, and translated into ten languages, adapted for the theatre and adopted by street entertainers. Twenty years on, the title was still serving as a marketing lure, having undergone such permutations as *Les Vrais Mystères de Paris*, *Les Nouveaux Mystères de Paris*, *Les Mystères du vieux Paris*, and *Les Mystères du nouveau Paris*. Imitations flourished not only in European provincial capitals but also in America, continuing right up until the turn of the century.

In England, newspaper entrepreneur G.W.M. Reynolds, already known for his successful poaching of Dickens's Mr Pickwick in *Pickwick Abroad* (1839), began a series entitled *The Mysteries of London*, which ran from 1844 until

---

[1] See Nora Atkinson, *Eugène Sue et le roman-feuilleton*, Paris, 1929, 10-11, 67-77; Jean-Louis Bory, *Eugène Sue, le roi du roman populaire*, Paris, 1962, 246-50, 270-95; and Pierre Orecchioni, "Eugène Sue: mesure d'un succès", *Europe, revue littéraire mensuelle*, 643-44 (November-December 1982), 157-66.

1856, establishing him as one of the best-selling novelists of the nineteenth century. While this probably originated in an attempt to corner the market generated by Sue's success, *The Mysteries of London* became a publishing phenomenon in its own right. Like its forerunner, it was not exempt from pirating, even having to change its name to *The Mysteries of the Court of London* when the title was hijacked in 1848; it was later republished with the subtitle *Stories of Life in the Modern Babylon.*[2] From the vantage point of the twentieth century, it would be easy to attribute this success to astute marketing and the burgeoning commercialism that is now taken for granted. However, while this undoubtedly played an important part, the extent and duration of the "mysteries" cult raises questions about the appeal of the mystery formula employed in these two works. Were they merely exploiting the mysteries of the nineteenth-century city, as some critics have suggested,[3] or were they influencing public opinion in the direction of change?

The publication of *Les Mystères de Paris* came at a favourable conjunction in the development of the French serial novel (*roman-feuilleton*) and in Sue's career. Two rival newspapers, Emile de Girardin's *La Presse* and Dutacq's *Le Siècle*, were launched in 1836, and both slashed subscription prices from eighty francs to forty francs, forcing other competing papers to do the same by relying on advertising and popular serials. A decade later, the number of readers regularly taking a newspaper had risen from 70,000 overall (1836) to 200,000 in Paris alone (1846).[4] Sue's previous novel, *Mathilde* (1841), had attracted a wide female readership with its presentation of the legal and domestic problems facing women trapped in unhappy marriages, enabling him to build on this success and confirming him in the direction of the *roman à thèse*.

Marie-Joseph Eugène Sue (1804-1857) had spent the first thirty-three years of his life lavishly dissipating an inherited fortune. His earlier novels had taken maritime or historical themes, showing clearly the influence of James Fenimore Cooper and Walter Scott, who both enjoyed great popularity in France in the 1830s; these early works had been published in the British periodical press, which, as Louis James has noted, relied heavily on French serials in the 1840s.[5] At the time, Sue was writing purely for his own pleasure; it was only following his bankruptcy in 1837 that he turned to writing as a matter of economic necessity. During this period, his interest in social affairs, as illustrated by the standpoint taken in *Mathilde*, was strengthened by his discovery of the working-class socialist network, leading allegedly to the impetuous claim "Je

[2] Trefor Thomas, "Introduction" to *The Mysteries of London*, Keele, 1996, viii. All quotes from *The Mysteries of London* are taken from this edition, but the article draws on the unabridged first series of *The Mysteries of London*, 2 vols, London, 1845, 1846.

[3] Asa Briggs, *Victorian Cities*, London, 1963, 60.

[4] Atkinson, 10.

[5] Louis James, *Fiction for the Working Man*, London, 1963, 136-37.

suis socialiste!" in 1841.[6] Although this ideological change appeared to have little effect on his lifestyle, or on his perception of society at the time of *Les Mystères de Paris*, earning him the disapprobation of Karl Marx among others, Sue's future work focused increasingly on working-class heroes and heroines. At the time of his death in 1857, in self-imposed exile from the Second Empire, he was working on a proletarian epic entitled *Les Mystères du peuple ou Histoire d'une famille de prolétaires à travers les âges*, which aimed to offer an alternative history of the French people from the position of the oppressed.

George William MacArthur Reynolds (1814-1879) inherited a fortune in 1830, upon which he moved to Paris and launched into his first publishing ventures, editing the *London and Paris Courier* and the literary section of the *Paris Literary Gazette*. His interest in contemporary French literature persisted long after his money ran out; on his return to England in 1835, he wrote articles and serials for various magazines in which the influence of his years in France was clearly felt, ranging from the travels of Pickwick in France to his translation of Hugo's *Chants du Crépuscule* (1836). He also published a series of articles on French literature, issued in volume form as *The Modern Literature of France* in 1839. Reynolds eventually started various publications of his own which reflected both his commercial acumen and his radical views; one of these, *Reynolds's Weekly Newspaper*, was to run until 1967. Politically, he was prominent in the Chartist movement and keen to see the revolutionary fervour of France take root in Britain; following the overthrow of the July Monarchy in February 1848, he spoke at a Chartist rally in Trafalgar Square, an event which was incorporated as an authorial aside in a chapter of the second series of the *Mysteries*. *The Mysteries of London* was issued in Penny Numbers, a format which aimed to attract all classes of reader, coinciding with the English translation of *Les Mystères de Paris* published by Chapman and Hall in 1845. Advertisements stressed not only "the thrilling interest of the tale" and the "vivid descriptions of London", but also the exposure of rogueries and "the fearlessness with which the cause of the industrious millions" was espoused. By May 1845, the combined sales of the weekly and monthly parts amounted to more than 30,000 copies.

In both cases, the selling points of the novels were the skill and pace of the narrative and the presentation of the underworld and criminal society that was hailed variously as lurid and sensational or as brave support for the underclass. Critics of Sue's novels in England spoke unanimously of the narrative power of his novels; even those critics who strongly censured *The Mysteries of Paris* for sensationalism and for presenting scenes of vice and iniquity, complained that they could not help reading to the end. Peter Brooks, in *Reading for the Plot*, argues that the recourse to the world of the "criminally deviant", simultaneously emerging in the work of Sue, Balzac, Hugo, Dickens and Dostoevsky, was tapping into a new seam of narrative material, "as if the

---

[6] Bory, 232.

underworld of the transgressive and dangerous social elements were the last fund of 'narratable' material in an increasingly bland social and literary system".[7] The plotting of thieves and assassins in the underworld district of the Cité, the notorious ninth *arrondissement* of Paris, lent itself easily to the plotting of both action and enigmas in the story, drawing on the popularity of Fenimore Cooper's tales of adventure and also on the fear of the area inspired by a perceived rise in crime.

Sue's "Preface" to *Les Mystères de Paris* played heavily on this double interest, and on the potential charge of immorality in a work which dared speak (albeit guardedly) of prostitution and murder. Most importantly, Sue solicited the entry of the reader into his fictional world, inviting them to witness sinister scenes in untrodden areas, to encounter fearful, hideous characters and to cross, somewhat transgressively, the boundaries of their own experience. Added piquancy was derived from the precision of the references Sue makes to specific Parisian streets and taverns, a technique much used by Balzac, and reminiscent of the work of Defoe. One immediate consequence of the work's success was the popularization of visits to the Cité using the novel as a guide book. This encouraged a blend of realism with the fictional plot lines of burglary, murder and abduction, playing heavily on the suspense that these generated.

Another influence in Sue's portrayal of the underworld was that of Ann Radcliffe's *Mysteries of Udolpho* (1794). Gothic elements are clearly revealed in the atmospheric tension created by the opening images of darkness and storm, the motifs of confinement and claustration, and the use of ghost imagery to describe the area. The opening chapter describes the conquest of this world made by a mysterious, heroic figure who is immediately caught up in overheard plots of burglary, feats of detection and questions of concealed identity. Much of the central energy of the text derives from the discovery and resolution of criminal plots by this upright hero, Rodolphe. The opening of *The Mysteries of London* works in a similar way, using the same motif of the thunderstorm to involve the reader in the terror of a handsome youth, lost in the London slums, who stumbles on a criminal cabal. The narrative is thus led naturally to follow the exploits of the criminals, and the escape of the youth, diverging in two directions – to the underworld and to "respectable" society. The reader is soon caught up in a struggle between good and bad elements of society, represented in a seemingly conventional way by the upright and the dangerous classes of the city.

The narrative and the criminal plotting are aided by the presentation of the underworld as labyrinth. In the case of *Les Mystères de Paris*, this relates back to the images of Paris as labyrinth, maze or abyss popularized by Louis Sébastien Mercier in his *Tableau de Paris* (1781-89), applying them not only to

---

[7] Peter Brooks, *Reading for the Plot: Design and Intention in Narrative*, London, 1984, 85.

the physical landscape of the capitals, but to a metaphoric perception of the city as polycentric and confusing, pathless, anonymous, and hostile. In fiction, the Cité and the London slums are characterized by the narrow, twisting streets, dead ends and hidden passages that distinguished them geographically, and perpetual tension engendered by motifs of entrapment and escape. Twenty years on, the same imagery would permeate the landscape of Victor Hugo's *Les Misérables* (1862) where the routes of escape include rooftops and sewers – overhead and underground routes in the city. In *Les Mystères de Paris*, the routes are linked by the river, which connects three of the major criminal haunts, including a subterranean tavern whose roof is hidden beneath the feet of the casual passer-by. The inevitable association of this underground network with the underworld of classical legend, and with hell, reinforces the sinister elements of the plot.

The image of the city as labyrinth, however, extends beyond the underworld and the "dangerous" areas of Paris, to the more respectable *arrondissements*, from which a similar maze of connections exists. The second book centres around a typical Parisian tenement in the rue du Temple, in which Rodolphe hires a room. This becomes the site of personal intrigue at several class levels. The aristocratic Mme d'Harville is enticed there by a bourgeois lover; the vivacious seamstress Rigolette budgets carefully to live on her meagre earnings; the hardworking jeweller Morel goes mad after a series of misfortunes. The Temple itself is another labyrinthine space devoted to the sale of second-hand goods; it reflects both the aspiration to material success through acquiring possessions and the "denuding and dispossession" of the original owners on their way down in life.[8] As such it becomes the site of further mysteries: in the drawer of an elegant writing desk Rodolphe discovers a letter relating to the plight of an aristocratic gentlewoman who has been swindled out of her fortune.

In ways such as this, material objects provide a linking device between the different areas of the city, highlighting the increasingly materialistic basis of power underpinning urban relations. At the centre of this web of connections, however, is the figure of a corrupt lawyer, Jacques Ferrand, whose offices become the organizing locus of the city, with links to all parts of Paris and all classes – the aristocracy, the clergy, the bourgeoisie, the working classes and the criminal classes. At a purely superficial level, the machinations of Ferrand provide the source and solution of the mysteries of Paris, making his exposure and punishment a central part of the narrative and locating the heart of the city's problems in the moral and financial corruption that Ferrand comes to symbolize.

Reynolds adopted this figuration of the labyrinthine city as a significant

---

[8] See Brian Rigby, "Things, Distinction and Decay", in *French Literature, Thought and Culture in the Nineteenth Century: Essays in honour of D.G. Charlton*, ed. Brian Rigby, London, 1993, 98.

feature in the organization of *The Mysteries of London*. Like Sue, his technique was to invite the reader on a journey of discovery, in which the voice of the narrator serves as guide:

> The reader who follows us through the mazes of our narrative, has yet to be introduced to many strange places – many hideous haunts of crime, abodes of poverty, dens of horror, and lurking-holes of perfidy – as well as many seats of wealthy voluptuousness and aristocratic dissipation (64).

The mazes of the narrative reveal the labyrinthine connections between "respectable" society and the underworld in matters of plot – burglaries, blackmailing, abduction – and in matters of politics – for example, bribery and corruption. The theme of finding the right path in the city becomes a major focus, linked to moral choice. This is illustrated primarily by two brothers, Eugene and Richard Markham, whose chosen paths of Vice and Virtue explore opposing ways of using the capital, but also by the many less significant characters who are metaphorically "lost" in the systems of power. The numerous first-person narratives or "histories" of underworld characters describe the attempts of each individual to establish their own path and to decipher the mystifying signs of the metropolis. Ambition for money or power is depicted as a common motivation for crime in all classes, from the burglaries and abductions carried out by Anthony Tidkins, the notorious "Resurrection-man" to the defrauding of foreign businessmen in fabricated speculations carried out by upwardly mobile swindlers. Anne Humpherys, in her article on the geometry of the city in *The Mysteries of London*, argues that the image of the maze figures the wrong turnings and dead ends encountered by individuals and that the correct path, once found, leads to an implied centre.[9] The monstrous heart of the city in Reynolds's eyes is identified in the *Prologue* as the royal throne, from which the systems of power perpetuate the "fearful contrasts" of grandeur and misery around the capital, the nation, and indeed the British Empire: "This is the parent of a mighty nation; and yet around that parent's seat the children crave for bread!" (4).

While Anne Humpherys argues that this monstrous centre of the novel is ultimately experienced by the reader as hollow and empty, it has great importance as a focal point. Far from destroying the atmosphere of suspense, this primary revelation sets new mysteries – concerning the behaviour of the aristocracy, or of those who aspire to it – in play. The most extreme case in point is a plot concerning a young boy, Henry Holford, who is sent by thieves to explore the potential for burgling Buckingham Palace. Holford becomes so intrigued by the grandeur of the Palace and the gossip he overhears while

---

[9] Anne Humpherys, "The Geometry of the Modern City: G.W.M. Reynolds and *The Mysteries of London*", *Browning Institute Studies* (11, 1983), 74.

hiding there that he returns a second and a third time, overhearing private conversations between Victoria and Prince Albert and once actually meeting the Prince. There is, of course, no connection of Victoria with the personal or criminal intrigues of the city. Instead, the corruption of fictional members of the aristocracy becomes the subject of interrogation, both in their private affairs and their direction of the public institutions of the capital.

One narrative path Reynolds found particularly fruitful was the exposé of institutions in the city often culled from topical debate, ranging from the letter-reading scandal at the General Post Office to a comparison of dietary charts in prisons and in workhouses. By blending fiction with contemporary events to secure the ongoing curiosity of his audience, Reynolds leads the reader into a blend of fictional narration and politicization. Somewhat voyeuristically, the reader is invited to peep behind closed doors at the secret motives and behaviour of those in power. One typical, inflammatory scene presents the Home Secretary giving directions to his inferiors concerning charges of abuse in the workhouse, the best way of suppressing opposition to the government, and the scapegoating of the poor for the crimes of the rich. The police force, legal system, workhouse and prisons all undergo extensive and ongoing criticism for their role in creating and perpetuating an unjust, dualistic metropolis. The energy of the narrative derives much of its power from exploring these power structures and the role they play in the development of individual characters, forever creating new histories, new plots and new enigmas. By the end of the first volume, Reynolds saw his role as one of initiation:

> ... as yet we have only drawn the veil partially aside from the mighty panorama of grandeur and misery which it is our task to display: – the reader has still to be initiated more deeply into the MYSTERIES OF LONDON (Volume 1, "Epilogue", 197).

The systematic revelation of bureaucratic as well as criminal secrets becomes a key principle in the structure of the narrative.

Reynolds's image of drawing aside a veil to reveal the truth highlights an important feature common to both novels: the use of disguise and of misrepresentation in the urban power struggle. This is a key element in *Les Mystères de Paris*, forming a major theme that links the superficial plot-level mysteries of Paris with a wider appreciation of the unreliability of appearances in the city. At its most obvious, this takes the form of physical disguise: an escaped convict disfigures his face with vitriol in order to escape detection by the Law; Rodolphe disguises himself as an ordinary worker in his expeditions into the low-life areas of the capital, for his own amusement and in order to gather information about the inhabitants of the Cité or the rue du Temple at first-hand. Questions of concealed identity initially fuel the suspense of the narrative by teasing the reader's curiosity; by concealing their identity with different clothes, characters exploit the anonymity of the city and highlight the importance of material signs and commodities as vital signifiers. Ferrand's deception of clients from all classes operates on precisely that principle; he creates an identity for himself as a pious, abstemious man in order to inspire trust and thus gain custom. He is eventually unmasked as avaricious and lustful, guilty of embezzlement, murder and rape. Of the two brothers in *The Mysteries of London* who seek their fortunes in the City, Eugene inspires the trust of businessmen in the city by establishing himself in an opulent mansion furnished on the proceeds of blackmail and credit; this facilitates his deception of rich and poor alike as he embarks on a career of deceit culminating in his appointment as a Member of Parliament. The younger brother, Richard, naively takes each acquaintance he makes at face value, and in consequence is swindled by "men-upon-town", who feign friendship in order to cheat him at cards and use him as a scapegoat for a forgery. The whole of the first volume relates his gradual realization of the discourse of deception seen operating in the modern Babylon. As Richard learns, to those who successfully manipulate the code, from speculators to card-sharpers, the city offers endless opportunity for power and material wealth. To those who interpret all signs as they stand, from innocent provincials to foreign Counts, Babylon retains its association with exploitation and slavery.

A second form of disguise uncovered by the text is that of language, in particular the underworld slang or argot of the Cité or the London rookeries. This was hailed as one of the selling points of the narrative in Sue's "Preface", where he speaks of argot as a barbarian language, full of references to blood and crime; one of the many commercial spin-offs was a glossary of argot, especially designed for readers of the book. Reynolds similarly included passages of underworld slang in *The Mysteries of London* – more often in the form of songs or poetry – which required substantial footnotes explaining every other word. These discourses are reminiscent in turn of the earlier usage of the term "mystery" to denote trades or crafts requiring initiation to their particular secrets, a point on which the mystery novels were keen to capitalize.

The twin themes of disguise and revelation or unmasking in the texts also relate to a deeper level of social concern that was encouraged by the initial acclaim for Sue's work as a plea for the working class. Behind the individual mysteries of personal intrigue lies the discovery of social injustice, especially with regard to women and to the working class artisans of the capital. The history of Mme d'Harville illustrates the evils of arranged marriage and of the powerlessness of married women; her epileptic husband commits suicide because he cannot free her by divorcing her. The budget Rigolette presents to Rodolphe cannot account for a single day of illness. The loss of a precious stone spells ruin for the honest jeweller Morel because he works on the breadline. The mysteries also integrated topical issues which featured highly in journalistic reportage, such as problems of theft and violence in particular areas, of inadequate housing and sanitation, of alcoholism, and of disease.

Rodolphe's search for a friend's lost son leads him not only to escaped murderers plotting crime but to the outcasts of society struggling to survive. The histories related by working-class characters reveal lives of hardship and exploitation, unfair prejudice against the poor in the legal system and the impossibility of escape from their position at the bottom of the social scale. Progressively, the narrative combines with comment on social issues, referring the reader to contemporary surveys on topics ranging from prisons to prostitution.

This element is expanded by Reynolds, who includes diagrams and extracts from newspapers to draw attention to abuses and injustices in society. Reynolds uses the topical image of the microscope to suggest that all appearances hide a physical or moral mystery:

> A drop of the purest water, magnified by that instrument some thousands of times, appears filled with horrible reptiles and monsters of revolting forms.
> Such is London.
> Fair and attractive as the mighty metropolis may appear to the superficial observer, it swarms with disgusting, loathsome, and venomous objects, wearing human shapes (58).

While comments such as these encourage a naively dualistic view of the city by splitting fictional characters into categories of "good" or "bad", they also indicate a preoccupation with identifying the sources of crime and sickness, as a preliminary to finding a solution.

The plot-level mysteries of the outset become increasingly welded to the physical unveiling of a diseased city in need of a cure. At times, they are almost inseparably connected – for example, the macabre insistence on subterranean settings with the removal of bodies from overcrowded cemeteries to the catacombs in Paris, or tales of body snatching coinciding with digressions on disease near graveyards. The Gothic motifs of darkness, obscurity and claustration relate strikingly to the reality of the suffocating darkness, damp and humidity of the overcrowded slum areas of both cities, as urban historians such as Louis Chevalier have shown.[10] The mysteries of the underworld also coincide with numerous reports and parliamentary commissions on urban problems that were emerging at the time. In France, the *Académie des Sciences morales et politiques* received twenty-one theses on the subject of "misère" set for their prize competition in 1840; the socialist writer Flora Tristan, who in 1844 dedicated her major work, *L'Union ouvrière*, to Sue, had published her *London Journal*, describing the appalling poverty of the city hidden beneath its grandeur, in the same year. The public health expert, Parent-Duchâtelet, had

---

[10] Louis Chevalier, *Classes laborieuses et classes dangereuses à Paris pendant la première moitié du dix-neuvième siècle*, Paris, 1958, translated by Frank Jellinek as *Labouring Classes and Dangerous Classes in Paris During the First Half of the Nineteenth Century*, London, 1973.

recently completed a major work on prostitution in Paris. The influence of these contemporary reports is evident throughout *Les Mystères de Paris* in footnotes or incorporated into the text in the increasingly didactic passages that characterize the later volumes of the work.

While Reynolds is not as scrupulous about attributing his sources, the narrative of *The Mysteries of London* frequently intercalates journalistic-style passages on similar issues, informing, giving statistics, and offering ideas towards a solution. These passages are often voiced by representative working-class characters discussing contemporary events in one of the "boozing-kens" of the metropolis, but also give rise to lengthy didactic sections in which Reynolds's political sentiments are overtly broadcast. Reynolds's descriptions of the slum areas of St Giles, Saffron Hill and Smithfield state that the deprivation of these districts formed an essential component of the urban experience and one of the key revelations of the title:

> These are the fearful mysteries of that hideous district which exists in the very heart of this great metropolis ... swarming with a population that is born, lives and dies, amidst squalor, penury, wretchedness and crime (43).

It is noticeable that the sections of both *Les Mystères de Paris* and *The Mysteries of London* that raise these issues are concerned with scenes in the Cité district or the London rookeries. The significance of associating the underworld with disease is not only the high mortality experienced in these poorer areas during recent outbreaks of cholera (1832), but also in the fear that they were hotbeds of an equally deadly civic disease – that of urban distress, leading to political unrest.

For Sue, this threat is manifested in his stand on crime, and his calls for prison reform. Characters such as le Chourineur and Fleur-de-Marie illustrate the extent to which the prisons were seen to perpetuate rather than discourage crime among the "dangerous" classes. Episodes set in the women's prison of Saint-Lazare posit intervention by the upper and middle classes as a healing agent restoring moral health to criminalized classes who, Sue argues, are fundamentally good at heart. Criticism of the male prison, La Force, and of the death penalty, focuses on the glamorizing of violence as a means to superiority and a lack of distinction between the motives for crime. Le Chourineur illustrates the redemptive power of such intervention by turning natural violence into a force for good. Reynolds gives several minor examples of this – a reformed gamester, for example, devotes his life to warning others of the path they are treading – but his central villain, Anthony Tidkins, serves more as a warning of latent revenge. Like many other characters in the work, Tidkins tells his own life story, relating how his attempts to live honestly as a child were successively crushed by circumstances and bureaucracy; hardened by a spell on the treadmill, he embarks on a life of crime, becoming in the text an almost demonized figure. The very excesses of the character are seen as an allegory for political discontent, fuelling a "demonic" backlash against years of aristocratic oppression. This view would be supported by Reynolds's perception of deprivation – with its corollary, depravation – as the central mystery of London.

In this context, the idea of initiation into the discourses of the city takes the reader onto more positive ground. Similarly, disguise illustrates understanding of the codes of the city and is used as a means to empowerment. Rodolphe's mastery of argot enables his integration in the Cité and discovery of the conditions there at first-hand; disguise enables him to provide, unseen, solutions to the problems of everyday people. Richard Markham uses his experience to save others from a similar fate and to track down other exploiters. Ellen Monroe disguises herself at a masquerade ball to repel an unwanted suitor, and dresses as a man to be able to cross London alone and warn a friend of danger. She has learnt to exploit the mystifying signs of the city for her own benefit.

It can be seen that the representation of the city as "mystery" works at several different levels. The first is, quite simply, the mysteries of the plot – the suspense on which the serial novels depended to attract their audience. At a second level, the authors reveal the appalling conditions in the "unknown" working-class areas, probing the bureaucratic and physical secrets of the city for an appropriate response to seemingly endless problems. This includes revelations about the various institutions that structure urban life. Perhaps not surprisingly, most of the fan letters Sue received during the serialization of *Les Mystères de Paris* focused on these two aspects.[11] To go beyond this suggests a third dimension that resists easy classification but which is perhaps best approached through the melodramatic or Manichean elements of the texts. Calls for social reform cohabit uneasily with superman heroes and irredeemable villains; there is also a tension between the avowed aim of elucidating the mysteries of the city and exploitation of the productive nature of these mysteries, which are generated afresh by each new character, theme or incident. The *Oxford English Dictionary* lists under mystery "something beyond human knowledge or comprehension"; in view of the constant failure to provide any human solution, the recourse to characters of almost mythic personality and power surely raises the question of whether the city itself can ever be mastered or fully understood?

In their comparisons of Paris and London with Babylon, Sue and Reynolds make frequent suggestions for reforming the city. However, these plans often seem to depend on distance from such contamination and corruption. Sue sets his model farm, Bouqueval, on the outskirts of Paris, where his heroine, a fallen woman, loses all taint of her degraded past. Reynolds refers repeatedly to the outskirts of London as a welcome respite from squalor and pollution, and, indeed, all his good and generous characters live outside the hub of the city.

---

[11] See Brynja Svane, *Les Lecteurs d'Eugène Sue, Le monde d'Eugène Sue II*, Copenhagen, 1986.

Urban historians have criticized novelists and the popular press for ignoring the existence of suburbia,[12] but several of Reynolds's settings reflect the attempts to build rural idylls at a safe distance from any moral or physical threat. More exotic alternatives, the fictional states of Gerolstein and Castelcicala, present a comparative, Utopian, New Jerusalem: a benevolent monarchy for Sue, a democratic republic for Reynolds. However, although the texts seem to offer them as a solution to specific problems, whether personal or political, this retreat from the city marks what Anne Humpherys has termed the "problem of closure ... an admission of defeat".[13] No excursions outside the capital are sustained, possibly because they offer none of the real-life enigmas of the fragmented and confusing metropolis.

Both *Les Mystères de Paris* and *The Mysteries of London* end with the conventional and unconvincing endings of death or marriage for all the central characters; the difference between them is their relation to the city. The final chapters of *Les Mystères de Paris* take place away from Paris, where the narrative – and, it seems, the characters – can no longer survive. The vitality is lost; the ending seems curiously unsatisfactory, reflecting the weakness inherent in the serial novel. In *The Mysteries of London*, an "Epilogue" closes the work by reflecting on the city rather than the characters; Reynolds comments on the richness of the metropolis as a theme and announces a second set of mysteries. By keeping the focus on the city, Reynolds was able to defer resolution to the "Mysteries" for another ten years. This was, perhaps, the clue to his success.

---

[12] Donald J. Olsen, *The Growth of Victorian London*, London, 1976, 26.

[13] Anne Humpherys, "Generic Strands and Urban Twists: The Victorian Mysteries Novel", *Victorian Studies*, XXXIV/4 (1990-91), 468-69.

URBAN ERASURES AND RENOVATIONS: SOPHIATOWN AND DISTRICT SIX IN POST-APARTHEID LITERATURES

JOHN A. STOTESBURY

City secrets

Writing and reading as an outsider to the South African experience, I have repeatedly found my outsider's touristic gaze fixed and fixated as much on the concrete architectonic structures of South African cities as on its people and their pain and survival. As I peered through the ice-striated porthole of a South African Airways plane as it circled over Johannesburg before my first visit there a decade ago, my first vision of South Africa was not of its people but its urban structures. In the hazy winter's morning sunlight after a night flight from London, Johannesburg appeared aridly brown, lacking the deciduous greenery of short Finnish summers or the darker, traffic-soiled foliage of London or any similar Western European city. But like any European city, variations in the density and evident wealth of residential districts were immediately visible: the spaced-out villas of the Northern Suburbs with their garden patches of unnaturally bright blueness contrasting with other areas packed with innumerable tiny off-white cuboid dwellings, side by side, row after row.

Johannesburg, for an outsider like me, remains a larger mystery than the Cape Town that I also faced on that first visit: where Johannesburg has an urban history of a hundred years, Cape Town has a history that spans centuries, since, from a Western perspective, it appears to have an urban shape and existence that has been created and narrativized by its inhabitants through a long process of familiarity in ways that Johannesburg lacks. But despite Cape Town's relatively long history of becoming, an insider such as the novelist Mike Nicol can still insist that, in his eyes, "after three and a half centuries Cape Town is in the early stages of imagining itself: while the writers' passion for their city is obvious, the number of books is yet to reach a critical mass – that point where a city starts existing in the mind as well as on the ground".[1] Despite Nicol's reservation, however, for me it has seemed that Johannesburg was only then awakening in

---

[1] Mike Nicol, "Written in the Wind", *Sunday Times* (Johannesburg), "Lifestyle" section, 11 July 1999, 8-9.

1991 to the hope of a new socio-political future, newly liberated from the myths of empire and the exploitation of cheap labour. Unlike Cape Town, Johannesburg even more has been a city still in the process of discovering its first true narrative.

Subjective observations such as these naturally contribute comparatively little to the proper debate over the South African urban experience, other than to remind us that an outsider's observations are no more than that: external, dependent upon more or less informed readings of the semiotics of structures proffered by buildings, communities, discourses. Narratives, in contrast, provide the illusion of offering up to their observer a major part of the secret of cities. As Italo Calvino's narrator remarks of the two types of inhabitants in his invisible city of Esmeralda, while for the ordinary citizen "the shortest distance between two points ... is not a straight line but a zigzag", even more for those with "secret and adventurous lives" the urban way is not straight or straightforward:

> ... cats, thieves, illicit lovers move along higher, discontinuous ways, dropping from a rooftop to a balcony, following gutterings with acrobats' steps. Below, the rats run in the darkness of the sewers, one behind the other's tail, along with conspirators and smugglers: they peep out of manholes and drainpipes, they slip through double bottoms and ditches, from one hiding place to another they drag crusts of cheese, contraband goods, kegs of gunpowder, crossing the city's compactness pierced by the spokes of underground passages.[2]

In brief, in the context of this paper Calvino's vision of the phantasmic city recalls the invisible intimacy of the ways of life of the city and further emphasizes what can be lost when districts or whole cities undergo erasure.

Writing in a different context of the "disavowal of location" and the erasure of a sense of locatedness in recent Asian American narratives, Rachel C. Lee argues for what she terms the "primacy of material locations to political identity and to the contingent, open-ended, and sometimes conflicted relationships engendered by sharing a living space".[3] If this holds true for locations other than the USA, then the impact of the physical destruction of material locations on the identity of their displaced inhabitants may be seen to be massive. Whether the greatest loss through urban erasure is that of the (often unfulfilled or only partially fulfilled) "promise of plenitude" which Hana Wirth-Nesher has detected in the ideal modern city,[4] or whether the loss is merely that of the unobserved and unobservable ways and movements of those who know the secrets of their own city, my present argument hinges on the speculation that erasure by acts of

---

[2] Italo Calvino, *Invisible Cities* (1972), trans. William Weaver, San Diego, 1974, 88-89.

[3] Rachel C. Lee, "The Erasure of Places and the Re-Siting of Empire in Wendy Law-Yone's *The Coffee Tree*", *Cultural Critique*, 35 (1996-97), 149, 173-74.

[4] Hana Wirth-Nesher, *City Codes: Reading the Modern Urban Novel*, Cambridge, 1996, 159.

warfare, or political will, or through time and decay nevertheless leaves traces which survive in a variety of memorializations.

Varieties of erasure
The purpose of this essay is to explore the urban spaces traversed by two very different literary narratives produced by South Africans since the decline of apartheid in the 1990s. Much has already been written and said about the apartheid destruction of those two famous South African city districts, Sophiatown, in the Johannesburg of the 1950s, and District Six in the heart of the "Mother City", Cape Town, in the late 1960s and early 1970s (for instance, in the writing of Alex la Guma, Richard Rive, Bloke Modisane and Don Mattera). Both acts of destruction resulted from the decision of the various apartheid governments to erase districts which offered locations for resistance and alternative modes of existence – in effect, of course, acts of environmental and ethnic cleansing.

In a treatment of the link between the spatial structures of everyday life and its cultural expressions, Paul Gready refers – paradoxically, given the relatively tiny geographical space which it occupied on the city map – to the "gargantuan reality" of Sophiatown, a reality which subsequent commentators and creative artists have found difficult to recapture in its entirety. Sophiatown, Gready suggests, was a "pressure cooker of societal potential and contradictions" and it

> offered unprecedented possibilities for blacks to choose and invent their society from the novel distractions of urban life .... [It was] open to a variety of interpretations, dreams, commitments, and methods of survival.[5]

In the chronology of apartheid, the precarious fragility of Sophiatown prefigures that of District Six: both "non-white" districts were razed to the ground, their populations were displaced to racially segregated districts of the cities, and attempts were made to erase their sites from memory. In the case of Sophiatown this attempted erasure was facilitated by the overtly triumphalist white reconstruction, re-settlement and re-naming of the district as Triomf, and although the suburb remains, it was renamed once more Sophiatown after the general election of 1994. District Six, in contrast, exists as a largely unredeveloped area in the midst of the city, a desolate site punctuated by a handful of undemolished church towers and minarets. Thus, unlike Sophiatown's re-embellishment in the form of the white suburban district built on its ruins, District Six remains an unresolved "urban homicide" – a deliberately terminated community – the evidence of the political crime preserved *in situ* as well as memorialized in the District Six Museum.

The South African experience of deliberate, politically-motivated erasure of urban space and identity is, of course, by no means unique in the world. For

---

[5] Paul Gready, "The Sophiatown Writers of the Fifties: The Unreal Reality of Their World", *Journal of Southern African Studies*, XVI/1 (1990), 139.

example, writing of the outcome of the Arab-Israeli conflict of 1948, Tom
Abowd has commented on a phenomenon that can be compared in detail with
the South African urban experience; in his words, "occasionally ... the Israeli
state has sought to demolish and to physically erase particular areas of
Palestinian habitation that obstruct Israeli visions for exclusive rule in what
mainstream Zionism regards as Israel's 'eternal' and 'unified' capital".
Identifying one such area, the Moroccan Quarter of the Old City of Jerusalem,
Abowd suggests that over the course of seven centuries the neighbourhood
consisted above all of "familial, religious and social" structures that had been
built "mainly of stone and brick", and their destruction after 1948, he suggests,
was an act of "colonial appropriation [which] suppressed histories not of
exclusive and monolithic quarters, but of fluidity, mixture, and inter-communal
interaction (if not always complete cooperation) across a vibrant and changing
urban space".[6]

If the Zionist quest for a reunified temporal and spiritual capital city remains
in some ways too sensitive or incomplete for radical comparison, then one might
also turn in general to the fate of modern cities in the twentieth century. In
addition to those suffering destruction from forces as diverse as urban
development and the decay occasioned by nature, whole cities such as
Stalingrad, Warsaw, Dresden, Hamburg, Hiroshima and Nagasaki have
undergone massive erasure in time of war. In the case of a city like Berlin the
architect Daniel Libeskind has identified a peculiar quality of its own related to
the process of its erasure and reconstruction:

> The incredible idea of demolishing the city is unique [*sic*] to Berlin. Streets in
> other cities such as Paris, New York and London seem to be sacred territory;
> nobody changes the street patterns in most cities of the world. This is not the case
> in Berlin. Berlin has always had the idea that if a house can be removed, the
> direction or course of a street can also be changed.[7]

In another report, Libeskind considers the post-reunification renovation of
Berlin's centre across the rubble of the former East-West border zone to be
"mediocrity on a mega-scale never before seen in such a city", and the same
article partially contradicts Libeskind's own view of the exceptional mutability
of Berlin as a city in its assessment of the "new" Potsdamer Platz, which is "one
of several planned 'centres' where modern blocks are being built *on an identical
street plan* to that of pre-war Berlin" (my emphasis).[8]

---

[6] Tom Abowd, "The Moroccan Quarter: A History of the Present", reissued from
Jerusalem Quarterly File, 7 (2000). Online: http://www.jfq-jerusalem.org/journal/2000/jqf
7abowd.html (3 May 2000).
[7] Daniel Libeskind, "Berlin Alexanderplatz: Ideologies of Design and Planning and the
Fate of Public Space", reissued from *The Journal of the International Institute* III/1
(1995); Online: http://www.umich.edu/~iinet/journal/vol3no1/berlin.html (3 May 2000).
[8] Toby Helm, "From the Ruins Emerges a Bland, Boring Berlin", *Electronic Telegraph*,

This desire for the creation of an illusion of some sense of urban continuity where erasure has been violent and widespread would also appear to be part of a process which can be identified in the transformation of Sophiatown from semi-informal African urban settlement to the formal inner-city Afrikaner suburb of Triomf. As Mike Nicol elsewhere points out,

> By 1960 Sophiatown was a memory. The same streets with the same names were still there but the new houses were occupied by whites. The suburb was now called Triomf.[9]

With its rigidly uniform gridwork of renovated residential streets ranging from Willie, Best and Sol in the north-west, to Gerty, Bertha and Toby in the south-east, all crossed by streets still retaining the self-assured, imperial names of Milner, Edward and Victoria, the Triomf of the apartheid regime, no less than Berlin under one regime after another, was an incredible idea. As such, however, it could scarcely exceed the incredibility of District Six, the grotesqueness of whose erasure prevented the very thought of a racialized physical renovation throughout the subsequent decades of apartheid.

Two narratives
Of the two narratives to be considered here, the first, and ostensibly the more conventional in generic terms, is Linda Fortune's autobiographical narrative of childhood and adolescence in District Six. *The House in Tyne Street: Childhood Memories of District Six* (1996) spans the years from the early 1950s up to her family's expulsion in 1971. The community she describes from her memories of her earliest years is traditional, patriarchal: the centre of Fortune's childhood is indisputably her father, whose death at the age of fifty-three fortuitously precedes the final dissolution of the District. Living in the midst of a multilingual and multicultural community, the child herself felt secure and integrated since "there was never a shortage of children to play with",[10] and as the adult narrator points out, "the people of Tyne Street, as all over in the District, always stood by one another" (120).

Important, too, is that as a child in the 1950s the narrator was aware of apartheid, but her familiarity was largely second-hand, transmitted orally by her mother's younger sister, known simply as "Auntie", who provides her with an idyllic and doubtless a-historical vision of a pre-apartheid Golden Age, but one that retains some kind of magical and recuperative significance for the child:

---

14 Sept. 2000; Online: wysiwyg://137/http://www.telegrap...FFFFrX&pg=/et/00/9/14/wber14.html. 14 Sept. 2000.

[9] Mike Nicol, *A Good-Looking Corpse*, London, 1991, 234.

[10] Linda Fortune, *The House in Tyne Street: Childhood Memories of District Six*, Cape Town, 1996, 20.

"When your mom and I were young there was no such thing as apartheid. People could marry whomever they wished and live wherever they chose. Here in this neighbourhood there lived Jewish, Indian, Native, Muslim, Christian and even Chinese people. They all got on well and we never had to lock our doors at night. People lived freely, and they had a lot of respect for each other. Life started to change when people began to move away one by one" (16-17).

And again, in mid-narrative, when in the 1960s Fortune and her teenage sister listen in on their mother discussing the first rumours of a threat to District Six,

"Shirley and I looked at each other. It was the first word we ever heard about any place being declared 'a white area.' We were worried, but soon we forgot about it because the grown-ups didn't talk about it again for a long time" (72).

Thirdly, in March 1966 the *Post*, a liberal Cape Town newspaper, published a photograph of the teenage Linda, representing her as an involuntary resistor to the threat of displacement and erroneously identifying her as a Muslim. But after she has expressed her initial indignation and anxiety, calm returns:

Nobody did anything. In our street nobody even did much objecting or fighting against what was about to happen. My mother said "We won't stand a chance against the government" (76-77).

Embedded, then, in Linda Fortune's narrative of displacement, are records of three successive discursive failures: firstly of communal history, secondly of communal rumour, and thirdly of the communal exhortation to resistance, each of which fails to awaken in Fortune any effective sense of the power of the apartheid state to alter the urban context of her life for ever. What finally achieves this end is the actual erasure of District Six. This comes about first through the expulsion of its inhabitants, racial group by racial group, and then through the demolition of the local cool-drink factory, shops, cinemas, pubs, homes: whole streetfuls of stone and brick made amorphous, their secret ways, so lovingly recorded in the first part of Fortune's memoir, instantaneously made not only not visible but lifeless.

My second narrative, Marlene van Niekerk's novel *Triomf*, first appeared in 1994 in Afrikaans, and was published in its first South African English translation in 1999 (the English text was further modified for international publication in the same year). *Triomf* is significant in post-apartheid writing not least for its linguistic and cultural hybridity. As Leon de Kock has pointed out in a discussion of the lengthy process of his translation of the Afrikaans original:

Triomf [is] a novel whose rejection of cultural exclusivity and whose internal subversion of Afrikaner metanarratives made its translation into a global language such as English an irresistible project, and yet whose very bastardization of idioms and codes specific to South Africa seemed to render such "globalization" impossible.

De Kock adds that the South African English translation (used here) has "sold well", and that the original Afrikaans version has sold some ten thousand copies: "very large in S[outh] A[frican] terms."[11]

Triomf tells the story of what might be termed the "gargantuan" Benade family, four individuals inhabiting a dilapidated house in the poor-white Afrikaner suburb of Triomf, whose lives are caught up in their own colonial history. Most dramatically, Mol and Pop Benade are the ageing parents of the epileptic Lambert, whose fortieth birthday is due to coincide with the first democratic elections in April 1994; but Mol and Pop happen also to be brother and sister. This ethnically charged incestuous relationship has long been compounded by Mol's sexual abuse at the hands of her own son, Lambert, but also, on occasion, at the hands of her second brother, Treppie, whose role is that of the frustrated Afrikaner intellectual, a violent and acerbic critic of his own dysfunctional family and of Afrikaner-dominated society alike.

This oddly structured family is complemented throughout by its symbiotic relationship with several generations of dogs whose *Ur-mutter* has been a "kaffir-dog" abandoned by its displaced black owner upon the destruction of Sophiatown. Each generation of the Benade dogs is melded mnemonically into the multiple structures of Triomf by being named after streets in the apartheid suburb, so that in the present time of the novel the family cohabits with the diminutive Gerty and her pup Toby, "who was the size of three dogs in one" (7),[12] the fruit of a violent chance encounter between Gerty and a policeman's Alsatian. Triomf's expression of sexuality is invariably aggressive and frequently illicit, deviant, and public – that is, urban – a deliberate fracturing of the Calvinist-inspired self-image of the white apartheid state.

This symbiosis of human and canine families, of Afrikaner whites and their "kaffir" predecessors, is taken further in a series of powerful images centred on the intricacies of inter-species (and, by extension, inter-ethnic) communication. Like most human pet-owners, the Benades converse with their dogs:

> When people tune in their voices to the dogs like this, the dogs know they're part of the company. That's a nice thing for a dog to know. And it's nice for people, too (11).

Thus, when the family reads in the press of a dog-fight racket run by Triomf policemen, Treppie's response consolidates the intimacy of the human-canine relationship: "If I understand correctly, you could say the whole of Jo'burg is one big pit bull terrier fight" (16-17) – a vision of the city which he and Lambert

---

[11] Leon De Kock, "Re-Bastardising a Bugger of a Text: The Case of *Triomf*, or, Here Tog, God Help Us: Trying to Translate the Untranslatable", unpublished conference abstract, included in an e-mail to the author, 3 August 2000.

[12] Marlene Van Niekerk, *Triomf* (Afrikaans orig. publ. 1994), trans. Leon de Kock, Johannesburg, 1999, 7. There is also an international English edition, London, 2000.

expand to absurdity in their own canine lamentation that appears to unite the suburb and the city as one:

> Suddenly Treppie slips off his crate and slides down onto his heels. He pretends he's walking on his back paws, like a trained poodle. Toby and Gerty run around him, jumping up and down.
> Then he goes down onto his knees, stretching his arms out in front of him with his knuckles on the floor. And then he lifts his nose up into the air, letting out a long dog-wail ....
> Treppie's crying like the dogs.
> Toby and Gerty's barking gets higher and thinner, until their voices break and they too give in to the crying. They sit next to Treppie with their front legs stretched out in front of them, their snouts lifted up into the air, just like him. The way they cry, all three of them, you'd swear they were in a little choir together.

With Lambert's participation, the howling of the quartet stimulates a predictable response: "If they carry on long and hard enough, then all the dogs will eventually join them. Martha Street's dogs and the other streets' dogs, until all the dogs are crying all the way to Ontdekkers and beyond" (17). In this process, the lamentations of the dysfunctional family traverse suburban boundaries, across species and racial strictures, beyond the logocentric absurdities of apartheid that are represented in Triomf in terms of stone and brick. Their message, indefinable at this early stage of the novel, echoes hollowly throughout the novel.

Feeling increasingly vulnerable as a result of old age and Lambert's unpredictable temperament, and engrossed in their community's fear of a potential black uprising against the whites on the forthcoming election day, the Benade family members individually devise plans for escape in the event of urban insurrection, from Triomf to the state border with Mozambique – yet another version of the Boer *trek* northwards away from the intolerable power of the Other. Lambert's self-appointed task consists of collecting used wine-box bags from the suburb's garbage cans and municipal refuse dump, which he fills with petrol for "when the shit hits the fan" (221), before burying them for safety in the foundations of his "den":

> Mol stares at the stuff Lambert has dug out of the earth [beneath the floor]. It's a helluva heap. Pieces of red brick, bits of smooth drainpipe, thick chunks of old cement, and that blue gravel you see on graves. Small bits of glass and other stuff shine in the muck. Lambert has already taken out most of the shiny things – for his collection, he says. He collects the strangest things (1).

A similar image recurs when the dog Gerty dies, and her burial by the Benades in their garden reintegrates her into the Sophiatown of her canine ancestors:

> The digging was a struggle. The earth was full of rubble, and they had to use the pick to wrench loose and lift out some of the big blocks of cement. They got only

three feet deep when Pop said enough. He was tired and Gerty didn't have to go six feet under, she was only a dog, after all (205).

Where the death and interment of the dog gesture towards the specific history of Triomf, the Benades' premonition of personal extinction and burial, triggered by Gerty's demise, again links the specificity of the canine and human suburban experience with colonialism and apartheid. Gerty's death provokes anxiety in Mol, fearful that Gerty will not rest peacefully in her Triomf/Sophiatown grave, for Mol has long been conscious of the unsolid foundations of the city:

> Jo'burg's like that. It's hollow on the inside. Not just one big hollow like a shell, but lots of dead mines with empty passageways and old tunnels. Treppie says that's why it's become so expensive to get buried in Jo'burg. There just isn't enough solid ground left for graves. And even if you do get a grave, he says, you still can't be so sure, 'cause most of the corpses fall through after a while (194).

When Mol eventually comes to die, she plans to be cremated: "Ash is light. It stays above ground .... You won't sink into the depths" (195).

Thus, throughout the novel the topographical layers, literal and metaphorical, in the presentation of Triomf – above the ruins of Sophiatown, and below that the remnants of Johannesburg's historical *raison d'être* as a colonial city in southern Africa – are emphatically *there*, just below the surface of the narrative, functioning as a motif which (as one reviewer has put it) "becomes a guiding metaphor for the social architecture of apartheid".[13]

Triomf, the novel, teems with friction, anger, conflict. The house which the Benades inhabit from the rise of Triomf upon the rubble of Sophiatown to its symbolic nadir in the elections of 1994 suffers physical abuse in almost as many ways as old Mol herself: Treppie's wrath and Lambert's epileptic and emotional seizures repeatedly inflict serious damage on its structure, threatening to reduce the house to another layer of the rubble upon which it has been constructed. The Benades' domicile is represented as both metaphor and metonym in relation to the Afrikaner and the apartheid state. At times it is riven by internal dissension, but at the same time it functions as a bastion against a hostile world, a latter-day fortress community set artificially apart from its larger urban and African context, a grim reminder of the worst aspects of the crucible of the Boers in the self-inflicted isolation it has endured throughout its history. The house's final indignity is to be invaded on election day itself by a paint company after the Benades have won a supermarket competition. The prize: to have the house repainted entirely white, an apparently cleansed, restored and infinitely paradoxical suburban sepulchre containing the living dead, an emblem of the hopelessly multivalent duplicity of the willing or unwilling victim-participants in the secret/overt history of the oppressor state.

---

[13] Review of *Triomf* by Marlene van Niekerk. "Reviews", Online: Amazon.co.uk.; http://www.amazon.co.uk/exec/obid...600334/sr=1-1/026-3783409-9794854. 3 May 2000.

For the Benades and, by extension, for their suburbanized Afrikaner community, poised on the brink of a radical shift in the power of the state, history would appear – in a Fukuyaman sense – to be at an end, their culture consigned to a toothless marginalization. The conclusion of possibly the final grand narrative of nineteenth-century European imperialism represented by the apartheid state appears to have ended in the meaningless howling of dogs and human citizens alike. What remains at the end of the twentieth century, as Francis Fukuyama speculates, is a search for "the basis of a new directional history",[14] which for the Benades and their like appears, at the crucial moment of change in their lives, to be somewhere in the heavens rather than in the crumbling certainties of their urban existence.

Thus, through several layers of discourse both of these urban narratives reveal, in Calvino's terms, the secret and adventurous ways of their districts, not least because both are concerned with city areas which now exist only in fragments of pots and plates, and memory. They appear to function as more than simply part of the familiar neo-Gothic record of South Africa dealt with in the resistance literatures of District Six and Sophiatown produced in the decades after their destruction. In the post-apartheid period, rather, these two generically disparate narratives re-present that urban experience at the moment of crucial social and political change in the mid-1990s. Since both narratives have been constructed upon the retrospective fact of the political futility of the apartheid urban erasures and all that such events once implied, new texts such as these cope with an apparently extinct past from an undeniably different perspective from that of their predecessors. How, then, do they represent the city that was there, but no longer exists? How do they proceed with the reconstruction of urban memory of communities once built of stone and brick but ruthlessly erased? And how, given the urgent agendas of the "new" South Africa for the development of social cohesion, do they set about the task of creating a sense of personal, ethnic and communal survival and continuity?

Renovations

It is tempting to search, perhaps simplistically, for comforting evidence of some kind of psychic recuperation and renovation after the destruction. One such example might be Linda Fortune's unbitter observation, after much of District Six had already disappeared, that "the only improvement was the unobstructed view of Table Mountain that could now be enjoyed!" (caption to photograph facing page 119). Urban erasure, it might be claimed from her positive tone, at least opened up alternative vistas, and in an important sense that may well be true, since it gave immeasurable stimulus to the resistance against apartheid. In this sense it can be argued that Van Niekerk's narrative strikes a different, less conciliatory, and also curiously depoliticized tone in the face of the future.

Near the end of the novel the Benades sit meditatively outside on the *stoep* of

[14] Francis Fukuyama, *The End of History and the Last Man*, Penguin, 1992, xv.

their freshly whitened home, the family now depleted by the death of the ever-ailing Pop:

> "Hey, Ma, stop staring into the sky like that, just now a Martian pisses into your eye," says Lambert.
> "I'm looking at Orion. Look, a man of stars with three jewels in his belt."
> "Where?" asks Lambert.
> "There," Treppie points for Lambert to see.
> "Light-blue my beloved, for ever and ever. Orion washes my feet."
> "What shit you talking now, Ma?" says Lambert (472).

The traditional Afrikaner family, as this passage briefly reflects, has some kind of potential for experiencing positive sentiments and discovering fresh perspectives on their existence, but in this narrative there is no final symbolic reinsertion of the dysfunctional Afrikaner into the mainstream of the South African urban narrative. As Ina Gräbe points out, however, though perhaps with some degree of understatement, "the positive aspect of their lifestyle emerges in the mastery of the art of survival in the face of considerable obstacles".[15]

Nevertheless, where *Triomf* undoubtedly succeeds is in its treatment of the South African city as a discursive site for examining the multidimensionality of the colonial and postcolonial experience. The city in *Triomf* is, in part, an architectonic phenomenon, where the human habitation of Johannesburg, *Egoli*, the city of gold, is epitomized in the relentless metaphorical delving of the novel into the social and political archaeology of the recent past. The habitation of the atavistic Benade family is an incessant reminder of the distorted value systems represented by the construction of a British (and Western) imperial urban culture upon that part of the African high terrain named Witwatersrand by the earliest European settlers. In this process, the behaviour of the Benades can be seen in the novel as entirely dependent on its location, which is contemporary Triomf, formerly Sophiatown, and soon to be "Sophiatown" again.

In sum: their fictional lives seem to be overwhelmingly predetermined in historical terms, and that history consists of the seemingly endlessly repetitive layering of lives and habitations, one upon the other, in historical time. If the atavism of the Benades can be criticized for its hyperbole, it can be argued that the same hyperbole accurately images the exaggerations and distortions occasioned by the colonial and imperial process, in particular in its South African urban guise.

An impressionistic conclusion of this kind tends, however, to beg the question. As Maria Balshaw and Liam Kennedy have recently cautioned, semiotic readings "that posit the city as analogous to language will all too often

---

[15] Ina Gräbe, "The Brutalization of Cultural and Universal Values in Marlene van Niekerk's *Triomf*: Relativity of Cultural Relativism or Redefinition of Universal Validity?", in *The Search for a New Alphabet: Literary Studies in a Changing World*, eds Harold Hendrix, Joost Koek, Sophie Levie, and Will van Peer, Amsterdam, 1996, 107.

decontextualise and relativise their object". They further warn that "while there can be no doubt that language plays an important part in shaping our comprehension of the city, representation also involves material, visual and psychic forms and practices that cannot be reduced to textuality".[16] But what my own cursory discussion of these two narratives indicates is the powerful sense of place in their treatments of the South African urban experience. As I have indicated in my analysis of Linda Fortune's apparently guileless memoir, for her the failure of early resistance to apartheid in District Six was in fact the failure of the word – that is, the text – to impress upon the District's citizens the imminence of their communal fate. Only when the physical environment of their urban lives was bulldozed from beneath their feet could they awaken to the reality. In contrast to this, Van Niekerk's textualization of the Sophiatown/ Triomf binary plays infinitely subtle games with the portentously emblematic lives of its Afrikaner family. But (*pace* numerous reviewers of the South African English translation and also Ina Gräbe, one of the first critics of the original Afrikaans version of the novel) I would argue that here, too, it is the *locus* (the house, district, city, state) which lives on beyond the farce and fury of its ephemeral human (and canine) inhabitants.

Finally, for both narratives, the struggle is between text and context; there would appear to be no final solution to the process set up in the movement between erasure and renovation, other than the preservation of memory and the founding of a discursive mode of literary archaeology designed to better explore the multilayered detritus of wasted pasts.

---

[16] Maria Balshaw and Liam Kennedy, "Introduction: Urban Space and Representation", in *Urban Space and Representation*, eds Maria Balshaw and Liam Kennedy, London, 2000, 4.

INVISIBLE AND BROKEN CITIES: THE IMAGE OF A QUEST IN NINETEENTH-CENTURY EUROPEAN TRAVEL BOOKS OR MOUNTAINEERING ACCOUNTS AND MODERN NATIVE AMERICAN FICTION

FRANÇOISE BESSON

At first sight the link between nineteenth-century European travel books or accounts of mountaineering and modern Native American fiction is not obvious and yet one can find challenging coincidences between these different types of writing – coincidences that reveal a profound vision of the world and man's quest in and questioning of the universe. Perhaps the perception of a direct link with nature may explain those correspondences. The modern city imagined in a natural place, or, more often, the ruins of the ancient city seen in the natural shapes of the world reveal man's quest. The link between the broken space and invisibility may be the key to the questions that man reads in a natural landscape that he has metamorphosed into a city. For ruins contain invisible spaces the imagination can endlessly fill. The often-used image of ruins in the landscape is also a shattered image of oneness, the broken city becoming an invisible city. The broken mirror of the organized town can be reconstituted by means of literary cities scattered in texts that reveal other invisible cities, which are the constructed images of an inner world.

The invisible modern city
In *Invisible Man* Ralph Ellison defines the narrator's invisibility as an image of the distorted vision of those who live in a white American town. According to the narrator, it is "a matter of construction of their *inner* eyes".[1] He shows the transformation of man by his fellow citizens' eyes into an invisible creature in terms of *construction*. This reveals the link between an invisible architecture and man's inner eye. In the novel, New York becomes the shattered city depriving the black man of his existence; elsewhere, for Scott Momaday in *House Made of Dawn*, Los Angeles deprives the Indian of his essence. The visible city generates

---

[1] Ralph Ellison, *Invisible Man*, Penguin, 1982, 7.

the black man's invisibility and the Indian's inner dislocation. What becomes obvious for the man who has been deprived of his roots – the *dis-location*, the estrangement from one's place, conveyed by invisibility or material dislocation – may reveal to all men the relationship between the land and the city which has been built and then destroyed. Invisible or ruined cities become the sign of their memory recovered, of their belonging to a common space.

As Ralph Ellison's phrase just quoted shows, language uses the architecture of the city to define a man's life or thought.[2] Language signals that man tries to define his own existence in terms of construction. The numerous literary mappings of real cities[3] reveal man's attempt at organizing his own self; his tendency to see the original, natural chaos as the image of an ancient city extends into his description of the modern visible city that is linked with his own experience and reveals his fear of dislocation. "The city has always sought to ward off the void", Nathalie Cochoy writes.[4] Perhaps the modern city seen in invisible landscapes or ruins full of empty spaces seen in natural chaos or any original landscape are the aesthetic expressions of man's tendency to fill up the empty or invisible spaces of his own inner world, those empty spaces which are questions visually transformed into broken or invisible cities.

The metaphor of the industrial town is present in some nineteenth-century accounts of mountaineering. When Henry Russell-Killough (the famous French Irish mountain climber referred to by Jules Verne in *Michel Strogoff*, who was probably his model for Phileas Fogg in *Le Tour du monde en quatre-vingts jours*) climbs the Pyrenean mountains, he compares the wild landscapes with

---

[2] The words *to build up, foundations, ways, crossroads, construct, deadlock, stone wall, monumental, to buttress*, used to depict man's life, inner world or thoughts, are borrowed from the lexical field of city space and of urban architecture.

[3] Let us take as examples Virginia Woolf's *Mrs Dalloway*, where the heroine's thoughts follow her movements in London, Joyce's painting of Dublin revealing Stephen's inner mazes through his movements in the Irish city in *A Portrait of the Artist as a Young Man*, E.M. Forster's vision of an Indian city, Chandrapore, as the image of the opposition between two worlds in *A Passage to India*, Lawrence Durrell's poetic image of Alexandria rebuilt by his own memories in *The Alexandria Quartet*, and all the American cities depicted by American writers to show the characters' inner worlds or journeys: Boston depicted by Henry James, Edith Wharton or Henry Miller, New York depicted by F.S. Fitzgerald, Ralph Ellison, Saul Bellow, Paul Auster and many others, Paterson, which is the core of William Carlos Williams's poetry, Los Angeles opposed to Walatowa (Jemez Pueblo) in the Native American vision given by N. Scott Momaday in *House Made of Dawn*, Paris painted by all the expatriate American writers or the Algerian city painted by Albert Camus. This is only a very small selection meant to show the essential role of the city in the writer's definition of man's inner world.

[4] "La ville a toujours tenté de conjurer le vide"; Nathalie Cochoy, "New York ou la cité invisible", Colloquium about *Images de la Ville*, 4 February, 1994, Université Toulouse Le Mirail, a paper published in *Séminaires d'études doctorales 1992-1996*, Toulouse, Université Toulouse-Le Mirail, 1996, 95. The editor is grateful to Robert Druce for most of the translations. The original of three longer quotes are in an Appendix.

cities – sometimes with a destroyed mythical Mediterranean city, but also with the modern, industrial town, which is exclusively English. Observing the landscape seen from the *Pic Long*, he thinks of London: "All the rest was in blackness and resembled London." To describe what he imagines when he climbs the *Canigou* in the clouds, he refers to Manchester:

> In all honesty I cannot speak of the view, for on each occasion I was climbing through dense cloud. One might have thought oneself to be in Manchester.[5]

Besides the hint of humour hidden behind Manchester's fog, another purpose may be read in the reference to the English city, which seems to emerge in the middle of a narrative situated around Pyrenean summits to allow the reader to see what cannot be seen and to understand that the landscape consists of an absence of image. The black colour in the first example and the clouds in the second appear as two forms of obstruction to the visible landscape. The reference to the stone being built, the city, becomes the only image emerging out of the natural stone – in the clouds or in darkness, through two natural images of the invisible. Industrial civilization generates an impressionistic painting in the "non-vision" of the Pyrenean landscape. From the visual nothingness there emerges the most unexpected image for a reader confronted with the travels and impressions of a romantic writer – the industrial city. The chaos, those shapes isolated from one another, appear as a fragmented image of the city: Russell sees a London concert hall in the Pyrenean fog, the chaos becomes a graveyard, the shapes of the mountain remind him of a factory and the *Vignemale* is a cathedral, like the leaves or the snow. Life, death and faith in the world beyond are summed up in the metaphorical image of the city, envisaged as a whole or fragmented, having its source in an English urban landscape descried where the climber cannot see the shapes of the mountain; and the allusion to the English city in the description of the Pyrenean mountains allows the climber to make the invisibility of the landscape visible. Perhaps the ruin of the modern city is contained in the memory of the standing city seen in an invisible world. Having become immaterial and invisible, it becomes the image of an absent world, a reflection of the ironical vision of the English industrial city in the fog perceived by Charles Dickens and an image of man's fate: his most modern, technical constructions may be the invisible veil seen in the mountain by a simple mountaineer.

But that modern city, hidden from the real landscape and only visible for the climber in his mind's eye, is perhaps the sign of an invisible world looming in his inner landscape and revealed to him by the invisible, which may have the shape of a mythical city.

---

[5] Henry Russell, *Souvenirs d'un montagnard*, Pau, 1888, 154, 279 ("Tout le reste était noir et ressemblait à Londres"; "Ma conscience m'interdit de parler de la vue, car chaque fois, je montai dans les nuages. On aurait pu se croire à Manchester").

The mythical city of the Mediterranean
Ruins have always attracted man's imagination. In the eighteenth century and at
the beginning of the nineteenth, they were praised to such an extent that people
protested against the restoration of ancient castles, which they thought thereby
lost their aesthetic dimension and their soul as ruins. Perhaps the broken building
had such a value to the romantic mind because of all the mysteries contained in
its absent space. The ruin is a piece of architecture built by man and destroyed by
time; its visible remains appear as the memory of a remote period and its hollow
space contains an invisible world that the human mind can try to fill with his
own memory and imagination. This is perhaps also why the metaphorical ruins
of the city recur in literature, revealing some strange correspondences between
such different genres as nineteenth-century European travel books or
mountaineering accounts and modern Native American novels or short stories.
All of them see the link between the visible and the invisible and seem to see the
essence of things in that invisible world perceived beyond the visible shapes and
sometimes expressed through the image of the mythical city.

The metaphor of the buried ancient city often recurs in British books relating
travels in the Alps or the Pyrenees or ascents in the various mountains of the
globe. Most of the time, the metaphor refers to the Mediterranean city; the Greek
temples or the Roman Coliseum emerge among a landscape of wild mountains
where what man has built over the past centuries is inserted within the virgin
mountain. There is a striking coincidence between the image of the
Mediterranean city in European travel books or accounts of mountaineering and
the image of the Native ruin of the city in Native American literature, as if the
city, built and destroyed by man and time, was the image in the landscape –
whatever the culture – of man's fate and his relationship with the land.

The key to the recurrence of the mythical city perhaps lies in the reference to
a mythical island that may contain all the memory of the world and all the quests
of each individual looking for his own island. The *Souvenirs d'un montagnard*
by Henry Russell are interspersed with metaphorical references, one of which
may reveal the meaning of the reference to the destroyed city. The granite blocks
in Montarouye Lake are compared to the "ruins of a drowned city";[6] moreover
as the Pyrenees above a sea of clouds are assimilated to the "sinister debris of a
drowned continent",[7] one may think of Atlantis. The emergence of that possible
fragment of the mysterious memory of the world mingling the real mountains
and the metaphorical sea around an island, whose very existence remains
mysterious and which emerges in the mountaineer's imagination in the shape of
metaphorical ruins, reveals Russell's and perhaps other writers' vision of
civilization in nature. Atlantis is the myth inscribed in the original landscape, the
city built by men and then destroyed, yet remaining alive as a dream in man's

---

[6] *Ibid.*, 242 ("décombres d'une ville noyée").
[7] *Ibid.*, 54 ("débris sinistres d'un continent noyé").

consciousness. It may be a key to the recurrence of the metaphor of Mediterranean ruined cities seen in natural landscapes.

If the Mediterranean city recurs more often than others in nineteenth-century British travel books and accounts of mountaineering, it is perhaps because it contains a mythical landscape that men, anywhere in the world, can re-appropriate through the imaginary world. Eden, the Lost Paradise looked for by all men, is supposed to be situated in a country of the Mediterranean. The great monotheistic religions have their roots in the Mediterranean world. The source of the spirituality of a great part of the world is situated between Jerusalem and the small Mediterranean towns situated in Judaea, Galilee or Egypt. Moreover, colonization and invasions have taken Mediterranean spirituality to countries that have their own myths and references to the Mediterranean are now mingled with African or Native American myths. As far as fiction is concerned, several literary myths – such as the pastoral – several forms of poetry (indeed, the very term *poetry*), the dramatic genres of comedy and tragedy, all have Mediterranean origins. The most famous travel book in the world, *The Odyssey*, is entirely situated within the boundaries of the Mediterranean, and the Bible contains the stories of many travels in a Mediterranean world. Literature all around the world and particularly in Anglo-Saxon countries often chooses Mediterranean borders to depict man's predicament and human vices. Shakespeare situated several plays in Mediterranean countries; and the Mediterranean world is very much present in American fiction, in the work of such novelists as Hemingway, Hawthorne, Fitzgerald or Henry James, as Paul Carmignani, in his article "Epiphanies méditerranéennes dans la littérature américaine", has shown.[8] Paul Carmignani also notes Mediterranean references in some descriptions of non-Mediterranean landscapes – in the case of writers having a close relationship with the landscape, the Mediterranean allusion maybe the sign of a particular quest. Therefore it is interesting to see to what extent nineteenth-century British travel books or accounts of mountaineering and some modern Native American novels meet in their references to Mediterranean cities or to the ruins as the destroyed image of the city – the inclusion of a built past in an eternal landscape. A Mediterranean reference may appear to represent a desire to re-appropriate an original past and insert it into one's own landscape from the moment there is a physical contact with it.

The Mediterranean reference is present in Native American fiction and in many European travel books or mountain climbing accounts, where metaphorical cities emerge from the chaos; most of the time they are ruined cities. When Russell uses the image of the destroyed city that the mountains reveal to him, it is the ruins of a non-English town, generally a Mediterranean city, like Rome or Palmyra. He compares the snow to a "capital city in flames",[9]

---

[8] Paul Carmignani, "Epiphanies méditerranéennes dans la littérature américaine", in *Méditerranée, Imaginaires de l'espace*, Cahiers de l'Université de Perpignan, 20, 1995.

[9] Russell, 329 ("capitale en feu").

which may sound like an allusion to the great fire of Rome. The seracs reappearing at the end of the summer "like the shapeless and eloquent rubble of an ancient city swallowed up by the sands of the desert and all at once laid bare by the simoon"[10] evoke Palmyra and its repeatedly crushed civilization, the very ruins of which could not be found until the seventeenth century. Russell's words seem to reveal man's fate. Only the elements control the landscape of the world. Even man-made landscapes – such as the human architecture of the city – depend on the will of nature. Sand swallows up a town, the wind unearths it. Man and his creations become derisory in front of the forces contained in the natural world, as James Erskine Murray reveals when he compares the *Marboré*, a Pyrenean mount, to the Mediterranean civilizations represented by Palmyra, Rome and Egypt:

> Such is a faint description of the winter garb worn by the Marboré; one of nature's grandest works; the contemplation of which strikes the beholder with awe and admiration, where –
> "We feel the present Deity, and taste
> The joy of God, to see his awful works;"
> and in comparison with which the noblest efforts of man's genius, the gorgeous ruins of antiquity, the Palmyras, and the Coliseums, nay, even the Pyramids, dwindle into insignificance.[11]

The same image is found in Henry David Inglis's travel book, when he says about the Marboré: "Contemplating a scene like this, how insignificant seem the proudest works of man – the most majestic ruins of antiquity – the Roman amphitheatres – even the Coloseum [*sic*]!"[12] F.H. Johnson compares the same mountain to "the ramparts of the celestial city", and, after comparing the "Great Chaos" to "a disordered circle of the Giant Druids" he describes the Cirque of Gavarnie:

> It reminds us first of a half-ruined temple, or a Circus Maximus of the giants hewn out of the earth rather than built by hands. Then of Martin's pictures of antedilluvian cities, with their huge foundations of frowning rock, and their marble towers far up into the night, gleaming among the "tingling stars" that are awakened by the impending tempest which destroyed all the world. Then again, that is the Palace of king, such as dwelt among the rocks in eastern lands and carved out *façades* and *entablatures* on precipices, while the whole earth within was hollow with their marble halls and swarming with concealed life, though outside, all was fixed and still.[13]

---

[10] *Ibid.*, 78 ("comme les débris informes et solennels d'une ville antique engloutie sous les sables du désert et déterrée soudain par le Simoun").

[11] James Erskine Murray, *A Summer in the Pyrenees*, London, 1837, II, 35.

[12] Henry David Inglis, *Switzerland, the South of France and the Pyrenees, in 1830 by Derwent Conway*, Edinburgh, 1831, II, 166.

[13] F.H. Johnson, *Winter Sketches in the South of France and the Pyrenees*, London, 1857,

Different cultures meet in this landscape drawing: through images, new spaces representing human constructions are born from the original creation. The hollows of the natural world are filled by the traveller's imagination and by his historical and aesthetic references that link his individual experience and the landscape he sees with the collective memory of the world represented by the city or the isolated religious monument. The Roman temple or the druids' monument, the cathedral, the Buddhist monasteries, the minarets of Russell's text, are the constructed spiritual signs isolated from the rest of the city and used to convey a syncretic vision of the natural landscape. The shift from the Roman "half-ruined temple" to the "antediluvian cities" derived from John Martin's paintings appears as an aesthetic recomposition of space where nature writes and paints the images of human memory.

The transposition of the cities of the greatest Mediterranean civilizations into the natural landscape also appears in John Milford's travel book. In the landscape of Gavarnie he sees the ruins of several cities: "Let us form an idea of vast perpendicular rocks, whose naked and rugged sides appear like the ruins of so many towns and fortifications, and whose tops are covered with an eternal snow."[14] Geology is replaced by human creation in a comparison framed by the natural shapes of the original mountain projecting its sharp lines onto a human landscape found in the image of destruction. Perhaps because of the natural chaos found in the mountain, perhaps also because of the physical link of the climber with the soil and the rock, the mountaineer, still more often than the simple traveller, sees the ruins of ancient cities in the landscapes he crosses. S.E.S. Allen, climbing the Rockies in 1896, wrote in the report of his ascent:

> The grey quartzite lay in slabs before us, level as a floor and polished by ancient ice. From the grooves and cracks of this ancient pavement grew long grass, as in the streets of some deserted city.[15]

The "grooves and cracks" are that hollow space allowing life to emerge as it allows imagination to fill it with an architecture of the past projecting the collective memory of the world into the individual experience. The city space takes mythical dimensions in the metamorphosis of geology into an abandoned town stemming from the past. Those empty spaces becoming deserted streets contain symbolical connotations referring to the inner world of an individual isolated in the wild world and linking the new landscapes he meets with a

---

282, 280, 285.

[14] John Milford, *Observations, Moral, Literary and Antiquarian, made during a Tour through the Pyrenees, South of France, Switzerland, the whole of Italy, and the Netherlands in the years 1814 and 1815,* London, 1818, I, 53.

[15] S.E.S. Allen, "Mountaineering in the Canadian Rockies", in *The Alpine Journal*, XVIII/134 (November 1896), 223.

universal human space conveyed by the image of deserted or destroyed cities. The anonymous city may become more precise and S.E.S. Allen shifts from the general deserted city to the Greek one:

> As we stepped upon its surface our hot faces were cooled by a whiff from the ice-fields and before us, the grey pavement gently sloping to meet it, lay a placid lake, a dark blue circle of about 1/2 mile in diameter. The glaciers clustered around its further end, whence floating blocks of ice dotted with white the sapphire surface, while behind and above rose the slopes of a grand amphitheatre, their ice-fields glowing like Pentelic marble in the mellow light of the afternoon sun, like a vast Dionysiac theatre, the upper tier of seats outlined against a Grecian sky (Allen, 226).

The description of the landscape is articulated around a shifting from the Canadian ices to the Mediterranean sky. Glacial geology is inscribed in a classical mythological time. The mountaineers see the human city destroyed where there is no living creature, no human element. They see the broken ancient city in the dismantled mountain.

The Mediterranean city (Rome, Palmyra, Greek or Egyptian cities) often recurs perhaps because Mediterranean civilizations may appear as the cradle of many cultures, from Europe to North Africa. Moreover, the very name of the sea, the Mediterranean, symbolically places it in the middle of all lands and ensures that Mediterranean civilizations are at the heart of the world. Of course, a mere geographical reference cannot encompass the memory of the whole world, but the symbol contained in the city built and then destroyed, the debris found in the original shapes of the landscape contain that universal dimension which cannot be linked with the distortion of universality found in colonialism. This vision of the ruined Mediterranean city in the original landscape of the mountain is simply the image of man's place in the world and of his link with the land, the land that gives him the clay or the stone with which his house, his city will be made. And this is perhaps why one can find some correspondences between the travellers' and climbers' visions of Mediterranean cities in mountainous landscapes and the Native American vision of ruins. There is a spiritual dimension in that vision of the mythical city. When most mountaineers and travellers see a multitude of precious stones in the colours of the mountains, they build a metaphorical New Jerusalem, the mythical Mediterranean city of the Book of Revelation, entirely covered with precious stones, the "celestial city" seen by Johnson in the Marboré. The memory of the world seems to be inscribed in those poetical paintings of the mountains seen through a physical experience.

The Mediterranean reference also appears in Native American literature as a multiple sign. In *The Ancient Child*, N. Scott Momaday quotes *Carmen*; one of the female characters has "Egyptian eyes", and there is a reference to a "loup de la Méditerranée" on a menu.[16] The Spanish presence in New Mexico justifies a

---

[16] N. Scott Momaday, *The Ancient Child*, New York, 1990, 137, 206.

text interspersed with Spanish words, as in *House Made of Dawn*. But the recurring Mediterranean reference to the horse looking like "the black Arabian of the Moors"[17] or to the centaur, the Greek mythological figure metaphorically integrated into a Native traditional ceremony, shows the mixture of the two cultures. The metaphorical references to the Greek writer Aesop, to Genesis and the Gospel According to John evoking Jerusalem also introduce the Mediterranean world into the Native landscape in a deep analysis of the value of the word. The blend of cultures is also emphasized by the reference to the city. The ruins of an old copper mine generate an allusion to Alesia, the Gallic city, the last place of resistance of a people in front of the Roman invasion:

> ... he was below and across the road from an old copper mine, a ghost, too, like the ancient towns that lay upon the ridge above and behind him, given up to the consuming earth and left alone amid the remnants of some old and curious haste: broken implements, red and eaten through with rust; charred and rotting wood; a thousand pieces of clear and green and amber glass upon the swollen ground, as if untold legions of ants had come to raise a siegeworks at Alesia (60-61).

A real world of fragments emerging from the colonizing past (illustrated by the mine which introduces the image of colonization into the landscape) generates a second image: a fragment of European memory is seen in the allusion to the town of Alesia appearing as the emblem of a dominant civilization crushing Native people. The Mediterranean colonizing world metaphorically transforming men into insects – but an organized society of insects – is projected onto the Native American landscape through the ruins of the mine left by another Mediterranean civilization, the Spanish, since the scene takes place in New Mexico. In *Tracks*, Louise Erdrich evokes "Christ in Gethsemane" when she speaks about one of the Native characters, Nanapush, telling the story of a little girl and talking about water:

> The light seemed brighter outside, unfading. I cursed all the talk of water and began a rosary in my thoughts. But I saw the sorrowful mystery, Christ in Gethsemane. He wept a river, and I could not keep from hearing the voice of Nanapush. In the old language there are a hundred ways to describe water and he used them all – its direction, color, source and volume.[18]

The storyteller becomes the sign of the spiritual link uniting the human being and the universe. The young woman feels her Indianness in her awareness of being a listener like all the listeners of the people she belongs to. The association of the old Indian storyteller with Christ is made through the place name, Gethsemane, the reference to the gardens of Jerusalem, the place of the

---

[17] N. Scott Momaday, *House Made of Dawn* (1966), New York, 1989, 79. Further references to this novel will be given in the text.
[18] Louise Erdrich, *Tracks*, London, 1994, 149.

beginning of Christ's Passion. The role of water, essential in Native American tradition as the element of fertility, of material life but also spiritual life, is revealed through the Christian reference to the Mediterranean garden and the vision becomes a syncretic one. The material reference, or the musical or the spiritual are all images of the Mediterranean presence in the Native American inner world. The Mediterranean inscription in the text appears as an image of a European original world embedded in the original American landscape. The signs of colonization (Christopher Columbus belonging to a Mediterranean world) and of a recovery of the essence of the landscape – the Mediterranean landscape and the Native American being really united in the transparency of the water – are both present and the Indian writer finds the spiritual Mediterranean city in the waters of her landscape, in the memory of the natural world. A sign and a message, the Mediterranean city reveals a world full of fragments that man can reconstitute as a whole shape.

The archaeological reference, the fragments of pottery found in the cave by the main character's grandfather in Momaday's *House Made of Dawn*, are also the broken image of a historical past becoming eternal in its union with the present of the discovery. Paul Carmignani quotes a chapter from *The Professor's House* by Willa Cather, "Tom Outland's Story", in which the fragments of pottery found by the protagonist in cave dwellings situated in New Mexico and belonging to an Indian tribe which vanished three hundred centuries before are strangely similar to fragments found in Crete Island. The young man is going to superimpose the Native American World and Mediterranean antiquity, thus blending several spaces and several times. As Paul Carmignani says:

> This superimposition may seem surprising, although many examples of it are to be found in the literature and the culture of the New World; and it may be explained by the presence, from the revolutionary times onward, of an underlying craving of the American psyche: the yearning for an Edenic past whose natural inheritor is the American Indian, who is more primitive and thus by definition closer to the origins of life and, above all, to its primordial innocence.[19]

We can find the reason for the proximity between European travellers' and climbers' accounts and Native American fiction in that "primordial innocence" that the mountaineer, the traveller and the Indian find in a direct, physical contact with the landscape. This vision of the universe reconciling fragments belonging to different worlds is particularly perceptible in the image of the ruins seen in the Native American landscape.

The Native American ruins of the city
The image of colonization revealed by the ruins of the copper mine is transcended to become a vision, the vision of man's questionings about his situation in the universe. Like nineteenth-century travellers and climbers seeing

---

[19] Carmignani, 95.

ancient ruined cities in the mountainous landscapes of the world, Native Americans reveal the link of man with the landscape through a spiritual archaeology where they are going to recover their own memory and their own world. The landscape described by N. Scott Momaday at the very beginning of *House Made of Dawn* evokes "crevices in the walls", hollow spaces, and ruins:

> The sun strikes the canyon floor only a few hours each day, and in winter the snow remains for a long time in the crevices of the walls. There is a town in the valley, and there are ruins of other towns in the canyon. In three directions from the town there are cultivated fields. Most of them lie to the west, across the river, on the slope of the plain. Now and then in winter, great angles of geese fly through the valley, and then the sky and the geese are the same colour and the air is hard and damp and smoke rises from the houses of the town (5).

The ruins are the image of the Native American memory inscribed in the landscape in which the Indian can find the collective voice of his people, where he can find his own life, his own memory in the town seen "like a scattering of bones in the heart of the land". The real ruins and the town seen as a scattered body appear as the image of a scattered memory that may be recovered in a mythical map inscribed in the landscape. The whole landscape becomes the Native city: "The canyon was a ladder to the plain" (55). The landscape becomes the kiva, the ceremonial place leading the Indian to see beyond the invisible border, to see beyond the visible. The "canyon walls" introduce a literary city where Shakespeare and Faulkner, joined by the sound and fury of the world, reveal the sense of the Native landscape, first defined, to the white reader, by the ruins of its cities:

> At the source of the rain the deep black bank of the sky swelled and roiled, moving slowly southward under the rock rims of the canyon walls. And in the cold and denser dark, with the sound and sight of the fury all around, Angela stood transfixed in the open door … (74-75).

The feminine white character discovers the sense of vision and reveals the meaning of the metaphorical city inscribed in the landscape through that literary wall of sight separating the sound and the fury of the world in a hidden inclusion of white literature.

The multiple real or metaphorical walls and houses scattered in the novel lead to the hero's recovery, the awareness of his belonging to the landscape, of his belonging to "the house made of dawn", his landscape and the Navajo chant becoming the common sign of the memory of the land and the memory of a people perhaps found in the image of the ruined city opposed to the modern city, Los Angeles, the angels' city without memory, the city of broken individuals, the real shattered city. Those cities, scattered in past European travel books or modern Native American novels, follow the same quest; the ruined or invisible cities seen in the natural landscape are the image of man's questions in front of the world, the image of a quest for a lost harmony with nature, which the broken city helps him to recover. The broken fragments become the riddle to be deciphered, the puzzle to be reconstituted. This is the puzzle of man's own self within the circle of the cosmos; man's memory and the vision of the organized but invisible or broken city in the natural landscape will appear as the image of the quest for his inner city.

The immaterial house as the sign of the construction of the poetic inner city
All those metaphorical cities – the mythical ruined Mediterranean city, the modern English one, the Native American city full of memory or the American city without memory – reveal man's need to organize his own inner space. The visions of destroyed cities rebuilt by man's imagination may reveal that dream of rebuilding a great house that looks like the ancestors' city and his own memory. The city is the human image of the organization of the world. Its streets and ways, its houses and monuments are the reflection of his own life in the space of the world: hence, perhaps, the allusion to the "house" to evoke man's place in the universe. Gaston Bachelard sees the house like a cosmos and he adds, "A huge cosmic house is potentially present whenever you dream of a house".[20] Michel Serres writes, "Why are we so deaf, so unable to understand, so unfamiliar with what is spoken and what is sung in our worldly house?"[21] The Navajo chant and Momaday's novel *House Made of Dawn* reveal another immaterial house made of time, of natural, cyclical time. The Indian must see that house to recover his own self through his own memory, which is the memory of his people and the memory of the land found both in the landscape and in the chant, the voice being contained in the shapes of the world as the voice of the sea echoes the hero's inner voice and the voice of the world at the same time. The quest for an ancestral house may be read in that repeated vision of ruined cities in the landscape, and it is perhaps explained by Bachelard's words:

> If we pass on from these faintly gleaming images to more compelling images, images that force us to recall occasions earlier in our past, then here the poets are our masters. With what power they prove that dwellings forever lost still live on in us. They force us to bring them back into existence, as though they had been waiting for an injection of fresh life-blood from us. How much better then would we live in our house! How our old memories would suddenly acquire the possibility of a new and living reality! We judge the past. A sort of regret that we

---

[20] Gaston Bachelard, *La poétique de l'espace*, Paris, 1992, 24, 61 ("La maison est vraiment un cosmos"; "Une immense maison cosmique est en puissance dans tout rêve de maison").

[21] Michel Serres, *Nouvelles du monde*, Paris, 1997, 130 ("Pourquoi cette surdité, cette incompréhension, cette étrangeté à ce qui se parle et se chante dans notre maison du monde?").

did not live our life in the old house intensely enough manifests itself in our souls, rises from the past and drowns us.[22]

Can we not say the same thing about the ancient city, our collective house built by our ancestors that the traveller tries to find in the wild space, trying to organize the stone into a work of art containing ways and spaces reflecting material and spiritual life in it? Perhaps the need to compare wild nature to the ancient ruined city to show visibly the fragility of man's works in comparison with the strength of nature reveals man's dream of recovering his most remote memory in the union of the wild land and the built city. Perhaps it reveals his desperate need to be in peace with time by associating the destroyed city and the eternal mountain. Observers fill the hollows of their inner cities with the ruins of their ancestors' constructions, as if to build their own works of art with the shapes of their memories. As Bachelard says:

> How frequently one has recalled Leonardo da Vinci's advice to painters lost for inspiration in face of nature, to examine with a dreamer's eye the cracks in an old wall! Is there not a chart of the universe to be found in the lines left by the hand of time in an ancient city-wall? Who has not discovered in a few cracks in a ceiling the map of a new continent? The poet knows all about that. But to tell in his fashion what are these worlds which chance has designed within the limits of a drawing or a dream, he must dwell within them. He finds a corner where for a while he can make his home in this world within a cracked ceiling.[23]

The ruined city may appear as the collective image in the universe of that cracked ceiling. The image of a lost city that man tries to recover within his mind and which is the reconciliation of his past and his present, of his landscape and the cosmos, of himself, time and space. By reconciling the ancient ruined city or the invisible modern town and the natural landscape metaphorically, he fills up the crevices of his inner space and tries to recover his lost city, his lost island, that Atlantis hidden in him that he desperately tries to discover in the fragments of his memory reshaped into a painting in words, a story which is his own individual story and the story of mankind inscribed in stone letters in all the landscapes of the world.

When he changes the mountain chaos poetically into a Greek monument or a Druidic temple, man asserts his vision of a superior order that he tries to compare with his own world. He romantically acknowledges the grandeur of nature in front of the fragility of Man revealed by the ruins, thus using poetry as a rampart in front of his own fears. He organizes the natural chaos, the original broken stone into an ancient ruined city and so doing he projects his fear of an essential dislocation of his being onto the landscape, a fear positively metamorphosed into aesthetic creation; and his vision of an invisible modern city in the fog reveals all

---

[22] Bachelard, 65.

[23] *Ibid.*, 136.

the hidden cities which may remain hidden in each of us, a puzzle reconstituted through natural invisibility. What is first an aesthetic, romantic image, is the expression of man's conscious or unconscious awareness of his situation in the universe, a situation between the natural, eternal world of the chaotic stone of the origins, and the architectural, temporal world of the built stone: a situation between nature and the city. By projecting the city into the natural world, by projecting the invisible organized construction into the natural landscape, by trying to find all the earthen fragments once used as everyday life objects, by trying to find all the broken fragments of life, Man tries to shape his own memory.

The superimposition of the ruined or invisible city on the natural landscape appears as a will of fighting against *dis-location*, of finding, through the memory of the world, one's true location, of finding one's whole self in the shape of the world. The chaos of the mountain thus becomes the eternal city that each individual bears within him, a city built from his consciousness of the link he has with the land, of his belonging to time and of the reciprocity of that relationship. Time, which allows the creation of a city and is responsible for its destruction, becomes the way to the invisible city. Man must take its streets to find that, if time makes ruins, those ruins were a city once and their memory is human memory. The broken images made by time reveal memory as the poetic inner city, looking like real Alexandria found again by Mountolive through a double journey in the desert and in his memory in Durrell's *Alexandria Quartet*. The invisible city or the invisible parts of the shattered city appear as the broken mirror placed in front of man's eyes in a natural landscape, a broken mirror that his awakening to the harmony with the world is to reconstitute.

The meaning of the broken city in the natural landscape may be found in those floods echoing one another in Native American mythology and in Christian religion. The flood, the natural original water recovering all the shapes of the world, preserves them in the depths of the ocean and the broken city swallowed up by the flood becomes the eternal invisible memory of the world. The sea, the fluid space of creation, the original, transparent and dark space, leading to the unseen world of its bottom and allowing its surface to reflect the sunlight, contains that hidden city, that Atlantis looked for everywhere in the world and perhaps present within each individual trying to understand his place in the universe by building his own city. The human heart and the human mind have their ways, their buildings, their cathedrals or their temples. And the contact with the natural world, with an original, eternal landscape perhaps reveals to the traveller the fragility of human constructions, the fragility of human victories over other men and over space and the need of a true house recognized in the natural space of the world, in the cyclical time of the universe and in the family link with one's people and with the land.

If nineteenth-century travellers and mountaineers meet modern Native Americans in the vision of ruins – real or imagined – in the natural landscape, it is perhaps because they all follow the Way. The Indian's Red Way and the mountaineer's way partake of the same union with nature, with the stone and the memory of the earth. This is perhaps why, in their writing, they hear the eternal breathing of the land remembered in the ruins of the city invisibly reshaped.

Appendix

Carmignani, 95.
Cette superposition peut surprendre, pourtant on en trouve maint exemple dans la littérature ou la culture du Nouveau-Monde et on peut l'expliquer par la présence, manifestée dès la période révolutionnaire, d'une double aspiration dans la psyché américaine: la nostalgie d'un passé édénique dont l'héritier sera tout naturellement l'Indien, plus primitif, et donc par définition, plus proche des origines et surtout de l'innocence primordiale.

Bachelard, 65.
Si nous passons de ces images tout en lueurs à des images qui insistent, qui nous obligent à nous souvenir plus avant dans notre passé, les poètes sont nos maîtres. Avec quelle force ils nous prouvent que les maisons à jamais perdues vivent en nous. En nous, elles insistent pour revivre, comme si elles attendaient de nous un supplément d'être. Comme nous habiterions mieux la maison! Comme nos vieux souvenirs ont subitement une vivante possibilité d'être! Nous jugeons le passé. Une sorte de remords de ne pas avoir vécu assez profondément dans la vieille maison vient de l'âme, monte du passé, nous submerge (65).

Bachelard, 136.
Que de fois n'a-t-on pas rappelé que Léonard de Vinci conseillait aux peintres en déficit d'inspiration devant la nature, de regarder d'un oeil rêveur les fissures d'un vieux mur ! N'y a-t-il pas un plan d'univers dans les lignes dessinées par le temps sur la vieille muraille? Qui n'a vu dans quelques lignes qui apparaissent en un plafond la carte d'un nouveau continent? Le poète sait tout cela. Mais pour dire à sa façon ce que sont ces univers créés par le hasard aux confins d'un dessin et d'une rêverie, il va les habiter. Il trouve un coin où séjourner dans ce monde du plafond craquelé.

NOTES ON CONTRIBUTORS

Ian Almond teaches English Literature at Bosphorus University, Istambul, Turkey. He has also taught at the universities of Bari (South Italy) and Kayseri (central Turkey). He is the author of *Sufism and Deconstruction: A Comparative Study of Derrida and Ibn' Arabia* (2004) and of many articles in journals such as *ELH*, *New Literary History*, *The Harvard Theological Review* and *German Life and Letters*.

Annelise Ballegaard Petersen teaches at the Institute of Literature, Media and Cultural Studies, University of Southern Denmark, Odense. She has published extensively on literature and urban culture, with a special focus on German Literature between 1890 and 1945. She has co-edited, with Svend Erik Larsen, *La rue – espace ouvert*, Odense, 1997.

C.C. Barfoot, who taught in the English Department, Leiden University, for over thirty years before his retirement in 2002, published *The Thread of Connection: Aspects of fate in the Novels of Jane Austen and Others* (1982); and has most recently edited *Victorian Keats and Romantic Carlyle: The Fusion and Confusion of Literary Periods* (1999), *Aldous Huxley between East and West* (2001), *"My Rebellious and Imperfect Eye": Observing Geoffrey Grigson* (2002, with R.M. Healey), and *"A Natural Delineation of Human Passions": The Historic Moment of* Lyrical Ballads (2004).

Françoise Besson is Professor of English Literature at Toulouse-Le Mirail University. Her research focuses mainly on the representation of landscape and the relationship between landscape and writing in English travel books, on Gothic novels and also on Native American literature, on which she has published many articles. Her books include *Pyrénées romanesque Pyrénées poétique dans le regard britannique* (2000), *Le Paysage pyrénées dans la litératuur de voyage et l'iconographie britannique du dix-neuvième siècle* (2000); *Le Lieu nomade dans le cinéma de Charles Chaplin* (2003) and, with Madeleine Vesson, *Au fils de coiffes: Tolouse et les pays d'oc* (2003).

Karlien van den Beukel lives in London. Her poems have appeared in *Angel Exhaust*, *Talus* and the anthology *Foil: Defining Poetry 1985-2000*. With Lucy Sheerman, she is co-editor of rempress, the Cambridge-based poetry imprint. Her current major research is on Edwin Denby, the New York City Ballet and the New York School of Poetry.

Kasia Boddy teaches in the English Department at University College London. She has published on various aspects of twentieth-century American literature, is co-editor of *The Virago Book of Twentieth-Century Fiction* (2000) and is currently completing a book on the representation of boxing.

Rocco Coronato teaches English Literature at the University of Siena. His research interests focus on the relationship between European and English Renaissance theatre, with a special stress on Jonson and Shakespeare and the Renaissance theories of laughter. He is the author of *Shakespeare's Neighbors: Theory Matters in the Bard and His Contemporaries* (2001) and *Jonson Versus Bakhtin: Carnival and the Grotesque* (2003).

Robert Druce joined the English Department, Leiden University, in 1975. He published *The Eye of Innocence: Children and Their Poetry* (1965 and 1972); a novel, *Firefang* (1972); *This Day Our Daily Fictions* (1988, rev. edn. 1992). He has lived in Suffolk since his retirement in 1996; and is a Senior Examiner for the International Baccalaureate.

James How was awarded a Ph.D. in English Literature by the University of Edinburgh and in 2003 he published a book based on his thesis, *Epistolary Spaces: English letter writing from the foundation of the Post Office to Richardson's* Clarissa. He now works as a civil servant in the Scottish Executive, advising on a number of policy issues.

Sara James wrote her doctoral thesis on the urban mystery novels of Eugène Sue and G.W.M. Reynolds and has published articles on Sue, Reynolds and Emile Zola. She is currently working on nineteenth-century women's writing in France and is Lecturer in French at Merton College, Oxford.

Daniel Karlin, teaches English literature at University College London and is the author of books and articles on Robert and Elizabeth Barrett Browning, on Rudyard Kipling and on Victorian poetry and fiction. He edited the new *Penguin Book of Victorian Verse* (1997) and is working on a book on Proust. At University College he convenes a course on "London in Literature" which studies the representation of the city from medieval to modern times.

Deborah Parsons is Lecturer in English Literature at the University of Birmingham. She is the author of *Streetwalking the Metropolis: Women, the City and Modernity* (2000) and *Djuna Barnes* (forthcoming). She is currently completing a book on *Madrid, Modernism and Modernity*, a reader on *Modernity and the Metropolis*, and has longer-term research interests in the cultural history of the circus and fairground in the late nineteenth and twentieth centuries.

Philip Rand holds degrees from Amherst College, Princeton University, and the University of Rome, La Sapienza. He has taught French Literature and the Russian language at Claremont McAlaster College in California, History of the English Language, Technique and Theory of Translation (Italian – English) at the *Scuola Superiore per Mediatori linguistici "Carlo Bo"* in Rome. His scholarly activities have focused on the literature of the Second Empire in France and treatments of the Franco-Prussian War in European Literature, most recently reflected in an article, "The Last Days of the Second Empire", in *The Subverting Vision of Edward Bulwer Lytton: Bicentenary Reflections* (2004).

Doc Rossi was Dean of The Umbra Institute, Perugia and has research interests in both literary and cultural studies and music. He has published articles on Shakespeare and Brecht, F. Scott Fitzgerald, and the Beat Generation, and also on Early Music and contemporary popular music, including two books, *The Original Jerry Donahue*, and a modern edition of Thomas Robinson's *New Citharen Lessons* (London 1609). He is currently working on a book-length study dealing with Shakespeare's influence on Brecht and another on the history of the cittern.

Alan Shelston, until recently Senior Lecturer in English Literature at the University of Manchester, has published critical essays on a number of nineteenth-century fiction, and in particular on Elizabeth Gaskell. He is editor, with John Chapple, of *The Further Letters of Mrs Gaskell* (2000).

John A. Stotesbury teaches at the University of Joensuu, Finland, since 1975 and specializes in colonial and postcolonial literatures, in particular South African. His publications include *Apartheid, Liberalism and Romance. A Critical Investigation of the Writing of Joy Packer* (1996); and co-editorship of *African Voices: Interviews with Thirteen African Writers* (1989), *Postcolonialism and Cultural Resistance* (1999), and an issue of *The Atlantic Literary Review* (New Delhi). In addition to articles on South African writing, his most recent publications include studies in the field of autobiography, photography and blindness. He has also co-edited *London in Literature: Visionary Mappings of the Metropolis* (2002).

Joachim von der Thüsen received his Ph.D. from Stanford University and teaches comparative literature at the University of Utrecht. His most recent book publication is a study of the transformations of the sublime around 1800: *Het Verlangen naar Huivering: Over het Sublieme, het Wrede en het Unheimliche* (1997).

Wim Tigges teaches English literature and Irish language and literature in the English Department of Leiden University. He has published on a variety of literary subjects, and edited *Moments of Moment: Aspects of the Literary Epiphany* (1999) and co-edited *Configuring Romanticism* (2003).

Valeria Tinkler-Villani has taught at Leiden University for thirty years. She is the author of *Visions of Dante in English Poetry* (1989), co-edited *"Exhibited by Candlelight": Sources and Developments in the Gothic Tradition* (1995) and has written articles on the Gothic, the City in Literature and particularly on the Rossetti family, the most recent article being "In the Footsteps of His Father? Dantean Allegory in Gabriele Rossetti and Dante Gabriel Rossetti" (2004).

Frederik Tygstrup, who teaches comparative literature at the University of Copenhagen, has published *The Fiction of Experience: The European Novel 1615-1857* (1992) and *In Search of Reality: Essays on the Modern Novel* (2000), both in Danish, and numerous articles on the history and theory of the novel, and on issues in literary theory.

INDEX

History and Representation
in Ford Madox Ford's Writings

Edited by Joseph Wiesenfarth

Amsterdam/New York, NY 2004. XI, 241 pp.
(International Ford Madox Ford Studies 3)

ISBN: 90-420-1613-2   € 50,-/US $ 63.-

History and Representation in Ford Madox Ford's Writings explores the idea of history across various genres: fiction, autobiography, books about places and cultures, criticism, and poetry. 'I wanted the Novelist in fact to appear in his really proud position as historian of his own time', wrote Ford. The twenty leading specialists assembled for this volume consider his writing about twentieth-century events, especially the First World War; and also his representations of the past, particularly in his fine trilogy about Henry VIII and Katharine Howard, *The Fifth Queen*. Ford's provocative dealings with the relationship between fiction and history is shown to anticipate postmodern thinking about historiography and narrative. The collection includes essays by two acclaimed novelists, Nicholas Delbanco and Alan Judd, assessing Ford's grasp of literary history, and his place in it.

USA/Canada: One Rockefeller Plaza, Ste. 1420, New York, NY 10020,
Tel. (212) 265-6360, Call toll-free (U.S. only) 1-800-225-3998,
Fax (212) 265-6402
All other countries: Tijnmuiden 7, 1046 AK Amsterdam, The Netherlands.
Tel. ++ 31 (0)20 611 48 21, Fax ++ 31 (0)20 447 29 79
Orders-queries@rodopi.nl   www.rodopi.nl
Please note that the exchange rate is subject to fluctuations

Ecrire en pays assiégé-Haïti-Writing Under Siege

Edité par Marie-Agnès Sourieau et
Kathleen M. Balutansky

Amsterdam/New York, NY 2004. 545 pp.
(Francopolyphonies 1)

ISBN: 90-420-1753-8   € 100,-/US $130.-

Jacques Stephen Alexis, Jacques Roumain, René Depestre, Marie Chauvet, Frankétienne, J. J. Dominique, Jean Métellus, Dany Laferrière, Yanick Lahens, Lyonel Trouillot et Edwidge Danticat sont quelques-uns des écrivains haïtiens dont l'écriture est marquée par le contexte politique d'Haïti. Les régimes dictatoriaux ont, en effet, affecté l'espace créatif, imposant un certain nombre de contraintes auxquelles ces écrivains, chacun à leur manière, ont ingénieusement riposté et réagi. Ce recueil d'essais critiques et d'entretiens tente d'illustrer et d'analyser comment les oeuvres romanesques, poétiques et théâtrales s'accommodent du « pays assiégé » et déploient des stratégies linguistiques et formelles permettant de transcender les forces d'oppression.

USA/Canada: One Rockefeller Plaza, Ste. 1420, New York, NY 10020,
Tel. (212) 265-6360, Call toll-free (U.S. only) 1-800-225-3998,
Fax (212) 265-6402
All other countries: Tijnmuiden 7, 1046 AK Amsterdam, The Netherlands.
Tel. ++ 31 (0)20 611 48 21, Fax ++ 31 (0)20 447 29 79
Orders-queries@rodopi.nl   www.rodopi.nl
Please note that the exchange rate is subject to fluctuations

Towards a Transcultural Future.
Literature and Society in a 'Post'-Colonial World. ASNEL Papers 9.1.

Edited by Geoffrey V. Davis, Peter H. Marsden,
Bénédicte Ledent and Marc Delrez.

Amsterdam/New York, NY 2004. XVI, 317 pp.
(Cross/Cultures 77)

ISBN: 90-420-1773-2   Bound   € 70,-/US $ 91.-

This collection has one central theoretical focus, viz. stock-taking essays on the present and future status of postcolonialism, transculturalism, nationalism, and globalization. These are complemented by 'special' angles of entry (e.g. 'dharmic ethics') and by considerations of the global impress of technology (African literary studies and the Internet). Further essays have a focus on literary-cultural studies in Australia (the South Asian experience) and New Zealand (ecopoetics; a Central European émigrée perspective on the nation; the unravelling of literary nationalism; transplantation and the trope of translation). The thematic umbrella, finally, covers studies of such topics as translation and interculturalism (the transcendental in Australian and Indian fiction; African Shakespeares; Canadian narrative and First-Nations story templates); anglophone / francophone relations (the writing and rewriting of crime fiction in Africa and the USA; utopian fiction in Quebec); and syncretism in post-apartheid South African theatre. Some of the authors treated in detail are: Janet Frame; Kapka Kassabova; Elizabeth Knox; Annamarie Jagose; Denys Trussell; David Malouf; Patrick White; Yasmine Gooneratne; Raja Rao; Robert Kroetsch; Thomas King; Chester Himes; Julius Nyerere; Ayi Kwei Armah; Léopold Sédar Senghor; Simon Njami; Abourahman Waberi; Lueen Conning; Nuruddin Farah; Athol Fugard; Frantz Fanon; Julia Kristeva; Shakespeare. The collection is rounded off by creative writing (prose, poetry, and drama) by Bernard Cohen, Jan Kemp, Vincent O'Sullivan, Andrew Sant, and Sujay Sood.

USA/Canada: One Rockefeller Plaza, Ste. 1420, New York, NY 10020,
Tel. (212) 265-6360, Call toll-free (U.S. only) 1-800-225-3998,
Fax (212) 265-6402
All other countries: Tijnmuiden 7, 1046 AK Amsterdam, The Netherlands.
Tel. ++ 31 (0)20 611 48 21, Fax ++ 31 (0)20 447 29 79
Orders-queries@rodopi.nl   www.rodopi.nl
Please note that the exchange rate is subject to fluctuations

Architectures of Poetry

Edited by María Eugenia Díaz Sánchez and Craig Douglas Dworkin

Amsterdam/New York, NY 2004. 143 pp.
(Internationale Forschungen zur Allgemeinen und Vergleichenden
Literaturwissenschaft 79)

ISBN: 90-420-1892-5   € 34,-/US $ 44.-

Architectures of Poetry is the first comprehensive accounting of the currently intense
dialogue between the sister arts of poetry and architecture. Refusing to take
either term in a metaphoric sense, the eleven essays collected in this volume
exemplify an exciting methodological direction for work in the humanities: a
"literal wager" that is willing to take the unintended suggestions of language as
reality. At the same time, they also provide close readings of the work of a
number of important writers. In addition to a suite of essays devoted to the team
of Arakawa and Madeline Gins, chapters focus on figures as diverse as Francesco
Borromini, Rainer Maria Rilke, Stéphane Mallarmé, Friedrich Achleitner, John
Cage and Lyn Hejinian.

Craig Dworkin is the author of *Reading the Illegible* (Northwestern UP, 2003) and
the editor of *Eclipse* (www.princeton.edu/eclipse) and *The UbuWeb Anthology of
Conceptual Writing* (www.ubu.com/concept). He teaches at Princeton University.

USA/Canada: One Rockefeller Plaza, Ste. 1420, New York, NY 10020,
Tel. (212) 265-6360, Call toll-free (U.S. only) 1-800-225-3998,
Fax (212) 265-6402
All other countries: Tijnmuiden 7, 1046 AK Amsterdam, The Netherlands.
Tel. ++ 31 (0)20 611 48 21, Fax ++ 31 (0)20 447 29 79
Orders-queries@rodopi.nl   www.rodopi.nl
Please note that the exchange rate is subject to fluctuations

The Mirror and the Veil
An Overview of American Online Diaries and Blogs

Viviane Serfaty

Amsterdam/New York, NY 2004. X, 144 pp.
(Amsterdam Monographs in American Studies 11)

ISBN: 90-420-1803-8   € 32,-/US $42.-

The Mirror and the Veil offers a unique perspective on the phenomenon of online personal diaries and blogs. Blending insights from literary criticism, from psychoanalytical theory and from social sciences, Viviane Serfaty identifies the historical roots of self-representational writing in America and studies the original features it has developed on the Internet. She perceptively analyzes the motivations of bloggers and the repercussions their writings may have on themselves and on American society at large. This book will be of interest to specialists in American Studies, to students in literature, communication, psychology and sociology, as well as to anyone endeavoring to understand the new set of practises created by Internet users in America.

USA/Canada: One Rockefeller Plaza, Ste. 1420, New York, NY 10020,
Tel. (212) 265-6360, Call toll-free (U.S. only) 1-800-225-3998,
Fax (212) 265-6402
All other countries: Tijnmuiden 7, 1046 AK Amsterdam, The Netherlands.
Tel. ++ 31 (0)20 611 48 21, Fax ++ 31 (0)20 447 29 79
Orders-queries@rodopi.nl   www.rodopi.nl
Please note that the exchange rate is subject to fluctuations

Beyond Scotland
New Contexts for Twentieth-Century Scottish Literature

Edited by Gerard Carruthers, David Goldie & Alastair Renfrew

Amsterdam/New York, NY 2004. 267 pp. (Scroll 2)

ISBN: 90-420-1883-6   € 54,-/US $ 70.-
ISBN: 90-420-1893-3   € 24,-/US $ 31.-
Textbook Editions (with a minimum of 10 copies)

Scottish creative writing in the twentieth century was notable for its willingness to explore and absorb the literatures of other times and other nations. From the engagement with Russian literature of Hugh MacDiarmid and Edwin Morgan, through to the interplay with continental literary theory, Scottish writers have proved active participants in a diverse international literary practice. Scottish criticism has, arguably, often been slow in appreciating the full extent of this exchange. Preoccupied with marking out its territory, with identifying an independent and distinctive tradition, Scottish criticism has occasionally blinded itself to the diversity and range of its writers. In stressing the importance of cultural independence, it has tended to overlook the many virtues of interdependence.

The essays in this book aim to offer a corrective view. They celebrate the achievement of Scottish writing in the twentieth century by offering a wider basis for appreciation than a narrow idea of 'Scottishness'. Each essay explores an aspect of Scottish writing in an individual foreign perspective; together they provide an enriching account of a national literary practice that has deep, and often surprisingly complex, roots in international culture.

USA/Canada: One Rockefeller Plaza, Ste. 1420, New York, NY 10020,
Tel. (212) 265-6360, Call toll-free (U.S. only) 1-800-225-3998,
Fax (212) 265-6402
All other countries: Tijnmuiden 7, 1046 AK Amsterdam, The Netherlands.
Tel. ++ 31 (0)20 611 48 21, Fax ++ 31 (0)20 447 29 79
Orders-queries@rodopi.nl   www.rodopi.nl
Please note that the exchange rate is subject to fluctuations